SURVIVING ALEX

SURVIVING ALEX

A MOTHER'S STORY OF LOVE, LOSS, AND ADDICTION

PATRICIA A. ROOS

RUTGERS UNIVERSITY PRESS

New Brunswick, Camden, and Newark, New Jersey
London and Oxford

Rutgers University Press is a department of Rutgers, The State University of New Jersey, one of the leading public research universities in the nation. By publishing worldwide, it furthers the University's mission of dedication to excellence in teaching, scholarship, research, and clinical care.

Library of Congress Cataloging-in-Publication Data

Names: Roos, Patricia A., author.
Title: Surviving Alex : a mother's story of love, loss, and addiction / Patricia A. Roos.
Description: New Brunswick : Rutgers University Press, [2024] | Includes
    bibliographical references and index.
Identifiers: LCCN 2023025500 | ISBN 9781978837027 (cloth) |
    ISBN 9781978837041 (epub) | ISBN 9781978837058 (pdf)
Subjects: LCSH: Clarke, Alex, 1989-2015. | Roos, Patricia A.—Family. |
    Drug abuse—Social aspects—United States. | Sons—Death. | Drugs—
    Overdose—United States. | Compulsive behavior—United States.
Classification: LCC HV5825 .R66 2024 | DDC 362.290973—dc23/eng/20231219
LC record available at https://lccn.loc.gov/2023025500

A British Cataloging-in-Publication record for this book is available from the British Library.

References to internet websites (URLs) were accurate at the time of writing. Neither the author nor Rutgers University Press is responsible for URLs that may have expired or changed since the manuscript was prepared.

∞ The paper used in this publication meets the requirements of the American National Standard for Information Sciences—Permanence of Paper for Printed Library Materials, ANSI Z39.48-1992.

rutgersuniversitypress.org

To Alex, our love survives.
And, to Chip, somehow we managed to survive with
our love intact. It was no easy feat.

"What do you say? There really are no words for that. There really aren't. Somebody tries to say, 'I'm sorry, I'm so sorry.' People say that to me. There's no language for it. Sorry doesn't do it. I think you should just hug people and mop their floor or something."

She tried to read a few books by writers about the death of their children but they annoyed her in the same way the comforters did. "Books that have been written about the death of a child, but are all about the author. And people who were trying to soothe me, were trying to soothe *me*. I never heard anything about him. They say it's about the living, it's not, it's about the dead."

She doesn't want "closure," she says. "It's such an American thing. I want what I got." Morrison gathers herself up. "Memory. And work. And"—she starts to laugh—"some more ibuprofen."

—Toni Morrison, on the death of her son Slade, who died from
pancreatic cancer at forty-five years of age,
interviewed in Emma Brockes, "Toni Morrison"

When you keep waking up in the middle of the night to scribble a note, always about one topic, you may as well realize it: you are writing a book.

—C. Wright Mills, "On Intellectual Craftsmanship"

CONTENTS

SURVIVING ALEX

Prologue

Mom and Dad, . . . I can't deal with my life anymore.
I'm tired of hurting you. . . . I will love you forever, Alex.

—Alex Clarke, May 2015

O N THE DAY after Mother's Day in 2015, my twenty-five-year-old son Alex died of a heroin overdose, alone in a trash-strewn vacant lot in Newark, New Jersey. My husband Chip and I were devastated, as any parent would be. All parents fear losing a child, and Alex was our only child. No family wants to be a member of that community of sorrow. With the raging overdose epidemic, more and more families are living through that incomparable loss. We had already spent years trying to understand how anxieties, an eating disorder, and then addiction entered our lives, and how we might help Alex live. Now, we were commencing a new process of surviving addiction's deadly aftermath. "What do we do now?" I whispered.

This book emerged directly from that question. Years later, I realize that everything I have done since Alex's eating disorder and addiction stole our "normal" lives has been an attempt to understand why and how this happened to Alex, and to us. How did this college-educated young man with such a promising future fall into crippling anxieties and alcohol and substance use to overdose on heroin? How can it be that our loving family and his countless friends were not enough to save him? And, the two questions all surviving family members ask at some point: What might we have done differently, and how will we survive the loss of our beautiful boy?

I learned much while living within the "insanity," a metaphor used in addiction and treatment systems to describe the reality of the lives of those addicted and their families. I realized soon enough that my questions were far too narrow. To do justice to Alex's story, I needed to direct my lens far more broadly than Alex and my family. My story— our story—is one that weaves together both the personal and the sociological. I write as a mother, but also as a sociologist. I understand what any mom would feel losing her child, but I also have sociological tools to see a bigger picture. I use both these vantage points to come to terms with Alex's addictions and death, to begin healing, and to challenge conventional ways of understanding and treating addiction.

Over nine years out from Alex's death, I have moved well beyond simple answers. When Alex first overdosed in October 2013, I joined Nar-Anon, the 12-step companion program to Narcotics Anonymous for family members. Then, the 12-step focus on addiction as a brain disease was reassuring. Nar-Anon's Three C's comforted me: we did not *cause* Alex's addiction, we could not *control* it, and we could not *cure* it. But the simplicity of that slogan leaves much unexamined. The real truth? If I knew then what I know now, I believe I might have made a difference, maybe even kept Alex alive.

I didn't fully understand the psychological pain that drove Alex first to an eating disorder when he was twelve, and then to alcohol and opioid addictions. Once addiction arrived, I was too ready to accept the conventional wisdom of what I now view as broken treatment systems. This knowledge breaks my heart, but I also know we did the best we could. Here I bring what I learned to others, both those who find themselves in my position, and perhaps as importantly to those who do not. One of the most valuable takeaways from my conversations with fellow travelers in grief is that yes, it happens to people who look like us, and yes, it happens to people who come from families like ours. It can happen to anyone.

I write in my own voice, that of an educated white woman, but with the hope of reaching a broader audience. My conversations with others have often been uncomfortable, if they happen at all. No one likes to talk with a mom about her dead son. It's as if addiction is catching, and it might infect their families. As a result, the continuing public silence about addiction and mental health disorders is deafening. I want to break that silence and make others feel less alone in their struggles.

In weaving together the personal and the sociological, I learned about the broader set of factors implicated in mental health and substance use disorders. First, my family is not unique. The number of deaths due to drug overdoses is staggering. According to the Centers for Disease Control (CDC), during the twelve-month period ending in February 2023, well over 105,000 Americans died of a drug overdose,[1] and between 1999 and 2020 more than 932,000 similarly died.[2] As overdoses continue to spiral out of control, many families are living through similar trauma with their addicted loved ones, nationally, in New Jersey, and even in our small central New Jersey town. Those who haven't lived with addiction want to believe it won't ever happen to them, but it already is: in 2021, 16 percent of the US population were classified as having an alcohol or drug use disorder.[3] A recent poll found that one in three Americans identify drug use as a problem in their families, a figure bandied about in the addiction community.[4]

Second, the addiction story is as much about mental health as it is about substance use. Using substances, whether they be alcohol or drugs or both, is a way of coping with pain.

Third, the substance use story is also about race, ethnicity, and socioeconomic status. As the demographics of substance use have shifted in recent years to what some call "cul-de-sac problems"—including middle- and upper-class white families—the public conversations have altered too, sadly in entirely predictable ways. But addiction happens in all races and socioeconomic statuses; this is an epidemic that crosses many social, demographic, and geographic boundaries.

Fourth, we cannot incarcerate our way out of the overdose crisis. With deinstitutionalization and mass incarceration, jails and prisons have become dumping grounds for those with substance use and mental health disorders. We need public policy solutions, both governmental and private, that promote treatment and prevention strategies over jails and prisons. Our public policies regarding substance use disorders should be guided by empathy and compassion, not punitive inhumanity.

Fifth, even amid a growing epidemic of prescription drugs, heroin, and now fentanyl and other synthetic drugs, the stigma toward, and discrimination against, those suffering from substance use and mental health disorders and their families is stark and raging.

The bottom line: as a sociologist, I know that conventional explanations for substance use treatment and public policy solutions are almost always conceived as ones of individual choice. According to this view, Alex made choices in his young life, and his death was simply an inevitable outcome of those bad choices. It was his "own fault," and if not his, then his parents. Indeed, some of those commenting on my first public op-ed about Alex's death made precisely this personal choice argument.[5]

There is a role for personal explanations, but this book is a sociological memoir. Focusing solely on the personal misses the larger picture. Good explanations need to be multifaceted and nuanced, moving beyond the personal to what sociologists call structural or systemic explanations. Such an approach recognizes that the factors producing overdoses are broad and nuanced. These include broken treatment systems; a revolving door between rehabs and sober living houses, often fostered by patient brokering; jails and prisons used as dumping grounds for those with substance use and mental health disorders; growing economic and racial inequality; out-of-control opioid prescriptions fueled by Big Pharma; lack of insurance parity between mental and physical health, and lack of regulators willing to support the 2008 federal law requiring parity; a political focus on criminal justice solutions rather than treatment; workplace bias against those with criminal records; the role of trauma in addiction; and the direct relationship of addiction to mental health as co-occurring disorders.

I read about these larger explanations, but I also lived through them. For those arguing "it's all choice," there is no place for such factors. But there is substantially more to the explanation of the overdose crisis than bad choices made by young people like Alex in the throes of addiction. Understanding the larger, systemic failures is key to understanding how to fix the problem, and the kinds of roles that government and private partnerships can play in developing solutions. If it's all personal choice, there is no place for collective efforts operating for the larger social good.

My story addresses many of these larger systemic concerns. My son is dead from heroin, and it is true enough to say he shares responsibility for that outcome. But there are larger truths, too. And we can understand those truths only by raising our eyes to look at larger social systems. Among the many things I learned are that being a loved child does not prevent addiction or ensure that addiction can be overcome. People make a lot of money from the existence of addiction. Schools and other institutions often look out for themselves more so than their students or clients.

This is a real story about real people, in families that loved and tried to do their best for their children. My fellow travelers in addiction and grief are people just like you and me. I shed light on the day-to-day insanity of addiction and mental health struggles, as well as the possibilities for recovery and resilience for surviving family members. Alex was not just one more 2015 overdose. I want people to see him as the living, brilliant child, and young man he was, the Alex we and his friends knew and loved.

In this book I include information I gathered over the years we lived with Alex's mental health and substance use disorders and struggled to survive its aftermath. In addition to reading voraciously on the topic, I drew from contemporaneous personal journals, picture albums, calendars, and scrapbooks. I talked with important people in Alex's life, including his friends, therapist, teachers, police officers, family members, and others who met him along the way. As Alex's medical heir, I collected intake and medical information from the institutions in which he resided, including rehabs, hospitals, detox centers, and jail. This information provided a wealth of information reported by social workers, doctors, psychiatrists, rehab staff, police officers, and jailers that flesh out my personal narrative. I look to my own and my family's interactions with Alex for greater understanding of our lives before and during his addiction, as well as in its aftermath. Most of those I spoke with were fine with me using their first names. For those who weren't, I use pseudonyms, or generic descriptions. I use the real names of the health care facilities or other institutions in which Alex resided during his years of mental health struggles and addiction, but I do not name individual doctors, psychiatrists, therapists, or medical staff.

In this book I bear witness to the struggle, stigma, and shame my family experienced during the years Alex suffered from addiction and mental health issues, including a life-threatening eating disorder. I also bear witness to the anguish we experienced before his death and to our grief after. Watching Alex succumb to addiction fostered a resilience I did not know I possessed and an education I never wanted but am compelled to share. I have experienced the entrenched inaction of politicians and the public to America's overdose crisis, the complicity of the criminal justice system and Big Pharma, the lack of insurance parity between physical and mental health, and the reality of broken treatment systems. There is lots of blame to go around. Bearing witness to these failures, and the harm they have done to many, led me to join a growing moral community of action, a community that seeks an alternative to the exclusive focus on the 12 steps approach to recovery. To make this different vision of recovery happen, things need to be done, and I am active in that effort. I describe an emergent moral community seeking to promote harm reduction principles, as cities, states, the federal government, the private sector, and dedicated individuals search for new solutions to the dual traumas of substance use and mental health disorders. That movement is growing, and it's well past time for a larger community of action. I view this book as part of that mission.

In that spirit, there are multiple ways to read this book, depending on how you are coming to this topic. The flow of the book reflects my own journey. In part I, I give you the perspective first of a mom in shock, then of the sociologist compelled to understand this worst case unfolding in my own home. In part II, I write about the "good old days" when Chip and I thought all was well with our "normal" family, and how cracks in that normality began to form that tore our family apart. In part III, I convey the day-to-day insanity of addiction, culminating in Alex's death. Finally, in part IV I reflect broadly on how I searched for social communities to help address Alex's substance use and mental health issues, and then move forward from Alex's death by learning about what we as a community can do. Chip adds his own perspective, as a dad and a sociologist. One possibility for reading this book is to follow how I wrote it, chronologically from our early lives with Alex, through to his death, and thereafter. Alternatively, one might choose to proceed directly to the insanity of our lives with addiction, followed by my reflections on the trauma, before returning to early chapters to see our lives before. The insanity I describe will be all too familiar for those families with addicted loved ones. For others, it could well suggest potential futures. Wherever you are on the addiction journey—an interested bystander, a person amid the insanity, or anywhere in between—reading this book could be hard. No one knows better than me how devastating the emotions of sorrow, guilt, and anger can be.

PART I

INTRODUCTION

CHAPTER 1

Day 1

Life changes in the instant. The ordinary instant.
—Joan Didion, *The Year of Magical Thinking*

TUESDAY, MAY 12, 2015, was my worst day. There were many bad days during Alex's years of psychological pain and addiction, but that day—that moment—is most seared in my memory. It was 2 P.M. and I was sitting at the desk in my home office, just back from a morning meeting. The sun shone brightly through the windows that looked out on our front walk. I watched as two black-clad official-looking strangers approached the door. My heart beat wildly and I could scarcely breathe. I shouted to my husband Chip, "It's not good news," as I raced to the door and opened it as my fears blurted out the question, "Is he okay?" The officers—one female and one male—introduced themselves as Newark, New Jersey, law enforcement officers. I didn't want to let them in the house because I knew instinctively what had happened—what letting them in would confirm. But I did invite them in, and on that beautiful Tuesday afternoon, our worst nightmare arrived.

After verifying that we were Alex's parents, the female detective told us that our twenty-five-year-old son Alex had died the previous day. The only details she could provide were that he was found in a vacant field, a place frequented by heroin addicts. There was a backpack near him, and a syringe. She showed us his driver's license but wouldn't give it to us. It was now "evidence." She did not know his time of death. A man working in a nearby building had found Alex the previous morning, Monday, May 11, so that is his official date of death. But I "know" in some deep way he died the previous evening, Mother's Day. That day will never again be my day.

Alex had been missing for six days. It was not the first time he had gone missing, nor the first time I had called around to hospitals and police stations trying to locate him. A few days earlier I had gone to the local Metuchen police station to declare him missing. By the time the notification went out, it was too late.

You could tell that the officers at my door had done this many times before with other families. They were caring yet matter-of-fact, asking if we needed emergency medical services, whether we had any questions, or if they could call anyone for us. We had many questions, but we knew the officers had no answers for us, and so we did not ask. They were gone in minutes. We were alone, staring at each other in horror. "What do we do now?"

Anyone who has experienced such shock knows how disorienting it is. One's life changes in an instant. Although I've seen scenes like this play out numerous times in movies and TV shows, living through it was quite different. We didn't scream, or sob. We were numb, in shock I suppose. But not from surprise. In some sense, we had been waiting for it. The tears came later, when I was interviewing Alex's buddies, his teachers, and others who knew or met him. They still come when I'm talking about Alex with my friends, when I see photos of holidays and birthdays, and when I'm writing, about good times or bad. Many of my friends' children are getting married, or having children, and even writing about that brings tears.

In one sense, Day 1 is the culmination of all that happened before, and it also holds the seeds for what will happen in the days, weeks, and years that follow. Most immediately, our family of five shrank to four. Although Alex was our only child, our nephew Hunter and niece Ginny had lived with us since they were sixteen and twelve. Their father Hal— Chip's brother—died suddenly in 2012, preceded by their mother Kathy eight years earlier. Although we could not replace their parents, Hunter and Ginny became ours to love and care for in new ways. We are family, and they are now our children. And with the losses they had already sustained in their lives, we knew that Alex's death would hit them hard.

After the officers left, we waited for Hunter and Ginny to arrive home. News travels fast and furiously in small towns. Our neighbors would soon learn Alex had died of a heroin overdose, and we didn't want either of them to hear about Alex through Metuchen's grapevine. Ginny was finishing her first year of high school, and we waited until she walked home. Hunter was in his first year of college at Rutgers, taking his last semester exam that morning. Chip went to pick him up at his dorm. Hunter and Ginny were devastated. Both were exceedingly close to Alex; he had been more of a brother than cousin. Both knew he had substance use issues, but they always assumed he would survive. Only Chip and I feared the worst. In fact, at some level we had been steeling ourselves for this possibility. Alex had already experienced multiple overdoses, from which he had miraculously recovered.

As one does, we began to make phone calls—to our family, friends, and colleagues. Our "first responders" arrived almost immediately. My friend Debby, the chair of my department, was the first to arrive and offer help. By mid-May, classes were over, and I had finished grading one class and was partway through the second. I handed Debby all my paperwork, giving her directions about how to grade my students' final papers. She arranged to have my teaching assistant and colleagues read the papers and assign grades. Chip's teaching assistants handled his final exam the following morning. Our students got their final grades that semester, never knowing the trauma that occurred in our lives.

I called our former neighbor Dori, who immediately signed off from her virtual workplace and was at our house in minutes. She remembers that day vividly and recalls me saying, "Well he finally did it, the police are here, he's gone." Looking back, Dori told me, "I feel like the shock of it didn't hit you guys till much later. . . . You weren't crying so hard that you couldn't tell me. You said it so matter-of[-factly]. OMG, she cannot be saying that, but you were." Dori, and later that day her husband, Joe, alerted the rest of our local tribe. We had been friends with Dori and Joe for decades, first as next-door neighbors and then as neighbors a few blocks away, after we moved into Hal and Kathy's house to better accommodate our new family of five. Dori and Joe knew all about Alex's anorexia and substance use. They had experienced much of the trauma with us, living through multiple ambulances and police coming to the house, helping me search for Alex when he went missing, and supporting us when overdoses occurred. That day Dori hugged me close, quietly trying to take on some of my pain. She returned the next day, and for many days thereafter.

Our neighbor Carolyn was in her kitchen when Dori called and told her simply, "Alex is dead." "What?" It took her a while to understand the reality of it. Her husband, Joe Sr., was on his way to work when Dori called. He turned around and drove home. Their son, Joe Jr., long a friend of Alex's, let out a wail of sorrow. They were all in shock, unable to cope with the enormity of Alex's loss. They came later that afternoon. Joe Sr. was there when Chip got home with Hunter. Chip remembered Joe Sr. was the first person to hug him as he returned home, and that he sobbed in his arms. Chip had warned Hunter on the ride home that the house would be filling with people. Best friends just know to show up when you need them. For Hunter, however, it was too much; he retreated to his room, to deal with his sorrow alone.

I asked Hunter about his memories of that day, and he remembered sensing tension in the car on the way home:

> I had an attitude about some shit, and obviously [Chip] was trying to figure out the right time to tell me. He pulled over . . . and was like, "Just so you know, Alex is dead." I was like, "What the f-ck?" . . . I remember being shocked but also relieved in a way, of just like, thank God this shit's finally over. It was a weird combination of those two feelings. . . . This was coming inevitably, so at least it's kind of done. . . . It felt very dreamlike in the way the same day my dad died, of just like, what the f-ck is going on?

I well remember the next day when Hunter wondered aloud what our family had done in previous lives to deserve the trauma visited on us in this one.

Our family members, none of whom lived nearby, also knew of Alex's substance use issues. We had not kept it from them, but they assumed he would recover. We could offer them no details about Alex's death because we knew so little. I told them they didn't need to come, but of course they all did—my sisters Marianne, Libby, and Christine, and my brother Bill and their families. Only my ninety-two-year-old mother and Chip's father and his wife were unable to make the trip. Chip's sister Lynn (we always call her Poo) was devastated. She had long been close to Alex and was often there to help him in Florida when he needed her most. He loved her deeply.

I began to think about how to alert our larger community of friends and colleagues, and to figure out how to survive. But first I needed sleep. When day turned to evening, I took enough Ambien to ensure I could sleep through the night, more than I had ever taken in the past. I needed to be alert the next day. There was no time for insomnia.

Ours was what most people would consider a "good family." In our family story, Alex had everything going for him. He was smart, athletic, wickedly funny, loving, and sensitive. He grew up in Metuchen, a small New Jersey town south of New York City, the only child of two college professors. He attended a small private school from first to twelfth grade, where he did well. He had a passion for baseball and played Little League and tournament baseball and varsity in high school. Chip and Alex twice spent a week at Cooperstown Father & Son Baseball Camp, in 2000 and 2001. Along the way, Alex earned a black belt in karate and excelled as a skateboarder. Everyone loved him, and he had many close friends. In telling our story, I describe us as a "good family." While I'm aware of the reductive nature of this trope, I still find it a useful, descriptive idiom. Until Alex got sick, we thought of ourselves as a "normal" suburban American family. We were white, well educated, and affluent enough not to worry too much about our bills. We thought—as many Americans do—that addiction was something that happened to other people, not people like us. We learned soon enough that addiction knows no class or race boundaries—it takes aim at all kinds of families.

I think about our story in a second way as well, describing how our lives progressed along "two roads," to different futures. The ideal road—what all parents want for their child—travels a straight line through an idyllic childhood, high school and college graduations, career success, a family of his own. A second road—the one that parents dread—heads directly into the storms, depression, anxiety, mental health disorders, substance use, and, in the worst case, death. No parent wants such a life for her child, but some children get that life. These two paths are not at opposite ends of the same continuum. Sometimes they run parallel, but frequently they intersect. Sometimes you can hop from one to the other, and sometimes you have a foot on each. Alex walked each of these roads, veering toward happiness, success, and sanity at some points in his life, and toward anxiety, despair, and addiction at other times. We walked with him.

As a sociologist, I have studied, taught, and understood that society is formed and informed by the relations between biography and history.[1] This book has a lot of biography in it: mine, my family's, and most importantly, Alex's. The book also has a lot of history, if we think of history as a collection of forces larger than any individual: policies with long roots, promoting ideas about drug use that have gone unquestioned until recently, and the utter failure of any institution in our society to diminish the horror and damage that some drugs can cause.

In the middle of all that, the individual and history, is the thing we call "family." There is great variation in what we mean by family, but whatever we're talking about, or think we're talking about, it is the individual family member and the contexts within which his or her drug use happens that involve families so deeply. Ultimately, my book is about what happens to families and ways they can respond productively to the practices of people who use drugs that can bring death. While what I write is shaped by my own distinct experience, I worked hard to open myself up to the experiences of families unlike mine, especially those who lack the resources we had to help Alex. Writing about families and addiction means that this is a sad book—good people die too soon. But it is also a hopeful book—including ideas about how things can be made better. These are my two roads, which I'll tell you about primarily by describing the roads Alex took throughout his life.

CHAPTER 2

Week 1

> I just wish Alex had allowed himself to feel and believe that
> the dark sky would clear, the clouds would eventually part,
> and pure, unadulterated sunshine would fill his life.
> —Ashley, May 17, 2015

WEEK 1 KEPT us occupied with the chores and rituals that follow a death in the family. First on the list was meeting with the funeral director. Jay had been Alex's Little League coach and his son a teammate. Sadly, we were also repeat clients, having used his services when Kathy died in 2004 and then Hal in 2012.

We decided on cremation, and spoke to Jay about our decision to hold a "celebration of life" instead of a traditional funeral. We scheduled it for the following weekend at the funeral home. Jay arranged to bring Alex's body from Newark. We paid $4,375 for Jay's services, our final parental expense. We then drove to Newark to meet with the detective who had come to our house, hoping to find out if there was anything more she could tell us.

Later in the week, once Alex's body had arrived, we returned to the funeral home. Jay had a list of Alex's possessions, which he gave us along with Alex's wallet, which held his driver's license, health insurance card, and various other IDs. I asked Jay if he was sure it was Alex, and he assured us it was.

We chose not to view Alex's body; we wanted to remember our vibrant Alex. I sometimes regret that choice, feeling I should have hugged him one last time. At that moment, however, the thought of seeing Alex dead was unbearable. Chip remains convinced we made the right decision. He had, after all, seen Hal, Kathy, and his mother after their deaths and didn't want to relive that experience with Alex. Maybe I would have had equal regrets had I chosen differently, but a mother wants to hug her child, and I often wish I had.

Perhaps because of that choice, for years I was not entirely convinced Alex had died. Jay could have been wrong. After all, he hadn't seen Alex for years. Maybe someone stole his ID. For months I "saw" Alex walking around downtown, or into our backyard. I could hear him telling us he'd just been "away." It was five years before we could manage to bring Alex's ashes home. They remained with Jay until December 17, 2019, the day Alex would have turned thirty. It seemed time. Yet, truth be told, all these years later I sometimes still see him walking around town. In her book *The Year of Magical Thinking*, Joan Didion describes how she couldn't give away her husband's shoes after he died because he would need them if he returned.[1] I had much the same thought as I—much later—began to clean out Alex's closet. Keeping his clothes was a way to keep him alive, in an alternate universe. Until we packed to sell our house in 2022, some of Alex's clothes and shoes remained in his closet— just in case. The shattering finality of it is impossible to comprehend.

We went back to Newark a few days later. This time the police gave us Alex's backpack. At home, I took out the few items I wanted to keep, including family photos I had given to Alex to keep him company at his last rehab, and then buried the ratty thing deep in the trash. One thing we did not do on our trips to Newark that week was visit the empty lot where Alex's body was found. We eventually did that seven years later, before leaving New Jersey, and wondered anew what transpired that May night.

My friend Carolyn tells me that I projected a tremendous calm and sense of purpose those first weeks as I shifted to "what we need to do now" mode. Carolyn saw it as strength; but I think it was my ability to compartmentalize. Maybe I got that from my father, who was career military. All I knew was that Chip and I needed to put one foot in front of the other. We finalized arrangements. We organized the "Celebration of Life." We looked at photo albums and shoeboxes full of pictures, selecting the ones we wanted to display at the service. And, we talked about Alex. We walked the paths ahead of us, and we survived Day 1,

Week 1, and the days since. We have Hunter and Ginny and each other. We moved forward, and for me with an added purpose.

Chip asked our friend April to help organize the service and coordinate with Jay. April made the posters, put photographs in frames, and ordered the flowers. Friends from work organized and paid for the repast. Many local friends—"our tribe," as I call them—pitched in to help; our house was full of people, but we felt alone.

I began the task of writing Alex's obituary and my eulogy, and decided to be public about Alex's cause of death. With addiction, stigma leads some parents to disown their children, even in death. One of Alex's friends told me about a mutual friend who died of an overdose. His parents responded by getting rid of all their son's stuff, refusing to hold a service, vowing to never talk about him again. I have heard other such stories. I have difficulty fathoming such a reaction, even while understanding that there is no single way to grieve and deal with the death of a child. I needed to celebrate the life of my child, to try to give meaning to a life cut short, to acknowledge all of who he was. I also felt strongly that I needed to take a public stand against the stigma, to step out of the shadows. I wanted to shine a light on addiction. So, in addition to the normal obit stuff—name, age, family members, and where to donate—I was honest:

> Our beloved son Alex died May 11, 2015. He was a beautiful, smart, and funny guy. He spent his entire school life at Wardlaw Hartridge School and received his BS degree in biology from Dickinson College in 2012. He was a gifted athlete and played varsity baseball at Wardlaw. Alex loved his Granny, EDM [electronic dance music], his dog Lexi, and eating sushi with his dad.
>
> In his short life, Alex struggled with mental illness and drug and alcohol addiction. He fought them hard, sometimes winning a reprieve from the crippling anxieties and addictions that ended his life. If you have lived with the insanity of drug addiction, you well understand our sorrow. Alex recently talked with us about his new "three year plan," and he successfully carried out the first few steps of it, being re-admitted to Rutgers to complete his master's degree and finding a new sober living program, one that had a lot of promise and a year-long support structure. It was not to be. We try to remember the periods of tranquility

in the past few years, and the joys and successes of his short life. For all of you who loved him, thanks for being there for him and for us.

In my Facebook post—the site of so many of our "good family" memories—I included two of my favorite Alex pictures, but was similarly brief and blunt: "Our beloved Alex died yesterday, presumably of a drug overdose, although we don't know for sure. We are beyond heartbroken. Lots of you loved him. We will always love him. We will have a celebration of his life and will let you know the details." I recommended a donation in his honor to Rutgers Recovery House "so that others suffering in recovery might live again." The recovery house, run by Rutgers University's Alcohol and Drug Assistance Program, was established in 1988, and was the first residential recovery program on any college campus. By May 2020, nearly sixty people had generously joined us in donating to the program in Alex's memory.

Who Was Alex?

We held Alex's Celebration of Life the Sunday after the detectives arrived, May 17. Chip had created a slide show of photographs set to three songs that reminded him of Alex—Bob Dylan's "Forever Young," Creedence Clearwater Revival's "Have You Ever Seen the Rain?" and the Grateful Dead's "New Speedway Boogie," which played on a continual loop during the service. In truth, the songs were not Alex's musical tastes, although he liked them well enough. His tastes ran to loud music, from EDM to house to rock, which had emanated from our basement, where he and his "basement friends" hung out. He had set up his laptop to DJ for his friends, mimicking his favorite EDM artists Diplo, DeadMau5, Zedd, and Swedish House Mafia. Alex thought it was funny that I liked EDM, but it reminded me of my disco era. I don't listen to EDM music now; it's not playing in the basement anymore. I do listen to Dylan, Creedence, and Grateful Dead as I write about Alex; I'm listening to them as I write this.

Jay had told us to prepare for about one hundred people; in fact, close to five hundred came. Every chair in the funeral home's largest room was taken, and people were standing in the aisles. Our far-flung family members were there, from Virginia, Kansas City, and Florida—aunts, uncles, and cousins. Especially heartwarming was seeing so many of Alex's friends from childhood, high school, and college. One of his college classmates brought a large, color poster that included remarkable tributes that had been posted on Alex's Facebook page. His high school friends had attended a wedding for two classmates on Saturday, and then came to Alex's memorial service on Sunday. Even the bride and groom. Surely, twenty-five-year-olds should not have to attend a classmate's memorial.

Many of our Rutgers colleagues were there, even as they had to do double duty that day at the university's commencement. Many local friends were there. Every member of my book club attended, which included a mom's group that started when our kids were in sixth grade and continued until they graduated from high school. Parents of Alex's friends whom we had befriended over the years came, including some we hadn't seen in years. As I looked out over the crowd, I saw my Nar-Anon friends, who had come out in force to support me. They more than anyone knew the terrors of addiction. They knew that at least for that day they had been spared the ultimate curse. Sorrow was etched deeply on their faces. Another friend brought her son, a heroin user who had been at Alex's first rehab with him. I urged him to be vigilant in his sobriety—and when I bumped into him years later walking in town, I was heartened to see that he was doing well. I hugged him, and as I stepped away burst into tears. Why couldn't that be Alex? Alex lived, he thrived, he strove, he struggled—but he died.

So many from our small New Jersey town paid their respects to us and to Alex that Sunday—far more people than I can name. And I was grateful that many of Hunter's and Ginny's friends came to support them, including Hunter's new Rutgers fraternity brothers.

Rituals are important. Birthday celebrations, marriages, and memorial services all help us remember the important people in our lives. For the first hour, hundreds of people stood in line to hug Chip, me, Hunter, and Ginny. They cried. We consoled. It was a strange, out-of-body experience. In the second hour, eulogies from friends, teachers, and family members provided evidence of Alex's happiness, his successes, his smarts, and wicked sense of humor, and the love he had for his family. He was a person who had had a life worth celebrating and remembering.

Chip went first. He's the emotional one; I'm the one who can more successfully compartmentalize. We recognize and admire these traits in each other, but often wish we were more like the other. Mostly, we've learned to live with our differences. Ever the editor, Chip always reads my drafts. He's my best editor, although I don't always take his advice. He supports my decision to write about Alex and to tell my story but has zero interest in writing about this trauma himself. He'd prefer to lose himself in his scholarly work, not to dwell in his personal worst cases. Nonetheless, Alex still comes to him frequently in vivid dreams, day and night. Sometimes they are soothing, sometimes immensely sad. I've heard him more than once sobbing in the middle of the night.

Chip spoke of the joy Alex brought to our lives:

> When Alex was clean and sober he was such a joy to be around. He was crazy funny, wickedly witty, incredibly smart, so easy to love. . . . Let me tell you some things that Alex loved:
>
> He loved sushi. I started him on that early and told him he couldn't order anything from the menu unless he learned the proper name of the fish. He loved Saba. That's mackerel, in case you don't know your proper sushi-words. And when we went to Pi's, long our favorite place to be together in the world, we'd walk through the door and an employee would yell out, "Hey, Mackerel King!" Pi himself gave Alex that name. . . .
>
> He loved that I dedicated my last book to him, although I don't know if he ever read it. The book is titled *Worst Cases*. My dedication reads, "For Alex, my best case." He will always be my best case.
>
> He loved his dog, Lexi. He chose Lexi's name (registered name: Lady Lexus of Metuchen). Alex taught Lexi some cool tricks, although he never picked up any poop. But he held Lexi's head in his lap when we put her to sleep.
>
> He loved electronic dance music, EDM. I decidedly do not like it. I told him it wasn't real music, just as I told him his snake wasn't a proper pet. He told me I was just an old man.

Alex had a special connection to his Aunt Poo, as we call her. She was always there for him, and never more so when Alex's addictions brought him to Florida, where she lives. She spoke of how even during that time, Alex could still be Alex:

> It was really a gift that [my daughter] Sara and I were able to spend time with him during that trip. He laughed and made fun of me for stupid stuff. He gave Sara advice about school and keeping her grades up. We played pool which gave him yet another reason to make fun of me. We cracked up laughing about how embarrassing it was when Pat would go to his games and yell, "Go sweetie!"
>
> We ate oysters. We shopped and I made fun of him for buying something to cover his premature grey. He told me I was a sissy because I thought the water was too cold to go into . . . in March . . . but he finally fessed up that it was too cold for him too. He thought Hunter rocked for getting into the fraternity that Hal was in. But most of all, he talked about him getting back to school and starting over.

Our former next-door neighbors, Dori and Joe, knew Alex as their "third kid" and loved him dearly. They spoke about how close he was with their two kids:

> We can remember like it was yesterday meeting Alex for the first time. He came to the front door, looked up at us, and could not wait to meet the kid next door. . . . He was almost three when we moved in. Instantly he became a great playmate with our daughter Jenna, and then also our son Matthew.
>
> He was older and wiser and the most coordinated little kid we ever met. Mastered the pogo stick in a day; he was doing crazy tricks on his bike by five; and then came the skateboard. Typical Alex, he practiced and practiced for hours and hours . . . very loudly in our driveway ☺ but you couldn't help but be impressed how dedicated he was to get better and better at it.
>
> A natural athlete, he took to baseball very quickly . . . But he did feel it was his big brother duty to reveal the truth about Santa Claus . . . and we're sure many other truths were shared in the backyard secret passage.

One of his Dickinson College professors, Tyson, spoke of the pleasure of having Alex in his Introduction to Sociology course six years earlier. Tyson expressed being somewhat daunted by the idea of

teaching someone who had not one, but two university professor sociologists as parents, but "Alex was the kind of kid you love to teach. The
kind of kid you'd want to hang around with—curious, totally tuned in,
in solidarity with his fellow classmates, and intent on bringing us all
insights, laughter, and levity." He gave an anecdote about Alex that rang
so true it left everyone laughing:

> Often when I teach an Intro to Sociology course I start with a quick poll
> to try and explain what sociologists do. A provocative favorite of mine
> is, "Raise your hand if you think teenagers are having more sex than
> they used to." Undoubtedly, most of the students' hands go up—
> reflecting the conventional wisdom which has it that kids are having
> more sex than they used to be having. Sociologists, of course, know that
> they really aren't having more sex, they are actually having less, and this
> is my way of showing what sociologists do. But before revealing the
> truth . . . I ask them, "How do you know that kids are having more sex?"
> and students give all sorts of reasons from things they learned or seen
> or read from media, schools, and parents, etc. . . . [On this occasion,] I
> realized Alex, who had been sitting quietly in the second row with a
> baseball cap on, still had his hand raised. I asked him, "Alex, how else do
> we know that teenagers are having more sex?" And then Alex, with an
> ever so slight smirk, perhaps lowering his voice a bit, stated, "personal
> experience."
>
> It took me a second to realize that he was totally aware of his humor
> and as soon as I laughed, the whole class erupted in laughter. This class-
> room moment captured what I knew of Alex—a popular kid who made
> people laugh with his warm, easygoing way.

One of the best things we learned as all the tributes poured in was
that so many of Alex's friends talked about him as "my best friend." Jeff,
one of those longtime best friends, understood Alex's dedication to
perfection, but also spoke of his inclination toward risk-taking:

> Thank you for coming today to honor my best friend Alex. . . . I first met
> Alex when I was eleven years old at Wardlaw Hartridge. We had bonded
> over our love for skateboarding and he invited me over to his house to
> hang out . . . and [we] became inseparable. I quickly became part of the
> Clarke family and I spent more time at their house than my own.

We did everything together, from going to school, to camp in the summers, vacations to LBI [Long Beach Island] and Georgia. I even spent my Christmases with his family.

Some of my best memories took place hanging out in his basement and around Metuchen with him. Thinking back on it, we spent most of our time being idiots and trying our best to get in trouble or hurt, but always having fun. Whether it was skating at the brand-new Metuchen Police Station and getting yelled at by the officers, or making snowboard jumps in the woods with Joe, we were always laughing and loving life.

Alex was one of the smartest guys I knew. He was a great student and was always there for me when I needed help in Chemistry and Physics. He was always doing the craziest things on the computer that I never understood, like making his own website, editing our skate videos, and of course figuring a way to crack the firewall at school so we could go on any website. . . .

One of my favorite memories of Alex was [at] Rexplex, the old skate park near Newark Airport. After a year of practicing, we finally had the guts to drop in on the 12-foot halfpipe. . . . He began to drop in and hesitated ever so slightly, which resulted in him falling off his skateboard and basically falling 12 feet to his face. . . . He jumped up off the floor laughing and smiling like he just had the time of his life. That was exactly who Alex was.

Alex's friend Ashley was unable to be at the service but sent me her tribute to read. She provided insight into the college-age Alex, appreciating his craziness, complexity, and smarts:

Oh . . . where to start? I can remember when I first saw Alex, I thought, "Who is this kid with his super shaggy hair, a tongue ring, and an attitude unlike one I had seen any other freshman on campus have?" I must say I was confused, but under that exterior was such a complex and wonderful man. It started with a "We should do dinner and a movie." . . . Well let me tell you we picked the WORST movie to watch . . . 28 Days Later, yeah that weird movie where people get infected with some monkey virus. . . . However, that was the universe doing me a huge favor. It allowed us to talk and not just about superficial stuff, but we really got to talk . . . to get to know each other. That's when I began to love the person we are all here for today. Alex was truly gifted, naturally SO smart, and boy did that tick me off sometimes. . . . We took several classes together our senior year and with very little effort he kicked my butt all the time; I think he got a kick out of it when he'd beat me on exams, even problem sets we did TOGETHER (how that happened I will never know). As we grew closer, I was welcomed into the Clarke household and it became a home away from home. . . . Oh what I'd give to walk into that house again and see his smiling face at the bottom of the stairs.

And, last was my turn. In a tremulous voice, I spoke my piece and explained why I was missing Alex that day. I include the full eulogy in the appendix. I described how Alex walked along two roads in his life, and how these roads intersected throughout his life. I wanted to emphasize the first road, to talk about Alex's charms, his kindness and generosity, and his loving relationship with Hunter and Ginny:

Alex was a very good person, a "good kid." He was movie-star good-looking, smart, and wickedly funny. Definitely takes after his father in that regard—no one describes me as funny. I am still in awe of the eulogy he gave for his Aunt Kathy when he was fourteen. He wrote it because of his love for Kathy. He was an excellent athlete, excelling in baseball in high school and earning a black belt in karate. He was kind, and generous to those he loved, and he loved fiercely and was fiercely loyal. Among those he loved were Hunter and Ginny. He was a bit peeved that his "only child" status was threatened when Hunter and Ginny came to live with us. Frankly it was funny to see Alex and Hunter's attempts at one-upmanship. . . . They became like brothers, squabbles and all.

Here is what Hunter remembers: "He was my friend, my role model, and my brother. I always looked up to him and aspired to be as outgoing and intelligent as he was, and I still do. My favorite memories growing up were being around Alex. . . . I'll always be grateful for everything he taught me and everything he did for me and my sister." For her part, Ginny remembers how kind Alex was: "I could have been that annoying younger cousin, but he helped me with my math homework, came into my room to chat, and played video games. He was a brother to me."

I also spoke about the darkness that had taken over Alex's life, the second road on which he traveled:

But Alex also had his demons. He had an eating disorder that almost killed him when he was twelve. After being hospitalized, he fought back with the help of our dog Lexi, good doctors, and his Wardlaw friends to mostly recover. But significant anxiety and panic attacks remained with him for the rest of his life, fueling self-medication through drinking, drugs, and a resurgent eating disorder. These got particularly bad in the last few years of his life. He was searching for something to fill the void. But drinking and drugs did the opposite, they drove away his friends, the friends who loved him so much.

. . . One reason I want to be open and honest about Alex's struggles is to find a way in which his life can continue to have meaning.

After the service, we had people over to our house for food. It's all pretty much a blur. I remember feeling thankful for the support of so many of our friends and neighbors. I also remember feeling that the stigma of an addict's death likely persisted in that room of good-heartened, well-intentioned people. Years later, Hunter expressed it well: "I'm sure that [the service] was nice for you guys. It just pissed me off so much that [for some of those people] he was just reduced to just an overdose. . . . So many people still have that stigma of 'Who is this f-cking junkie?' And that shit pissed me off the most."

Week 1 was the longest week of my life. But it was not the hardest. That came after. We didn't know how to pick up the pieces and learn to live our lives again. We sought help. The following week we met with Dr. O, a psychologist we had talked with over the years to help find ways we could help Alex and help ourselves cope. Dr. O had treated Alex as well during his high school years, and especially once his substance use began. He gave us much insight into Alex's traumas. I rejoined my Nar-Anon group. They were glad to see me and welcomed me back. A friend gave us the name of a counselor who sponsored a group of parents who had lost a child to substance use. As I describe more fully in chapter 12, each group helped me at that point in my life. I also met with a *Rutgers News* staff member, Ken, who had previously helped Chip and me write op-eds related to our scholarly interests. He coached me on how to use my grief for good, through my writing.

The weekend after the service, we drove out to Montauk with Hunter and Ginny to visit our friends Judy and Mike. Montauk had long provided a respite from our trauma, and it did that again. We introduced Hunter and Ginny to our favorite walks overlooking the Atlantic Ocean, and the beautiful Montauk beaches. It was good to get away; it was the respite we needed. Judy, a former dissertation adviser of Chip's, and a former colleague of mine at Stony Brook, was nurturing as always. They fed us well and engaged us in supportive conversations.

A few days earlier I had pulled out a blank journal and begun to write in it. My first line: "5/20/15—finally, a use for this journal—toward a book *Remembering Alex*." That weekend I began to think more about how to write about our experiences. Judy helped me frame some of those ideas. While there, I read sections of sociologist Carolyn Ellis's book on the death of her husband and mentor Gene Weinstein and became intrigued with the way sociologists write about death and dying.[2] My story would be different, but I began to see how sociology could elucidate my narrative.

On our way toward home, we stopped to visit our friends Donna and Mark in Port Jefferson, where Chip and I had lived during our Stony Brook years. In conversation, Donna remembered Alex as "a sweet, gentle person." As I looked at Donna's two grown daughters who had joined us—friends of Alex over the years—I wondered anew why Alex hadn't been able to make the same transition to adulthood they had.

Over the following weeks, I learned more about how to move forward. I had routinely met friends, colleagues, and students for breakfast or lunch, and relished those opportunities for friendship and fellowship. Recognizing my need for renewed community, I slowly began meeting friends and colleagues for meals. Some friends had endured similar kinds of trauma and we spoke of that; others just wanted to see how I was doing. Resuming those get-togethers was comforting. I made an appointment for Ginny and me for a spa day. Dori, Carolyn, and I visited the Presby Iris Gardens in Montclair and ate hot fudge sundaes at Holsten's, the location of Tony Soprano's last supper. Dori and I returned to our regular chick-flick movie dates. Book club friends Joanne and Carolyn took me out to dinner, and we reminisced about our kids. As I tried to figure out how to survive my altered life, I endeavored to avoid talking about Alex all the time. Regaining normality to me also meant keeping up on the lives of my friends and their kids.

In July 2015, we took another step toward normalcy and traveled to my nephew Greg's wedding in Wisconsin. While it was a pleasure—even a delight—to celebrate with Greg and Meg, and much of my extended family, even at weddings one can't get away from sadness. I met another mom who had lost her son to an overdose a few months before Alex. We compared notes; there is solace in talking with others who know exactly how you feel.

As I contemplated the upcoming holidays, I knew I needed to get away from New Jersey. I was able to convince Chip, Hunter, and Ginny, along with Poo and Sara, who had long spent Christmas with us, to escape. We flew to a beach resort in Costa Rica for ten days. We spent time at the pool, ate at a different restaurant every night, went zip-lining and ATV driving, and celebrated Christmas with a makeshift tree the kids put together to surprise us. The formula worked, and we spent the next three Christmases away from home, traveling to Antigua in 2016, Jamaica in 2017, and then to Anna Maria Island in Florida in 2018. We were lucky we had the financial resources to escape; they helped us to heal. I know many families are not so lucky.

By 2019, we were ready to be home for the holidays and we've celebrated Christmas at home every year since. Each year we put up Alex's stocking, along with Granny's, Hal's, and Kathy's. We have even found some joy.

CHAPTER 3

Context

> Perhaps the most fruitful distinction with which the sociological
> imagination works is between 'the personal troubles of milieu'
> and 'the public issues of social structure.' . . . Know that
> many personal troubles cannot be solved merely as troubles,
> but must be understood in terms of public issues—and
> in terms of the problems of history-making.
> —C. Wright Mills, *The Sociological Imagination*

FROM THE TIME Alex began to suffer from anorexia, and then later also with addiction, I struggled to understand how a "good family" like ours could have landed in such a terrible place. I had to confront my assumptions that tragedies like mine did not happen to people like me, the kind of suburbanites thought protected from the dark world of drug misuse. Being academically minded, I read as many books and articles as I could and sought out anyone who had studied or dealt with the issues. I needed context for my family's suffering.

I quickly realized that our family was a living example of what I had been teaching and writing throughout my career. Our personal troubles were devastating but were part of larger public issues. What we saw and experienced as our own problems were but threads in a larger tapestry of social forces of which we were only dimly aware. I read voraciously about America's linked problems of substance use and mental health disorders, always filtering these readings through my knowledge of Alex's experiences, and ours along with his. We suffered alone, but the suffering could be understood only as part of larger social structures.

I read academic tomes, journalistic accounts, and memoirs—often at the same time. I read all the new books as they were published, among them Maia Szalavitz's *Unbroken Brain* and her more recent *Undoing Drugs*, Princeton economists Anne Case and Angus Deaton's *Deaths of Despair and the Future of Capitalism*, Johann Hari's *Chasing the Scream*, Carl Erik Fisher's *The Urge*, and many more—integrating what I was reading with what I had already learned (for a full list, see the "Relevant Sources" section at the end of the book).[1] I attended conferences on addiction and public health, and learned that the addiction story is often as much about mental health as it is about substance use. I discovered who the overdose crisis affected, and how its demography and geography changed over time. Since 1999 the epidemic itself has morphed from prescription drugs to heroin to fentanyl and drugs such as xylazine (often called tranq) used in veterinary medicine. Countless Americans continue to die, and few are paying attention. Each year there are more overdoses to add to the misery. Families suffer what I have come to call "surplus misery." How could they not think "why us?"

In this chapter, I share what I learned about how to think, research, and write about addiction. I not only add my personal story to the growing library of books and articles shining a light on addiction but offer a sociological perspective critical to developing effective policy approaches to address it. Our "personal troubles," as Mills taught us, must be understood in the context of "public issues of social structure." My story is not just a rendition of an individual life. We all live within a broader social context, and we can't really understand how and why people live as they do without understanding those contexts. This broader understanding of Alex's life and death helped me walk with him along his two roads, and ultimately sustained me in my grief.

The Numbers

I know not everyone loves numbers, but they provide an essential tool to understanding the big picture. So, let's take a closer look at overdose data. The number of Americans dying from drug overdoses is staggering. Between 1999 and 2020, more than 932,000 people died of a drug overdose.[2] During the twelve-month period ending in February 2023, approximately 105,000 Americans died the same way.[3]

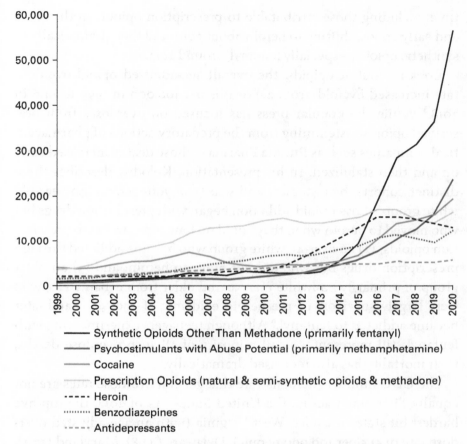

FIGURE 3.1. National Drug-Involved Overdose Deaths,* Number among All Ages, 1999–2020.
*Includes deaths with underlying causes of unintentional drug poisoning (X40-X44), suicide drug poisoning (X60-X64), homicide drug poisoning (X85), or drug poisoning of undetermined intent (Y10-Y14), as coded in the International Classification of Diseases, 10th revision.
Source: Andrew Kolodny, "Where We Stand & How We Move Forward: The Current State of the Opioid Crisis," keynote address, Knock Out Opioid Abuse Day, Learning Series Webinar, Partnership for a Drug-Free New Jersey and NJ Cares, October 6, 2022, https://knockoutday.drugfreenj.org/wp-content /uploads/2022/10/KOOAD_10_6_webinar.pdf.

In Figure 3.1, Andrew Kolodny presents data from the Centers for Disease Control and Prevention (CDC) demonstrating the drugs that contribute to U.S. overdose numbers, opioids and nonopioids alike, including prescription opioids, heroin, cocaine, methamphetamine, and synthetic opioids.[4] Trends in overdose statistics vary strikingly over time, including those attributable to prescription opioids in the 1990s and early 2000s, shifting to heroin about 2010, and then dramatically to synthetic opioids, especially fentanyl, around 2013.

Looking first at opioids, the overall age-adjusted opioid overdose rate increased fivefold, from 2.9 deaths per 100,000 in 1999 to 14.6 in 2018.[5] While the popular press has focused on overdoses from prescribed opioids—stemming from the predatory actions of pharmaceutical companies such as Purdue Pharma—those deaths increased early on and then stabilized. In his presentation, Kolodny describes three distinct cohorts, by age, race, and sex: (1) a younger, 20–40-year-old white group whose opioid addiction began with prescription drugs but who moved to heroin when they could no longer get access to prescription opioids; (2) an over-40 white group who became addicted through prescription drugs but who did not move to heroin; and (3) an older group of primarily nonwhite men 50 and older from urban areas, who were largely survivors of the heroin epidemic of the 1970s and later became addicted to fentanyl.[6] Although teenagers experimenting with fentanyl still represent a small minority of all such overdose deaths, their mortality has also increased dramatically.[7]

The CDC numbers demonstrate that general overdose rates are not equally distributed across the United States. As of 2018, the top-five hardest-hit states included West Virginia (with an age-adjusted overdose rate of 51.5 per 100,000 people), Delaware (43.8), Maryland (37.2), Pennsylvania (36.1), and Ohio (35.9). The five states with the lowest overdose rates were South Dakota (6.9), Nebraska (7.4), Iowa (9.6), North Dakota (10.2), and Texas (10.4). New Jersey, where we raised Alex, ranked 8th in the list of overdose states, at 33.1 per 100,000 people, only slightly lower than the top five. Alex died of a heroin overdose in 2015, and as the trend lines show, this was right at the height of heroin overdoses nationally.[8] This upward trend in drug overdoses between 1999 and 2018 occurred for both men and women, although males were more likely than females to die. In 2018 the age-adjusted rate of drug overdose for men was 27.9 per 100,000 men, up from 8.2 in 1999. The equivalent figures for women were 13.6 in 2018, up from 3.9 in 1999.[9]

Drug overdoses also varied by race for both men and women. While the upward trend in overdoses occurred for all races for both men and women, early in the epidemic black men were more likely to die than their white counterparts (in 1999, 11.5 per 100,000 vs. 8.1). By 2005, the race difference reversed, with white men more likely to die of overdose than black men. By 2016, overdose deaths were 28.8 per 100,000 for white men versus 24.0 for black men. If one looks only at non-Hispanic men, the white-black difference in 2016 was even larger (32.7 vs. 24.7), and the comparable figures for Native American and Hispanic men were 17.7 and 13.9, respectively. Among women, whites have always been more likely to overdose than blacks. Previously the difference was small: in 1999, 4.0 (white women) to 3.9 (black women). The gap, however, widened: in 2016 it was 15.2 for white women versus 10.0 for black women. In general, race differences in drug overdoses within sex between 1999 and 2016 were similar for opioid-specific overdose rates (as opposed to all overdoses).[10]

To provide some perspective on these numbers, Case and Deaton noted that by 2017 the annual number of drug overdose deaths was "greater than the peak annual number of deaths from HIV, from guns, or from automobile crashes. It is greater than the total number of Americans who died in Vietnam. The cumulative total from 2000 to 2017 is greater than the total number of Americans who died in the two world wars."[11]

Why and How?

The same way statistics are revealing, so too are historical perspectives on addiction. To make sense of Alex's and our experiences, I found it essential to take a dive into America's history of addiction to help flesh out the "why questions" that we struggled with, and to put these statistical trends into perspective. As historian David Herzberg's *White Market Drugs* well describes, the current overdose crisis in the United States is only the latest in a series of drug crises that have persisted for well over a century.[12] In Herzberg's telling, over the years, "pharmaceuticals" and "drugs" evolved as two distinct strands: the regulation of legal, medical prescribing of pharmaceuticals to whites through "white markets" on the one hand, and the controlling of illegal, nonmedical drugs sold in "informal markets" to urban blacks and immigrants, on the other. This distinction goes back well over a century and has long been a binary one linked to race.

Small-town and suburban communities in the United States have repeatedly suffered crises of addiction and overdose from legal pharmaceuticals sold in white markets. These have occurred over three distinct periods in American history: (1) the rise in opioids and cocaine at the turn of the twentieth century; (2) the increased sales of pharmaceutical sedatives and stimulants from the 1930s to the 1970s; and (3) the spiraling medical sales of sedatives, stimulants, and opioids at the turn of the twenty-first century. Despite presumed therapeutic intent of physicians and pharmaceutical companies, lack of consumer protections led to increased addiction among white communities, more so than among black, brown, and poorer communities who had less access to legally prescribed medicines. While addictive drugs certainly have their medical benefits, addiction is also an outcome of poorly regulated markets that serve to increase company profits at the expense of consumer interests.[13]

While physicians and pharmaceutical companies have often treated consumers of white market prescription medicines as "legitimate addicts," those who purchased drugs for nonmedical use in informal markets are viewed as "dope fiends."[14] All nonmedical use of drugs was seen as unlawful and harmful, morally stigmatized, and actively controlled through drug wars perpetrated especially against communities of color. These attitudes became entrenched in policies enacted by the U.S. government, through its so-called war on drugs.[15] By most reports, the war on drugs' first and most effective proponent was Harry Anslinger, who in 1930 became the founding commissioner of the U.S. Federal Bureau of Narcotics, formerly the Bureau of Prohibition. He served in that position for thirty-two years, through five presidents, Republican and Democrat alike (Herbert Hoover, Franklin Roosevelt, Harry Truman, Dwight Eisenhower, and John Kennedy). Although the agency's name had changed, Aslinger's focus remained prohibition, and harsh and punitive penalties became the government's go-to response to illegal drug use, particularly by nonwhites.[16]

Over the years, the war on drugs has been a bipartisan battle cry. President Richard Nixon endorsed it, and in the late 1980s President

Ronald Reagan and First Lady Nancy Reagan amplified the call. President Joe Biden advocated tough-minded drug policies during his Senate years, and Hillary Clinton similarly embraced harsh drug policies. Both have since moderated their views. As Michelle Alexander describes so powerfully in *The New Jim Crow*, under these national policies, mass incarceration—especially of black and brown Americans—meant that throwing people into jails and prisons became the accepted response, even for minor drug offenses.[17]

The war on drugs rhetoric continues to infect how society and law enforcement deal with addiction to this day—something we personally witnessed. For example, it contributed to the stigmatizing of legitimate uses of drug maintenance programs. Historically doctors prescribed morphine maintenance for "respectable" consumers (those who were white, native-born, and working). Methadone maintenance for opioid withdrawal, in contrast, was not officially sanctioned until the 1960s and not approved by the Food and Drug Administration (FDA) until 1972. One reason for this delay was because its consumers—more often blacks and Hispanics, or "socioeconomic problem addicts"—were seen as less respectable.[18] Race and class prejudice was systematically built into how addiction was defined, but also into proposed solutions.

While the war on drugs was raging on the front lawns of America, the backdoors were left wide open for the legal marketing and encouraged use of addictive prescription drugs for pain management, most notoriously OxyContin. Pharmaceutical companies such as Purdue Pharma worked relentlessly in the 1980s and 1990s to advocate for the use of opioids, by freeing them from burdensome governmental and industry regulations, leading to huge increases in the sales of opioids and dramatic profits.[19] Pharmaceutical companies touted their drugs as nonaddictive, based on one "study" in the *New England Journal of Medicine* claiming an addiction rate of less than 1 percent among those with no history of addiction.[20] As journalists and activists have since pointed out, this was not research at all, simply a letter to the editor that became the basis for advertising lies Purdue Pharma used repeatedly in their advertising.[21] Drug companies also funded marketing, and co-opted professional and regulatory organizations to change long-standing medical standards to encourage opioid use for pain. In 2001, the Joint

Commission on the Accreditation of Healthcare Organizations developed new standards that defined pain as the "Fifth Vital Sign," which proved to be a huge win for opioid-producing companies.[22]

From inside the pharmaceutical industry, the ensuing overdose crisis was blamed not on the companies profiting from opioids (which they did handsomely) but on those who abused drugs. In the words of Purdue Pharma's president, Richard Sackler: "We have to hammer on the abusers in every possible way. They are the culprits and the problem. They are reckless criminals." Sackler argued that restrictions on opioid distribution would only hurt "legitimate pain patients."[23] Such strategies represented a renewed racialization of addiction, and furthermore allowed those marketing dangerous drugs to avoid responsibility. We all know what happened: "In the early twenty-first century, then, the United States faced the worst of both worlds: morgues filling up with fatal drug overdoses even as prisons continued to fill with drug offenders. It was the most terrible manifestation yet of the basic structural flaws that had dogged American drug policy for a century."[24]

What does all this mean for Americans? As the overdose crisis surged, it became harder for pharmaceutical companies to maintain their focus on "criminal abusers" when those abusing drugs were white kids from rural and suburban areas, especially those from regions suffering economic deprivation. As the victims became the white kids next door, attitudes toward those suffering from addiction slowly began to shift. The National Institute for Drug Abuse (NIDA) remade addiction into a chronic brain disease. Even traditional forms of opioid maintenance such as methadone maintenance were re-created with a different consumer—white kids like Alex—in mind. Buprenorphine (aka Suboxone), used to treat opiate addiction, was FDA approved in 2002, and regulations were eased to allow it to be prescribed in physicians' offices (and reduced even further in 2020 when the COVID-19 pandemic hit). Indeed, Alex took full advantage of Suboxone during his years of addiction.

Emerging in more recent years has been a new emphasis on harm reduction policies, which focus less on punitive strategies that criminalize drugs and more on reducing the harm and risks associated with drug use. Such policies humanize those addicted, thus reducing stigma and enhancing opportunities for successful treatment. Although many other countries have adopted harm reduction strategies, the United States has not moved very far along this new policy track.[25] Nonetheless, progress is visible: punitive drug laws are slowly being revisited in some states and naloxone (aka Narcan) is now widely available to emergency services and the police, often the first responders to overdoses. Alex benefited from these policy changes: Narcan brought him back to life multiple times. As Herzberg opines, reformers are "[reorienting] drug policy so that it is structured around safe and unsafe use rather than medical and nonmedical use ... [in] an effort to dismantle the medicine-drug divide."[26]

Who?

As I found out in the worst possible way, heroin had arrived in my small New Jersey town by the 2010s. Until then, if I thought about heroin, which I didn't much, I assumed it was primarily a big-city, poor-neighborhood phenomenon. Yet long before then, it was devastating vast parts of Middle America. Like most white middle-class Americans, I was mostly ignorant of this destruction, until it literally hit home. Two of the first books I read about the overdose epidemic were Sam Quinones's *Dreamland* and Beth Macy's *Dopesick*.[27] Quinones and Macy dug deep into America's addiction crisis, describing its devastating effects on small-town rural and suburban America, as well as its shift into wealthier suburbs. By the time they were writing, heroin had reached white main-street America. Quinones tells the story of those most affected early on by addiction, the canaries in the proverbial coal mine. He interviewed the families of young people from Ohio, West Virginia, Oregon, Kentucky, and other states devastated by heroin overdoses, and many of them were the sons and daughters of the white suburban middle class.

In *Dreamland*, we hear the story of Purdue Pharma, which made millions profiting from peddling opioids, ostensibly to those suffering from chronic pain but clearly reaching America's young. We hear as well of the middle-level dealers selling the black tar heroin that was killing people, and the always overwhelmed law enforcement officers trying but failing to stem the tide of heroin use, addiction, and death. Whether it is black tar heroin in the Midwest and the West, or the white powder heroin more common in the East, kids from every background were being addicted in record numbers. These interweaving stories are compelling, describing how dealers—many from the same small town in Nayarit, Mexico—sold heroin like hamburgers on street corners. This was capitalism at its most successful, although now it was killing not only people you didn't know, but also your and your neighbors' kids.

Dopesick tracks a similar story, describing opiate addiction in western Virginia—Appalachian country—bordering Tennessee, West Virginia, and Kentucky. For two decades, Macy reported on the heroin epidemic for the *Roanoke Times*, documenting the relentless toll of opioid overdoses among Americans from every walk of life and the role of Purdue Pharma's OxyContin in fueling the epidemic. The interviews with devastated moms are heartrending. I readily understand the grief these moms felt when their sons and daughters died. Many more Americans now understand this grief. Opioid addiction—and drug addiction more generally—is an equal opportunity problem. It is white and black, red and blue, rich and poor, rural and urban, and it wears blue jeans and suits. No group or geographic region is spared. People are dying of overdoses in record numbers. Not surprisingly, the increasing numbers, and the change in the composition of who is addicted, led to increased media and political attention. Stories of addiction and loss now pop up daily in the national and local press. It's also shown up in our movie theaters.

In *The Least of Us*, Quinones turns his lens to the next stage of the addiction crisis, the shift to synthetic fentanyl and methamphetamines, with their illicit origins in China and, eventually, Mexico.[28] Quinones tells heartbreaking stories of how these drugs destroyed the lives of the kids next door, and their friends and families. Part of the story is the economic devastation of small-town America, including the closing of automobile factories and machine shops in Muncie, Indiana; truck-axle factories in Hardin County, Ohio; and glass factories in Clarksburg, West Virginia. As the economies of small towns and cities were decimated, drugs flooded the deteriorating neighborhoods, addicting large swaths of people. And things went from bad to worse when the method for producing meth shifted from ephedrine to the highly toxic P2P, leaving a mental health "apocalypse" in its wake.[29]

As a sociologist specializing in gender and labor, I knew how profoundly social and economic forces shape people's life chances, and addiction. In *Deaths of Despair and the Future of Capitalism*, Case and Deaton add this structural context to the addiction story. They point to the culprit in their title, describing how social and economic forces that pervade capitalism fail many Americans. Although remaining bullish about capitalism, their work documents the dramatic surge in deaths from suicide, alcoholism, and drug overdose—or "deaths of despair"—that have driven down life expectancy rates in the United States to historically low levels. CDC data demonstrate that mortality death rates between 1990 and 2017 due to drug, alcohol, and suicide tripled for those with less than a bachelor's degree (BA), for both men and women, while those with a BA remained essentially constant.[30]

Increasing mortality due to deaths of despair in recent years has been driven primarily by whites, echoing an increase among blacks earlier in the twentieth century.[31] One might say that white Americans are now catching up on the despair black Americans have long experienced. Reflecting the distinction between rates of change and overall levels of mortality, however, black mortality rates remain higher than white rates, due to racially biased policies and practices. Thanks to pushback against those biased policies, there has been some progress in reducing the race gap since 1970, for several reasons: (1) the black mortality rate declined faster than white's; (2) progress among blacks stalled during the 1980s, when the crack and HIV crises hit them hard; and (3) blacks were less likely than whites to die from opioid overdoses, suicide, and alcoholism at the beginning of the twenty-first century because they had less access to the prescription opioids that drove those deaths. Progress toward race equality halted after 2013, when blacks began to suffer higher mortality from fentanyl and other synthetic opioids.[32]

In Case and Deaton's view, educational achievement is key: between 1992 and 2017 the rate of deaths of despair increased most dramatically for whites without a BA, followed by the comparable group among blacks. Blacks and whites with BAs had the lowest mortality rates from drugs, alcohol, and suicide; their death rates remained essentially flat from 1992 to 2017. Overall, 90 percent of overdose deaths are among those without a college degree.[33]

As a sociologist, I found analyzing these numbers and trends helpful as my first step in trying to make sense of how this tragedy arrived at our front door. Yet the statistics left me wondering why my Alex, with his college degree and loving family, ended up dying a "death of despair." To answer that question, I needed a more personal understanding of the addiction story. Addiction had literally entered my house, so my take on it became intensely personal.

To gain insight into my family's situation, I broadened my readings from scholarship and journalism to memoirs. These personal narratives describe mental health and addiction in raw and unfiltered ways, showing how it destroys the lives of children, families, neighbors, and friends. They help us experience the immediacy of addiction and associated mental health crises, the daily insanity for the addicted and those who love them. While Alex was still in active addiction, I read with hope about those who confronted eating disorders and addiction and survived. I desperately wanted the positive outcomes of David Sheff (*Beautiful Boy*), William Cope Moyers (*Broken*), and Maia Szalavitz (*Unbroken Brain*). Later, I read David Carr (*The Night of the Gun*), Hunter Biden (*Beautiful Things*), Ryan Hampton (*American Fix*), Harriet Brown (*Brave Girl Eating*), and Marya Hornbacher (*Wasted*). I agonized over the addiction stories of Nic Sheff (*Tweak* and *We All Fall Down*) and more recently Keri Blakinger's *Corrections in Ink* and Matthew Perry's *Friends, Lovers, and the Big Terrible Thing*. Novelists have also begun to address addiction, most notably Barbara Kingsolver in her Pulitzer prize-winning novel *Demon Copperhead*, which tackles the history and reality of substance use in Appalachia, and its horrific consequences for families and society. [34] All these authors are white, perhaps reflecting the fact that addiction has now entered their homes, and not just those of unknown "others."

Imagining Alex in the squalid conditions these authors describe was terrifying to contemplate, and yet from everything I learned he lived through a very similar hell. All these memoirs describe success stories. We root for those addicted and their families, and in these memoirs our hopes are rewarded. And of course, the subjects in each have survived to tell their stories. My story has a very different ending; Alex didn't survive to pen his own heroic narrative. It is left to me to tell his (and my) story. I would desperately have preferred to have been one of those parents who wrote about their harrowing journey with their surviving child.

In *Surviving Alex*, I extend these authors' experiences to examine what happens when your loved one dies. I found only two such memoirs. Jessie Dunleavy's *Cover My Dreams in Ink* describes the 2017 fentanyl overdose of her thirty-four-year-old son Paul.[35] Dunleavy's book is a searing reminder of the toll of the overdose epidemic on young Americans and their families, and an indictment of our existing policies and treatment programs. She shows how young people like Paul fall through the cracks of educational, medical, and legal institutions that should have saved him. Multiple systemic failures left Dunleavy to contend alone with increasingly severe consequences. All of this is familiar; our family contended with similar systemic failures.

W.J.T. Mitchell's *Mental Traveler* narrates the death by suicide of his thirty-eight-year-old son Gabe.[36] The Mitchells' twenty-year odyssey of despair and sorrow is a gripping memoir of a young man suffering from schizophrenia and other mental health disorders, but also the travails of his family who supported him. Mitchell demonstrates how academic understandings and personal experiences can inform each other. His is a story infused with scholarly insights as a professor at the University of Chicago. Similarly, mine builds on sociological insights.

These ways of thinking about addiction sharpened my understanding of the American overdose crisis. They reframed my developing ideas, complicating my search for answers to what happened to my family. If Case and Deaton are right, Alex was in the 10 percent of those who overdosed and died who had a BA. Why wasn't his college degree and his middle-class upbringing protective, as their work indicates it was for so many others? For the most part, Alex didn't turn to heroin from prescription drugs. He wasn't prescribed opioids from "white markets" but found them through "informal markets." At one point he did have a legal prescription for Xanax, and he later misused prescribed Suboxone.

These theories, arguments, and statistics do not fully explain Alex's story, but they provide a foundation for understanding the public and political approaches to the overdose crisis, which I explore in chapters 12 and 13. They also give context for how the medical, educational, and geographic community treated us during Alex's short life. As I explained above, the existing war on drugs mentality and zero tolerance policies lead to a punitive approach to dealing with addiction. Jail sentences have long been the accepted response for those who not only sell drugs, but who do drugs. And like many low-level users, Alex did spend time in jail, and spent years facing severe legal troubles. At that time, harm reduction approaches were scarcely on the scene, a deficit that hurt Alex's chances for recovery. Significant headway is yet to come with respect to harm reduction as a politically acceptable approach to addiction, a point I return to in chapter 13.

Thinking, Researching, and Writing about Addiction

After years of reading, I knew about the history of the overdose crisis and the pain it caused so many American families. My sociologist self needed to go the next step, to connect what I was learning to what had happened to Alex. Why did the methods we tried fail? How should policies be fixed, so others can avoid this pain? As a mother, I needed to know what happened to Alex. As a sociologist, I compared the models of explanation available and found one clearly superior to the rest. If we can adopt the harm reduction model more widely, we can make a huge difference in solving the addiction crisis.

To understand this model, let's start with how the *Diagnostic and Statistical Manual of Mental Disorders, Fifth Edition* (DSM-5) classifies addiction. DSM-5 is the foundation of how we treat mental disorders today. It classifies addiction as "a severe substance use disorder" that is "best understood as compulsive use of a substance or compulsive engagement in a behavior despite ongoing negative consequences."[37] Researchers, policymakers, and your average American tend to think about how that compulsion to addiction develops in one of three distinct ways.

First, the moral argument dictates that addiction is simply a voluntary choice, likely evolving from individual "defects of character." While many researchers have moved on from this perspective, it remains a strong point of view among politicians and the public generally. Many Americans, regardless of their level of education, still believe that the opportunity for change lies within the individual, who simply needs to be ready for change. Indeed, this perspective remains the go-to explanation in the United States for understanding, treating, and policing addiction. We have treatment and medical systems heavily focused on 12-step programs, a political sphere that relies on criminal justice remedies, insurance systems and state regulatory agencies that fail those addicted, and a popular media that pushes the choice paradigm. The underlying argument is that we need to change the individual choices made by defective people, by force if necessary. And the many "success" memoirs of survivors who are in sustained recovery because they mustered the fortitude to change reinforce that view. Or, invoking the paradigm, they proved to be "less defective" than those who succumbed.

Alternatively, in argument number two, many now define addiction a chronic brain disease, where the drug hijacks the brain, leading to addiction's negative consequences. Nora Volkow and her colleagues at NIDA are proponents of this approach, which has gained adherents over recent years, especially as white, middle-class people have increasingly become addicted. Through years of research on rats, and more recently through human brain imaging, researchers have demonstrated the physical differences in the brains of those addicted and those not. Many of us remember hearing about the rats who continued to press a lever for heroin until they died. Subsequent brain imaging research revealed that those addicted have fewer dopamine receptors, which results in reducing the ability of the prefrontal cortex to exert control. An important implication of these studies is that those who keep using drugs do so to remain stable, and no longer to feel pleasure.[38] In my view, this research is an improvement on the personal choice perspective because it allows for extra-individual causes for addiction, such as stress, differing economic resources, and trauma. The brain disease model views addiction as "involuntary and uncontrollable compulsions," which call for compassion and treatment. This idea of addiction as a brain disease now permeates the language of 12-step programs, the preferred treatment in rehab and sober living programs.

These two approaches are often described as a "dichotomy of free choice versus total compulsion" and have long been the accepted models for examining addiction.[39] In 2012, the National Center on Addiction and Substance Abuse at Columbia University (now renamed Partnership to End Addiction) published an authoritative report on the topic, which came down clearly on the side of "brain disease."[40] Addiction, the report argued, is a "complex brain disease with significant behavioral characteristics.... [It] typically originates with use in adolescence when the brain is still developing and is more vulnerable to their effects. If untreated, it can become a chronic and relapsing condition."[41] The report described only two "models for understanding addiction": the moral model (which argued that addiction was a "failure of personal responsibility or morality") and the disease model (which acknowledged the roles of biology and genetics).[42]

But there is a third approach that has gained ground in recent years, one that conceptualizes addiction as a type of learning disorder, like developmental disorders such as autism and attention-deficit/hyperactivity disorder. Having parented Alex and lived through his harrowing years of addiction, I found this perspective most compelling and closest to our experience. Yet, this approach is not yet well accepted in entrenched treatment programs or in social and political conversations that continue unabated to focus almost entirely on the morality mantras of "free choice" and "compulsion."

Maia Szalavitz, a leading proponent of this approach, survived addiction to heroin and cocaine in the 1980s when she was in her twenties. She went on to become one of the foremost American journalists of addiction. She rejects the "broken brain" depiction of addiction and asserts there are three critical elements to the phenomenon: (1) the behavior has a psychological purpose; (2) the specific learning pathways involved cause the behavior to become nearly automatic and compulsive; and (3) the behavior does not stop when it is no longer adaptive, meaning it continues even though there is no longer any psychological benefit from the behavior.[43]

In short, under this perspective, addiction is best viewed as a coping mechanism for pain, not a personality flaw or brain disease. Szalavitz, and other adherents to this view, emphasize the social and political implications of addiction over approaches focused on a medical or character flaw. Given the failings of current treatment and criminal justice policies, this insight is a crucial one. As I describe more fully in chapter 11, taking into account learning, as Szalavitz recommends, allows researchers and practitioners to focus on the physical and psychological pain that precedes addiction, including trauma.

Psychologists such as Stanton Peele have also argued against the view of addiction as a chronic brain disease, believing instead that those with substance use disorders mature out of their addiction when their cultural contexts change.[44] Based on research studies by Lee Robins and Norman Zinberg, Peele, Szalavitz, and Fisher note the experiences of Vietnam veterans who took opium and heroin overseas, but gave it up once they returned home to their "normal lives." Scientists have long known that while the brain reaches its adult size around age fourteen, it continues to mature, not fully developing until the mid- to late twenties.[45] One of the last areas of the brain to mature is the front part—the prefrontal cortex—responsible for impulse control and planning. As a result, teens are more likely to engage in risky behavior and less likely to consider the consequences of their actions. Consistent with this, the vast majority of substance use disorders begin in adolescence (90 percent), and most end with or without treatment by age thirty.[46]

To my mind, this focus on social context on the development and persistence of addiction—Szalavitz calls it "set and setting"—provides a more convincing explanation for addiction. It brings to mind Bruce Alexander's Rat Park experiments in the late 1970s. In one, he found that isolating rats in cages led them to fatal doses of heroin, whereas providing them a sense of community with their fellow rats encouraged resistance to the drug. While not all attempts to replicate the Rat Park experiments succeeded, most did.[47]

Other social scientists have also argued for the importance of social context, noting that a single injection of heroin will not, contrary to public opinion, lead to addiction. Most addicts do not in fact die and can lead functional lives. The "one hit and you're hooked" view of addiction is false.[48] In fact, the vast majority of drug users (~70 percent), including heroin users, do not meet the DSM-5 definition of addiction. In this view pre-existing conditions or vulnerabilities such as psychological disorders (like depression or anxiety) or socioeconomic factors (like poverty, unemployment, incarceration, and racism) are the real precursors to addiction. Researchers attribute addiction to "unprocessed pain" from "society's wounds": "This is the core of the addiction-as-dislocation theory. Beyond soothing the concrete effects of physical dislocation, people use drugs to address an alienation from cultural supports. This kind of alienation is what Émile Durkheim, the founder of modern sociology, called anomie: the social condition of a breakdown of norms and values, resulting in an existential lack of connection to meaning and purpose. Both this sense of dislocation and the actions of addiction supply industries, some scholars argue, are the core drivers of today's opioid epidemic."[49] It's thus not the organic properties of drugs that lead to addiction, as brain disease researchers argue. Rather, it's the environments in which people live that precondition one to choose drugs, "to seek euphoria or numbness through drugs . . . biographies matter."[50] Genetic predispositions can lead to addiction, just as they do for other neurodevelopmental conditions like schizophrenia, depression, and autism. In fact, studies have shown addiction is often a co-occurring disorder with one or more of these conditions, up to 98 percent in some studies.[51]

As I searched for explanations, as a sociologist I knew that free choice was a nonstarter. I found the brain disease perspective more convincing. It made sense to me that heroin had taken over Alex's brain. Like others with substance use issues, he was a different person on drugs. There was no more of that happy child. He was simply the drug-seeking addict, with a maniacal drive for heroin, and he would lie, cheat, and steal to get it. We don't fully know the lengths he went to get drugs, but we did learn about his forays into dangerous parts of many cities, and into multiple experiences with gun-wielding drug dealers. We know about him selling drugs to support his own habit, a common occurrence among low-level drug users. So, I know what the drug did to him. But I also know that the brain disease explanation only goes so far. How did Alex get to the point that he took that first hit? And most importantly, why did he keep injecting heroin even when he knew that it was destroying his life? I kept searching.

Amidst the despair over Alex's addiction, reading Szalavitz gave me my first aha moment. Although *Unbroken Brain* was not published until

2016—one year after Alex died—Szalavitz's work began to appear in interviews and magazine articles prior to then. Her perspective—more social science–oriented than other work—helped me make sense of what was happening to Alex. She explains well what I was experiencing in my front-row seat to addiction: why the punitive policies undergirding much of U.S. policy on addiction fail, why the traditional U.S. treatment system is inferior, and why current public policy approaches are broken. She argued that addiction occurs only in certain contexts, that it's a pattern of learned behavior.[52]

These researchers and activists changed the trajectory of my search for why, and my views of current treatment programs. It provided me a language and a blueprint for writing about the insanity of addiction. Although this approach still runs counter to widely accepted norms in the recovery community, many are beginning to make similar arguments. In her memoir about surviving alcohol addiction, Leslie Jamison champions a more pluralistic approach to addiction recovery, moving away from punitive treatment and incarceration to treatment approaches like harm reduction and medication-assisted recovery. Journalists like Michael Pollan, and researchers and policy professionals, are advocating for this perspective, precisely because it's a more holistic approach that values the humanity of those contending with substance use and mental health disorders. To my mind, it also better addresses the corrosive effects of stigma and leads to more effective public and private policy strategies.[53]

I've heard activists describe harm reduction as a strategy that "meets people where they are but doesn't leave them there." Maia Szalavitz was the first to explore harm reduction in historical perspective, and others have documented how harm reduction methods have successfully reduced overdoses and addiction in a number of other countries (e.g., Portugal, Switzerland, Uruguay, and Vancouver, Canada).[54] While those in the policy world and addiction researchers may know about harm reduction, those of us outside these circles remain largely unfamiliar with it. My memoir brings these ideas to a larger public, while providing a strong challenge to extant treatment and policy options, a topic I return to in chapter 13.

PART II

NORMALITY AND ANXIETY

CHAPTER 4

"A Good Family"

"The Dream"
Ther was an old man from peru.
He dreamed he was eating his shoe.
He awakened to find it was all in his mind but was never actually there.
—Alex Clarke, date unknown

LOVE FOR A CHILD "is a singular love, because it is a love whose foundation is not physical attraction, or pleasure, or intellect, but fear. . . . Every day, your first thought is not 'I love him' but 'How is he?' The world, overnight, rearranges itself into an obstacle course of terrors."[1] Before the troubles began, I assumed we were "a good family," a normal middle-class family, exempt from the dark side of addictions. For reasons I can no longer fathom, my neighbor Dori and I used to trade horrific stories about the things that happened to children. I remember a story about a child who died when snow fell off the roof, burying him in his own backyard. I wondered at the time what I would do if Alex—my only child—died under a snow drift, little realizing the avalanche of troubles that would eventually bury him. I now know that bad things happen to good people.

In these next chapters, I write about our family's early years when we lived our lives blissfully ignorant of the future that would come. I look back on those years and appreciate all the opportunities that we enjoyed as a family: two steady incomes, good health care, excellent schools, a vibrant community, and many good friends. In that safe bubble, we walked along that first road together, enjoying the happy (if tiring) years of baby and toddlerhood and the progression to early school years. But when Alex was twelve and in middle school, the cracks began to appear. Entering adolescence, his anorexia and mental health issues emerged, and he began to walk on that second road, the one parents dread, with potholes and detours. And then, thankfully, for a while at least, Alex gained weight and his mental health issues receded. The old Alex was back, walking confidently along that first road. But we soon learned that these two roads are not at opposite ends of a single continuum. They run parallel to each other, and frequently intersect. We walked with him along both those roads for the rest of his life.

Pat and Chip

Lee "Chip" Clarke was a Southern boy born in Georgia and raised in Florida, the first child of hospital administrator Ben and teacher Katherine. His sister Poo and brother Hal were two and four years younger, respectively. In 1979, after graduating from Florida State University, he left for graduate school at Stony Brook University on Long Island, where he earned his PhD in sociology. Despite his over forty years up north, Chip still speaks with a southern accent, which when talking to his family reverts to a thick drawl.

I was an Army brat. My father Bill was a civil engineer, and my mom Miriam a proud Army wife who met her future husband when she was eighteen, on a blind date at West Point. I am the second of five boomers, with an older brother, Bill, and three younger sisters, Libby, Marianne, and Christine. We were stationed in Oklahoma when I was born, and soon moved to Germany for three years. Then we moved back to the States, transferring from base to base. By the time I was twenty-five, I had moved twenty-five times. During my mid-teens, we spent four wonderful years at West Point, where my father was a professor of civil engineering. West Point was a kid's paradise, a place where we were protected from the outside world. We ice skated a block from our house, played in the local woods, swam in dammed-up creeks, sat on the field during Army home football games, and wandered by ourselves from one end of the base to the other. As kids we learned and embraced West Point's motto: "Duty, Honor, Country." I still remember my father's question to us when he arrived home from work: "So what do you have to say for yourself?" Perhaps that's why my siblings and I all ended up in service-related occupations. And we have all had a lot to say for ourselves. This book is part of that legacy from my father. Our journey with Alex, and my continuing journey with him ever present within me, have given me something to say.

Just before my sophomore year in high school, my dad's service took us to Washington, DC, where he attended the National War College, and then to Honolulu, where he became Hawaii's district engineer. I spent my last two high school years at the well-respected Punahou School, a private K-12 school that President Barack Obama later attended. I found the school, and then leaned on my parents to pay the private school tuition. Those years were amazing, walking barefoot at school, surfing at many Hawaiian beaches, dancing hula, Tahitian, and Māori semiprofessionally, and being challenged intellectually at the best school in Honolulu. After my graduation in 1968, my father retired and relocated the family to Southern California. I attended the University of California, Davis, and married my first husband. In 1974 we relocated to the University of California, Los Angeles, for our PhDs. In 1978, I moved to Washington, DC, to work on my dissertation and serve as a research assistant at the National Academy of Sciences. After completing my dissertation, and getting divorced along the way, in 1981 I moved to my first faculty position at Stony Brook as an assistant professor of sociology.

And Stony Brook is where Chip's and my worlds crossed. Despite a seven-year age difference, we fell in love. I was drawn to his deprecating wit, keen insights, and southern drawl. He always made me laugh. As different as we were, we made it work. By 1987, Chip had his doctorate in sociology and a postdoctoral fellowship under his belt and accepted a visiting scholar position at the Russell Sage Foundation in New York City. I had been granted tenure at Stony Brook and was starting a sabbatical year for research and writing. We moved to a subsidized one-bedroom apartment in a newly refurbished building on 3rd and 64th St., a short walk to Chip's office. I worked out of the apartment. We sold our cars and had nothing tying us down. For the first time as a couple, we had extra money. I remember that Christmas, enjoying three movies one right after the other. We sampled expensive restaurants and splurged once on Le Bernardin. We enjoyed Broadway, went to museums, and explored the city. I walked in Central Park every day. We became expert tour guides for visiting family members. In July 1988 we married. It was a magical twelve months.

During that year, a member of the hiring department at Rutgers' Sociology Department asked whether I'd be interested in moving. As it turned out, the department had two openings. Chip and I applied and got offers: tenured for me and tenure-track for him. We moved to Highland Park, New Jersey, near the university. Chip began teaching in September, while I commuted to Stony Brook for the fall semester, to pay back my sabbatical year. I joined him in January 1989.

The new academic year brought welcome financial security and the sense of being on track. By mid-spring I was pregnant with Alex. On December 17, 1989, Lee Alexander Roos Clarke arrived, in the middle of our second year at Rutgers, a week early and a bit small, but otherwise perfect. We bought a house in Metuchen, about a twenty-minute drive from Rutgers and fifty minutes by train from New York City. There was a lot to celebrate that Christmas. Everything had fallen into place. We both had great academic jobs, at the same university, a home of our own, and, best of all—Alex. We were thrilled with our little family.

Pat, Chip, and Alex

Alex's early years were idyllic, and uneventful. He was a happy baby and easy child. Chip and I were utterly besotted and so too were our families. Alex was the first grandkid on Chip's side and the Florida Clarkes became our frequent visitors. Christmases were now at our house, and any life celebration was an excuse for a trip north. We often traveled to Florida (Chip's family) or Virginia (mine), to visit relatives. Alex's early years were filled with family. He became especially close to Granny (Chip's mom), whom he learned to speed dial, and to Chip's sister Poo, as well as his brother Hal and his wife Kathy, particularly after they moved near us in Metuchen.

We were the beneficiaries of love not only from the many members of our extended family but also from friends, both local and distant. In writing this story, I opened boxes of keepsakes from Alex's childhood. I particularly loved his preschool "My Family" drawings. In his pictures,

Alex often expanded our small three-person nuclear family to include his cousins Elizabeth and Gregory, and sometimes his cherished baby doll Ryla—a name he chose for a reason I no longer remember. Ryla survives in the keepsakes box, along with Bow Wow (his favorite stuffed dog) and Blankie (his blanket). We have multiple photos of him fast asleep, hugging all of them. A dreamcatcher stood guard next to his bed. I'm not sure it caught all of Alex's bad dreams, but it did help him fall asleep again. I wish it could have done that forever.

Over the last few years, I've reorganized my old photos into albums, first into physical photo albums and then digitally. They reminded me how Alex was always smiling, always laughing. There he is smiling as Granny reads to him, playing with his earliest buddy Zach, climbing in boxes, or tussling with Chip on the living room floor. Or he is wearing his Superboy pj's, staring with awe at the Christmas tree, searching for Easter eggs, riding his trike, sledding down snowbanks, playing with his toys, or sitting on my lap. Nearly all those early pictures are get-togethers with the Rooses or the Clarkes, or sometimes with other surrogate family. There he is, as a toddler, laughing uproariously as he and his cousin Greg step naked into a big silver washing tub or hug each other with abandon as we sit in my sister Marianne and her husband David's backyard in Winchester, Virginia. He's laughing again, as he hugs Hal or Poo in their dad's pool in West Palm Beach. And, always there is Alex in Chip's arms or on his lap, happy, contented, goofy—the seeds of his wit developing through osmosis from his dad.

In July 1995, Alex was proud to serve as the ring bearer in Hal and Kathy's wedding. Dressed in the same tuxedo as Hal and Chip, he was thrilled to be an important part of the festivities. One of my favorite pictures is from a 1998 Clarke trip to Disney World. A beaming Alex is happily enveloped in a hug from a huge Tigger. During spring break 2001 we arranged a Clarke family vacation on the Keys, staying in Islamorada, where they all went jet skiing. By eleven years old, Alex was also ready to embrace risk, joining Chip for parasailing. Later that year, when we visited Marianne and David in Montana, Alex was all smiles, racing around on a four-wheeler, enjoying Yosemite, and shooting guns as if he were in a Western.

In July 1996, we celebrated my parents' fiftieth wedding anniversary at Capon Springs, a resort in West Virginia. The whole family was there: my brother and sisters and all their kids. There is a photo of Alex and his cousin Eileen in clown faces, their dour expressions suggesting they might not be that happy with all that face paint. Another photo shows Alex and Eileen reciting the Pledge of Allegiance at the resort's morning flag-raising ceremony, and then one with their arms playfully thrown around their cousin Greg. A few years later in August 1999, the Roos family met again in Williamsburg. And there again, Alex, Greg, and Eileen were smiling widely in their eighteenth-century garb, marching in a revolutionary brigade with their stick guns. When I interviewed Greg for this book, he remembered those times, describing Alex as "a really, really energetic kid. He had insane amounts of energy . . . [and] he could be a bit of a smart-ass."

Eileen, too, remembered those childhood times together, as well as Alex's emerging independence:

> As we reached late elementary and middle school, Alex seemed to get much cooler right as I barreled into an extended awkward phase. An age gap of a year is also immense when you are in middle school. But Alex was still kind to his dorky younger cousin. He and I at one point walked around your neighborhood in Metuchen, which already seemed like a very grown-up experience to me since I was still going everywhere with an adult. Alex led the way. One of the stops was at Chip's mother's house [Granny was visiting Hal's house]. I don't remember what was said, but I was struck by how much she and Alex clearly loved each other.

It was never hard to catch Alex smiling—whether at family celebrations, his preschool and kindergarten graduations, playing with friends, visiting our work friends, running on the beach, holding his younger cousins, or on various vacations. When we traveled for work, we often added time for sightseeing with family or far-flung friends, trips that are wonderful memories for me. During spring break 1997, we extended a talk Chip gave at Oxford University to enjoy England, with Alex and Granny. In addition to the expected tourist photos, the highlight of our visit was our expedition to a London park, which happened to be hosting that year's Pride Parade. We emerged out of the London

Underground amid the crush of humanity arriving for the parade. Alex was transfixed by the hordes of people, the loud whistles, the costumes, the excitement. His first question to me was "Why do they have their butts hanging out?" We stayed for a long time, learning both cultural and history lessons.

In August 1998, we visited San Francisco for the annual meeting of our professional association and stayed on to tour Alcatraz and visit our friends Linda and Bruce down the peninsula. Alex loved the Alcatraz tour, posing for the obligatory prison bars photo. And there he is laughing with new friends Miles and Jack, frolicking on the beach at Half Moon Bay. One of our special places was our regular visits to Chick and Barbara's Hillsdale, New York, home in the Berkshires. Chick was Chip's dissertation adviser, and we always visited in October, enjoying the change of leaves and the views of the Catskills and the Taconic ranges off the back porch. When Alex got older, he enjoyed helping Chick chop wood and cut down trees. Alex's other surrogate grandparents were Judy—another of Chip's dissertation advisers—and her husband Mike, who live in Montauk. We visited them often, enjoying our Montauk crabs and clambering into their jeep to run their Vizslas on the beach. Once our German shepherd Lexi arrived on the scene, we brought her with us, although she preferred to ride in the jeep with us during those early morning beach runs.

Our lives were mostly centered in our small Metuchen community those early years, and especially in our backyard that opened into that of our neighbors Dori and Joe. Our local tribe would typically include Carolyn and Joe Sr. and Janis and John. Our collective set of kids— there were nine of them—played Manhunt and performed in backyard plays they spent hours rehearsing. One of their favorite songs for the backyard productions was the late nineties hit "Blue (Da Ba Dee)" by Eiffel 65. Watching them perform "I'm blue, da ba dee da ba daa" had us all in hysterics. Dori remembered Alex's "goofy dance moves and how very serious he was to get the show just right."

Alex, Jenna, and Matt were best buddies for years. We celebrated every holiday on the calendar, most memorably Halloween, Christmas, Easter, and the Fourth of July, when our illegal fireworks were legendary. They spent hours in an overgrown area of bushes in their backyard, which they called their "secret passage." As Dori told me in my interview with her, "Alex was my third child. . . . What a distinctive voice he had. And just a really good laugh." We spent some wonderful times with them, in Bermuda over spring break 1995, in the Outer Banks in North Carolina in June 1999, and we brought them to our magical place—Hillsdale, New York—in October 2000 and October 2002.

Once Hal and Kathy and their kids Hunter and Ginny moved in a half mile away in 2001, some of our backyard fun moved to their backyard, where we hung out, with kids playing for hours in the pool. But our backyard remained "fun central," especially once we got our playground equipment—the Clubhouse, as the kids called it—complete with fort, slide, and ladder. There were other lazy days at the Metuchen pool, or short jaunts to local sights. Alex had one of those old-fashioned, idyllic childhoods, where parents sit out in the backyard and kids put on musical productions and ride bikes and skateboards around town.

School

We had long expected that Alex would attend public school. In fact, we chose Metuchen because of its highly regarded schools. But when Alex was in kindergarten at a Y-sponsored school in Metuchen, we vacationed in St. Lucia on our 1996 spring break. Alex had a great week at the kids camp, joining the others in camp activities, making friends, putting on plays. And that is where I got my first inkling of Alex's daredevil instincts. We have pictures of him clambering up tall ladders to take a turn on the flying trapeze, and then somersaulting down to the trampoline many feet below. Of course, he was tethered and under watchful eyes, but his exhilaration was evident. If only there had been tethers, safety nets, and spotters later in his life.

But that trip to St. Lucia was important for another reason. We met a couple from our area who spoke enthusiastically about the Wardlaw-Hartridge School, a private school in the town next to ours that their son attended. That chance meeting changed our lives. Once home, we checked it out. As college professors, we were impressed with the school's focus on academics, the diversity by race and ethnicity of their student body, its small classes, and its high expectations for students. We had concerns about whether our middle-class family would fit in with affluent prep school families but learned that about half the student body were children of faculty and families like ours, for whom a private school price tag would be a stretch, but doable. At the time, we felt that by enrolling Alex in Wardlaw we were prioritizing his education. The decision took a big bite out of our family budget for the next twelve years. But it also led to years of agonizing over whether this was the right decision for Alex.

Alex began first grade at Wardlaw in 1996 and graduated twelve years later, almost a "lifer." There was busing for some of the early years but eventually we drove him to and from school. Our twenty-minute commute to school in the morning and then back in the afternoon turned out to be a bonus of unexpectedly enjoyable family time and conversation. I remember some terrific conversations during those trips, which lasted until Alex turned seventeen and we agreed to help him buy a car. After that, he drove himself to school.

We found lots to love about Wardlaw. Alex's teachers were great and caring. The classes were small; his graduating class had fewer than fifty students. As a result, the students were close. He had many great friends there, including Omari, James, AlexF,[2] Blair, Adam, and Latisha in primary school, and Jeff and Jordan in middle and high schools, among many others. His friends, like the student body, were racially diverse—which was always one of Wardlaw's strengths and appeal. In my interview with one of his friends, Latisha talked about her earliest memories of Alex: "Basically he had a lot of energy . . . he and [AlexF] were making really interesting, fun games. . . . They were very complex, like a battleship game. Then they were always inclusive, so whoever wanted to play was allowed to play. . . . [The games] were very intellectual." She described Alex as "the leader of the pack who was athletic and smart, but also cared about how everyone was doing. He was very deeply emotional in making sure everyone was okay with what they were doing and where they were at."

Surprisingly for two progressive parents, we loved the uniforms, and not knowing any better at the time—at least at first—Alex liked them too. First- and second-grade uniforms were a yellow polo shirt with khaki pants. Once boys got to third grade, a tie and jacket replaced the polo shirt. The pictures of a beaming Alex preparing for his first day of third grade bring a smile. They show him intently learning to tie his long tie—clip-ons were not for him. He felt so snazzy, and I have to say he did look good.

In June 2001, Alex graduated from Wardlaw's lower school, ready to transition to middle school. There was, of course, a ceremony with remarks from the head of the lower school, who mentioned each member of the fifth grade graduating class. "Calling Dr. Clarke, calling Dr. Clarke," he began. Alex wanted to be a doctor, and that's what the lower school head predicted for his future—anticipating, as we all did, that Alex would continue to travel along the first road.

The Athlete

Alex's athletic abilities emerged early. Our neighbor Dori wondered "how these two intellectual college professors ended up with the most athletic kid in the neighborhood." We wondered too. He rode a two-wheeler at age five. Alex put his mind toward mastering skateboarding and did. Tony Hawk, whose pictures adorned Alex's bedroom in middle school, was his idol.

He practiced skateboarding alone and for hours on end with his middle school buddies, AlexF and Jeff. They made several videos showing off their prowess. In speaking with me later, Jeff recalled the two of them skateboarding everywhere in Metuchen—by the local police station, in front of businesses—and getting yelled at. He remembered Alex's determination, and what became a theme in Alex's life: his willingness to take risks.

When Alex expressed an interest in karate at age five, we signed him up for karate training in Metuchen. Alex really connected with his instructors, who not only guided him through the training but also emphasized the importance of good values. I still have a copy of the speech nine-year-old Alex gave at a graduation at the Metuchen Black Belt Institute on December 2, 1999:

What my family means to me?

My family means everything to me. My mom help . . . well used to help me with my homework. She doesn't now because my teacher said "your parents may not help you with your homework." My mom also reads with me, she talks to me, and she plays games with me.

My mom, dad, and all of my relatives love me very much. They all teach me respect and they are very good at it. They also teach me to be honest to almost everybody.

My mom and dad both help me study for school, and they tell me to "check over your homework."

My grandmother, granny, is very sweet to me and all of my cousins. She loves me, and plays the games I want to play.

I think my mom, dad, and all my relatives are the best.

Alex took karate lessons for many years, and after his anorexia in middle school, Mr. Matland and Colin were especially kind and supportive, helping him to earn his black belt in July 2003.

In addition to karate, from the age of five we signed him up for many of the town's sports programs: basketball, soccer, and baseball. He played soccer until his junior year in high school and always liked pickup basketball, but his real love was baseball. Beginning with tee-ball in 1995, he played on town teams through age twelve and was chosen for the travel tournament teams every year he was eligible. He played a variety of positions but excelled at pitcher and second base. We were there for every game and loved to watch him play. I used to say he had ice water in his veins. On more than one occasion he struck out multiple batters, with bases loaded and the game hanging in the balance. In 2000 and 2001, he and Chip went to Cooperstown for a weeklong Father & Son Baseball Camp. He loved everything baseball and kept up his love for the sport through high school, winning letters on Wardlaw's middle school and varsity baseball teams. We were immensely proud of him. He was learning skills useful to a life full of success.

We thought Alex was smarter, cleverer, and wittier than either of us, and also better looking. Of course, we were biased, and I understand we all like to think that about our kids. But from what we could see, he was doing well in school, had many friends, and could make people laugh with his incisive wit. He was writing stories and poetry that were not homework. They wouldn't have won any poetry awards, but we loved them nonetheless, misspellings and all. They bespoke the future we imagined for him—successful, intellectual, engaged, creative. Those early years were magical. We have such fond memories. Alex was well on his way down the best-case road toward success and happiness.

But it was not to be.

CHAPTER 5

Widening Cracks

*Mama, it's like throwing a dime in the ditch, jumping in after it,
and only then realizing that there was no ladder to get out.*

—Alex Clarke, age twelve, the night before
hospital admission, November 11, 2002

THE FIRST TROUBLES slipped in quietly during the summer of 2002. Alex played baseball that summer and his team made it to the July championships. My picture albums make it crystal clear that by late summer 2002 my beautiful boy had stopped smiling and laughing. By August, both his smile and his spirit had evaporated. We visited my first cousin Jack and his wife Lorna in Maine that month, and then traveled up to Boothbay Harbor for the wedding of Lynne and Eric, two former graduate students. He was quite timid at the reception, not at all his typical spirited self. It quickly became apparent that he was losing too much weight. We began to check out medical options. Alex was twelve, in the seventh grade, and in the throes of what we came to learn was full-blown anxiety. Cracks were beginning to grow in my "good family."

As I began to write this chapter—and examining my photos more carefully—I realized Alex's anorexia began a year after 9/11. Somehow, I had misremembered these crises as occurring at the same time. Metuchen is a bedroom community with commuter rail to New York City, and the terror attacks sent those of us in the greater New York area reeling. Driving Alex to school the day after, we heard on the radio that a Metuchen dad had died in the falling towers. As I burst into tears, Alex calmly told me, "Mom, it's the circle of life." We'd recently seen the *Lion King* on Broadway, but even so his calmness that terrifying week was unnerving. Perhaps it was his way of asserting control when everything around him was beginning to be out of control.

To this day, I wonder if Alex's anxiety and anorexia emerged as a traumatic response to 9/11. Chip and I raised that possibility with several rehab doctors over the years, but no one gave it much credence. Years later though, several doctors described Alex as manifesting symptoms of post-traumatic stress disorder, but neither Alex nor we had any ready explanation for any trauma diagnosis. If 9/11 was a trigger, we'll never know. Alex had been overly reactive to such issues before. Before his anorexia, he had obsessed over mad cow disease and West Nile virus. In his academic work, Chip studies the preparation for, and responses to, disasters and crises—for example, worst cases, toxic spills, terrorism, earthquakes, plane crashes, and pandemics. He had bought Alex a jokey "mad cow" T-shirt during a work trip to France in early 2001, where mad cow disease had been a "worst case" discussion topic. When Alex learned that mad cow disease was caused by contaminated beef, he refused to eat meat for a month. And later, at our friends Chick and Barbara's wedding in Napa in mid-2001, he worried obsessively about West Nile virus. At the time we chalked these up to Alex being sensitive and a worrier. Looking back, perhaps they were warning signs.

There are other confounding factors I must consider. Both Chip and I have family histories of anxiety, panic attacks, eating disorders, and alcoholism, and Alex eventually developed all of these. Earlier in her life, Chip's mom suffered from eating disorders and alcoholism. By the time I met her, she was open about her alcoholism and proud of her years of sobriety, which she maintained until the day she died. Chip's sister Poo had a girlhood bout with bulimia, which she thankfully grew out of. Chip was long a heavy drinker. After the family deaths he took it to excess, until he stopped entirely. My mom's side of the family suffered with weight issues, quite possibly an epigenetic throwback to the Irish famine that brought our great-great-grandfather to Philadelphia in the 1850s. I, for one, was always dieting well into my adult years, even when I looked fine. In graduate school, I also suffered anxiety and panic attacks, manifested as fear of being in closed-in public places. As I matured successfully into my academic career, my anxiety lessened, and my panic attacks receded. To this day though I sit on aisle seats in movies, Broadway shows, concerts, and planes, in case I need to flee. These family histories meant Alex had a predisposition to alcoholism and mental health issues, and we talked with him about these from a very young age.

As Alex's anorexia progressed that fall, I began a journal. One of the first things I wrote about was Alex obsessing about a photograph of himself in a bathing suit from a Florida Keys vacation in 2001. He thought he looked chubby. I look at that picture now, as I did then, and thought it unremarkable. He certainly didn't look overweight; Alex had never been overweight. But that picture loomed large for him that fall, and he worried about his weight incessantly.

Alex attributed his disordered eating to discussions that fall in his health class on the epidemic of childhood obesity and eating disorders. More likely, it was merely more fuel to a fire that was already raging. Given his weight anxieties, the timing couldn't have been worse. He asked Chip how to get a "six pack," and in an off-handed dad sort of way, Chip suggested crunches and avoiding McDonald's. Alex took the advice to heart—and then to extremes. At first, we didn't think much of it. Fast food isn't great for anyone, and exercising is. And, besides, don't all kids approaching adolescence worry about their bodies? Parents, but not kids, know that "baby fat" is normal and typically disappears by high school, especially for youngsters as physically active as Alex.

I can now see, in retrospect, the clear symptoms of anorexia: obsessive exercising and refusing food. Our pediatrician became alarmed and sent us to a pediatric cardiologist for a consultation because Alex's heart rate was so low. The cardiologist told us that if Alex were an adult, he'd be ordering a pacemaker. He told Alex frankly he could die if he didn't eat, and that he should think about food as medicine. But from that point on, Alex refused to eat. His pediatrician recommended a therapist, and prescribed Zoloft. The therapy appointments were a disaster; Alex scarcely talked. He was shutting down both physically and psychologically.

Things came to a head on November 11, 2002, when Alex was getting ready for school. After refusing to eat breakfast, I gave him two options, eat and go to school, or go to the emergency room. His reply? "I might as well start [treatment], so I can be around other people like myself." "You can't make me eat," he argued. "You're right," I admitted, "I can't. You'll have to make that decision yourself." Reflecting his confused state of mind, he pleaded, "Don't leave it to me." Even back then he talked about having no self-esteem. He said the kids ignored him, and that the girls paid more attention to him with an eating disorder. His friend AlexF told a different story: "I clearly remember being in a lunchroom one day and being, like, 'Hey, why don't you come sit with us?' I couldn't understand why he was distant." Reflecting his state of mind at the time, his friend Omari, who had moved away before the start of that school year, remembers calling Alex around his birthday: "I remember him being sad, like just hearing sadness on the phone . . . and [him] feeling alone."

I found an eating disorders program twenty minutes away at Somerset Medical Center. I drove Alex to their emergency room that morning, hoping he'd be able to move directly into the program. But after being admitted to the emergency room, and kept overnight, we learned from the Eating Disorders Unit (EDU) director there was no room available until the following Monday, November 18. Because he was so young, and the only male at the time, they wanted to put him in a room by himself, across from the nurse's station. Somerset released him at 6 P.M. on Tuesday, November 12. At home, he continued to refuse food.

Two days later, Chip took him to our pediatrician, who insisted on sending him back to intensive care, this time at our local JFK Hospital. The pediatric cardiologist in charge of his care was alarmed. After examination, she conferred with Chip and said that his heart rate had dropped so low that if he had a heart attack, she "wasn't sure we could bring him back." Later, in yet another test, she added a stimulant to his intravenous line to determine if his heart would respond. I watched Alex as his heart rate increased from 35 to over 140 in a few minutes, and he had a look of terror in his eyes. He remained at JFK for four days, under the care of a multidisciplinary team of pediatricians, dieticians, a psychiatrist, endocrinologist, social worker, and many caring nurses. Chip and I were there every day from morning until bedtime. Friends and family visited. During his stay, Alex wrote several poems, including this one:

The hospital is boring,
the nurses say I'm snoring.
They gave me a pound cake
and 3 apples a day.
They say when my heart rate goes up
I don't have to stay. (I'm looking forward to that day.)
I want to go home and play with my friends,
So I can be happy and joyful again.
I try to look up and never down,
It's a little hard when you're wearing a frown.
Soon I'll be fine, I'll be back in school,
My heart rate is fine, I'm no fool.

As promised, on November 18 the Somerset EDU opened a room for Alex. He and we were equally terrified as we left him alone that night. He was scared to stay, and we left crying, realizing we had just committed our twelve-year-old son to a psychiatric facility requiring forty-eight-hour notice to leave. That night, and often over the next few months he remained at the EDU, I awakened at night to hear Chip sobbing uncontrollably. All we could do was hug each other.

On Day 1 Alex weighed sixty-eight pounds, 75 percent his normal weight. Reading my journal entries, I can see that those next few months were always two steps forward, one step back, and sometimes three steps back. For a while, he seemed happier at the EDU than he did on his occasional day visits home. He told me he felt a sense of calmness, being with his "friends," typically adolescent girls who vied for his attention and older anorexic women who doted on him. As one of only two boys in the unit (another boy arrived shortly after Alex), and precocious and sensitive at that, he luxuriated in their attention. He got all the devotion he sought. Anorexia is often seen as a "girl's disease," but the National Eating Disorders Association estimates that one in three of those struggling with an eating disorder is male. Furthermore, "subclinical eating disordered behaviors (include binge eating, purging, laxative abuse, and fasting for weight loss) are nearly as common among men as they are among women."[1] Nonetheless, fewer males seek treatment for their disordered eating, so it was not surprising that so few males were at the

EDU. Alex, too, viewed anorexia as a "girl's disease," a point that brought him much shame in high school, college, and beyond.

The EDU program was based on Skinnerian operant behavioral therapy, with rewards (such as home passes) given for meeting caloric goals. Slowly but surely the program increased the number of calories he ate, but the process was unbearably slow. The EDU director and Alex's therapist warned us that until he gained more weight, we'd hear "his starvation talking." Alex and I talked about one of his EDU friends who had dropped to 50 percent her appropriate weight. He thought her "scary," but also expressed interest in what I thought he looked like. He believed being thin made him "unique" and "special." We tried, unsuccessfully, to convince him that there are healthier ways to be unique, like being a good student, or a good saxophone player. But he was clear that if he got back to a healthy weight, his "self-esteem would be shot."

I learned later from an EDU journal he kept that he felt safe being there: "I think I like it better in the Hospital than out of it because I'm not as stressed out in here. It's like there's nothing that can hurt me in here no one else can annoy me or hurt me in here either. . . . I like to look forward to good things and then I transition thinking about the good things to thinking about the bad things."

Earlier that fall, we resorted to bribery to bring Alex some joy, buying a puppy. I had no experience with dogs, having grown up without them. But I was game to try. Chip had a German shepherd when he was young, so that was the breed we chose. Lexi brought us such joy for the next nine years. Before Alex got his first day pass, we brought her to visit him. Playing with her was the one thing that gave him solace. Alex was still so painfully thin in those pictures and videos, but they show the first tentative smiles we'd seen in months.

By December 14, Alex had reached seventy-six pounds, and for the first time got a day pass to come home. He looked better. Though scrawny, he was no longer emaciated. We spent most of the day trimming the Christmas tree, and went next door to visit with Dori, Joe, and the kids. He didn't engage much, mostly just listened to us talk, as if after a month away he didn't fit in anymore. The next day, Alex returned for an early thirteenth birthday party, just for the family, at Hal and Kathy's house. He seemed to enjoy the party, romping in the backyard with Lexi. Driving back to the EDU that night, he told Chip, "This was just the right amount of time to be home."

On December 16, the day before his thirteenth birthday, Alex wrote in his EDU journal:

> Tomorrow is my birthday, I'm excited. I had a family meeting today. It was productful [sic]. My mom broke out in tears. I said I wanted to die. I felt really bad I hurt her feelings. My dad seemed pretty sad too. When I die of this eating disorder, I want someone to give this journal to my parents.
>
> Mom, dad, I love you so much. There's nothing in the world that can change my mind about that. There is nothing you did to contribute to my eating disorder. It is myself being stubborn. I'm about to cry. I'm so sorry for hurting you like this. I hate myself for it. I'm sorry for all of the responsibilities I left for you, like dog, dog. I totally f-cked up christmas [He must be referring to our early birthday dinner]. I'm hurting all of my family. I hate it. There is really nothing wrong with you. I wish I could get better for you guys. And I wish for you that I wanted to get better. I wish there was something I could do to help you. I just wish everyone was happy. I feel like I just can't do it. I'm helpless. I love you so much. You are the best parents ever. I wish I never got into this disorder because now I like it. I get a lot of attention from it and I like it. Bye.
>
> [Later that night] I've changed my mind. I want to get better. I don't want to die. I'm going to make everyone happy, even me. I love myself. Tomorrow's my birthday. I am excited.

He called me that night to talk about how he had reconsidered, describing his eating disorder as "boring," wanting instead to play baseball and "do more interesting things." The call did not, however, reflect turning a corner. His starvation was still talking. He remained unable to give up his eating disorder and was still more comfortable in the EDU than at home. It broke our hearts to celebrate his birthday in the EDU on December 17. Chip, Hal, and I hung out with him, and they gave us some extra visiting time to celebrate. I brought thirteen candles and lit them up on a plate in his room.

When I went in for visiting hours on December 20, he told me about a conversation he had with his EDU friends about drugs. Most of the older women there had tried drugs, and he was taken by what they were telling him and curious. "What is Special K?" he asked, Being unfamiliar with Special K, a nickname for the drug ketamine, I had little information for him. I didn't know that world. He claimed he had no interest in drugs himself. But his fascination was troubling. From that day forward, I worried that the die had been cast. I have thought often, then and since, that just as prisoners learn more about crime in jail, and rehab clients acquire new drug-seeking and using behaviors, Alex's interactions with anorexia patients in the EDU—particularly the adult women who doted on him—exposed him to information that led him to drugs, as well as taught him additional food restriction techniques.

A seven-hour pass home on December 21 felt like a "three steps back" day. Alex declared that he liked coming home because he could eat less. The trauma that day wreaked havoc with our psyches and patience. As always, we had to cajole him to eat (a plain bagel for lunch and a turkey sandwich and carrot for dinner). Chip got irritated and distant, and Alex asked why he was angry. You could hear the psychological jargon he had been learning, although to us it sounded more like psychobabble: "I'm not responsible for your feelings, and if Daddy is angry, I'm not responsible for it." Trying to salvage the day, I was too desperate to say anything. He claimed that "going to Somerset made it worse because I've learned more about food." On the way back to the EDU that evening, he told me he wanted the eating disorder to kill him, so that he wouldn't have to disappoint us: "If I weren't around, you wouldn't have to worry so much." How wrong he was—how could he not know that? Clearly, he wasn't ready to come home.

Reflecting the chaotic nature of the disease, the very next day we had a terrific time during his eight-hour pass. He ran out of the hospital declaring, "I'm free!" I took him to the mall to buy a Christmas present for Chip, and some Abercrombie & Fitch clothes for himself. He was in great spirits. As we drove to the mall, he couldn't decide if he wanted to be a professional baseball player or heart surgeon. After his comments the day before, it was exhilarating to hear him contemplate his future in positive terms. He played with Lexi, and then went with Chip to play pool. On the way home he told Chip, "This was the best day pass I've had." We were living the chaotic nature of the disease, but these moments gave us hope.

Christmas was another good day. During his seven-hour pass, Alex smiled while playing with Lexi. We celebrated the holidays with Hal and Kathy at their home, and Alex seemed happy, very loving, hugging both of us. He even joined us as the "piece of cheese" in our traditional family hugs, something that hadn't happened for a very long time. It was wonderful to see his spirits up. We were thrilled that he ate, and we tried hard not to police his food. Two days later, he called crying because they denied him a pass because he had only gained one pound for the week. We convinced ourselves that maybe this meant he really did want to come home.

At more than one of my visits, and in family therapy, we talked about whether Alex should move to public school. His EDU friends encouraged him to go public because, as they told him, "private school isn't reality." He believed we'd never let him make the move, but that wasn't the case at all. We were very open to the possibility. I encouraged him to take responsibility for his choices, advising him to explore his options. I suggested he visit the local public school and go to classes with one of his neighborhood friends, James or Sam. But he worried about change, and he didn't want to make the decision himself. Eventually though, he did choose to remain at Wardlaw to avoid going through another transition. I continue to second-guess our decision to send him to a private school in the first place and then to have him stay. While there were many positive outcomes from his private school experience, there's little doubt in my mind it contributed to his self-esteem issues. It made him jealous that some of his schoolmates were rich: "I want my family, and my life," he told me, "but in their house." He expressed worries more than once that we were going bankrupt—which was far from the case.

It was a dark end to a difficult fall. Visiting Alex on New Year's Eve, I arrived at his room when he was still in his therapy group. I noticed a questionnaire he had partially filled out sitting on his bed. As I skimmed his answers, I saw familiar themes: "My mom and dad make all my decisions for me" and "They run my life." He also said he wanted to totally change his life. He was still thinking about death and dying, which he described as a "rational" thing to do. It broke my heart.

On the first day of 2003, Alex got a seven-hour pass for New Year's Day. They arrived with big news: he and Chip had stopped for McDonald's on the way home, which Alex hadn't touched in well over a year. We went to see a Harry Potter movie, and then came home and hung out as a family. He did well for both lunch and dinner, although we learned the next day that he had lost one and a half pounds. On January 4, Chip and Alex got subs, and later in the day went to play pool and get Dunkin' Donuts. At home we played some Trivial Pursuit before taking him back. Two good days, we thought, to start the New Year.

January 8 was a red-letter day: we checked Alex out of inpatient care and brought him home. After more than seven weeks of inpatient treatment, he had reached eighty-five pounds. The EDU director reported that Alex's attitude had improved. We talked about his readmit weight—eighty pounds—but thankfully he never reached that weight again. We learned how not to be the food police. He was permitted some exercise, walking was okay, and eventually he could go back to karate, PE class, and baseball. He seemed happy to be home.

Stage 2 had begun. On January 9 we brought Alex to the Partial Hospitalization Program. He was back to Somerset Medical Center from 8:30 A.M. to 4 P.M. each day. To remain in the program, he was required to "complete" three meals a day. That first day he recognized and hugged a few former EDU patients, and we were struck anew that no matter where he went, many people loved him. One week into the program, his nutritionist threatened to throw him out unless he completed his daily food requirements. Finally, and fortunately, he did indeed "complete." He maintained his weight and gained more. Eventually, Alex progressed to the Intensive Outpatient Program (IOP), getting to Somerset at 8:30 A.M. and leaving at 1:30 P.M.

At one point early on Alex felt so overwhelmed he crawled into Lexi's cage and said he wanted to go back to the hospital. But overall, he adapted well to returning home and thankfully moved past those early terrors. He was very loving and happy, and exhibited no stress about returning to school. His first weekend home, he spent a few hours on Saturday with his friend James, and on Sunday skateboarded with AlexF. He was afraid he had overdone the exercising, and he had. But I was so happy to see him having fun like a normal kid, I wasn't about to intervene. Thankfully the scale didn't show a weight loss. Everything always revolved around that damn scale.

He wrote a few more poems that January, among them this one:

The more you try,
The more you get.
The higher you fly,
The better you'll feel.
So keep doin what you're doin,
And complete those meals.

Alex began his return to school on a part-time basis on January 23, while still juggling the demands of the EDU programs. We were thankful for the school's counselor, Peggy, who came to visit Alex in the hospital and kept in touch with Teresa, who ran the EDU's teaching component. Together they kept Alex current on his schoolwork. Peggy also kept in constant email discussion with me throughout Alex's ordeal. She, Alex, and I talked several times about the best way for him to return to school. She also prepared Alex's classmates for his return, asking that they "give him some space." With Alex's permission, she talked with them about anorexia and how his transition back to school would look, cautioning that "if you don't tell people what's going on they make up their own stories. . . . I remember the kids being really pretty good about this. . . . [I told them that] what he's looking for is acceptance and being back in his routine."

According to my journal notes, Alex felt like he fit right back in, being up to date in history, ahead in math, and behind in Latin. One of his teachers reported that "Alex volunteered some answers, and they were correct!" Peggy emailed me that the kids were happy to see him. Several friends saved a seat for him at lunch, and he bought food and ate it. My favorite sentence from Peggy's email: "It was wonderful to see him smile several times." After his first day, Alex told Chip he'd rather be at school than at the EDU. I wondered at the time, and since, whether he would have received the same warm welcome if he'd been at a larger public school. Wardlaw's teachers and staff were clearly watching the kids more closely than would likely happen in public schools.

When I interviewed Peggy for this book, she described her first memories of Alex. The year before, he had been in her "transitions program," which prepared sixth graders for the move to middle school. She remembers: "I remember moments . . . when he would kind of throw in a little zinger, which would indicate that little quizzical look on his face really was not as quizzical as I thought it was. The wheels were turning, and when he was ready, he was going to express an opinion . . . I do remember an occasional edginess to something that he said. Maybe it got laughter out of other people. . . . I see his face very clearly." This sounds so much like Alex.

Alex's last day at the IOP was February 21. After three and a half months of hospital life, including Thanksgiving, his thirteenth birthday, Christmas, and New Year's Day, on February 24 he finally returned to school full time. Slowly but surely, behavioral therapy helped him gain back most of the weight he lost, and the old Alex finally began to re-emerge. He had tired of the hospital, and wanted to be home, especially to hug Lexi. His poetry was sometimes silly, sometimes thoughtful. But one poem Alex wrote in Somerset that February expressed his love for his father and was profound, demonstrating Alex's sensitivity and complexity. He submitted it to Wardlaw's literary journal, *The Hyphen*, which included it in its 2003–2004 edition:

Through the Rain and Shine
After the pain, it's not that bad.
After the emotional rain, I'm not that sad.
I can see the light at the end of the tunnel,
I think it's going to be all right,
The end is coming into sight.
I'm sorry for all of the bad days,
Maybe that was just a phase.
It doesn't matter now, it's all going to be perfectly fine,
Life's going to be just divine.
Why did it have to be me,
I am a good person as you can see.
Finally, I'm in the blue, and I don't have to worry,
The best part is, there will be less days of fury.
I meant to stay out of your way,
But I didn't mean to ruin your days.
I hope we can work it out,

We can be happy without a doubt.
Even if we can't, I'll still care for you,
And I'll always be there for you.
I hope we'll be all right, so we can have fun,
And more importantly be father and son.

All told, Alex spent over seven weeks in inpatient treatment, and another six weeks in partial hospitalization programs. Months of psychological and nutritional therapy followed. But he was home, and back in school. He seemed happy with Lexi, his family, his doctors, and his school and neighborhood friends. His friends welcomed him back with open arms.

I have only two remaining entries in my journal from that time. On March 9, 2003, I wrote that Alex's transition was going well and summarized his progress. He was comfortable enough to spend the night at his friend AlexF's house, and to begin to play middle school baseball again. AlexF came with us to Chick and Barbara's place in Hillsdale. Our Alex still looks thin in those pictures, but he has some tentative smiles. He ate what we made, and continued to eat "fear food," like donuts and pizza. He still had flashes of anxiety, such as breaking out into hives before school tests, but with therapy he was learning to calm himself.

The best indicator of Alex's upward trajectory is the last entry in my journal on September 12, 2003. I hadn't written anything about his condition since the previous March. The news was all good: the summer was super, Alex was making lots of friends, and enjoying himself. Over the summer he and his two buddies James and Jeff were counselors in training at Mill Road Day Camp. Half of the day he worked with younger kids, and the rest of the day hung out with his friends. He told us, "Here I'm someone, and last year [at a different camp] I was nobody." The older counselors said he did an excellent job working with his young campers. Jeff remembers: "We had an awesome friendship. We were like glued to the hip I feel, like, from like, sixth, seventh grade, whenever we met, until probably when I left Wardlaw [after sophomore year]. The best memories I guess were at camp. We were always hanging out together during the summers. And then whenever we weren't in school, we were always hanging out at your house or going to the skate park or going to the mall. Getting in trouble and getting yelled at by [the police]. You know, the usual stuff."

Mostly, however, Alex spent that summer hanging with a new pack of neighborhood kids, especially Joe Jr., who remembers meeting Alex at a neighborhood barbeque: "I saw a young boy my age and I got so excited that there was someone my age in the neighborhood" to supplement the "bunch of girls." They skated and rode bikes, spending days at Edison Skate Park. And for the first time, Alex began to spend time with some of the neighborhood girls, who often stopped by the house to say hi. After Alex died, one of them—Dani—wrote on his Facebook page: "There's something in us as human beings that makes us want to ignore bad things. You always faced the negatives, and made them positive for all of us as friends. Even as young kids you were so happy, so funny and so full of life. I think of you every time I see heat lightning and remember you saying 'Dani look, look how cool it is!'" And the big news that summer: Alex earned his black belt in karate, completing the training he had begun when he was five years old. It was a remarkable challenge he had set for himself. A year later, he received another star on his black belt.

In my September journal entry I wrote about how well Alex's eighth-grade school year had started off. He particularly loved his Latin and art teachers. To my surprise, he asked my advice about running for student council president, and we talked through the pros and cons. He decided to throw his hat into the ring and was demonstrably happy when he was elected, and was especially thrilled by the response of classmates who, he reported, "whistled, yelled, and clapped" when his win was announced. Afterward, we talked about how to run meetings, and how to bring things up for a vote. He wanted to be prepared.

I talked with one of Alex's teachers about his time in middle school. She used to joke with Alex about his long hair: "I know he went through his hair transition, like short and long. I would always tell him . . . you have beautiful hair, but you need to cut it. . . . You look like you're getting ready to skateboard . . . the typical stereotype of a skate boarder. And they're like, 'Yeah, that's us. We're the cool kids.'" I learned for the first time during that interview that she had grown concerned about Alex's eating and recommended that the school administration "look into this because something's [wrong]" when he was "battling food and struggling to eat an apple . . . he's just losing too much weight." She told me that when he returned, "I knew he was back on the mend, you can tell. His complexion changed, his color changed, and his personality came back. He was happy again. . . . He was feeling good."

In talking with me, so many of Alex's friends described him as "my best friend," as I've noted before. His lower school friend Omari was typical: "He was like my first friend that I can really recall . . . the first person I ever invited over to my house." And AlexF described him as "the first friend I met in school . . . from there it was like best friends from the very beginning. From first grade all the way through I'd say to end of middle school, beginning of high school" (when he moved to a different high school). James too: "Alex was probably my best friend, my closest friend." As he got older, Alex collected even more best friends.

His friendship with Jeff deepened in those first few months back to school. As Jeff remembers it: "I vividly remember the first time we hung out, we came and we were skating on your driveway." And from that moment on, they were best friends. Typically, they met to skate, but they also made several short movies. Two chronicled their skating exploits. Another was a remake of Kanye West's song "Jesus Walks." Alex was smiling again in those videos.

As 2003 ended, we had our Alex back from his troubles. We were thrilled when he asked for a cheeseburger, and when he wanted Dunkin'. We were a happy family once again. The pictures from Thanksgiving, Alex's birthday, and Christmas show him smiling and laughing. I got a terrific picture of Alex and his friends AlexF, Jeff, and James on his fourteenth birthday, acting the goofy (and normal) kids they were. What a difference a year makes.

As Alex's eighth-grade school year progressed into the spring of 2004, Chip and I began to feel hopeful we had dodged a bullet. Our family was back walking along the best-case road. In June, Granny joined us to celebrate Alex's graduation from Wardlaw-Hartridge middle school. And it was truly a celebration.

We hoped that the good times meant that all was well. Alex's encounter with anorexia, however, was traumatic, and it left scars that continued to haunt him. He mostly didn't talk about that time; he was embarrassed. His Wardlaw friends knew about it, because they knew he left, and then returned. But with others he seldom talked about his experience, even those to whom he was very close.

In his later writings at rehab, though, Alex spoke of the long-term effects of his anorexia. In January 2014, at his third rehab in the Ambrosia Treatment Center, he wrote of the shame and insecurity he experienced in response to the prompt "When did I first learn that others were more important than me?"

There are certain instances in my life in which I feel as if I put myself first and that I am important. However, there are many instances in which others are more important than me. This is an essay in which I describe this latter feeling, and when I first began to think in this manner.

I first began to feel as if others were more important than me in middle school, around the age of 12. This was the time in which I became more aware of myself and my environment. I started to notice differences between myself and others around me. In addition, I began to become somewhat of a perfectionist. I felt that if I was not the best at everything I did, I was a failure. I was able to accomplish this in both my academics, as well as my baseball career. I got practically straight A's, and I was by far the best player on my baseball team.

It was 7th grade in which things got much worse for me and my grades and baseball career began to slip. I was hospitalized for 4 months, and I was not able to play ball or do any school work during that time. It was only because I went to a private school that I was able to graduate 7th grade because they made an exception for me the next year of school. I was physically an 8th grader; however, I was still a 7th grader mentally. I felt as if I was left behind, and that everyone else had progressed, while I was left to play catch-up.

I was now no longer able to be the best at my academic or my baseball teams, and I believe it was around this time that I started thinking that my peers were better than me at practically every aspect of life, and in turn were more important and interesting than me. I then began to look towards others to determine how to live the way I do. Soon after, my peers began drinking and smoking, so I did as well to fit in. Then, due to my addictive personality, I took drinking and drugging to an extreme and made it a lifestyle, which landed me in multiple rehabs through the past two years.

Reading his journal entry now, years later, some things don't match up. At the time, I was in frequent communication with Peggy, Wardlaw's counselor, and as far as I knew (and had been told), Alex was able to keep up with most of his schoolwork during his hospitalization. I was never told that Wardlaw made academic exceptions for him, and, to my knowledge, they never did. But, of course, that's not what's important. What matters, and what I only learned later, is that Alex felt "left behind" and "left to play catch-up." That he had that perception feels right, so too does his stated need for perfection. Although he eventually physically matured—growing to nearly six feet tall—and became academically more sophisticated, I don't think he ever really felt he had progressed emotionally or socially. For much of the rest of his life, he felt "left behind."

CHAPTER 6

Calm before the Storm

> Of course, we're made up of what we've forgotten too, what we've
> tried to bury or suppress. Some forgetting is necessary and the mind
> works to shield us from things that are too painful; even so, some
> aspect of trauma lives on in the body, from which it can reemerge
> unexpectedly. . . . Those memories—some intrusive, some lovely—
> seem now to have a grander significance, like signposts on a
> path. It's a path I can see now only because I have followed it
> backward, attempting to find a moment of revelation, evidence
> of something being set in motion.
>
> —Natasha Trethewey, *Memorial Drive: A Daughter's Memoir*

AS 2004 DAWNED, a relative calm returned to our lives. We held our breath, wanting so much to believe that Alex and our family had successfully weathered the storms of Alex's anorexia. I was certainly no longer naïve enough to think that such trauma only happens in other people's lives. I knew that if it happened to us, it could happen to anyone, and if it happened once, it could happen again.

As middle school turned into high school, we began to relax. Things were good. Alex was a successful athlete, and he did well academically. He went on a school trip to Italy and Greece. He got a job, saved enough for a used Volkswagen GTI, and had a longtime girlfriend. His friend circle widened, and our basement became a frequent gathering place. Just like his dad, he would sign off from conversations with "peace, man." Things were largely peaceful, and life was normal, "chill" as Alex often described it. Or at least it appeared that way to us.

Walking along the First Road

We have many happy memories from Alex's high school years. He excelled academically, taking eight honors and seven advanced placement courses. He made the honor roll each year. He graduated with an A- average. His interests were eclectic. He took Latin and was chosen for the Latin National Honor Society. He played the sax and made it to first chair in the school's orchestra. During his last semester, the local Rotary Club honored him as a "high school student of the month." As for any parent, those achievements made us proud.

In going through Alex's scrapbooks, I found two English assignments that describe the young man Alex was becoming. The first was a ninth-grade essay about "the person I most admire," describing the admiration he had for his dad:

> My father has served as my role model ever since I was very young . . . in part because he is able to manage four jobs at once: being a college professor, being a sociologist, researching disasters, and being a father/husband. My father has published many articles, three books, and two edited books, and still finds time to help me out with all my problems. . . . When my father teaches his Introduction to Sociology class, he is loud, he walks around the room, he is enthusiastic, and he makes funny jokes. . . . The characteristic about my father that truly makes him my role model is the fact that he has a phenomenal sense of humor. . . . Luckily for me, my father's extraordinary sense of humor has rubbed off on me. As many of my peers know, I have a good sense of humor, and if you ask my mother, she would tell you that it is akin to my father's.

Given Alex's later issues with addiction, the second assignment—an eleven-page research paper on brain development and teen behavior Alex wrote for his junior year English class—has stayed with me. In the paper, which was well researched and with an extensive bibliography, Alex argued that a major reason teens make risky decisions is "the slow growth of the prefrontal cortex, which affects the limbic system of the brain that deals with emotion, motivation, and memory. It affects judgment, and how well an individual can articulate his or her feelings." Even as Alex began to use drugs, he knew this research.

This academic knowledge didn't reduce his impulsivity or risk-taking, but, interestingly, the only rehab conversations he ever recalled liking were the ones about the biology and chemistry of the brain. As I reread this essay so many years later, I could only shake my head at one of his teacher's comments. In response to Alex's point that some legal scholars argue that teen drug users should be tried as juveniles until they are in their early twenties, his teacher had remarked: "Only bleeding-heart liberals would say this." While I know this was likely intended as a joke, the comment is undergirded by a mindset I came across often and one that infuses how our political and criminal justice system deals with addiction. I spent many years during Alex's substance use years fighting such mindsets by making this exact point about the underdeveloped young adult brain to anyone who would listen. I thought if he could survive until his late twenties, he might overcome his substance use. Alex didn't live long enough to test my theory. He died at twenty-five, the average age at which neuroscientists assert the brain typically reaches maturity.

In addition to academics, in high school Alex continued to be involved in student council. In ninth and tenth grades his classmates elected him class vice president. He played sports each year: soccer for his first two years, and baseball for all four years. I still have a copy of a local newspaper report: "Freshman Alex Clarke pitched the last two [innings], combining for a no-hitter." He still had that ice water in his veins that manifested so clearly during his little league days. In 2006 he was named to the first team in Wardlaw's conference. And in the final baseball game of his high school career the local media noted that "Alex Clarke doubled home the winning run."

Alex maintained his early interest in becoming a doctor. He explored medicine during his high school years by spending time as a junior volunteer at JFK, the same hospital to which ambulances would later take him for overdoses. He also attended a ten-day program at Georgetown University run by the National Youth Leadership Forum (NYLF) on medicine, which he described in an essay he wrote for college applications: "NYLF is one of my most memorable experiences, and it further encouraged my ambition to practice medicine, specifically surgery. This program consisted of a 10-day curriculum in which we studied with leading scientists in their fields. We learned about medical ethics, history, cures for diseases, and even practiced some medical procedures. We visited several medical schools, and observed medical students at work. This was inspiring because it made me believe that this could be me in a few short years." I remember Alex excitedly regaling us that summer with his NYLF experiences and practicing sewing "stitches" on a banana.

As soon as he got his driver's license, Alex was itching to earn money to buy a car. He had been earning some money umpiring Metuchen Little League games, but by the end of sophomore year he was looking for more than pocket change. Chip remembers shopping in Boro Hardware with Alex one day that May. Boro's owner, Steve, hired many Metuchen teens over the years. Chip asked Steve whether he had "any use for a useless teenager." Steve's response? "Yes, I do!" As they walked out to the car, Alex was both thrilled and terrified, proclaiming, "The first time he yells at me, I'm going to cry." As it turned out, Alex loved working there and stayed for several years. Just like his dad, who as a teen had worked at a Florida hardware store, Alex enjoyed learning about hardware. And to my knowledge, he never once cried at work.

Our photographs provide tangible evidence of those good times: Alex and his girlfriend Katie at her junior and senior proms; Alex and his friend Jeff at an April 2005 New York City auto show; Jeff joining us at a June 2005 celebration at Callaway Gardens in Georgia; Joe Jr. trekking to Hillsdale with us for our annual leaves trip in October 2005; Alex playing big brother to cousins Ginny and Sara on a visit to the Statue of Liberty over Christmas in 2005; Alex attending his cousin Elizabeth's wedding with us in Montana in 2006, and later that year helping to celebrate my parent's sixtieth wedding anniversary in Virginia. One picture from March 2005 remains my iPhone wallpaper. It's a regal photo of our German shepherd Lexi lying behind Alex with his paws resting on Alex's chest. Alex's arms are thrown backward around Lexi's neck. Alex loved that dog, and Lexi loved that boy.

In addition to these well-photographed moments, there are lots of other, everyday memories that never made it into albums. Our basement was where Alex's neighborhood and school friends spent time. They'd knock at the front or side door and stop to talk before heading downstairs. We loved these "basement people," as we called them. One of our favorites was Katie, whom Alex met the summer before his senior year. They were together for four years, attending two proms and maintaining a long-distance relationship during college (Dickinson College in Carlisle, Pennsylvania, for Alex and West Virginia University for Katie). Although they eventually moved on to new relationships, they kept in touch. All these years later Katie still describes him with affection: "[as] a perfectly rounded person, ... super social [with] tons of friends, ... a straight-A student and ... brilliant."

During these years, Chip and Alex got out their pool sticks on a regular basis, frequenting several local pool halls. Chip taught Alex how to shoot pool, but it wasn't too long before Alex could beat him. Another favorite haunt for them was the Metuchen Diner, where they always ordered the same thing (burgers and two slices of lemon meringue pie), sat and talked, and joked incessantly with their favorite waitress Rose. And then, there was their beloved sushi. Fish was mostly their thing. They would get out their "sticks" and head off, typically to Mr. Pi's, where (as regular customers) their pictures were on the wall. When Mr. Pi's went out of business not too long ago, Chip raced to the restaurant to get those pictures off the wall.

As it came time to apply to college, we hoped Alex would choose Rutgers University, where, given our faculty status, he could have gone tuition-free. We made the requisite college trips, and he decided to apply early decision to Cornell, his stretch school, but didn't get in. He then decided on early decision II to Dickinson College, and though he applied as well to Rutgers and several others, upon his acceptance by Dickinson in February 2008, he became set on going there. We convinced ourselves at the time that he might fly beneath the radar at a big school like Rutgers, and thus might do better at a small school, and so acceded to Alex's choice. Both Hunter and Ginny later chose Rutgers and found their way beautifully there. I have no doubt Alex would have done so as well. I wish he had chosen to be closer to home at the university we know so well.

Intersecting with the Second Road

Along with the good came the bad. As he progressed through high school, Alex also veered sharply toward the second road. We began to see warning signs. It was clear he was drinking too much and also experimenting with marijuana, dangerous enough in any family but particularly in a family such as ours with a history of alcoholism and anxiety disorders. It is easy for parents to be confused about such behavior, and we were. Many teenagers drink and smoke pot, with no lasting ill effects. Many go through angst and risky experimentation, eventually maturing out of it. But for Alex the risks turned out to be far greater. The anxiety that had emerged during his anorexia lingered, and later developed into full-fledged panic attacks. We learned much later from his therapist, Dr. O, that Alex started drinking heavily soon after his hospitalization to self-medicate, to soothe his anxieties, and to enhance his shattered self-esteem. He told Dr. O that his "daily life was torture." The chatter inside his head—and I mean this metaphorically because to my knowledge he did not hear voices—was always about what he had done wrong that day. He told Dr. O that he worried his friends were laughing at him. He felt he was not good enough. He focused on his failures. The ironic thing is that, in truth, he was very successful, and his family and friends loved him. But he couldn't see it.

Perhaps Alex is the best one to describe his slide into addiction. During his first rehab experience at Advanced Health and Education in the fall of 2013, five years after he graduated from high school, he reflected upon what had brought him to that point. In a November 7 letter addressed to us, he wrote about honesty. It's not clear how much he's writing to his counselors as opposed to us, but his words are nonetheless illuminating:

> Throughout my quest towards sobriety at Advanced Health, I have begun to understand that honesty is a central aspect of recovery. . . . As you probably know, I began drinking casually around freshman year of high school at age 13. The first beer I drank by myself was from your fridge, with [a friend] in his back yard. Like most alcoholic stories, my drinking remained relatively under control for a few years until I went to Puerto Rico with the baseball team on spring break. It was there

when I first got drunk with the rest of the team because I wanted to fit in. I started drinking in a problematic manner junior or senior year of high school. I remember first making my own fake ID and then buying a fake ID and using them to buy liquor in Plainfield, getting rides there from [a friend] even before I could drive. I went there so often, I actually didn't even need to bring my fake ID with me because I was such a regular. This actually worked out in my favor one time when a cop stopped me coming out of the store, and decided to get the store owner in trouble instead of me when he saw I didn't have a fake. Throughout my junior year, I smoked weed consistently, and sold to support my habit. I also drove drunk a number of times, and it is a miracle that I didn't get a DUI before I actually did." [He goes on to talk about his college years.]

External factors intervened as well. On September 4, 2004, just as Alex was beginning high school, the first of many family deaths occurred that shook our family to its core. Hal's wife Kathy died of severe prolapse of the mitral valve, one month shy of her forty-second birthday. Her sudden and shocking death distressed Alex. As we prepared for her memorial service, we didn't think to ask him if he wanted to say anything. He still seemed so young and was only a year out from his hospitalization. But one day that difficult week, Alex wrote a beautiful eulogy. He was so poised and articulate as he spoke before hundreds of Kathy's and our friends in the First Presbyterian Church of Metuchen. Wardlaw had trained him well to write and deliver a beautiful speech, which included this excerpt:

Among those wonderful memories . . . when I was around five years old. Kathy was always telling me she was born with a special gift, the gift to find money wherever it was, simply by smelling it. So, about every time I was around her I would show her my money, she would smell it, and then I would hide it. No matter where I hid the money, she would always find it. To this day, I still believe she was born with a special gift, not the gift to be able to find money with her nose, but the gift to love, the gift to make you feel special, and the gift to make everyone in the room smile.

That Thanksgiving was particularly miserable. Neither Hal nor we felt like hosting a celebration. Our small family of six went instead to a Thanksgiving dinner at the Sheraton, where Hal worked. My pictures of that dinner show Alex, Hunter, and Ginny making funny faces, trying to make us laugh. I'm sure we laughed, but nobody was happy. Alex still remembered Kathy fondly many years later as he was writing college essays, one of which recalled his eulogy for a beloved aunt who had died way too young: "As I looked out into the crowd of over three hundred people and noticed the deep pain in every one of their eyes . . . I told a few comical stories involving my aunt and me. . . . I was able to show that although their loved ones might die, it is important to remember the happy times you have had with them."

Other incidents during Alex's high school years contributed to our concern. During the summer before his senior year, he and two of his friends decided to jump the fence at the local town pool. They invited Katie and her friend along. Katie related what happened:

> K: [A friend and I] were just hanging out at my house. We weren't
>   doing anything and it was getting kind of late. And I got a text
>   message or a call from Alex. And . . . he was like you want to
>   hang out? . . . And they picked . . . us up, and [said] we're going
>   to go swimming . . . not knowing what we were getting our-
>   selves into. [We went] to the Metuchen Pool. . . . We jumped
>   the fence and went swimming. And it was innocent, but it was
>   stupid for sure. . . . And then the cops came and we ran from
>   them, and we all know how that ended.
> PR: Did they take you guys to the police station too?
> K: They did. They took us. They individually had our parents pick
>   us up, which was the worst part of it, and then we were all
>   grounded.
> PR: Yeah. I'm surprised your mom didn't say you are not allowed
>   to see this guy again.
> K: Yeah. I mean, I guess they didn't.
> PR: Oh God, what an introduction.
> K: That was our first date.

They were all lucky they didn't get police citations that night, or worse. And Katie's parents didn't forbid her from seeing Alex after that "first date." I remember later apologizing to Katie's parents, whom we got to know well, and they were understanding. As parents, we all know that kids do risky things—indeed, most kids do many stupid things. We just hope that the risky things they do don't kill them.

As Alex was nearing the end of his high school career, we became concerned that he might have some reading issues that could negatively affect him in college. He was doing very well in school, but his standardized test scores were not reflecting his abilities. He did much better on math and science SATs (Math 620 and Biology 610), which required less reading skills, than on English (590) and Latin (450).

During the summer before his senior year, we had him evaluated by an educational psychologist. After two days of testing, the results showed that Alex had a slow reading rate. His reading comprehension for short pieces was high average, but for longer pieces his comprehension was substantially weaker because he could not finish within the time limits. The psychologist suggested that the weaknesses that showed up in testing had been masked at Wardlaw because teachers may have allowed Alex extra time to finish in-class tests. She found that "under timed constraints, Alex's performance is relatively weak as he has a difficult time working quickly." Comparing his test results with his junior year research paper, she observed that "a review of a research paper completed for school last year was a better indicator of good writing when not placed under pressure of either time or thought."

Based on her testing, the psychologist explained that Alex ranked over the 90th percentile for many of the untimed tests he took, but on timed tests, his results were in the single digits. His process speed was ranked at the 5th percentile, his visual matching at the 6th, his retrieval fluency at the 2nd, his decision speed at the 8th, and his rapid picture naming at the 5th. She noted she "never sees this huge discrepancy."

After getting these results, we took Alex to a behavioral optometrist to evaluate the functioning of his eyes as related to learning. The optometrist diagnosed Alex with convergence insufficiency, accommodative insufficiency and infacility, and oculomotor dysfunction, summarized as "significant binocular, oculomotor, and accommodative deficits." In other words, Alex's eyes didn't coordinate effectively, so that when he read and then looked up at a distance, his eyes took some time to adjust.

Slow processing speed led to reading learning disabilities, a finding consistent with the psychological test results. Based on these results, the College Board approved his accommodation request for additional time, as did Wardlaw, and later Dickinson.

In May 2011, as Alex was considering applying to graduate school, we returned to the behavioral optometrist, and contacted a second educational psychologist. The optometrist confirmed her original report of "significant binocular, oculomotor, and accommodative deficits." The educational psychology results were broadly consistent with the testing from four years earlier. Alex's cognitive abilities were high, but he showed weaknesses in processing speed, cognitive fluency, and oral reading accuracy. He was unable to complete the reading comprehension section, although he did well on those questions he did answer. This time around, the psychologist also found clear evidence of Alex's anxieties: "Alex experiences a significant amount of anxiety related to his academic performance. He worried about tests even when he studies sufficiently for them. He feels anxiety during tests and exams, and he has difficulty relaxing. In addition, he experiences inattention, distractibility and he struggles to stand or sit still. He struggles to inhibit impulsive responses and sustain working memory. Alex has difficulty remembering things and may lose track of what he is doing."

Her formal diagnosis was "DSM-IV-TR 315.9, Learning Disorder, Not Otherwise Specified. Characterized by Deficits in Processing Speed that Impede Academic Fluency." In addition to recommending that Alex continue to be granted extra time for test taking, she recommended individual psychotherapy. Reading her report anew, I was struck by her behavioral assessment. Her testing and examination showed that Alex's anxiety fell in the clinically significant range, as did his inattention/hyperactivity score, which fell in the "at-risk range." He also fell into the clinically significant range on the mania scale: "He can never seem to relax, ideas almost always race through his mind, and he often has a hard time slowing down. He has trouble sitting still, and can't seem to turn off his mind."

These assessments ring true. Alex did seem overly anxious, he did have a hard time relaxing, and he was always on the go. Many of his friends described Alex as always wanting friends around.

Reflecting the psychologist's assessment, I can now see this as part of the issues Alex had to address. In addition to being embarrassed about anorexia, his diagnosis of learning disorder hugely frustrated him. This was simply not the image he had of himself. Thankfully, he agreed to accept the accommodations offered, and met with the Dickinson administrators once he was on campus to ensure that he received them.

The most serious and troubling incident in Alex's high school years occurred during his last semester, when he brought liquor to the winter dance. His friend Evan described the incident, which is consistent with what I heard from Alex and others: "[Alex] had his privileges taken away [for] alcohol at a dance ... [in a] Gatorade bottle.... Yeah, but he was just an idiot with it, and he was dancing with a girl. He had the bottle in his back pocket. [One of the teachers brought a friend] to the dance to be a chaperone. Her friend ... snatched the bottle out of his back pocket without him noticing and just took a whiff of it. We all saw, we're like, he's being dumb right now." I interviewed the teacher who chaperoned the dance, and her memory was broadly similar: "I remember him coming in, and he was stumbling all over, and I can smell it on him. And he had a Gatorade bottle in his pocket.... And my friend, he was there with me, he was a police officer in another township.... He called you guys and said he either needed to call Edison Police or [have Alex] go home with you guys.... And he certainly wasn't driving [his girlfriend] home."

As Alex described in his rehab writing, drinking and smoking marijuana was a regular occurrence for him and his high school friends. All those I interviewed said pretty much the same thing. One of his close friends, Evan, described their early high school experience: "Freshman year is about the age that all of us kind of discovered alcohol and marijuana. ... I would say freshman year you could bet at least 50 percent of us had tried it. Then each year it increased more and more."

Interestingly, early on Alex viewed marijuana as objectionable. That same friend described how he and Alex became close sophomore year, when they were in Latin class together:

He was always bookish and yet trying to be a skater at the same time. He would hear me and [another student] talking. We'd talk about something we did. . . . He overheard me talking about the first time I smoked pot. He was like, "You guys are dumb." Sophomore year is when him and I started to really bond. It probably was the marijuana and alcohol that started that. I mean, not only that. It's not. But we f-cking just had good times whenever we hung out. Just do dumb stuff and have a good time. . . . Like I said, he was always getting his work done and having fun.

When the Wardlaw administration found out about Alex's behavior, they suspended him for a week, among other "serious disciplinary actions." By Thursday of the following week, the upper school head sent Alex a note (bold in the original):

January 24, 2008

Dear Alex,

As you know, you attended the Semi-Formal with alcohol in your possession. Because, as stated in our Student and Parent Handbook, "**Possessing**, using, dealing in, or being under the influence of illicit drugs, **alcoholic beverages** or tobacco will likely lead to serious disciplinary action, including probation, suspension, or expulsion, even as a first offense" I asked the J-Board to examine this situation and make it's [sic] disciplinary recommendation to me.

The J-Board recommendation were as follows:
1. The student should be placed on "**Social Probation**" until June 6, 2008. . . .
2. The student must participate in an "**Alcohol Evaluation**" as soon as possible. Its results must be shared with me. Failure to do so should result in immediate expulsion from Wardlaw-Hartridge.
3. If the Alcohol Evaluation determines that an "**Intervention**" is necessary, the student must enroll in such a program. If enrolled, the program's director must share treatment progress with me. Failure to do so should result in immediate expulsion from Wardlaw-Hartridge.
4. Five days of **out-of-school suspension** to begin on Friday, January 25. Alex may return to school on January 26 if item 2 above has been completed. . . .

What strikes me all these years later is the letter's harsh and punitive tone. In addition to the sanctions, the head of the school also wrote to all the colleges to which Alex had applied to tell them of his suspension.

In retrospect, the school's punitive response isn't surprising for those of us who know the history of U.S. drug policies. The school's disciplinary policy on "**possessing**, using, dealing in, or being under the influence of illicit drugs, **alcoholic beverages**" reflects the broader society's criminal justice policies. As I described in chapter 3, U.S. history provides ample evidence that our justice system was (and still is) focused on the war on drugs.

This punitive approach quickly found its way into schools, where zero tolerance, abstinence, and criminal justice policies flourished in the 1980s and 1990s.[1] Schools began to mete out severe sanctions to policy infractions for alcohol and drug use, including exclusionary practices like suspensions and expulsions. These practices occurred despite warnings from the American Psychological Association, among others, that such policies were ineffective and unfairly administered, leading to higher suspension rates, especially for black and brown students. Back then, most Americans simply accepted these harsh policies without question, believing that students' illegal actions with alcohol and drugs required harsh consequences. Even Chip and I at the time understood the school's right to punish those violating its rules. We did, however, take issue with the severity of their response.

At the time I was immensely saddened by the school's rigid, punishing response, so different from its reaction to his anorexia five years earlier. When Alex got sick in seventh grade, the school's previous administrators enveloped him in a supportive, caring community. Those administrators, and his fellow students, were important to Alex's successful recovery and re-entry to middle school life. He was not stigmatized, and instead was treated with empathy by his school community, teachers, administrators, and students alike.

This time the response was strikingly different. Rather than consider Alex's recent history of self-harming behavior, they looked at him with blinders, seeing only that he had broken the rules and was engaging in illegal behavior that needed to stop. Period. I can only think that they thought this stern approach would "teach him a lesson," and would deter other students from engaging in similar behavior. This time there was no community and no empathy, only punishment. In a small school like Wardlaw, Alex had essentially been placed in the stocks. Sadly, in addition to piling on the stigma, the school's response failed. At college, less than a year later, Alex's alcohol and drug use intensified.

Over the years I have become increasingly convinced that Wardlaw's singular punitive approach was ill-advised. There is some promising new research on how harm reduction strategies can reduce the punitive effects of school disciplinary policies and yield a better outcome. Several school districts have begun to experiment with new policies, to good advantage. Restorative justice approaches are designed to emphasize relational social engagement and trust in the community over social control and punishment. Initial results in several states, including Colorado, Georgia, and Connecticut, show dramatic declines in suspensions and expulsions after their legislatures repealed statewide zero tolerance policies. These changes are part of a trend, beginning in 2011, whereby state legislatures began to reform school-based criminal justice policies.[2] More generally, research shows that adopting harm reduction strategies has reduced morbidity and mortality linked to risky health behavior, in comparison with traditional abstinence policies.[3]

As angry as we were, we were thankful that the school's head provided a broader context in his letter to the colleges that had accepted Alex. That letter is so different in tone than the school's "sanctions" letter. As I recall none of the colleges rescinded their acceptances.

My anger nevertheless festered for the remainder of the school year. Once Alex graduated, and was safely away from reprisals, I sent a long, angry letter to the school's top administrators, dated June 20, 2008. A few of its points:

> As I reflect back on our many years at Wardlaw Hartridge, I am immensely saddened by having to leave the school with such ill will. I write in hopes that in the future you might avoid the kinds of actions that were so disrespectful of our family, and that left us with such anger toward a school we have known and loved for so many years. . . .
>
> In our minds, the school's true value came through loud and clear when Alex was hospitalized with a medical crisis in 7th grade. [Peggy] worked with Alex and us, helping Alex to integrate back into the school.

His classmates likewise welcomed him back with open arms and were always there for him. We felt truly blessed that we were in the Wardlaw community. That was truly Wardlaw at its best, a caring community taking care of one of its own. The school's teachers and administrators provided individualized understanding and empathy, and worked with us to do what was best for Alex.

This year has been Wardlaw at its worst, and a trying one for Alex and us. . . . Your reaction to his behavior, however, was vastly excessive and overly moralistic. We certainly did not receive the kind of individualized understanding and empathy we had previously, and which should be the hallmark of a Wardlaw education. Here was an opportunity to work with us in a respectful way to do what was right for Alex. . . .

I urge you to work with parents to develop a more realistic set of consequences for behavioral misdeeds of teenagers, and a fairer system of adjudicating them.

I did not remember writing this letter until I began this chapter and looked through my files, but I still agree with its sentiments. They were my views on school discipline, well before I ever learned anything about harm reduction, and remain so. Perhaps not surprisingly, I never received a response.

As I look back to that time, from the perspective of years later, there are a few takeaways. I recognize my (still existing) outrage at how the school meted out discipline. We agreed that Alex's actions were inappropriate but felt that a different school response would have yielded better outcomes. I believe this still. Alex was stigmatized and singled out among his peers. More generally, what sense does it make to separate students from schoolwork via suspension?

As I write about these incidents from so long ago, I searched online to see whether the school's policies might have changed since Alex's graduation. Wardlaw's 2019–2020 *Student & Parent Handbook* shows that suspensions and expulsions are still listed as possible consequences of infractions. "Social probation" is still on the books, which for Alex lasted the remainder of his last semester. Clearly my letter fell on deaf ears.

For comparative purposes, I looked up the Metuchen High School (MHS)'s policy on alcohol and drugs in their 2020–2021 *Parent-Student*

Handbook. While students are not permitted to be in unlawful possession of drugs or alcohol at school, or at any student activities, infractions require removal until parents are contacted, and "referral to the
Student Assistance Program. . . . Second offenses could result in expulsion." And for evening school activities, "any student suspected or
observed to be under the influence of alcohol or drugs will not be
admitted. Parents/guardians and/or the police will be notified."

To better understand how these policies worked in practice, I interviewed the retiring principal of MHS. While Bruce didn't know Alex
personally, we knew him relatively well from Hunter's and Ginny's years
at MHS. By way of context, as of April 2022, Metuchen had approximately fifteen thousand residents. It's a relatively small suburban New
Jersey town, primarily white, educated, and middle-class, and part of
the broader New York City exurb. Census data from 2020 show that
approximately 68 percent of the residents are whites, 16 percent Asian,
6 percent blacks, 8 percent two or more races, and 10 percent Hispanic
(of any race). Its nickname, "the Brainy Boro," is well deserved: 97 percent
of its residents aged twenty-five years or older have graduated from high
school, and 62 percent have at least a bachelor's degree. In 2020 the
median household income was $136,067 (in 2020 dollars), the median
value of owner-occupied housing units was $462,200, and the poverty
rate a low 3.3 percent.[4] As befits a small town, the high school and local
police work together closely. Bruce described it as a useful and cordial
relationship. Illustrative of this, when I asked him how he heard about
Alex's death, he reported: "I actually heard about it through the police
department. The police department does a pretty good job of alerting us
of any kind of a possible drug death, or a death due to auto, or there may
be an impact in the building, an emotional impact of some kind. I also
think that one of my guidance counselors might have also told me. It
was a concern because at that time I believe Ginny was in the high
school. . . . We were concerned with Ginny's well-being."

I asked Bruce specifically how the school responded to violations of
the alcohol and drug policies during his tenure:

We sent all those kids [suspected of drug or alcohol consumption] out
for drug tests. . . . The parent actually has to come in and take the

student for the test. Many times, it's eye-opening for the parent because they didn't realize that their child ever had a problem of any form. [In addition, the school suspends students with positive drug or alcohol tests for three days.] I think it's a little bit foolish, but it's like a three-day suspension where the student's out of school. But before the student comes back into the building, the student needs be in some kind of a rehab program.... They need to show evidence that they're enrolled [continuously] in a program.... Then we also will have them get involved in speaking, on a weekly basis if not more, with our student systems coordinator [a branch of the Counseling Department].... Generally the counselor usually has some pretty strong and good conversations with that student. They really connect with the student. What it is, it's a resource in the building when a kid is having that dark moment, that they can excuse themselves and go and speak with that student systems counselor.

MHS has thirty-eight cameras on the premises. And, by law, the school has the legal right to look through students' personal property, including backpacks, lockers, and even their cars, if they have reasonable suspicion that a student has violated a school rule or the law.[5] The local police, on the other hand, must meet the higher standard of probable cause to conduct a search. Bruce talked about his "regular relationship" with the local police. They alert him to parties with underage drinking, and he warns the police if he hears of any upcoming gatherings. He lets the police know when a student is sent out for a drug test. The school also works actively with a police officer, whose responsibilities include working as a "juvenile detective."

During Bruce's twelve years at the school, no student was expelled for drugs or alcohol. I asked about the number of suspensions in an average year: "My population is 750 students the past year. But I would say on a regular year ... I'd say three to five, probably hovering more around three to be honest with you. Because the other thing with all this now, too, is that kids are pretty in tune with how to beat us.... I maybe had one or two over my twelve years here where a kid was actually selling, either in the phys ed locker rooms or in a bathroom or whatever. But again, the police get involved [if student is selling drugs]."[6]

I was intrigued to learn about Bruce's negative attitudes toward the school's suspension policy, and its experimentation with restorative justice programs:

We've been using restorative justice to try to cut down our suspension numbers. Just tell a kid he's suspended, what good is that? We've all realized it, and it's not only in Metuchen, but it's across the county and across the state. . . . Yes, we've begun to use it here with a number of our students and not just students that have been suspended, but students who may be chronically late to school, which would initiate a detention. What we've started to do is . . . provide community service type of opportunities. So, we try to turn around and make it a real learning experience, educational experience in that you made a mistake. We're not going to suspend you. We're not going to have something that's going to be on a school record or on a disciplinary record. Yes. I think it has been successful. I think that we've taken some of our students and basically what we're doing is we're saying, "Look, they're not going to crucify you for what you did. We want you to learn from what you did. We want you to turn it into a good thing, as opposed to continue down that same path." . . . We haven't done it really long enough to really be able to project out that this is really working.

It was gratifying to learn that this small community in which I lived is trying out a new approach to school discipline, one that is more holistic and empathic than the traditional punitive approaches in place in many U.S. high schools, including the one Alex attended. Few people I've talked with over the years have heard of harm reduction; more, however, knew of restorative justice. As I look back to Alex's high school experiences, I wish Wardlaw had been as enlightened. It's too complex a question to know whether a different disciplinary approach might have made a difference for Alex. Perhaps not. But layering a new level of trauma on existing mental health issues certainly didn't help.

We saw both highs and lows during Alex's high school years and traveled with him on both the first and second roads. We hoped that he would mature as he went out on his own to college. One thing he already had was a large community of friends, from the neighborhood and from school. That community was about to dramatically increase as he moved to college. To close out this chapter, I include a few of the memories I heard from his friends, fleshing out a picture of the young man he was. They provide a good counterpoint to his negative contemporaneous self-descriptions.

His friend Mark told me:

> So, my first memory of him is, he's a very, was a very outgoing guy. . . . So he is somebody who I found, it was super easy to fall into a friendship with. . . . You can drop him into a room and he's walking out probably invited to a wedding and making friends and doing all that stuff, so it was really comfortable for me to become his friend and use that as a way to open up my horizons, meet a ton of new people. He was so generous in terms of bringing me around to his friends. . . . Oh yeah. I'm sure you hear this a lot, but he was definitely my best friend. I don't know if I was his, but he was 100 percent my best friend and I mean, he is still so with me today.

I loved what his friend Latisha said about their friendship:

> Because we were at this smaller school . . . it was like a family, not just friendships, everyone was looking out for the best interests. He was the leader of the pack who was athletic and smart, but also cared about how everyone was doing. He was very deeply emotional in making sure everyone was okay with what they were doing and where they were at.
>
> For me, my mom died when I was young, it was like eighth-grade summer, going into freshman year. . . . He would always just be like, "Tish, how are you doing? Are you okay? What's good?" I'm like, "Oh, I'm good, yeah, yeah, yeah." He was like, "All right, well, just checking on you," that kind of thing, where most dudes aren't that emotionally aware of how people are feeling and what they're doing. [Alex and his friend AlexF] were funny and smart, but they also were emotionally aware of what people were going through, not just worried about themselves. . . .
>
> He was very aware, he had like, spidey senses of people's emotions and feelings, and he was always just trying to make sure people were in a good spirit and people were in a good mood. Whether that was making people laugh, telling stories, or joking and clowning in the best possible way, never from a place of malice. . . .

Of course, it's behind this façade of, "I'm just a dude, I'm just cool, I'm chilling, I'm having fun," and guys come over, we'll hang out and chill, "You want a beer? You want a soda? Tish, you don't drink, you want a Coke?" Whatever it is, it's behind this mask of, I'm just the cool guy.

My interview with Jordan, one of his closest high school friends, showed both the positives and negatives of Alex's demeanor:

J: And then throughout the whole baseball season, I just remember Alex and I were very close, and then from then on, he was my best friend at Wardlaw.

PR: Yeah, and what drew you to him? What drew him to you?

J: I mean, what is there not to be drawn to from Alex? He was always just so cool.

I'm sure everyone has said that. He was just an infectious personality to be around.

He always was right on the edge, whether that was. . . . Like when he got caught jumping in the pool with his girlfriend. That was pushing, going to the edge. [He was] pushing the envelope in that sense. Yeah. I mean, . . . I don't know whether he was just bored with normal things, and this just excited him. I mean, you think about that. . . . [I just watched] *Free Solo*, where the guy that rock climbed without a rope, and basically normal life is just boring to him. . . . By climbing without a rope, it triggers something in his brain that that's how he wants to live. So, you wonder if Alex pushing himself to the edge on everything that he did was how his brain wanted to function.

PR: Yeah. It's interesting that you talk about *Free Solo* because several people have said he reminds them of Alex. And his name was Alex, wasn't it?

J: Alex Honnold, yeah.

PR: Yeah. And people said that [he] even looks like Alex, and I saw pictures of him online, and he does look like an older version of Alex, right?

J: Except that . . . our Alex . . . was very good socially. When he talked to my parents, my parents loved him, and he was charming.

PR: He knew how to charm people.

J: Right, and when he's with a group of people, our age, he was always the center of attention.

How do these affectionate quotes from his friends square with an Alex who later in his life could see no way out of his addictions? He was smart, funny, good-looking. In the "Senior Superlatives" of his high school yearbook, his peers voted him "Class Flirt." His "senior prediction" was "after three years at Dickinson realizes he's too good-looking for college and decides to become a Hollister model/Chippendales dancer with his good buddy Jordan." Of course, neither he nor Jordan became models, and each graduated from college four years later. How could he not see all those who loved him—all who saw the good and positive in him—his family and his friends? This is the pain and confusion that remains in the hearts and minds of survivors, friends, and family alike. I have no answer to the self-destruction of addiction. I can ask lots of questions about our own behavior, questions we ask ourselves ad nauseam: Was private school a mistake? Should we have reacted differently to his school suspension? Was there something else we could have done that would have inoculated him from the resurgence of his anorexia, and his drug-taking? Ultimately, why did Alex travel along the second road to his death when so many of his peers did not, even those who were caught up in drinking and drugs along the way? To search for answers, I asked his friends for their insights, which I provide in subsequent chapters. Jordan clearly adds a useful piece to the puzzle here. I never heard Alex say that normal life was boring to him, but I long thought he was pushing himself to the edge on everything he did. He was fearless, but not always in a good sense. Maybe that was how his brain wanted to function. But, along with those edgy actions came considerable anxieties.

Alex's first Christmas, 1989, Highland Park, NJ. Alex was born about a week before Christmas. We used this photo for our Christmas card that year. (Photo credit: Patricia A. Roos)

Alex and Aunt Poo (Chip's sister), summer 1994, Metuchen, NJ. Poo visited us frequently and was always playing with Alex. He loved her deeply. She was there for him, and especially so when Alex traveled to Florida for substance use treatment. Chip writes about giving up on Alex. Poo never did. (Photo credit: Patricia A. Roos)

Alex and Granny (Chip's mom), November 1994, West Palm Beach, FL. Granny was a presence in Alex's life from Day 1. She visited us in Jersey, and we visited her in Florida, multiple times a year. We were always thankful she didn't see Alex at his worst. (Photo credit: Patricia A. Roos)

Alex with view of the World Trade Center, August 1995, New York. We traveled to the Statue of Liberty, and on the ferry caught the World Trade Center in the background, where so many lives would be lost six years later. (Photo credit: Lee Clarke)

Alex and cousins Elizabeth and Gregory, August 1995, Metuchen, NJ. My sister
Marianne, her husband David, and their kids visited us in Metuchen that year, the
first of many visits in New Jersey, Virginia, Minnesota, and Montana. (Photo
credit: Patricia A. Roos)

Alex's first day of school, September 1996, Metuchen, NJ. Wearing his spiffy new uniform, Alex paused for pictures before his first day at Wardlaw Hartridge's lower school. He was about six years away from anorexia, and seventeen years from heroin. (Photo credit: Patricia A. Roos)

Chip, Alex, and Pat, July 1996, Capon Springs, WV. We celebrated my parents'
fiftieth wedding anniversary with the entire Roos clan at Capon Springs, a resort in
West Virginia. Alex especially loved playing with his cousins Eileen (my brother
Bill's daughter), Elizabeth, and Greg. My sister Libby took a great family picture
that day. (Photo credit: Elizabeth J. Roos)

Alex and Hunter, October 1998, Edison, NJ. Alex walking with Hunter after a Wardlaw Hartridge soccer game. Hal (Chip's brother), Kathy, Hunter, and Ginny lived half a mile from us, and Hunter and Alex were already more like brothers than cousins. (Photo credit: Hal Clarke)

Alex and cousins Audrey and Clara, April 2001, Arlington, VA. At a Roos get-together in Arlington, Alex met up with my sister Christine, her husband Matt, and their two kids Audrey and Clara (Nicole was not yet born). He loved those cousins. Years later, Clara produced a documentary podcast about the opioid epidemic during her junior year at Ithaca College's Roy H. Park School of Communications entitled *About Alex*. (Photo credit: Patricia A. Roos)

Alex, August 2002, Cooperstown, NY. In August 2001 and August 2002, Chip and Alex traveled to Cooperstown for a father-son baseball camp. Alex loved all things baseball, and still had that perfect baseball pose and focus. (Photo credit: Lee Clarke)

Alex and Lexi, late summer 2002, southern NJ. By late summer we decided to purchase a German shepherd dog. Alex chose her name, Lady Lexus of Metuchen, Lexi for short. We traveled to the breeder, choosing the dog who climbed right into Alex's lap. By this time, Alex was losing weight. The next time he saw Lexi he was in the hospital. You can see a bit of hope for the future in Alex's tentative smile. (Photo credit: Lee Clarke)

Lexi and Alex, March, 2005, Metuchen, NJ. My favorite picture of Alex and Lexi. Such a regal picture of Lexi, and a sweet picture of fifteen-year-old Alex. That dog loved Alex, and he loved that dog. This picture won first prize at a picture-taking event at Alex's school that year (truth be told, I think everyone won a prize). (Photo credit: Patricia A. Roos)

Hunter, Ginny, and Alex, Thanksgiving 2004, Edison, NJ. After Hal's wife Kathy died in September 2004, none of us felt like hosting Thanksgiving. Instead, we went to eat at the local Sheraton, where Hal worked. The kids were making funny faces, trying to make us laugh. I'm sure we laughed, but none of us were happy. (Photo credit: Patricia A. Roos)

Pat and Alex, Spring 2004, Hillsdale, NY. We trekked at least yearly to Hillsdale to visit Chick and Barbara Perrow and see the leaves change. But this year, we visited in the spring as well. I love this picture of Alex and me in our special place. He was looking good, having gained back much of his lost weight. And, once again, he was smiling. (Photo credit: Lee Clarke)

Chip, Sara, Alex, and Ginny, December 2005, Ellis Island, NY. Poo and Sara joined us for most Christmas breaks. That Christmas, their visits included Ellis Island. They had the New York City skyline in the background again, but this time the Twin Towers were gone. (Photo credit: Lynn Clarke Moran)

Chip and Alex, August 2006, Red Lodge, MT. This is my favorite picture of Chip and Alex, and to this day it serves as my screensaver. That year we traveled to Montana for my niece Elizabeth and Phil's wedding, and my sister Libby caught them in a sweet father-son moment. (Photo credit: Elizabeth J. Roos)

Alex, fall 2007, Roosevelt Park, Edison, NJ. Chip loves this graduation picture, taken in the fall of Alex's senior year of high school. The suit Chip wore when we married fit Alex like a glove. Alex loved that. (Photo credit: Lee Clarke)

Alex, May 2012, Dickinson College, Carlisle, PA. Another of my favorite pictures of Alex. Hal caught him smiling widely, right after he picked up his diploma at his Dickinson College commencement. Later that day, we packed up Alex's things, and brought him back to Metuchen. One month later we lost Granny, and later that summer, Hal. (Photo credit: Hal Clarke)

Alex, Eileen, and Hunter, May 2013, University of Virginia, Charlottesville, VA. Alex and Hunter joined us for a family trip to my niece Eileen's University of Virginia graduation. We had such a great time that weekend, a brief respite before addiction insanity took over our lives. (Photo credit: Patricia A. Roos)

Alex, April 2015, The Shores Treatment & Recovery Center, Port Saint Lucie, FL. Poo and Sara visited Alex whenever his addictions brought him to Florida. That day Poo treated them to oysters. Although anorexia and bulimia meant he was way too thin, he was doing well that day. He planned to head back to Jersey to once again begin his Rutgers graduate program and live in a sober living house right off campus. But it was not to be. (Photo credit: Lynn Clarke Moran)

PART III

DESCENT INTO INSANITY

CHAPTER 7

College Days

> When you're a parent, there's a story you are deeply invested
> in, it's not your story and you're not going to get to know how it
> turns out—at least, not unless you're very unlucky. . . . Parenting
> is a hostage situation: you're in the car, but your child is the
> one driving it—and he doesn't know how to drive. You can't get
> out, because you decided to love him before you knew who
> he was—before he even was anyone. . . . He needs your
> help, at least for now.
>
> —Agnes Callard, "Parenting and Panic"

AFTER HIS ACADEMICALLY successful but sometimes difficult high school years, Alex went to a small, well-respected liberal arts college in Carlisle, Pennsylvania—Dickinson College. We were able to assemble the funds to pay for Dickinson's nearly $50,000 yearly cost from a small college fund my father set up for each of his grandkids, and a $7,500 per year grant from a small family foundation. For the remainder, we paid from our college savings account, investments, and current income. We were lucky we had those resources, so he was not saddled with student loans, as many kids are. Those loans would have added considerably to his later anxieties. We made the investment in the hope that Dickinson would be the right place for him to stay on track.

Alex was thrilled to be away from home, far from parents surveilling his day-to-day life. But while the balance between the first and second roads was more toward good than bad in high school, by college the second road got a lot bumpier. Academically, he continued to do well; his grades were excellent. We held our breath, though we could never have guessed how much worse it would get. From his first semester, he encountered problems, mostly due to alcohol. He blacked out on several occasions and had difficult run-ins with the local Carlisle emergency services and police. Over his college years he ended up in the hospital several times with a blood alcohol content sufficient to kill him. We seriously contemplated cutting off his college funding, but because he continued to do so well academically, we were lulled into the hope, some might call it magical thinking, that he would outgrow this behavior. How could things be bad if he was going to class, getting good grades, and heading toward graduation?

The day we moved Alex to Dickinson on August 20, 2008, remains a vivid memory. The day started with a parents' orientation session after Alex, Chip, and I transferred Alex's boxes from our car to his rather small double in the basement of Drayer Hall. We met his roommate, a member of the Dickinson soccer team, who had moved in earlier because practice had already started. We left to attend the parents' reception. Alex walked us out and after we said our good-byes and gave final hugs. Chip said, nearly sotto voce, "Have fun." Alex murmured back, "Oh, I will."

We headed back to Metuchen tearful but nonetheless hopeful that Alex was off to a good start. The move-in had gone smoothly, the orientation was well done, and his roommate seemed nice. For the next few days, Alex attended orientation, got his ID card, learned about the campus, and generally got acclimated to college life. He readily felt at home, and quickly made a lot of friends. Whenever we visited over those next four years, it seemed every other person we ran into on campus would call out "Hey, Clarke," a new nickname that had stuck.

Alex's academic success continued in college. Still contemplating a future as a surgeon, he majored in biology and minored in computer science. He took a raft of difficult science courses, including biology, physics, computer science, chemistry, ecology, immunology, and microbiology, supplementing these with Latin, English, psychology, and sociology. He earned A's for two intro biology courses from Rutgers during the summer of 2010. He did very well in the organic chemistry sequence, always viewed as the weed-out courses for medical school. His final grade point average was 3.43, a respectable A-.

It's the nature of college life that parents know less about what their kids are up to than in high school. Yet, Alex was not absent from our lives. We visited him at Dickinson several times, and he came home for summer, school breaks, and holidays. Because he had a car, he occasionally drove the two and a half hours home for visits. All things considered, we saw him, and his basement friends, a lot over those years.

Alex and Katie remained a couple throughout Alex's first three years of college. They split up right before Alex's senior year. Katie told their story, which hints at some of the darker aspects of Alex's personality:

He wasn't sure he wanted a girlfriend in college, and we kind of had decided we were going to break up when he left, but then I guess we just changed our mind, or he changed his mind, or whatever it was. . . . I visited a couple of times when I was still [in high school] . . . and then when I was at West Virginia I would visit him as well, and he'd visit me so, and we dated until it was almost exactly four years.

I felt like I was just constantly being lied to. And I guess I hadn't matured enough to realize that it wasn't going to change, and it wasn't working, because we had broken up for small periods of time throughout our relationship. He actually cheated on me once when we were pretty early on in our relationship, and that I guess started the trust issues. . . . The lying in general, I don't think it had to do with drinking or drugs. . . . Alex, he was very social, and he was a party animal, he was very flirtatious. . . . I don't think he didn't love me, or didn't want to be with me. I think that he just wanted to have his cake and eat it too.

Ashley soon came into Alex's and our lives. He introduced us at his twenty-second birthday celebration at the Metuchen Inn on December 17, 2011. We warmed to Ashley immediately, and she became a fixture at our house for the next several years. It was reassuring to us that Alex chose girlfriends who were truly nice people and that they chose to be with him. We enjoyed Ashley's company, and the feeling seems to have been reciprocated. In talking with me for this book Ashley described her first introduction to us: "I remember being a little bit nervous, but at the same time I was like, whoever raised this kid, they have to be pretty down-to-earth good people. And it was a super easy introduction, which was nice."

Ashley became friendly with Alex during their junior year, when they took some of the same classes and found they had friends in common. She had been acquainted with Alex before and knew him as a popular kid on campus. She talked with me about how Alex was a different person outside of class than in class, where he wore his popular façade. She spoke of how he reflected on things but wasn't talkative about it. Ashley and I had a conversation recently about whether patience was one of Alex's virtues. I had never much thought Alex was particularly patient, but Ashley provided a more nuanced observation:

> I wouldn't have characterized Alex as a patient person. What he wanted, he wanted. He wanted it then, right now, but he was very patient with me. And in a way that I think he knew I needed someone to be patient with me, and that was a small way that he regularly showed me that he cared. . . . He would sit with me for hours even if I was up until two in the morning most times. He would sit there and try to motivate me to continue to push through, which is something that I really appreciated then because I needed that reinforcement, but I also needed to be doing the amount of work that I was doing.

On reflection, I recognized this as well. When he wanted something, Alex could be quite impatient. But for others he had the capacity for great patience and deep kindness. He had long, patient conversations with Granny, as she questioned him over the years about his school and social activities, and he was especially patient with his younger cousins, Ginny and Hunter. On many occasions, he helped Ginny with her homework, patiently explaining convoluted math or science concepts, and gave Hunter guidance about how to navigate college. I never saw impatience on those occasions.

During his senior year, Alex lived in an on-campus two-bedroom apartment with his friend Tim. Although he was in a fraternity, he never lived in their housing. Tim provided useful insight into Alex's mindset:

> I think he put a lot of pressure on himself. He always wanted to do well. His grades were definitely really important to him. . . . People were very kind of highbrow and super-judgmental [reflecting Dickinson's

middle-class culture] and would place you in these categories very quickly, and Alex was always wanting to be like, "Screw that." Like if you're one of my people, you're one of my people, period. . . . That was one of the best things about him. It's just like I don't care what other groups, what others say. Like if you're cool with me, here we go. This is what we're doing right now. So, it was interesting because I feel like the role in the fraternity for him, he wanted to be part of a group but he also was so fiercely independent and I feel like that played . . . a huge role in it too. [He wanted] to be a member of that group but still [had] the need to kind of be like, "Screw your authority, man. It's not going to get to me."

By Christmas senior year, Alex, Ashley, Tim and his girlfriend were ready to celebrate the holidays. As Ashley recounted it: "[Alex told us,] 'I want a massive Christmas tree.' And I was like, 'Okay.' I wouldn't have guessed, but I was like, 'Let's go shopping for one.' . . . The four of us decorated that tree, and then we made stockings and hung those stockings. I think we had Christmas dinner. I think he wanted to make it feel like home. . . . I think we left that Christmas tree up there until he graduated."

These reflections from Alex's friends provide important insights into his temperament during his college years. His friends were prodigious, and they loved him dearly. And he loved his good friends like family and loved having fun. But he also wanted good grades and did what he needed to do well academically. Tim also pointed to a different side of Alex, a strong independent streak that wasn't so visible to me at the time but now makes a lot of sense.

In chapter 6, I quoted from Alex's rehab statement on honesty, written at the Advanced Health and Education Treatment Center in November 2013. In it he described his slide into addiction, beginning in his high school years; he also wrote about his college years:

As I entered college, my drinking and smoking habits both increased. One counselor at Advanced Health said that alcoholics suffer from an inferiority complex, and I can really relate to this. I felt like I had to drink in excess to fit in with everyone else. It only made matters worse that I was constantly rejected from parties my roommates were invited to because they were on the soccer team. I was also rejected from my first-choice fraternity because of this. As you know from my arrest records and hospital visits, my alcohol problem continued to worsen throughout college. Throughout these 4 years, I decided to experiment with cocaine, ecstasy, mushrooms, acid, and pain killers. I never really did any one in excess, but I liked the feeling of getting out of myself, and being someone different who was able to socialize without fear. During my senior year, I decided to pick up selling weed again, and I proceeded to sell 1–2 pounds a week. From this, I made a lot of money, and I also got a lot of respect from my friends, and to be honest, it was the first time in a while that I felt included, and accepted, and needed at school. [He goes on to talk about his post-college years.]

It wasn't long before Alex found trouble at Dickinson, or perhaps trouble found him. During Alex's first semester there, homecoming was scheduled for three days in early November 2008. Parents were invited, classes were open, departments had open houses, and there was a football game and various student performances. Right before we left for Carlisle, I got a call from the local Carlisle police informing me that Alex had been arrested for underage drinking.

At the time, I did not know that he'd had a previous incident on October 2 and had met with the associate dean of students on October 30, just two days before his November 1 arrest. He was issued a "written warning" for underage drinking. After the arrest, Alex received a letter from Dickinson's director of student conduct, requiring his attendance at a November 13 hearing for violating Dickinson's community standards. An incident report sent with the letter recounted:

At approximately 12:25 A.M., officers were dispatched to the 200 block of West Pomfret Street where a resident was complaining of a disorderly crowd of people leaving a party. Officers arrived, and the complainant, who wished to remain anonymous, pointed out an individual who had tried to pick a fight with him . . . when [the complainant] told the young man to keep it down, the young man threatened to "kick his ass." . . . As I came to talk to him, the complainant followed me up and pointed him out, demanding if Clarke still wanted to "kick my ass now that the cops are here." I told the complainant to go home and not cause a further confrontation on the street. He did so and I was unable to locate him later on.

While talking to Clarke, it became apparent to me that he was intoxicated. His speech was slurry and he was making up words such as "accommodative," his eyes were glassy, and he exuded an odor of alcohol. I asked Clarke if he had been drinking, and he stated that he had not drunk anything. I asked him if he blew into a PBT [portable breath test device], if it would register, and he stated he wasn't sure. At that point, [the officer] saw the top of a silver flask sticking out of his pocket. He pulled it out and upon investigation the flask contained vodka and orange juice.

Clarke was asked if he had ID, and he stated that he did not. I asked him how old he was and he stated that he was 18. I placed Clarke under arrest, and a search of his pockets revealed his Dickinson identification.

Clarke was made to blow into a portable breath test machine, and the reading was positive for alcohol at a .195. Clarke finally admitted that he had been drinking, stating that it was "what college kids do." His mother was contacted and indicated that she would be in the station on 11/1/08 to talk with me.

Because it was a first-time offense, Alex was allowed to do community service. The arrest was treated as a traffic citation, and not included in his permanent record. When the police officer called me, I wrote down the name of the arresting officer, and asked for his working hours. Once we arrived in Carlisle, we brought Alex to the police station so that he could apologize. On December 18, he appeared before a judge and the matter was adjudicated. He paid $112 for court costs. No doubt he benefited from being a white college student. As we know from many research studies, police interactions with black and brown young people can lead to much harsher, even tragic outcomes.

In its own proceedings, Dickinson found him "responsible for alcohol (underage possession/consumption), alcohol (public intoxication), dishonesty and deception, and disorderly and disruptive behavior." He was put on "conduct probation until 3/1/09," with the warning that "further violations of the Dickinson College community standards will result in more serious sanctions including the possibility of suspension from the college." He was also required to speak with us.

Later that academic year, on January 19, 2009, he was again called before a disciplinary hearing, charged with underage possession of alcohol, violations of resident hall policies, and alcohol drinking games. In that instance, his resident assistant found Alex, his roommate and four other students playing beer pong, although none of the students appeared drunk. This time Alex was lucky. He was held responsible only for excessive noise, a violation of residence hall policies. This new letter, however, provided an important warning: "Alex, during the hearing we talked about the number of first-year students with 3 or more violations of College policy. This number is very small, you are one of the five. Please take the time to reflect on the negative image you are presenting to the College community. From our meeting, I gather that the negative image is not a true testament to your character and hope that as you move forward, you portray your true character."

Colleges are in a tough situation. They face huge problems with underage drinking, especially binge drinking among new college students like Alex. Most colleges do what they can to address this problem. Dickinson handled Alex's serious alcohol incidents responsibly, especially given its location in conservative, rural Pennsylvania. As one of his college friends later noted:

> Especially the environment we were in. In some degree, you're in a very small liberal arts school in the middle of central Pennsylvania. There's very little to do.... [It's] a very unique dynamic where Carlisle is, between the township where the city and the students and the vast difference in socioeconomic class and resentment from locals to the students and the students are on this pedestal. So, there's a very large shift that happens with every class that comes in. There's only so much a school can do to mitigate that line in the sand.

Exacerbating that difficult fall of 2008 was the death of my father at eighty-nine years of age on September 14. Because Arlington National Cemetery had a long wait list, we were unable to bury him until December 11. We picked up Alex in Carlisle after he'd completed his first semester exams and brought him to Virginia. The service was one that befits the Army officer that he was, with all the pomp and circumstance one might expect from military funeral honors.

As Alex's first semester ended, we worried about what lay ahead. We saw his self-destructive behavior, and now the college knew about it.

We thought perhaps he'd settle down. Many young people go through such experimentation and mature into responsible adults. That's what we hoped for Alex. But he always thought he was invincible. He thought he could handle it; he always believed he could function. And for a while he did. But things were about to get worse.

One of the more dramatic, and disturbing, incidents during Alex's college years happened toward the end of spring semester. He had joined a fraternity, Kappa Sigma, and, we learned, had traveled to Penn State for a fraternity event. On Saturday, April 18, 2009, Alex called us to say he was in the hospital and needed our help. He was plainly under the influence and could not tell me what had happened, how badly he had been hurt, and he did not say where he was. We assumed he was in Carlisle, so Chip jumped in the car and started driving there to bring him home. After talking with some health care workers in his hospital room, I learned that he was in the Mount Nittany Medical Center, in State College, Pennsylvania. I called Chip's cell phone, and he changed course, driving the four hours to "Happy Valley," quite the misnomer, I remember thinking at the time.

By the time Chip got to the hospital, Alex was beginning to remember how he got there. He also realized he was missing one of his front teeth. He thought he had fallen on a curb, outside a fraternity party. After talking with friends, Alex pieced together the story: a fraternity bouncer had knocked out his front tooth. The bouncer evidently had no interest in letting a brother from a different fraternity, not to mention college, into their party, especially one who was clearly already drunk and likely belligerent.

Alex's friend Mark remembered hearing about the Penn State episode. Mark was a year behind Alex in college, and attended Penn State:

> That was actually the first time that he was at Penn State for fraternity reasons. That chapter that opened at Penn State was new. So, he was actually brought in as a part of the group that I guess runs the ceremony, maybe, or does some of the official things. . . .
>
> I think he was probably trying to go to a different fraternity and based on the state that he was in and the fact that he was not a student there, they probably said no, and that probably did not sit too well with

him at that moment in time. And he definitely did not mince his words when he was angry at somebody or unhappy at the way things were going for him. So, I can imagine that it would be something that could rouse a reaction from a certain type of person that might have been at the door that evening.

Alex's future roommate Tim corroborated much of this story. He remembered it happened the weekend before he first met Alex:

One of the first times I really met Alex [was when I was] with [several friends]. . . . He comes back and he pops his front tooth out and he just starts smiling. He had just gotten back from Penn State because he had gone for the weekend, and he had gotten his tooth punched out, and I didn't really know him that well at this point, and he starts cracking these jokes, and I'm like, who is this guy without a tooth. . . . He's so okay with this right now. Like this weekend sounds absolutely insane, what he just went through, and he just kept cracking jokes, . . . [Alex described what happened].. They were partying and they'd been drinking all day and he said something to one guy, I think, like trying to get into a party or something and the guy just punched him in the tooth and knocked it out.

We helped Alex deal with his dental emergency. Thankfully, our dentist came in that weekend to fit him with a partial denture before Alex headed back to Dickinson. He was back in December for a dental implant from our oral surgeon, and eventually the dentist fit him for a crown. We paid out of pocket for the dental and oral surgeon costs. Luckily our medical insurance paid for nearly all the $7,600 in medical costs at the Mount Nittany Medical Center: ambulance service, emergency room, cat scans of the head and body, and lab work. Looking back on these incidents, I realize once again how fortunate Chip and I were to have the kind of health care coverage and savings that we could manage these expenses. We didn't have to take an extra job or assume debt to help our child. What would a parent do who couldn't afford to replace a front tooth? Things could have been much worse. But at the time, it was bad enough to feel life-threatening to us.

The Penn State incident finally ended in March 2010, when a crisis management claims adjuster working for the fraternity that hired the bouncer paid Alex a settlement: he received two checks totaling $2,500 in partial payment for dental and medical costs. We hoped at the time that the long-term consequences from his blackout drinking would give him multiple reasons to change his behavior. But as his joking interaction with Tim the following weekend suggests, Alex didn't draw the lessons we hoped he would.

That the lesson hadn't been learned continued to unsettle us both emotionally and financially. In going back through my papers, I found receipts for two payments to Carlisle Fire and Rescue Services that reminded me of the roller coaster we were on. Cumberland-Goodwill Fire Rescue was called for BLS (basic life support) treatment, once in May 2009 and another time in October 2009, for "possession of a small amount of marijuana for personal use" and "public drunkenness." We hired a local lawyer for that infraction. On May 8, 2012, days before his graduation, that lawyer delivered. Alex received word that his Petition for Expungement was officially granted: "The arresting agency . . . the Federal Bureau of Investigation . . . and all criminal justice agencies . . . shall expunge and destroy the official and unofficial arrest and other criminal records, files, and other documents pertaining to the captioned proceedings." Thankfully, we had the resources to keep his record clean at this point. The fact that Alex was a middle-class white kid with two PhDs for parents clearly helped.

I know of no other major incidents during his junior and senior year. This doesn't mean that his drinking and drug taking ceased; it just means he didn't get caught.[1] By his own admission in his rehab statement, he began to experiment with cocaine, ecstasy, mushrooms, acid, Adderall, and pain killers. Moreover, during his senior year he began to sell marijuana. Any of these could have gotten him suspended or, more likely, expelled from school or arrested again. Alex was fortunate that to this point he had evaded the harsh reality of U.S. drug laws. In many ways, college is a "no consequences zone." The harsh reality of the real life that follows college is difficult for many young people to adjust to. And so it was for Alex.

The question I still have is: Why did he feel the need to lose himself so thoroughly in drinking and drugs? My interviews with Alex's friends, those who knew him best during those years, suggested some answers. His friends saw him as high-energy, the life of the party, their best friend—but several saw a darker side. He later told his therapist that he sometimes took tests while drunk, yet he still did well academically. And there was lots more.

One high school friend told me: "[He was always] making jokes and playful and having fun. . . . [But] there were these moments where Alex wasn't Alex. There was like a [time when] just being drunk took over. Not in a negative way. He wasn't aggressive or mean or rude. It was just a . . . there was no boundaries. . . . It was just that he was intoxicated and almost invincible to a degree. On a weekend visit to Alex at Dickinson, his Wardlaw friend Jordan saw that Alex had taken a disturbing turn: "Basically, from when I got there, [I saw] it was just partying and drugs. . . . It was like a lot of weed, and I think [for Alex and others] it got into coke or Adderall. . . . I remember when I got there, it was great to see him. Dickinson's beautiful. [But] the first thing we did was hop in a car, use a fake ID, go get beer. Immediately started drinking. Going to a party. Basically, right when we woke up, Alex was ready to smoke weed." Jordan, who did not smoke or use drugs, cut the visit short, and left early to drive back to his college.

Amy became one of Alex's best friends at Dickinson, though like Ashley, her first impression wasn't particularly positive. She also offered insight into Alex's personality:

As you know, we had like twelve to twenty friends who are named Alex, and we had to go by all of their last names. The first time I met Clarke was in, I believe it was in his dorm's basement. My first impression of him was like, "Ah, what a cocky jerk over there." He had this hat on, and that long mop of hair . . . [but from then on] we hung out there. I was like, "Oh, this guy's great! So much fun."

I never had any bad times or difficult times with him. He was always consistently an excellent friend. There was a little period of time when he first started dating Ashley that he was just seeing her all the time. I was like, "Dude." Because this is when Ashley and I weren't close. I was like, "Clarke, you are picking her over me. What the hell? You hang out with her all the time. You never see me."

He was like, "What do you want me to do? She's my girlfriend." I was like, "Hang out with me too! We've been best friends for like four years . . . what the hell?" He was like, "I'm not going to pick either of you. I'm picking both of you. You both have to get over this and be friends now" . . . [and] he brought Ashley and I back together.

During school breaks, some of Alex's Dickinson friends who lived nearby became part of the basement group. Amy's identical twin Jane, a student at another college, was one of them. She recalled that her main experience of Alex

> was getting to come and hang out in your basement, because it was a nice just laid back place to be and a safe place to be. We didn't have to go to a bar, we didn't really have to do anything. . . .
>
> Because during college, he was just the happiest guy. . . . But one reason why I loved going to hang out with him, and he was always without a doubt my favorite of Amy's friends because he made me feel so welcome from the get-go. Went out of his way to make me feel like I had a place at his home and at your home.
>
> [I never saw] panic attacks, but loneliness, yeah. That's when he would call me and be like, "Hey, do you want to come down and hang out?" . . . I know he was a very lonely person.
>
> He was attractive, funny, good to be around, welcoming. People loved him. But it was just, I don't know. Sometimes people just, I think, really . . . they have some kind of almost darkness inside them that doesn't really come from anywhere and they look for an escape. And there really isn't one, unless you want to address that darkness head on. That's a really difficult thing to do.

Ashley also reflected on this aspect of Alex's personality:

> In retrospect, I think Alex was far more insecure than anyone realized. He wasn't always the most talkative person, and I think when he drank, he was more talkative and he was more interactive and he felt free in a way. So, I don't know if sort of internally it helped calm him enough that he could interact with people more freely, and then he would feel good about having good interactions with people. It's hard for me to say though what level of drinking was to have fun and what drinking was to

make him feel better. Because especially once he left Dickinson, I think a lot of his drinking was more isolated.

When viewed together, Alex's friends present a portrait of a young man with insecurity, panic attacks, and the need for approval. There were two sides of Alex: one where he was "the happiest" and one where he was "the loneliest." They loved him deeply, but in retrospect they also saw his inner demons. While Alex's college friends often partook and partied, I learned in my interviews that some had struggled at times with their own issues and demons, for a few specifically related to the grief of losing Alex. Nonetheless they matured into their late twenties (and now early thirties). Unlike Alex, they successfully accomplished their "transition to adulthood." I'm left still questioning and trying to understand why Alex was unable to make that same transition.

Career issues exacerbated Alex's insecurities. Like many young people today, he did not see an easy path forward to the work he wanted to do; becoming a doctor or dentist seemed to require a perfect record that he could not achieve. At his private high school and then college, he felt the pressure not just to achieve but to overachieve. As he got closer to graduation, he worried that his grades and test scores might not be good enough for medical school, so he decided to apply to dental school instead. But he soon learned that getting into dental school was as hard, or even harder, than medical school. I found a draft of Alex's personal statement for his dental school application in which he discussed how the deaths of Hal and Kathy had sparked his desire for a career in health care. He wrote:

I remain curious about the complex interactions and processes that must occur every day within the human body, simply for it to survive. I hope to use this curiosity, coupled with my knowledge and interest in computer programming, to delve more deeply into the complex inner workings of the human body. Computers now play a major role in the evolution of our knowledge of the health field, and it can be said that without modern technology, health practitioners would be much less successful, and the number of patients who are helped every day from potentially life-threatening illnesses would be significantly reduced. I hope to be able to help this process of discovery and invention of new technology to better health outcomes.

Alex's difficulties with standardized tests haunted him anew when he had to take the Dental Admission Test (DAT). He applied for accommodations for the DAT (as well as the Medical College Admission Test) but was turned down. Although he took a prep course, his August 2011 DAT scores were disappointing. The test scored eight categories: perceptual ability, quantitative reasoning, reading comprehension, biology, general chemistry, organic chemistry, total science, and academic average. With no accommodations, his academic average (in percentiles) was 77.6, ranging from a low of 52.2 for reading comprehension to a respectable 84.7 for quantitative reasoning. Most of his scores were in the high 70s. These percentiles indicate "what percent of examinees received the same or a lower standard score." His low scores in reading comprehension dragged down his average.

Even with these scores, he was invited to interview at both New York University (NYU)'s College of Dentistry and Tuft University's School of Dental Medicine and reported that each went well. He received no acceptances but was placed on the waiting list status at NYU and Tufts. NYU contacted him a week before classes began to ask if he was still interested if someone didn't show up, and he replied yes without hesitation. Ultimately, however, no slot opened for him.

As parents, we tried to support Alex as best we could. We understood that he had learning challenges that had complicated his search for a career. With a supportive family behind him, we were confident that he would find his way to something else just as satisfying. But Alex did not share that hope. It's not overstating to say that this outcome shattered his self-esteem and shook his confidence to the core. He told us and several friends that he felt like a failure. He knew he could do the work of academic science and felt he was on the track to success. Unlike many of his friends, he found it enormously difficult to shift his career plans. Already prone to anxiety and insecurity, he could not shake off the rejection, self-doubt, and sense of failure, and it dogged him for the rest of his life.

Even though he hit some potholes along the way during his years at Dickinson, Alex appeared to be traveling the road we had hoped for him, working diligently on his college courses, and building his résumé to support his career aspirations. The summer of 2011 he had an internship as a lab employee at Rutgers, conducting polymerase chain reaction (PCR) analysis on wt. (wild type, or normal) and transgenic mice DNA, to study the effects of the overexpression of the intestinal monoacylg-lycerol lipase (MGL) gene. To understand what this means, I turned to my sister Christine who has a PhD in biomedical engineering from the University of Virginia, and who currently works at Cornell University's College of Veterinary Medicine. She described this as interesting work. PCR analysis multiplies the number of DNA strands to allow research-ers to detect the amount of DNA in a sample. COVID-19 tests, for exam-ple, are PCR tests that amplify a virus's genes sufficiently to detect it. In this case, Alex was conducting PCR analyses on wild type and transgenic mice, comparing normal mice to those with a gene "introduced" via the experiment. The results of the experiments showed that transgenic mice with overexpressed MGL were more likely to be obese.

Alex also volunteered as a patient care intern at JFK Hospital in Edi-son, New Jersey, an emergency room volunteer at the Harrisburg Hos-pital; as an American Red Cross volunteer in Carlisle; and as an outreach volunteer for the Dickinson College Dental Society. He also worked in our local dentist's office, the same dentist who implanted the crown after his front tooth was knocked out.

Alex graduated right on time from Dickinson College. The college put on a beautiful commencement weekend, with a baccalaureate cere-mony on May 19 and commencement exercises on the lawn in front of Old West, the first building to be erected on the campus, on a gorgeous Sunday, May 20, 2012. The speaker that day was the then director of the Central Intelligence Agency, David Petraeus, whose wife had gradu-ated from Dickinson. We were thrilled that several family members were able to join us for the graduation, including my sisters Marianne and Christine, and their families, as well as my brother Bill, Chip's mom, and his brother Hal with Hunter and Ginny.

We celebrated with a family dinner the night before at a local restaurant. I look often at those graduation pictures. There is one where a beaming Alex has his arm around Granny. Another shows Hal with Ginny and Hunter. Alex was so proud of himself and his accomplishments. Alex's cousin Eileen later remarked about what she heard about that celebratory family dinner: "I distinctly remember hearing [my dad] talk about how thoughtful Alex had been to everyone and particularly to Chip's mom. His comments stuck with me in part because, in my dad's book, being kind to one's grandparents is pretty much the highest praise he can give."

In celebration of his graduation, I compiled pictures of Alex throughout his life, appropriately titled "Alex Clarke: In Honor of His Graduation from Dickinson College, Carlisle, PA. Story to Date! May 20, 2012." They ranged from his newborn picture at St. Peter's Hospital on December 17, 1989, to his first Christmas picture when he was just days old, to photos of his first buddies Jenna, Matt, and Zach, his later buddies AlexF, Jeff, and James, his grandparents, parents, the Roos and Clarke cousins, Ashley, and Lexi. There are photos from school, sports, and vacations, and fun times that represent a joyful collage that captured the many wonderful people and good times in Alex's life. While there was other history too, Alex's successes had us hoping those were part of a buried past. As we found, the "story to date" kept spooling ahead. The months and years to come were full of heartache, pain, and immense grief. Our family would splinter and was almost destroyed as we lost family members and then our beautiful boy, first to addiction and then to death.

CHAPTER 8

Summer of 2012

Early on, the McIlvaines [a family who lost their son on 9/11] spoke to a therapist who warned them that each member of their family would grieve differently. *Imagine that you're all at the top of a mountain,* she told them, *but you all have broken bones, so you can't help each other. You each have to find your own way down.*

It was a helpful metaphor [but there's a problem with it]: "That suggests everyone will *make it* down, . . . some people never get down the mountain at all."

—Jennifer Senior, "What Bobby McIlvaine Left Behind"

IN THE SUMMER OF 2012, our family began to unravel. It was the "summer from hell." The hell began the December before, when our beloved German shepherd Lexi died from a neurological condition. She had been declining in health for several months. When she could no longer walk, or even stand up, we knew it was time. Alex drove home from Dickinson, and the three of us sat on the floor of the Raritan Animal Hospital as they put her to sleep. Lexi's head was in Alex's lap as she died, and he cried uncontrollably. His companion of nine years, the dog that had helped him through his bout with anorexia, was now gone. It hit him hard.

Things got worse, very quickly. Exactly one month after attending Alex's graduation, Granny died suddenly of a staph infection from MRSA while hospitalized from complications for lung cancer. She was eighty years old. As we have seen in earlier chapters, Alex was very close to Granny, and he was devastated. We all flew down for a memorial service at Granny's condo in West Palm Beach, Florida.

Just six weeks later, Chip's brother Hal died suddenly of atherosclerosis two days shy of his fifty-first birthday. Hal and his kids Hunter and Ginny lived within walking distance, and we were often together. We were shattered by the sudden loss of Hal, just eight years after Kathy's, Ginny and Hunter most of all. We could see the toll Hal's death had on Alex. Hunter and Ginny came to live with us. Overnight our small family of three grew to five. As sad as the circumstances were—and then became—having Hunter and Ginny in our lives has been an immense blessing.

During the last eight years of Hal's life, he quit his job to stay home. He got to know many of Hunter and Ginny's friends and their parents, donating his time to their school and sports activities. Without a job, Hal had no health insurance. How does one ever pay cash for heart failure? Hal's death brought home the deep defects in our health care system that so many Americans suffer from to this day. If there was ever a good example of the need for universal health care, this is it.

It seemed to us like the whole town of Metuchen turned out for Hal's memorial service that Saturday, August 4, 2012, at the local First Presbyterian Church. Hal knew lots of people in town. The backyard pool parties that he kept up even after he lost Kathy were famous, happening most weekends over the summer. The cabana was full of hamburgers, hot dogs, Popsicles, soda, beer, and every snack imaginable.

As it had been for Kathy, the First Presbyterian Church was once again full to the rafters that Saturday, with nary a seat left open. We sat up front and looked out at all the friends from far and wide. The eulogies were heartfelt, with lots of levity interspersed throughout. We all knew that Hal, like Chip, had a remarkable sense of humor. We heard from Hal's sister Poo and his dad. Chip and I both spoke, as well as six of Hal's friends. Portions of my eulogy speak to that summer's trauma, and the community that coalesced to support us:

As I began to write these words, it was Thursday morning, August 2, and reminders popped up on my calendar and Facebook page that said, "Hal Clarke's birthday." When Hal died this past Monday, it was twenty-four years to the day from when he stood as best man at our wedding. It was just last year, also on our anniversary, that we celebrated Hal's fiftieth birthday. I still remember the amazing video Chip and others put together for that celebration, which rivaled the ones Hal orchestrated for Chip's and Poo's respective fiftieth birthdays.

And then Monday—it was as if time stood still. We came together as a family again. Poo and Sara were here from Florida within fourteen hours. Alex had been on an internship in Kansas City, Missouri, and he packed up all his bags and was home within twenty-four hours. And then the rest of our family arrived to share in our grief. . . . And that brings me to community: the phrase that immediately comes to mind is "It takes a village." . . . From those very first dark minutes on Monday our Metuchen friends came together to provide support . . . and Hal's huge network also organized immediately to wrap us in their collective embrace.

In closing, everyone asks me, "How are the kids?" Of course, the answer is "devastated," the same as the rest of us. As [twelve-year-old] Ginny was sitting around talking with Poo, Sara, and me last night, she had a pretty good analogy: "It's like winning the lottery, except in reverse." Sounds right to me. Hal was such a big presence in all our lives, it's hard to know how we'll live without him. But, we will. Hunter and Ginny are strong and resilient, and with their continued strength we'll reconfigure our combined family. But it will continue to "take a village."

That larger community persevered. When Hal died, the Metuchen moms he had befriended ensured we had months of homemade dinners. His friends arranged to have a local street named after him: "Hal Clarke Way" was appropriately located at the town's Little League stadium.

At first Hunter and Ginny moved in with us, but our house was small. Chip moved over to Hal's house with the kids, and I went back and forth the half mile between our two homes. Ultimately, we decided to add a second story to Hal's house so Ginny and Hunter could stay in their childhood home and our new larger family could all be together. During the renovation we were all back in our house. Mugsy and Cali, the two cats we inherited from Hal, joined us, now as indoor rather than outdoor cats. It was a tight squeeze, but we figured it out. I moved my study into the living room to give Hunter a bedroom. Ginny took over Alex's bedroom on the second floor, and Alex had the basement. The next eighteen months were mainly ones of sorrow and learning to be a family of five, along with dealing with the chaos of managing a major home renovation. We moved into our renovated home on April 1, 2014, right as the backyard cherry tree burst into bloom. With all the trauma, I hoped that it was an omen of strength and renewal.

The summer that Hal died, Alex was working in Kansas City, Missouri, for a summer internship at my sister and brother-in-law's small business, Travois, which funds affordable housing and economic development for Indian reservations. Among other things, he was working on increasing options for dental services on Indian reservations. He was living in Marianne and David's house while they were in Montana. Alex was enjoying the internship and especially the time getting to know his cousin Greg, three years older. Greg recounted:

> We spent a lot of our time in and out of the office probably hanging out during the work day. . . . [Alex's girlfriend Ashley] came out for a little while too, so it was fun to get to meet her and see Alex with a friend from back home. . . . It was fun to get to know him as an adult, not necessarily just family or cousin.
>
> We talked a lot about music. . . . I was building my record collection, and I had a completely different interest in music than he did. I was much more on the American, folk, bluegrass, a little bit country, and he was definitely more into . . . the electronic music and the EDM stuff.
>
> We argued about barbecue and cooking a lot. . . . I don't think he really cared for Kansas City barbecue, and I loved it, so we would get in the typical arguments of "Kansas City has the best barbecue," and I think we made it a goal to try as many different barbecue restaurants while he was here.

Greg didn't recall seeing any signs of Alex's eating disorder: "Often we would go to lunch together. We would have been working in the same office, and there was plenty of places to go eat down the street. So, we would always go and get pizza at this New York–style pizza joint down the street. It never seemed to come up, and he looked like he was a really healthy kid." Greg did think Alex "was drinking probably a little bit too much," but saw no evidence of heroin: "While he was here, I didn't notice him using or doing anything else. Maybe at the EDM concerts [Alex went to]. . . . I was still obviously very much into beer, so I was still trying to catalog what beers I was drinking, and we would try a bunch of different things." (Greg would eventually launch a successful brewery in Kansas City, Stockyards Brewing Co.)

Greg also remembered that Alex felt lonely, so he made an effort to spend time with him: "I remember him being a little bit lonely, probably not having his own group of friends here outside of family and some work people. Especially being in a massive house by yourself, that will just feel lonely. [Alex would come over to the house] or I would end up at my parents' house, because they had a much larger area to hang out in. But I think he came with me to a couple different beer festivals." Alex was indeed lonely that summer he spent in Kansas City. Worried about him, Chip flew out to Kansas City to spend a few days to help him get situated. Marianne and David were having major construction done on their house. Amid the chaos, Alex lived in a few rooms near the kitchen. During this same period, Granny had started to seriously deteriorate, and Chip started to write her obituary while in Kansas City. Alex was taken aback and asked Chip whether he really thought that necessary. A few weeks later, Granny was dead, and Chip gave that obituary. In truth none of us, least of all Alex, was prepared for her death.

When Chip called Alex just a few weeks later to tell him that Hal had died, Ashley was visiting. She recalled:

We were sitting and watching TV [when Chip called] . . . but he didn't really say anything. I knew that something was wrong, but I couldn't hear the other side of the conversation. . . . After he got off the phone, . . . I was like, "Something is obviously very wrong, and what is it?" So, I don't know if it was just he needed a second to process it. I mean he was obviously in shock, and he was very upset.

Then when he told me, I sort of went into a doer sort of mode. What do we need to do, we need to get you packed right now? We need to like get flights, and yeah. So, I don't know if I was speaking with you or I was speaking with Chip, but like we were trying to coordinate because he went into this silent autopilot. I don't think we talked pretty much that entire night. . . . [On the flight back] we sat and we drank our flight home. That was a tough few days because I don't think any of us really knew how to handle it. I think I was so worried about him, but he would not engage. He really just didn't talk.

Alex cut short his internship and came home for good. We were all lost, but Alex especially so. Unlike when Kathy died, he didn't have it in him to write a eulogy for the service. The death of Hal following so soon after Granny had left him in shock.

On the heels of these deeply felt losses came disappointment when the two dental schools that had placed him on the waiting list did not come through. I suggested he look at the then new Rutgers Professional Science Master's program that seemed right up his alley. He agreed and though he applied late was accepted almost immediately. He described his new life plan in his application to the program:

> My long term plan is to reapply to dental school. I see the Rutgers Professional Science Master's Program as an important and strategic step toward that goal, allowing me to advance my understanding and knowledge of both business and science skill sets necessary to establish and operate a successful dental practice. [He described his Travois internship as supporting] the company's goal of improving housing and economic development on Native American Indian reservations. . . . I gained insight into the kinds of business deals that must occur behind the scenes of large medical projects. Travois was in the process of writing grants to secure dental clinics for Indian reservations, and I was able to participate in that application process. [The Travois experience plus his experience with bench science the previous summer at Rutgers] reflects the two sides of professional science: the bench science in science labs, as well as the business side that applies that science.

Alex began the two-year program that fall, with the goal of earning a Master of Business and Science degree in December 2013, with a concentration in personal care science. Chip and I had our fingers crossed.

Even before the new academic year began, however, Alex veered back sharply to the second road. On August 22, 2012, at 3:21 A.M., he was pulled over in Mantoloking, New Jersey, on a DUI charge.

As one of two friends who were with him described it:

> The plan was to go to Bar A [Bar Anticipation on the Jersey Shore, a
> popular Jersey shore hangout]. Alex was going to drive us to Bar A,
> then we were going to take a car to [the other friend's] aunt's house,
> which was ten minutes away from Bar A. Then get Alex's car the next
> morning. We drank so much alcohol at Bar A . . . they kicked us out. . . .
> Next thing I know the car was pulled over and they told us to get out of
> the car. When the cops asked [Alex] to get out of the car, he had his
> wallet and his phone in his lap . . . and it all fell out. . . . They were like,
> all right, you're getting a DUI test. Alex claims he did well during the
> test, but then I was standing on the barrier . . . and I just start vomit-
> ing. . . . The next thing I knew, I woke up in some Jersey Shore police
> station. . . . We were there overnight . . . it was me and [the other friend]
> sitting in the police station lobby. Alex was nowhere to be seen—he
> was locked up.

The other friend's memory was consistent, albeit also vague:

> I think I probably thought it was not as bad, but it was probably because
> I was pissed drunk at that point. I don't think I was in the frame of mind
> to be like, "Hey, man, I think we should pull over and we should figure
> something out." And it was also, it was at that point. . . . This was the
> other mistake [we made] driving like twenty minutes from the bar to
> my great aunt's house, down the Jersey Shore. And at that point Uber
> didn't exist, so you would've had to try to find a taxi to drive thirty min-
> utes at two in the morning and it was just a decision that I can't even
> rationalize at this point, because there is no kind of way to think about
> it in that way. It was just a mistake all around.

Neither could remember how they got home. I remember Alex arriving home very early that morning without his car. He told us what had
happened, and I knew right away that he was at a critical juncture in his
life. As a college professor and researcher, I knew that Alex was headed
directly into New Jersey's criminal justice system.

We hired a lawyer (Al), and I started to keep a list of costs, planning to
make Alex responsible for reimbursing us. The wheels of justice moved
slowly. On August 26, 2013—more than a year after his arrest—Alex

was convicted of DUI in Mantoloking Municipal Court. That day's charges were $614, including a fine of $256, and add-ons for the Safe Neighborhoods Services Fund ($75), Victims of Crime Compensation Office ($50), a surcharge of $200, and other costs of $33. Other monetary and nonmonetary consequences soon followed. New Jersey's Motor Vehicle Commission suspended his license for nine months. In addition, he was required to "satisfy the requirements of the Intoxicated Driving Program (IDP) and the Intoxicated Driver Resource Center (IDRC), including immediate payment of a $100 IDP administrative fee" and a $230 fee to attend the mandatory six-session class. Added to that, for the next three years he was required to pay an annual $1,000 surcharge to the New Jersey Division of Motor Vehicles for drivers convicted of driving while intoxicated. None of that included legal fees.

The nonmonetary penalties generated even more anxiety. He now had a record. Constant paperwork arrived from the IDRC threatening legal action and warrants for his arrest when he failed to appear for hearings. As we traveled down this second road with Alex, I often thought about how fortunate he was to have parents with the ability to pay these expenses. We wondered what those who weren't from two-earner, middle-class families would do. Those without means are the ones truly in the crosshairs of the criminal justice system. Their fate is simply to languish in jail, the modern equivalent of debtors' prison.

Over the next few years, we paid much more for Alex's medical and legal costs. We would have paid more to keep him alive. The consequences for his future were very real, and he feared there was no way he would be able to extricate himself from the legal web that now held him tight. He and we hoped the worst was behind us, but unfortunately that wasn't even close to the truth. By the time he entered his first rehab at the Advanced Health and Education Treatment Center in November 2013, he was beginning to see the writing on the wall, although even then he still had hope. In the conclusion of his rehab essay on honesty, which I quoted in chapters 6 and 7, he wrote:

> After college, I continued drinking the same way, and my use of drugs
> subsided for a while until all of the deaths happened in the family. After

this, I started trying roxies [Roxicodone, a brand of oxycodone] with [one of his friends] and really enjoyed the feeling. In my opinion, it never really got out of control, and I continued to do them a few times a month, until I decided to switch to heroin. Even when I did this, however, I kept my drug use to a few times a month. . . . I am not trying to rationalize or minimize my drug use, I am just trying to tell you the full story.

Now, my alcohol and drug use has obviously landed me in rehab, and I have learned, and am continuing to learn, a great deal about the chemistry of addiction and the consequences my addiction has inflicted upon both of you, my friends, and myself. I know that I have dug myself a pretty large hole, but I know I can prove to you and myself that I can eventually climb my way out by "walking the walk" and showing you I can live a sober, happy, and successful life.

After my stay here, I really hope that you both will let me come home to live with you guys, and help with the move to the new house. I plan to take all the suggestions AA has taught me, including going to as many meetings as possible, working the 12 steps, and staying sober one day at a time. I know I have let you down in the past, so I am willing to do whatever it takes to come home and regain your trust.

This was the period when Alex's friends began to see his insecurities, the darkness he tried so hard to hide with his devil-may-care attitude. Not that they always recognized it so clearly at the time. But by the time I interviewed his friends in their late twenties, they were more cognizant of Alex's pain. Indeed, some had experienced similar pain in their own lives.

Alex was beginning to see how his drinking was a problem. After graduation, and shortly before his DUI, Ashley had warned us that he was drinking and driving, and Alex was none too happy when we confronted him with it. As Ashley remembered:

I think the first time that he felt like his life was over was when he got the DUI. I think he sort of panicked when he found out that I had told you guys that I was worried about his behavior. . . . He knew it was me. He texted me and he's like, "Did you really tell my parents either that I was drinking and driving or that you were worried about my behavior?" I think because he knew that I was one of the only people that would say something to you guys. I didn't feel good having to go and tell you guys that. If I wasn't genuinely concerned about him, I wouldn't have. . . . He had expressed that he was concerned too, and we weren't sure what rock bottom was going to be.

Losing so many who were close to him took its toll. Alex's Dickinson friend Tim remarked on the difficulties and pressures Alex felt adjusting to the loss of Granny and Hal and becoming a "big brother" to two new siblings. After I talked with Tim about the deaths in our family in the summer of 2012, he said:

That helps me figure a little bit more out about why about a year after we graduated, there was such a marked change [in Alex]. . . . I think it was just different, and I think it's really going from an only child to all the sudden kind of this older-sibling role-model role. . . . I think it weighed on him a little bit, but it was more I think he was so lost and he didn't know what he was doing. [He realized,] "I know I have Hunter and Ginny and I need to look out for them." . . . But now all of a sudden it's like, "I'm the older brother. . . . You're living with me."

Tim also noted that the collapse of Alex's dental school aspirations took a toll: "When the dentistry thing didn't work out, I always asked him, 'Well, what do you think is next? If dentistry's not next, what is next?' He could never come up with that next step. . . . All of those pressures, and just the way he carried himself because he always cared about doing well. That was important to him." Ashley had comparable conversations. When she asked Alex why he was interested in dental school rather than med school, she said he replied, "It was sort of a balance of confidence, like I can do that pretty easily and make a career out of it and be comfortable." Ashley continued: "But I do remember once he was home and he was applying for jobs and wasn't really sure what he wanted to do, that stressed him out. I think things not working out as easily as he thought that they were going to was really difficult for him." And, finally, Jeff recalled a very similar conversation with Alex toward the end of his life:

[One thing that] really hit hard and I think kind of just got him depressed . . . was dental school and I think he was having issues getting in. . . . That just like hit him really hard. . . . Now he doesn't know what the hell to do with his life. He's like, "I don't know what I'm doing next. Like I don't have a goal. I'm trying to figure it out." . . . [He just took drinking and smoking] . . . to another level. . . . I just moved on and stopped. . . . At the end it seemed like it was more to cover the pain of whatever he was going through. . . . So I had career goals. [I just] got sucked into I guess being an adult, and got sucked into the career life.

By the end of the summer of 2012, the insecurities and anxiety that drove Alex's anorexia returned in force. So much had left him shaken: the loss of loved ones, his reconfigured family, the collapse of the professional life he had long planned. His high school and college friends began to move on with their lives, with some distancing themselves from him because of his behavior. At the same time, his personal actions drove him into debt and then into the criminal justice system. The ability to cope seemed to allude him and his feelings of hopelessness grew. Over the ensuing months he fell into more serious drug and alcohol use. We scrambled to try to get ahead of it, but Alex was already on the on-ramp speeding to the second road of addiction. It didn't take long for the worst to take over Alex's and our lives.

CHAPTER 9

Worst Case

If the drive to get intoxicated is in all of us, and if 90 percent
of people can use drugs without becoming addicted, what is
happening with the 10 percent who can't?
—Johann Hari, *Chasing the Scream*

Addiction isn't just taking drugs. It is a pattern of learned behavior.
It only develops when vulnerable people interact with potentially
addictive experiences at the wrong time, in the wrong places,
and in the wrong pattern for them.
—Maia Szalavitz, *Unbroken Brain*

RESEARCHERS HAVE LONG found that higher education and supportive communities protect against addiction.[1] Alex had a family
who loved and supported him. But family was not his only community,
particularly after he got to college. Many of Alex's friends admitted to
drinking too much or taking drugs. Some saw themselves simply as
Alex's friends—just teenage and just-past-teenage "kids"—too imma-
ture, inexperienced, and self-involved to have been enablers of Alex's
destructive behavior. And, of course, there were people we never knew
and never met who formed another part of his community, people who
not only had no interest in friendship or protecting him from addiction,
but actively sought to draw him into the insanity. Why was he drawn
into that web, from which he couldn't extricate himself?

As his friends matured into their twenties, they successfully transitioned to adulthood. Or as Alex's friend Jeff put it, they "got sucked
into ... being an adult, and ... into the career life." Of course, those
well into their careers can suffer, or continue to suffer, from addiction

issues (Philip Seymour Hoffman and—much later—Matthew Perry come to mind),[2] but research indicates that most young people age out of addiction as they mature.[3] Several of Alex's friends who experimented with more serious drugs, including opioids, left them behind as they transitioned into post-collegiate adulthood.

If, as Johann Hari and others have argued, nine out of ten people can use drugs without becoming hooked, why is it that Alex moved further down the second road to addiction? Why was he among the vulnerable 10 percent who are unable to find and take the exit ramp? Alex's anorexia showed us that he was susceptible to mental health issues. It had taken him years to begin to move beyond the trauma of his eating disorder. But it now seems that he substituted drinking, which was easier to hide and more socially acceptable, for self-deprivation, and slipped into alcoholism. Then, too, there were the events of the summer of 2012, which created fertile ground for Alex's anxieties, insecurities, and self-doubts to grow. In so many ways Alex's childhood should have given him self-esteem, resilience, and the support structure to succeed. Why his demons held him in a stranglehold is a question I still ask today. The one thing I am sure of is that we need to look beyond personal choice, the singular explanation that most of us fall back on. It's analogous to telling a depressed person to "snap out of it" or to "think about the good things in your life." That's like telling them, as one of my friends put it, "if you tried harder, your teeth would be straight."[4]

Alex started the Rutgers Master of Business and Science degree as planned, and we were hopeful that it would provide the opportunity to move forward with his life, and for a while it looked like it was working. He did well his first year. As he anticipated, the program was a nice mix of both business and science courses.[5] He became a "Certified Sustainability Manager" and completed a Rutgers "Mini-MBA in Social Media Marketing." He finished the year with a grade point average of 3.75.

But, in truth, he was just biding his time, in the hope that these additional credentials would translate into dental school acceptance in round two. And he came close to succeeding, making it to the wait list for two well-respected dental schools. I wanted him to see that there was a way for him to find success. But his positive experiences in the

Rutgers program were insufficiently rewarding to put the stop to his descent into addiction when more setbacks arrived. Late one night in early May 2013, coming home from the train station after a trip to New York City, Alex crashed his car into a neighbor's yard, totaling the car and racking up over $6,000 in damages. Luckily no one, including him, was injured, but we paid those charges, adding them to the growing debt we expected Alex to eventually repay us. They added to his growing sense of failure and hopelessness, digging a hole from which he could not get out.

The week after that crash we drove with Alex and Hunter to my niece Eileen's graduation from the University of Virginia. That weekend we saw another side of Alex, as Eileen remembered:

> [The night before my graduation] as I was leaving from the dorm where you all were staying to go celebrate on the Corner, I invited Alex to come. Alex seemed excited, but then suddenly he glanced over to where Hunter was standing out of earshot. He then turned back to me and said that, as much as he wished he could join me, he didn't want to leave Hunter (who was underage) alone for the night. Hunter, of course, had just lost Hal less than a year before. I think many other twenty-three-year-olds would have jumped at the opportunity to bar hop rather than go to bed early on an uncomfortable dorm bed. Alex, however, chose to stay behind to be there for someone who was hurting. It was a small moment, but one that I think said a lot about his character and how much he loved his family. It is also the moment that I always think of when I remember Alex.

We also used the trip for Hunter, who was finishing his junior year in high school, to check out both the University of Virginia and James Madison University. All in all, it was normal family time.

The bright spot of our family road trip soon faded. New York University and Tufts rejected his re-applications to dental school. This time there was no wait list and no prospect of late admission. On August 26, his conviction for the previous year's DUI came through and he lost his driver's license for nine months. In an instant, his freedom of mobility disappeared and the reality of the monetary and nonmonetary consequences of the DUI conviction hit him full-on. He was beginning to fall into debt and was totally dependent on us, with no job in sight. His insecurities skyrocketed along with resurgent panic attacks. Whereas before, Alex's escapes were through alcohol, weed, and Molly (aka ecstasy), he now turned to the hard, more deadly stuff, including, as we soon learned, heroin. At the same time, New Jersey's criminal justice system tightened its grip.

On the Road, Scene 1: Introduction to Rehabs and 12-Step Programs

Aug. 28–Sept. 12, 2013: Princeton House, North Brunswick, NJ (intensive outpatient; rehab #1).

Oct. 11, 2013: Heroin overdose, at home.

Oct. 11–12, 2013: JFK Hospital, Edison, NJ.

Oct. 13–17, 2013: Summit Oaks Hospital, Summit, NJ (detox).

Oct. 17–Nov. 22, 2013: Advanced Health and Education, Eatontown, NJ (inpatient; rehab #2).

Nov. 24, 2013: Relapsed, to JFK Hospital, Edison, NJ.

As far as we have been able to piece together, Alex's introduction to opioids was in the form of Oxy's in college (i.e., oxycodone, the basis for the now infamous OxyContin prescription pain medicine, produced and marketed by Purdue Pharma). In retrospect, what we learned about his road to hard core heroin use aligns with Maia Szalavitz's description of the descent into addiction. Alex's vulnerabilities were potentiated by the box in which he found himself. For him—as for Szalavitz—his interactions (perhaps experiments) with potentially addictive experiences like heroin came "at the wrong time, in the wrong places, and in the wrong pattern."[6]

Like most Americans who have been untouched by drugs, we were ignorant of heroin and addiction. Our knowledge, if you could call it that, came mostly from TV shows and movies. We knew no one who had a child with a serious drug habit nor anyone who had lost a child to overdose. As college professors we were aware, of course, that students drank and smoked marijuana, but we'd never known of a student's hard drug use. As our fears about Alex's drug and alcohol use intensified, we learned about TV actor Cory Monteith's death from a heroin overdose in July 2013 at age thirty-one, and then Philip Seymour Hoffman's overdose in February 2014, at forty-six. By that point, we were paying full attention, and were terrified.

I began to read up on addiction, learning that it was not just the famous who died from overdoses, but increasingly the "kid next door," including white suburban kids like Alex. As he headed down the road to intensified substance use, the statistics of overdose deaths were already staggering: the number of people dying from heroin overdoses nationally had quadrupled between 2002 and 2013, reaching 8,200 by 2013.[7] This rapid increase occurred across all demographic groups, including whites and blacks, men and women, the young and old. More worrisome to us, New Jersey newspapers were reporting that the state's rate was more than three times the national one. Heroin had become the leading cause of death in New Jersey, exceeding homicide, suicide, car accidents, and AIDS.[8] And those addicted to heroin were no longer strangers. There were now faces to put with those statistics, someone's son, daughter, father, mother, cousin, or neighbor. The big picture really hit home when that face belonged to our kid.[9]

By the summer of 2013, Alex was speeding down the second road and quickly spiraling out of control into hard core substance use. Alex had used Roxicodone (Roxies, or "blues"), a brand name for oxycodone, a highly addictive, semi-synthetic opioid prescribed for pain. He bought his stash on the informal black market. To our knowledge, he never had a prescription for OxyContin and never needed it for treating any physical pain. Somehow, however, he found access to drugs that had been diverted for illegal use, or perhaps had been illegally manufactured. Like many legal users of prescription drugs who switched to heroin when their Oxy supply was cut off, or because they became too expensive, Alex turned to heroin. As he later explained to us, and told his friends, he went to a dealer to buy Roxies and when the dealer had none, came home with heroin instead. As one of his friends described it: "It was some Asian guy . . . at Fox and Hound. . . . The guy was like, I don't have any blues, but I have heroin and it's cheaper. . . . Even though previously we had explicitly said we would never [do] heroin. . . . That's why it floored me when he just flat out said he tried heroin."

Connor, a friend of Alex's from college, admitted to snorting heroin with him that summer. His introduction to heroin was much like Alex's: "I talked to my pill guy after abstaining for a long time. He's like, 'I don't have pills. I have dope' [a street term that included heroin]. And I said, "All right, pardon my language, f-ck it. Whatever, I just need to get high." He remembered one night with Alex:

> I have one memory of snorting heroin with Alex in your basement, and just falling asleep after ordering dinner, and then waking up the next day and going home. And then, after that, I don't really, because I was out of school [he graduated in May 2013, one year after Alex] for ... [only] a few months before I went to treatment and got sober, like capital-S sober, like all mood- and mind-altering substances.... So really that summer was the only time that me and Alex like hung out. ... After that, it was really a pretty rapid descent into ruining my own life, to be honest.

Connor told me that he never injected heroin. In March 2014, he entered his one and only rehab. By the time of my interview with him, he had been sober for eight years, and was looking forward to a career in law, specializing in harm reduction. Having gone through addiction and come out the other side, Connor described his fork-in-the road decision leading to his decision to get sober:

> C: A lot of people did [drugs] with me, ... but there's a certain
>   point at which they went this way, and I went that way.
> PR: What are the two ways you are referring to?
> C: Crippling, life-ruining, damn-near-fatal drug addiction, and
>   normal. That's what I would say. There's a certain point at
>   which the person that you were going and partying with is like,
>   "Oh that's enough." Or like, I don't necessarily know what their
>   thought process is, because I didn't share it, but there's a point
>   at which everyone has wild memories from college and a lot of
>   them just stopped, and they became functioning members
>   of society afterwards."

I learned more about Alex's illegal drug use after he died by register-ing with the State of New Jersey as his medical heir. This enabled me to obtain intake and medical information from every institution in which he resided, including rehabs, hospitals, detox centers, and jail. I learned a lot from those reports, as well as from Alex's rehab writings. As mentioned in previous chapters, he reported to the intake interviewers that his drug use began with weed in high school, followed by cocaine, acid, ecstasy, mushrooms, Oxy's (30mg), and amphetamines in college. After college, he added Percodan, Percocet, Dilaudid, Roxies, intravenous (IV) heroin, Xanax (legal and illegal), and Suboxone (legal and illegal) to his drug repertoire. Throughout these years, he also drank excessively, reporting that he had imbibed gin or rum daily for the past ten years. His drugs of choice during his worst, and final, years were IV heroin, Xanax, and the ever-present alcohol.

Our introduction to the U.S. recovery system began late that August 2013, before we knew about his heroin habit. We were more than aware his drinking was out of control, and we suspected he was experimenting with hard drugs. His May 12 accident, and the DUI arrest and ensuing conviction, were huge, blinking, red alerts. He recognized he had a problem. On August 28, two days after he learned about his license suspension, I went with Alex to sign him up for an intensive outpatient program (IOP) at Princeton House in North Brunswick, the first of what would be multiple rehabs over the next two years for his polysubstance use. I drove him several times per week to participate in the program, but within weeks they kicked him out. On September 12 he tested positive for barbiturates and alcohol, but at that point had no marijuana, benzodiazepines, cocaine, or opiates in his system. The counselors told us Alex needed more care than they could provide and recommended inpatient residential treatment programs.

In writings from a later rehab stay, Alex admitted he had sabotaged his recovery at Princeton House:

> I consistently disregarded the advice of my multiple therapists. I continued drinking and drugging the entire time I was in treatment [at Princeton House].
>
> I started hooking up with one of the girls I met in IOP, and we ended up drinking together, doing blues and shooting heroin.
>
> After IOP, I ignored my therapists' recommendations of seeking a higher level of care and tried to control my drinking/drugging on my own.

I went to a doctor and manipulated my life story to her in order to obtain a Xanax script, [which I used] in combination with drinking, which led to frequent blackouts.

At this same time, Alex had begun the second year of his master's program. The day after he was kicked out of Princeton House, I spoke with him about his options as I saw them, which I summarized in my journal on September 13: "The options are getting fewer, but as I see it there are two acceptable ones. . . . Doing nothing is not an option. 1) Stay enrolled in school, but go to one of the [recommended] therapists, while staying sober. . . . If you go this route, you need to meet with the therapist at least once a week. And you need to attend all your classes. . . . 2) The other option is to go directly to rehab [in-house treatment]."

He chose to remain in school, at least for a few more weeks, and agreed to meet regularly with Dr. O, as well as another mental health/ drug counselor. Soon after, however, Alex's friend Joe Jr. alerted us to his heroin use:

> J: I specifically remember . . . we made a pact that if it ever gets out of control, we got to speak up and say something to the other person's [parents]. . . . [Alex] took this like shady phone call and he was sitting in the back seat like, "Yo, can I come pick up that thing." And then I was like, holy shit, this is not fun anymore. This, it's like a real deal. That's why I went and spoke to Chip. . . . That was like really hard for me, too.
>
> PR: Do you regret that?
>
> J: No, no, not for a second. If it was me, I would hope and expect him to do the same. . . . I wouldn't have been able to live with myself if I didn't present it to you guys.

Joe's telling us had real consequences for his relationship with Alex: "He really didn't like me. He thought I was ratting him out."

In response to Joe's warning, we asked his new girlfriend KatieK[10] whether she knew he was using heroin, and she did not. KatieK, who was then nineteen, met Alex at the Cheesecake Factory. Learning of Alex's heroin use, she broke off their relationship, but remained friends with him during his early years in rehab.

As he sank further into addiction, Alex opened to her about his feelings:

K: I know his dog passing was very traumatic for him. I know that he was dealing with some eating disorders. [He told me] he was in the hospital for a couple months. . . . When he talked about your relatives passing, I know that definitely did have an effect on him.

PR: Did you see him—being lonely?

K: Yeah, I could see that. . . . He would just get in a really dark place. And I'm sure that can make him feel lonely, and I think he also would see sometimes his friends really moving forward. I know he really struggled with not finding a job.

PR: Did you ever see him have any panic attacks?

K: One time he went to the park down the street and called me and I met him there and he was kind of like hyperventilating a little bit. . . . [Another time] he had called me saying he rode his bike to the mall. So, I went to go get him and we were just sitting in the food court and . . . he had a lot of anxiety.

PR: Did you ever learn that he was doing heroin?

K: I wasn't totally ignorant to it. I feel like I did know there was something going on here deeper than drinking. He had some kind of addiction. But [our conversion with her] confirmed it. And I remember that's when I woke up and I was upstairs and you guys sat me down and talked to me about it. . . . That's not why [I left]. I stayed in his life after that [but as a friend].

Alex's world grew smaller, as most of his friends left, or he pushed them away, as with Joe. We could see he was deteriorating rapidly. We stepped up our surveillance efforts, but it didn't take long for things to escalate. On October 11, Alex overdosed on heroin for the first time we were aware of. When he didn't answer our knocks to his basement bedroom, we took the door off its hinges to find him unresponsive on the floor with a needle and heroin packets next to him. We had never before seen heroin and were as ignorant as most parents suddenly thrust into addiction. How could a few grains of white powder—something so innocuous-looking—be that deadly?

We called 911 and by the time emergency services (EMS) arrived, Alex was awake, and he walked to the ambulance. They took him to JFK Hospital, the same hospital where he had worked as a "junior volunteer" just a few years earlier. Our lives, and how we thought about our lives, had changed forever. We were now the parents of a heroin user. At this point the local police did not criminalize his behavior, seeing him as a "victim." They told us to get rid of the drugs and paraphernalia. We did, but to no avail. This was just the beginning. Alex overdosed again and again over the next eighteen months; the police and paramedics became fixtures at our house, reviving him over and over.

Sadly, disappointingly, and somewhat surprisingly, the physicians and nurses at JFK, and other hospitals where Alex was admitted over the following years, were less empathic than the police. I often overheard health care staff berating Alex for his "choices." It pains me to say that I often acted as if I didn't hear them, unwilling to confront the stigma directed at him and us. Of course, those who work in health care are not immune to the persistent stereotypes about addiction—they too can believe (and many plainly do) that substance use is solely a choice, or a manifestation of "defects of character." Indeed, we learned early on in our journey that stigma remains stark and raging. But I still am left wondering why health care professionals back then did not have a more informed, up-to-date view of addiction and believe many of them still don't.

After his overdose, it was clear that Alex's days in the Professional Science Master's program were over. I canceled his fall term. Alex was on a different road now, one that led out of graduate school and into holy hell. After two days at JFK, on October 13 Alex was transferred to Summit Oaks Hospital for detox. The Summit paperwork gave his diagnoses as major depression and alcohol use, with a history of blackouts, tremors, nausea, diarrhea, and anxiety. He was twenty-three. The doctors prescribed Keppra, Inderal, Lexapro, and Suboxone for detoxing. Then on October 17 he was transferred directly to his first inpatient rehab, Advanced Health and Education, an addiction treatment center in Eatontown, New Jersey. His admission was arranged by his mental health counselor. Advanced Health was considered an outpatient partial care/IOP with free optional support housing.

It was here that I really began to experience the absolute hell that is health care in America. I imagine that for those without insurance, having a child with substance use is next to impossible. Even for those of us lucky enough to have good coverage, the process of tangling with insurance companies is horrific. Gone were the days that we simply paid our premiums and got little back. Managing and following the paperwork alone was nightmarish. There were frequent rejections, requiring hours of phone calls with service providers and our insurance company, Blue Cross/Blue Shield. Luckily Advanced Health was quite competent on that front, helping me through the initial paperwork, ensuring that our insurance covered Alex's housing even though the program was not officially residential. Advanced Health had the system worked out and knew how to get paid. And, while I don't know it for sure, I assume the mental health counselor who referred Alex there and helped make the arrangements received a bounty for his services. As I traveled this road alongside Alex, I soon began to learn about patient brokering, endemic to the recovery business.

As I will describe further, Alex hated 12-step programs, the Alcoholics Anonymous (AA)/Narcotics Anonymous (NA) programs that form the core of most rehabs. Unfortunately, they were then, and still are, the only game in town. 12-step programs work for some people, but the failure rate is high. Despite his antipathy, Alex made some progress his first month of treatment, and I felt hopeful. But he fell between the cracks in their support system, mostly participating in group therapy sessions and seldom seeing individual therapists or psychiatrists. Ultimately, we were not impressed with Advanced Health's rehab offerings, which were light on therapy and heavy on group activities run by those in recovery, a staple at most rehabs—no doubt because it is, in part, more profitable. During Alex's first weeks there, one counselor died of an overdose, and they found heroin in the building. We were heartened to learn from his counselor that Alex resisted the drug when it was offered. It was during Alex's time at Advanced Health that I began to describe him as a "chemistry experiment." The number of medications he was prescribed seemed excessive. In addition to Keppra, Lexapro, and Inderal, his prescriptions now included, for reasons that remain a mystery to me, the antibiotics minocycline and amoxicillin, and quetiapine (aka Seroquel), an antipsychotic also prescribed off-label for insomnia. And it got worse.

On November 4, we called Advanced Health to express our concern, criticizing the lack of psychiatric therapy. The clinical progress notes I later read stated that Alex was recognizing relapse triggers, his emotional responses to anger issues, and the need to maintain behaviors that place him at risk of returning to drugs. But they also noted that Alex intended to use marijuana again once he completed the program, a theme that recurred throughout his rehab experiences. He never believed in abstinence, and always candidly expressed the desire to drink in moderation—a notion anathema to rehabs governed by strict 12-step orthodoxy.

In response to Alex's antipathy to 12-step methods, we resorted to the tried and true: "fake it until you make it" or "make the group your higher power," but Alex would have none of it. By the time he finished up at Advanced Health, however, he was saying more of the "right" things. For better or worse, he had learned to parrot the 12-step lingo. He had certainly learned what his counselors and we wanted to hear. Maybe it did touch him in some way; it's hard to know. But I do know it was ultimately unsuccessful.

In a November 7 letter he addressed to us, he wrote about "honesty," which I excerpted in chapters 6–8. His words were revealing. I can't say whether the beliefs and insights he wrote about reflected what he truly thought or only what he knew he should say, but I have no reason to disbelieve his descriptions about his history of substance use, including a detailed description of his illegal drinking and drug behavior since middle school. Toward the end of the letter, he expressed his desire to "eventually climb my way out by 'walking the walk' and showing you I can live a sober, happy, and successful life." Although the 12-step recovery process trained Alex to use that language, it's also true we wanted to hear it and wanted to believe it.

Our hopes were soon dashed. After thirty-six days in rehab, Alex was released on November 22. Chip picked him up without me because I was in Virginia visiting family. As I was on my way home on Amtrak two days later, Chip texted me that he was bringing Alex to JFK. He had overdosed again. We were now living on the treadmill that is addiction and addiction treatment, a treadmill that goes round and round, never advancing. We found ourselves cycling time and again through overdoses, naloxone (aka Narcan; see below), hospitals, detoxes, and rehabs. I hadn't even been able to enjoy the brief two-day respite before the insanity began anew.

This time, Alex was out the same day from JFK and came immediately home. We began to ferry him to appointments with a new psychiatrist, his therapist Dr. O, and to his same mental health/addiction counselor. We enjoyed some relative calm through Thanksgiving and the Christmas holidays, though it didn't help when one of his friends brought Roxies to our home for Thanksgiving Day. Alex admitted it to us, making us even more on edge, ever vigilant. And right after Christmas, the insanity returned with a vengeance.

On the Road, Scene 2: Florida, the "Non"-Recovery Capital of the World

Dec. 30, 2013: Heroin overdose, at home.

Dec. 30, 2013–Jan. 2, 2014: JFK Hospital, Edison, NJ.

Jan. 7–Feb. 7, 2014: Ambrosia Treatment Center, Port St. Lucie, FL (inpatient; rehab #3).

Feb. 1–3, 2014: Family visit to Florida, Ambrosia; family meeting Feb. 2.

Feb. 3, 2014: Relapsed, discharged himself against medical advice (AMA), and went to a Love's Truck Stop (Greyhound bus station, I-95, Fort Pierce, FL).

Feb. 7–9, 2014: Living Right, Lake Worth, FL (sober living house).

Feb. 9–10, 2014: Overnight at Serenity Now, West Palm Beach, FL (detox).

Feb. 10, 2014: Spent day in West Palm Beach; walked to Granny's condo; overnight with Poo and Todd.

Feb. 11–12, 2014: Back to New Jersey; Days Inn, Edison, NJ, for two nights.

Feb. 13, 2014: Home, with the flu.

Alex told us that he believed that if he could get a job, he would be fine, that he'd be able to drink in moderation and live a "normal" life.

We would have liked to have had the same belief, but we never had a chance to test the theory. On December 30, 2013, the worst visited us yet again. Alex was in Chip's office working on his résumé and applying for jobs online. I heard the crash from the back room, where we were watching television. We ran to find Alex on the floor, seizing and turning royal blue. Chip did CPR, chest compressions and rescue breaths. One of us called 911, although neither of us can remember who. Chip was able to get a faint pulse. As soon as they saw the red lights, our neighbors Joe and Dori came running over. The paramedics, who had arrived quickly, stuck a needle in Alex's neck and Narcan brought him back. Metuchen paramedics and police officers had only recently begun to stock Narcan. It is a miracle drug, and this was just the first of several times that Narcan saved Alex's life. When I got to the hospital, Alex was crying and mouthing "I'm sorry." He vowed he would never do it again. But heroin had him in its grip.

Dori described the scene: "I remember you shaking, oh, God, I just remember you shaking, shaking, shaking. And I looked [and] thought again, every time I felt so bad for Alex, but I was also so pissed off at him. I was like stop doing this to your parents, my friends . . . [and] yourself." I will forever remember that night: the flashing lights, the police officers, the EMS, Chip doing chest compressions, me racing out front to wait for the ambulance, sitting in our living room with Dori and Joe as Chip then the EMS worked on Alex, the two of us following the ambulance to JFK. I don't remember being pissed off at Alex that night, I was too afraid he would die. But anger was certainly something I often felt as we traveled along the second road of addiction with Alex.

Alex returned home from JFK on January 2, 2014, and by January 7 headed down to a new rehab, Ambrosia Treatment Center, in Port St. Lucie, Florida. We were desperate to get him into treatment, and frankly we wanted him out of the house. We still had two teenagers at home who needed us, and dealing with the everyday car-wreck insanity of Alex's addiction was too much. Finding another rehab was the only thing we knew to do. Online and "in the rooms" (a term used to indicate AA fellowship groups), I'd heard positive things about Florida rehabs, so I did my research and found Ambrosia in Port St. Lucie. Once I secured a spot for him, and he agreed to go, several snowstorms canceled multiple flights, delaying his departure by nearly a week. Each passing hour in New Jersey increased Alex's risk of death. When the only seat that became available was first class, we snapped it up. But the $900 first-class seat also meant free drinks. We warned him against drinking, to no avail. We watched him waiting in the departure line, chatting up another traveler, about Xanax we later learned. Alex bummed one before he was even on the plane. Between that and the free drinks, he blacked out a half hour out of West Palm Beach.

Poo, who was waiting at the West Palm Beach airport, picks up the story from there:

> I was waiting just outside the security checkpoint, and I knew the flight had landed. And I watched everybody come up the terminal walkway, and there's the typical crowd of people as everybody leaves at the same time. Then there was nobody, and it was late. I think it was 10 or 10:30, maybe later in the night, the airport wasn't busy at all. . . . And I said [to the Ambrosia guy], I don't see him, but I know he got on the plane. . . . I saw the sheriffs go that way, I just said to myself, "They're going for Alex." . . . Then a few minutes later, they brought him out of the jet way on a stretcher. Yeah, the Ambrosia guy . . . was there to take him. They had agreed . . . to let me say hello and give him a hug.

> By then, he was just argumentative, and mean-spirited, but they wouldn't let him off the gurney. Then the sheriffs were standing around and typical—"I'm the cop and you're the bad person" kind of mentality, and they were pretty rude as I remember. Then that made [Alex], of course, more mouthy.

Despite that inauspicious start to rehab #3, I hoped that Ambrosia would do better than Advanced Health. It didn't. Ambrosia sent me very little in response to my records request. I didn't press for more, and don't know if they held anything back. But I did receive a copy of Alex's intake interview, which was revealing. Alex described his last drug usage as January 6 (the day before), including heroin (four bags), Xanax, and alcohol. He was open about the consequences and contributing factors to his addiction, his change in living situation, his frequent alcohol and drug binges, poor impulse control, poor judgment, family problems, and depression. He told them about selling drugs to support his habit and stealing from and manipulating us. He acknowledged that he had "lost faith in myself and the trust of my family." He said he was "tired of fighting addiction on my own," and stated, "My reason for treatment is to get sober and my goal is to get on with my life" and "Drugs kept me away from doing the things I like."

But, like every rehab he attended, Ambrosia was a 12-step facility. He told the intake interviewers: "I have never done the steps or [gotten a] sponsor before." He struggled "with his trust in having faith in a Higher Power." On January 24 I talked with his primary counselor. At that point, she described a ninety-day inpatient target, which heartened me. From the outset, I thought the idea of a thirty-day rehab was an implausible and cruel joke. I never believed anyone could beat addiction in a month, and the evidence supports me on this point.[11] At Advanced Health, as noted above, Alex had been discharged after thirty-six days of residential treatment and relapsed in two days. Clearly, he needed more.

His primary counselor also reported that he "thinks the whole world is out to get him" and "that he cannot connect the dots, what is his part, even when pointed out." She advocated the 12-step philosophy as the best way to get to "psychic change." "But [he's] not willing to consider that this [program is] going to work. . . . [He's] not going to go to meetings when he gets out of here." She also reported that Alex was unwilling to talk about his anorexia in group, and "this secret is killing him, holding him back. Honesty is a huge factor here, and he can't share truth and honesty." With respect to honesty, she also asked, "Might he be gay?" She had noticed that he was close to their openly gay clients. She figured that if he wasn't being honest about his anorexia, perhaps he wasn't being honest about his sexuality either.

I know from Alex's intake interview, and essays he wrote while at Ambrosia, that he spoke openly of his anorexia: when asked about any traumatic events, he reported the family deaths and his hospitalization for anorexia in the seventh grade. Perhaps he didn't talk about it in group, as his counselor reported, but he had been open about it to the intake staff. I don't really know the answer to the sexuality question. It's hard to know if he questioned his sexuality. But the evidence I have indicates he viewed himself as heterosexual. Sounding like many twelve-year-old boys, his EDU journal was full of references to "hot" and "so pretty" girls, especially the one who "looks like Britney Spears." By the time he was twenty-four years old, he described himself in the Ambrosia interview as heterosexual, and that he had "always had this orientation." He also consistently reported no past or current sexual, psychological, or physical abuse or trauma. At the time and then later, none of his friends mentioned or alluded to Alex being gay. If Alex had been gay, I suspect he would have known that Chip and I would have been accepting.

Five days after I suffered an emergency appendectomy, we flew down on February 1 to participate in a family education meeting and to help Alex find sober aftercare. The family meeting occurred on February 2, and before leaving for New Jersey we toured Living Right, a sober house in Lake Worth. During our meeting with his rehab counselor, we learned that they had found Alex drinking Purell hand sanitizer. I later read how common this is and that it can be fatal or lead to vision loss.

The most frequent refrain I heard from Alex during that trip, and often thereafter, was "I'm not like these people." He was likely referring to his education and middle-class background. Poo heard similar complaints from him: "How many times did he say 'I don't belong here? I'm not like these people.' And from a socioeconomic perspective, he was a 100 percent right." Poo thought that led to his loneliness: "I can remember a lot of times when I went to see him . . . and I'd feel so bad for leaving him, because he felt so alone, and he really was." Few of Alex's peers at Ambrosia had college degrees, and he felt different because he did. Despite these differences, however, he always reported good relationships with his rehab peers, and my interviews bore that out. Perhaps he realized that in important ways he was more similar than he liked to believe.

Many of his rehab peers had the same co-occurring issues, dual diagnoses of mental health issues and substance use. That combination, as I came to appreciate, is incredibly hard to manage. He understood intellectually that he had both sets of issues; he could analyze it and talk about it. But he didn't seem to be able to understand how to move ahead. He revisited these themes in every rehab he attended. Poo describes his typical response: "Sometimes I think he just didn't have an answer. So, the easy answer was to bolt, or to use, or to rebel, or some combination of all of that." Did anyone have the answer? For sure, we were all having a hard time finding it.

Chip and I flew home February 3, the day after the Ambrosia family meeting. That evening, Ambrosia called to report Alex missing. We initially believed that they had kicked him out, drove him to a nearby Greyhound bus station, and dropped him off. The records I later received from Ambrosia stated that Alex used drugs and discharged himself against medical advice (AMA), which appears more likely the case. Chip called his friend Ken, a Palm Beach County police detective, to ask him to help find Alex. Remarkably, Ken found him almost immediately. Before describing his interaction with Alex on February 3, 2014, Ken told me: "I always looked at Alex like my nephew. I've always been a part of your family, as you know, and watching Alex grow up was remarkable. He was such a bright, talented young guy, I just knew that he had the whole world in front of him and could achieve anything he wanted to achieve. . . . Alex always had an inquisitive mind about himself, I thought. He was always full of energy and had a great sense of humor like his dad." He continued:

> Fort Pierce is a city, [with several highways running through it] both the Florida Turnpike and I-95 . . . and U.S. Highway 1 to the east. . . . I didn't know if Alex had any money, but I basically took a look at the map and got on Google and googled truck stops and Greyhound bus stations [and found] a Love's Truck Stop. I was probably a half hour outside of Fort Pierce at that time when I decided that would be my first target. . . . And I pulled in, and lo and behold there was Alex sitting on the curb next to an Arby's restaurant. The Love's Truck Stop . . . is a combination truck stop. It has a gas station, it has a convenience store, and it has an Arby's restaurant.

The Love's Truck Stop is twelve minutes by car from Ambrosia, so Alex could have walked there, or perhaps someone from the rehab dropped him off. Ken described what happened next:

> And so I discreetly pulled up and got out of my car. I watched him for a minute, just to see what condition he was in. And he seemed fine, he

seemed a little out of sorts. . . . So, I walked up to him and sat down on the curb beside him about three feet away.

I said, "Hey man, how you doing?" And he was very friendly and out-going, he didn't seem afraid or anything. . . . I felt that it was a little bit of an altered state of mind. . . . I could tell he was a little high. His eyes were dilated. I mean he showed some of the classic signs of somebody that may have just smoked a joint or maybe had tried some drugs.

[I said,] "Your name's Alex, right?" And he goes, "Yeah, how'd you know that man?" And I said, "Well, you probably know me, at least by name." And he goes, "Who are you?" I said, "I'm Kenny."

And Alex said, "Man, I know you," just like that, and we both chuck-led. He said, "Man, what the heck are you doing here?" And I said, "Your dad reached out to me tonight, told me that you had left your facility where you were rehabbing . . . he asked me to come and see if I could find you and maybe help you out."

Ken had already contacted the Fort Pierce Police Department, alert-ing them to the situation, and letting them know he was an off-duty police officer from Palm Beach County and was carrying a gun:

And as I was speaking to Alex, [I asked him,] "Hey, where'd you get that Snickers bar?" He said, "I stole it from the convenience store." And I said, "Then you obviously don't have any money, right?" And he goes, "No, I don't have a dime on me and I was really hungry."

And I said, "You know what? I haven't had dinner either. There's an Arby's right here. Why don't we go inside and have dinner?" And he goes, "Really, man?" And I said, "Yep, let's go have dinner." . . . [We were] about halfway through dinner and Alex said that he needed to go to the bathroom. . . . He was in there for a long period of time, probably about four or five minutes, and so I decided to walk into the bathroom . . . and thought he was injecting at that time. And I walked out of the bathroom and . . . got on my phone, called the sergeant back and asked him if he could send a couple patrol deputies [to] escort him back to the facility. . . . I could tell at that point that Alex was definitely high and it was intensifying, his rush if you will, from whatever drug he had just taken. . . . We talked about you, we talked about Chip and Grandma, and his aunt too, and just general conversations.

And I saw the law enforcement vehicle from Fort Pierce Police Department pull in around the side, and a young female officer and a young male officer came into the restaurant. [I told Alex,] "I don't think you're going to be that happy with me, but I'm only here because I care about you and I love you. I'm here because your parents want me to be here. [I asked the local police department] to send out a couple patrol officers to come and talk to you and try to get you to go back to the facility."

And he said he understood, and I motioned the officers to come over, and they were both very, very professional and very polite to Alex, and explained to him that they're here to offer him a ride back to the facility. And they asked him if he was willing to go and wanted to go, and he said, "Yes," and he gave me a hug, and off he went. He got in a patrol car with the officers who were treating him not as a bad guy, but as some-body's child. They were very compassionate. The girl was pretty emotional.

I think Alex is . . . very outgoing. And I didn't sense any fear at all. And I remember thinking to myself, "Wow, here's a young boy. He's out on the highway sitting on a curb at a truck stop, and he literally is show-ing no fear." I mean he looked like a kid sitting on the bench at Disney World eating a Snickers bar. His hair was blowing in the wind, it was curly.

I asked Ken if Alex had a backpack or suitcase with him, and he replied: "Nothing. He only had the clothes he had on." Ken's story is consistent with Alex having walked out of the facility. If he had been kicked out, presumably he would have had his backpack and suitcase and it's unlikely he would have readily agreed to return, or that they would have taken him back.

Alex finished out his remaining few days at Ambrosia. We had a con-versation with him and his counselor as he was preparing to transfer to Living Right, the sober living house we had toured earlier that week. No longer under discussion was the plan for ninety days. His stay at Ambrosia was not pleasant for him or them. He barely lasted the last few days, and they were happy to get rid of him, moving this problem client out of their facility to a sober living house. It was our repeated experience that rehabs only and always viewed relapses as the fault of their clients and interpreted the relapse as evidence of the client's need to start over at Day 1, in 12-step language. Little, if anything, is said about the responsibility of the treatment center. This Florida treatment center, in the "recovery capital of the world," failed Alex, and this was reflected in their discharge notes:

PROGNOSIS: poor
MOTIVATION: poor
LEVEL OF USE AT DC [DISCHARGE]: poor
AA/NA ATTENDANCE: good
HALFWAY HOUSE: sunset; IOP [He was rejected at Sunset and went instead to Living Right.]

I was thankful that my sister Libby, a nurse by training with years of experience, was able to help me decipher these and other medical record designations. She patiently explained all the abbreviations medical personnel use in their voluminous record taking, helping me to better understand Alex's medical experiences, both good and bad.

After twenty-nine days, Ambrosia was turning over their problematic client to the next place in line for insurance dollars. Ambrosia's discharge summary states:

Client completed 29 days of Tx. Client worked through latent withdrawal, client did not share any part of his treatment plan but did discuss his secret of being hospitalized for anorexia at age 12, client relapsed while in treatment, a week before his discharge, client was baker acted [a Florida law that allows individuals to be held for up to seventy-two hours for mental health examination] during his stay at ambrosia after trying to leave AMA, client was discharged to a halfway house in west palm beach and was recommend [sic] to attend IOP.

At discharge, Alex walked away with the following prescribed medications: gabapentin, one 300mg tablet three times a day for anxiety; quetiapine, two 200mg tablets every night at bedtime for insomnia; paroxetine, one 300mg tablet daily for depression; and minocycline, one 100mg tablet daily for acne.

While neither we nor Alex was happy with Ambrosia, the one thing I am thankful for is that they encouraged him to write, and he began and filled out a red spiral notebook. We often thought Alex was simply lost in pain and lacked understanding about how he had reached this point in his life. He raged at his confinement to us and his counselors. But his writings show a lot of introspection, self-knowledge, and insight. That red notebook seems to have meant something to him. He held on to it, brought it home, continued to write in it, and it survives still. He filled it with voluminous amount of his writing, reacting to prompts such as "When did I first learn that others were more important than me?"; "My pain"; "9 times I have sabotaged my recovery"; "What it will take to obtain long-term recovery?" In one essay, Alex identifies the pain he felt most of his life and points to his anorexia as the first manifestation of his anxiety and source of pain:

My Pain

In this letter I will address "my pain," where it has come from, how it has affected me, and how I plan to recover from it.

As many alcoholics will probably say, much of the pain I have experienced in my life has resulted from my use of alcohol. This is also true for me. However, prior to my use of alcohol and drugs, much of my pain resulted from my eating disorder when I was 12 years old. For some reason, I got it into my mind that I was not good enough the way I was, which caused me to be self-conscious about the way I looked. Because of that, I starved myself to the point to where my heart slowed down to the extent that it almost stopped. The doctors told my parents that if my heart did stop, they most likely would not be able to restart it again because I was too weak. I had lost the will to live, and actually prayed every day not to wake up the next morning.

After this, I was forced into a program in Somerset, NJ, in which I stayed for the next 4 months, going through extensive therapy, regaining much of the weight I had lost, and the confidence I had lost. Once I got out, I continued to see serious therapists, where I tried to work through my issues. Since then, I have been embarrassed and ashamed of this period of my life because I thought it was a girl disease, and it made me look weak.

I think these thoughts quickly led to my alcohol and drug use because I picked up my first drink just a few months after I got out of the hospital. This quickly turned into a problem throughout my high school years, and got much worse when I joined a fraternity in college. It is hard to describe the extent to which the pain that my substance abuse has caused me, but I have been arrested 3 separate times, and been to the hospital many more as a direct result of it. I have yet again been on the brink of death, again feeling hopeless, and again wanting not to wake up each morning.

Throughout my multiple stays at rehab, and in Ambrosia in particular, I am learning to be comfortable with who I am as an individual. I am trying to turn my life around and reverse the downward spiral my life has begun to take. In the process, I am learning to identify my triggers, and how to cope with them so that I never have to resort to using alcohol, drugs, or my eating disorder again to run from my pain. Instead, I can deal with my feelings like an adult, and move past this rough patch in my life, as I did when I was 12. Hopefully, by doing this I can make my alcohol and drug abuse be but a minor blip on the radar in an otherwise happy and successful life.

On February 7, Alex moved into Living Right, a sober living house in Lake Worth, Florida. He was going to be closer to Poo, which gave us some comfort. But as Ambrosia had predicted, he was not ready, and soon returned to drug use. On February 9, the owner of Living Right called to let us know that Alex and three other young men were caught with crack cocaine. All four were booted out and sent to Serenity Now, a detox facility where Alex spent the night. As I was writing this chapter, I did an online search for Living Right, and learned that in March 2017 the owner we met was arrested on forty-eight counts of patient brokering, and in October 2017 he was charged with an additional forty-three counts. His arrest was part of the Palm Beach County Sober Home Task Force's enforcement program targeting owners and operators of drug treatment centers and sober homes who were "buying and selling insured addicts." The *Palm Beach Post* reported in October 2017 that twenty-eight owners and operators had been charged during the past eight months.[12] I have no information on whether he was convicted, but I can no longer find a listing for Living Right sober house in Lake Worth. This information makes me question whether Alex ever had a chance in them.

On February 10, after detox, Alex simply walked out and found his way to Granny's West Palm Beach condo, which was still in the family after her 2012 death. Poo described what happened next:

I remember getting a call from ... the building manager. ... She said, "Your nephew Alex is here." And I just don't remember if we knew he had bolted, I think we did. He was saying he wanted the key to his grandmother's apartment. That he was a relative. He must've been really messed up because that makes no sense. I mean, the idea that anybody would give him a key and just tell him, go in.

She called me, and I think while I was on the line I called Chip, and [he said], "Do not allow him entry." ... I don't think [Alex] was unpleasant, I think I remember that the [manager] said he was extremely polite and respectful. He didn't like the answer, but he wasn't argumentative, and she never felt unsafe and never felt like she needed to call the cops, but he went next door to the park that's immediately south of the building. ...

He had been trying to go to a homeless shelter [and had been] doing research, and they wouldn't take him, because it wasn't just like, "Let me just check in and leave when I wanted." ... They wanted a commitment from him, that he would stay, try to get a job, to do something more than just "I want to sleep here and leave in the morning." So, nobody would take him, and/or there were no beds available.

We were surprised that Alex would even know how to get to Granny's condo because he hadn't been there in years. But get there he did. My best recollection, based on notes in my calendar, is that Poo was ultimately able to get Alex on the phone and went to pick him up at a nearby park. While he was still sitting in the park, we talked him into coming home, and arranged a plane ticket for the next day. We realized that we'd offloaded our problem onto Poo, and it wasn't right to burden her. We had to get Alex back to New Jersey. Poo brought him to her house that night. We told Poo and her husband Todd to put away any cash, valuables, and meds. We picked Alex up at Newark Airport the following day. Over Christmas break of 2022, I was back in Granny's condo, now a renovated home for family visitors. Poo took me to the nearby park to show me where she found Alex that day in 2014, sitting against a tree in the middle of the park. It was quiet, with a beautiful view of the intracoastal. I tried to understand Alex's mindset that day, but to this day it eludes me.

We had been taught by the rehab industry about the dangers of "enabling," and the need to "teach him consequences." It was a repeated mantra that we accepted as truth because we had no other truth. Rather than bring Alex back into the house, we paid for a week at a Days Inn near our home, where he promptly met and got drugs from motel neighbors. When I went there the next day, he told me he had overdosed and suffered seizures. When he developed the flu two days later, I brought him home. To this day, we regret our decision to put him in that motel. We learned then, and later, that punishing a drug user's behavior never works.

Alex's first suicide note was the last essay in the red notebook he began at Ambrosia. All indications are that he wrote this while at the Days Inn, although I didn't find the notebook until after he died:

> I love all of you, and I'm sorry for what I have done to you by destroying my life, and yours in the process. I am at a point now that I physically and mentally cannot handle my life anymore. Obviously I can't control my drinking, and I can't stop thinking about it. It's emotionally draining. I know you have had to deal with a lot of death in the family recently and I am sorry I will be throwing salt on the wound with my own death. I know I am acting selfish and self-centered by taking my own life, but I just can't go on like this. I can't handle my alcoholism or my eating disorder, which has been acting up recently worse than ever. I wake up every day hating my life, what I have become, and what I have done to you all. I know I cannot change the past, and for that I apologize, but by taking my own life, I hope you will recover sometime soon and finally have some sense of peace in your life. I don't want you to worry about me anymore, and finally you won't have to once I am laid to rest. Please forgive me for hurting you this one last time, but at least it is finally over. Just know that I love you and everything you all have done for me.
>
> Love, Alex

How I wish I could tell him how wrong he was. None of us, not Chip nor I, nor the rest of our family and his friends, are at peace with his decision to die. We never will be.

On the Road, Scene 3: Some Peace: Suboxone and Therapy
Feb. 21–June 24, 2014: Suboxone outpatient treatment.
Feb. 25, 2014–July 3, 2014: Rutgers Program for Addictions Consultation and Treatment (PACT) (met weekly); Community

Reinforcement and Family Training (CRAFT) family therapy (8 sessions), Rutgers University, Piscataway, NJ.

Apr. 1, 2014: Move to new home.

Apr. 8–10, 2014: Travel to Washington, DC, with friend; arrest for marijuana possession and hindering arrest on NJ Turnpike.

June 1–2, 2014: Overdose, to JFK Hospital, Edison, NJ.

Improbably, what followed was a period of peacefulness. Alex was adamant about not wanting to return to rehab, and we agreed they had proven unsuccessful thus far. We were ready to try something different. I had learned from my research that most people who recover do so on their own, and it had become clear to us that recovery wouldn't happen until Alex was ready. So, to help him be ready, we developed a make-shift IOP. As a backup, I searched for non-12-step rehabs. I talked with a rehab consultant, but the $5,000 up-front referral fee was too steep for our budget, especially given the costs we had already borne. Alex found a new psychiatrist and went back to meeting with Dr. O on a regular basis. He had heard about and wanted to try Suboxone sublingual films, a combination of buprenorphine and naloxone like methadone that counters the effects of opioids. Suboxone is often touted as a wonder drug, with a highly successful track record of treating heroin addiction, and for a while it worked. Alex researched and arranged for an appointment with a Suboxone doctor and stayed clean for four months—we think—meeting weekly with the doctor from February 21 to June 24, 2014. At my insistence, he also entered the Rutgers PACT, where he met weekly with a therapist. Chip and I participated in an eight-week CRAFT program for families of those who use drugs. Both programs were run through the Rutgers Graduate School of Applied and Professional Psychology. We had multiple family therapy sessions and were hopeful we were making progress.

Another happy development was the completion of the renovation of Hal's house. On April 1, 2014, we made the move to our new home, half a mile from where we had lived for twenty-four years. After living on top of one another for the previous year, it was a pleasure to be able to spread out. Each of the kids chose their room color, window treatments, and decorations. Alex chose a beautiful red—"spicy quesadilla," our decorator called it—for his now first-floor room. He had his two ball python snakes from college and bought a betta fish. No matter what difficulties he went through, he always took care of those pets, except for when he was in rehab, when we had the honor. He also loved Hal's cats, Mugsy and Cali, who now lived with us.

After a few months, however, our makeshift IOP began to show cracks. On April 8, 2014, Alex's college friend Alan drove down to Washington, DC, and took Alex with him. The state police pulled them over on the New Jersey Turnpike, arresting them for marijuana possession and hindering arrest. Alan told me about it in my interview with him:

> We were driving down to DC for a work event that I had to go to, to visit some friends from his fraternity in college. That was always something I kind of regretted because I thought we'd be fine. You know, smoking a little pot on the way down to DC but then we got caught and ended up being a bad situation. . . .
>
> We were just getting pulled over. They must have seen us emptying out a cigarette and trying to fill it with marijuana at a rest stop. [We had just gotten back on the turnpike, when we got pulled over.] It escalated because Alex tried to consume it and eat it and hide it. It was a minuscule amount of marijuana. We weren't going to be getting in a terrible amount of trouble. We were still very scared, obviously. I think the situation escalated because he tried to hide it and eat it and swallow it. The cops were forceful. They tried to force him to throw up on the trunk of my car. From then, it was what's done has been done. They were pretty polite. They just at that point brought us back to the Island rest stop, where we were on the Turnpike. Then they let us go a couple hours later.
>
> We drew some charges for possession of marijuana, I believe. I do remember we were questioned in the same room. Alex had a litany of prescription drugs on him. All prescribed to him. I remember the cop just making a comment like this was an obscene amount of prescription drugs to be carrying at a given time. He must have just gotten out of a clinic or something. I couldn't even tell you what they were. Alex had no problem with them going through his things. None of them were out of line of being prescribed anything. He didn't have anything else on him. . . .
>
> The charges were dropped because Alex passed away. . . . They never produced the evidence that they referenced and had. They had a body cam or something that would have shown the actions during the

arrest. They were never willing to produce it so then they dropped. . . . We kept asking for it. I think we went to a hearing. I might be wrong on timing here because it's not something I like to keep in my head. They never produced. We went down, they still didn't produce it, and I think the judge gave them one more time to produce it, being the prosecutor or the police and they never showed. Then I didn't think I had to be there but maybe I was there for it, and they dismissed the charges.

Alan was convinced that the charges were only dropped because Alex died: "I know for a fact . . . Because that was the reason it [was] dismissed." He genuinely regretted the incident, adding, "I took the onus. It was my wanting to smoke a joint that got us in that situation. I felt really guilty about it to him, and to you and Chip. It was not. . . . Obviously he was fine with it but it was an unnecessary happenstance and could have been avoided. It was always, to this day was always something I regret. Wish it didn't happen, but you can't take back your actions at times."

I remember Alex calling me when they got to DC, and his description of the events was similar. He was distraught that he would now have a New Jersey arrest record (the DUI in New Jersey is a traffic, not a criminal, offense, and thus not reportable on a criminal database). We hired Al, the same lawyer who had represented him for the DUI. I recall the same sequence of events his friend describes, with the police refusing to provide evidence they claimed to have. But Alex would never know the charges against him were dismissed. And, of course, a few years later—in February 2021—New Jersey decriminalized marijuana altogether. Today, he would not have been arrested for marijuana possession, especially because he was not the driver. Ironically, he hadn't even smoked the marijuana he tried to ingest: he tested clean several days later at his Suboxone doctor visit. We were pissed-off at both Alex and Alan. Although it was a relatively minor transgression and only one incident among many that fed Alex's panic and trauma, it loomed large for him.

There were otherwise signs of progress those months. Most importantly, to our knowledge he remained clean for his weekly checkups at the

Suboxone doctor, for a while at least. During that period, he went on a number of job interviews, including several for insurance sales. We supported him fully in his job search and ferried him to interviews. He spent several weeks studying for his New Jersey insurance license and was pleased when he passed the state test and received it. He had interviews with Farmers and Aflac, and both were interested in bringing him on board. I don't know whether he disclosed his arrest and rehab records. After everything that had happened, here was a real opportunity to move forward, and he was excited about it.

But with this progress, there were also setbacks. Toward the end of the time he was on Suboxone, I watched him carry a bottle of urine into the testing room. I alerted the doctor, and they began to watch him more closely. While traveling on a train to northern New Jersey for an insurance training session, he had a panic attack and had to leave the train. He arrived at the training sweaty and anxious, and eventually found his way home. Although we didn't know it until later, at some point he stopped taking his Suboxone and began selling it to finance his resurgent heroin and Xanax habits. By June 1 he was back in JFK Hospital with another overdose. Our carefully crafted IOP fell apart.

To close this chapter, I move my gaze from these specific events to chronicle how Alex's substance use, and the events and consequences that flowed from it, affected our family. We transitioned from parents in "a good family" to parents of a child who drove while drunk, was arrested for possession, used and sold drugs, and was repeatedly booted out of rehabs. What was it like to be caught in that insanity—the word of choice for families with loved ones who use substances? To put it mildly, it was a harrowing ride we could not have imagined or been prepared for. We were two college professors working full time, living in a quiet suburban community, and raising three young people.

In preparing this chapter I looked at our calendars from those times. Our days were filled with the regular craziness of life with jobs and kids—days we taught or prepared for classes or had scheduled research, various doctors' appointments, Hunter's test prep and college visits, Hunter's and Ginny's sports games and school appointments, and work and family travel. Trying to manage normal family life with all the added insanity of addiction was overwhelming. Looking back, I don't know how we did it. Thus far I've only described the first few miles of our travel down the second road to addiction. In the next chapter I report how much worse it became. Sadly, any family suffering through addiction will tell you remarkably similar stories. I know because I've talked with them. They've become my community.

During the summer of 2013, we began a vicious cycle of detox, rehab, release, overdose, and Narcan—repeat. Alex went to rehabs in New Jersey and Florida, the "non"-recovery capital of the world. He attended hundreds of 12-step sessions, both in rehabs and out. He tried Suboxone and went to multiple psychiatrists and psychologists. He was admitted to countless hospitals and rehabs. He threatened suicide. He totaled his car, then mine, and did damage to several others. His anorexia returned in full force, this time with bulimia. He stole money from us, and when we became more observant, he stole from unlocked cars, which landed him in jail. With each incident, his options narrowed, and he lost friends.

The Alex we had nurtured and knew disappeared. This new Alex was usually angry. He would lock himself in the bathroom and shoot up. Substance users try to hide what they are doing. We found syringes and heroin packets hidden in his bedroom: in an old baseball bag, in the ceiling panels, under the mattress. Our spoons began to disappear, until we found them bent and burned on the bottom. The 12-step program admonishes family members to leave the drugs and paraphernalia and to let their loved one "hit bottom." We could not do that. The syringes and heroin packets we found, if left for Alex, might be the very ones to kill him. Rock bottom for Alex, we feared, would be his death. Our scavenger hunts uncovered small bottles of clear grain alcohol (Everclear) and bottles of rum, stashed away in his room. Usually we confiscated those as well, although not always. For some reason, they seemed less dangerous, although logically we knew that is not the case for an alcoholic. After Alex died, syringes and bottles still showed up. When I donated some of Alex's jeans to a church rummage sale, I found several syringes taped inside the pants. Luckily, I found them while still in the church parking lot. Years later, I came across the random small bottle of gin, hidden in with the plastic bags in the back reaches of the kitchen cabinets.

The "new" Alex would disappear in the middle of the night, getting his drug "friends" to drive him to dealers in Plainfield or Newark. Without a car, he would walk, skateboard, or bike down to the liquor stores in town. After we cut off his money and canceled credit cards, he took to begging at the train station and elsewhere. He sold his belongings: watches, sunglasses, the Xbox we bought him for Christmas, anything of potential value he could get his hands on. He tried to sell his bass guitar, but we hid it at Dori and Joe's house. I woke up on numerous occasions to find him stealing money from my purse, which I had hidden under the bed or between the mattresses. He stole our prescription medicines, especially Ambien. One night I found him holding Chip's new bottle of Ambien, with twenty-four of the thirty 10mg pills already gone. He had already swallowed seven of them. Who knew that if you take multiple Ambien but stay awake long enough, you can get high enough to hallucinate?

When we learned or read about other families losing family heirlooms, we bought a safe. We took our wedding rings to our safety deposit box. Losing Chip's grandmother's engagement and wedding rings, which are now my rings, would have truly broken my heart. We kept our cars locked with our medicines in the trunk, and the car keys in our pillowcases. Once, Alex tried to break into Chip's car, causing hundreds of dollars of damage. Another night he stole Hunter's car to drive to Plainfield to buy Xanax and heroin. When he crashed that car into someone's mailbox, there was another $2,600 in damages. I took a video of him one night staggering around in the kitchen, passing out on the floor, waking up again; he never noticed. He was embarrassed when I showed him the video the next day, but not enough to stay clean. Drugs had literally become his life; his rehab and drug "friends" had replaced those from his childhood and school.

Heroin had narrowed his life to the four walls of his room. He had no money, no real friends, no girlfriend, no car, no school, no job—no life outside of drugs. He was furious, railing at the world and us. A few friends would occasionally come by for a visit, but for the most part his vast circle of local, high school, and college friends was gone. Who wants to witness a friend destroy his life, and who can blame them for cutting ties? Family remained, but he screamed at us for trying to control his behavior. He was, after all, twenty-four at the time, and had already enjoyed the freedom of college life.

I understand that "a good family" is a loaded term that is often used to perpetuate a stereotype of white, middle-class, intact families who believe in education, save money, and make it honestly. I use the term as shorthand, however, not as a stereotype. Good families—caring, involved families—are not supposed to have a child who falls prey to addiction. But as these last years demonstrated, the truth is much more complex. Once you go public about addiction you find out that many of your friends and family have suffered through the same insanity of drug or alcohol use. Many have told me about their kids, siblings, cousins, parents, neighbors, and friends. I didn't know then, but now I do. And people know about us, I made sure of that. I want to put real faces on the overdose epidemic, to reduce stigma and to advocate for better, more effective treatment options. Of course, good families who are black, poor, immigrants, or live in the inner city already know the scourge of addiction, because many lived it well before we did. With the recent surge of fentanyl overdoses, they are living it anew. Addiction is an equal opportunity scourge and problem.

Alex was always prone to risky behavior, and he'd try just about anything, so it isn't hard to imagine him curious about heroin. But today's heroin (and now fentanyl) bears scant resemblance to drugs of the 1970s and 1980s. A middle-class suburban kid back then never saw heroin, which along with fentanyl is now everywhere. They are also cheap, nearly pure, and perhaps most importantly have lost their stigma. Today's young people have lots of discretionary income and cars, and drugs come to them like pizza. Alex found heroin, even when he had no car and no money, no matter what city or state he was in. Even after we cut him off from cars, money, and credit cards, he begged and stole to finance his habit.

As Alex descended further into the insanity of drug use, we often wondered where our beautiful boy had gone. He existed in the flesh, but his persona was someone we didn't know, and he acted in ways we didn't understand. Occasionally we got glimpses of our Alex, and wondered what we could do to keep him alive and help him to recover. But as he continued to deteriorate, our hopes and dreams for him faded as well. In their place were now only desperate nightmares that morphed into night (and day) terrors and desperation.

CHAPTER 10

End of the Road

For a while, they would mourn him, because they were good
people, the best, and he was sorry for that—but eventually
they would see that their lives were better without him in it.
They would see how much time he had stolen from them. . . . He
hoped they would forgive him. . . . He was releasing them—he
loved them most of all, and this was what you did for
people you loved: you gave them their freedom.

—Hanya Yanagihara, *A Little Life*

BY HAPPENSTANCE, I began this chapter on what would have been Alex's thirty-second birthday. I woke up thinking of him, as I often do. I'd love to talk with him about what we've been up to. So much has happened in the years since he turned twenty-five: technological change, which he would have easily mastered; new music he would have played loudly; Chip's and my well-deserved work retirements; our relocation to Washington, DC; Hunter's and Ginny's many educational and work successes; and so much more. I still long for the conversations we would have had with the "old" Alex, even to discuss the political polarization that has divided our nation and the COVID-19 pandemic that killed so many and disrupted the lives of so many more. No doubt, he would have found the COVID-19 lockdowns even more depressing than the lonely isolation he had been living with. The anniversary of Alex's birthday comes with nightmare memories. But then again, everything in the last year of his life was traumatizing, for him and for us. Death is the ultimate end of the road, but how one travels along that road is important to consider. I turn now to those last few miles.

I resonate with W.J.T. Mitchell's description of his son Gabe's death by suicide: "But the word I recall being repeated endlessly, like a tolling bell in those days, is 'unimaginable.' I have often wondered why people always say that the death of a child is unimaginable—'I can't imagine what you are going through' is the routine expression of sympathy. My sense is just the opposite. It is all too imaginable. It may be one of the primary foundations of imagination, especially when driven by all the fears that are built into the parenting of any child, let alone one who seems especially vulnerable."[1] Like Mitchell, I didn't see Alex's death as unimaginable. It was entirely imaginable. I had been worrying about Alex from the moment he was born, indeed before he was born. I imagined all the worst cases that might befall him. I don't know if that was a manifestation of the anxiety I was already prone to or whether most moms have the same worries. With Alex's anorexia my inchoate "what if" concerns became more sharply defined. By the time we reached the on-ramp to the fast lane of that second road—Alex's substance use— my imagination was primed, and my worry was through the roof.

During Alex's years of addiction, and after his death, I tried to understand what Alex was thinking when he wrote his suicide notes. I've tried to imagine what he was thinking when he injected that last shot of heroin, which stopped his heart. It's unnerving how Jude's thoughts on suicide in Hanya Yanagihara's novel *A Little Life* sound like Alex. Was it suicide, or just that he needed to satisfy an insatiable craving? Are the two mutually exclusive? It tears at my heart to believe that Alex might have purposely overdosed.

Even when Alex was railing against us for searching his room, throwing away his stash, locking our cars and hiding the keys, he knew we loved him. And we knew he loved us. He told us many times that he was sorry for destroying his own life and ours; we believed, and still believe, that to be true. I do not doubt he believed his death would give us freedom. It is easy to accept that he had concluded recovery was out of reach—his rehabs had universally failed—and that he could no longer live in this world. Nonetheless, he still wanted us to recover and find peace in our lives. You could even say he promised us peace. But how could he ever believe that we could find lasting peace in this life with-

END OF THE ROAD 173

out him? In the end, he would leave us no peace. I can only hope that perhaps he found a kind of peace for himself.

On the Road, Scene 4: Arrest, Suicide Attempt, Psychiatric Acute Care, and Back to the Eating Disorders Unit

June 26, 2014: Drove to Newark, totaled my car, arrested for heroin possession.

June 27, 2014: Suicide attempt, at home.

June 27–July 3, 2014: Rutgers University Behavioral Health Care (UBHC), Piscataway, NJ, acute care, discharged to Summit Oaks Hospital.

July 16, 2014: JFK Hospital, Edison, NJ (for seizure and concussion, after fall).

July 22–25, 2014: Somerset Medical Center Eating Disorders Unit (rehab #4).

July 25, 2014: Signed out against medical advice (AMA), train to Plainfield, NJ.

July 25–26, 2014: Overnight at Plainfield Police Station.

Hunter graduated from high school on June 19, 2014. One week later our informal intensive outpatient program (IOP) collapsed in a spectacular fashion. On Monday June 23, I drove Alex to meet with his Community Reinforcement and Family Training (CRAFT) therapist, and on the next day I took him to the doctor who prescribed his buprenorphine/naloxone (aka Suboxone), for what would be his last appointment. Two days later, early on Thursday morning June 26, Alex snuck out of the house with my car keys and headed to Newark on Route 78 to buy heroin. He lost control of the car and crashed into a concrete barrier, totaling my car. From what we were able to piece together from talking with Alex, the tow truck driver he called dropped him off in downtown Newark, where he was subsequently arrested for possession of heroin and a syringe, with intent to use. Alex had called to let me know about the accident and tell us he was unhurt, but he didn't mention the arrests until later that evening. That second New Jersey arrest hung over his head, and led to several arrest warrants when rehab stays kept him from court appointments.

He used a credit card we had lent him for a job interview to buy a train ticket back to Metuchen. Judging from the credit card statement we subsequently received he spent much of the rest of the day wandering from restaurants to convenience stores. That day and night, Chip and I went into Manhattan for a long-planned date to meet relatives and friends for dinner and then to see Bryan Cranston in *LBJ* on Broadway. We were anxious the entire evening, not knowing where Alex was. We returned home late to find him catatonic on the back porch. We were able to get him to bed. Sleep was more elusive for us.

The next morning, I walked into Alex's room to check on him and caught him attempting to shoot up with bleach. I called for Chip, who found a suicide note on Alex's bedside table:

> Dad, Mom, Hunter, Ginny. I will preface this message by saying there is no good end in sight for me. I can't stand my life. Nothing seems to work out. And now with this on my record I literally have no hope of being successful. I know I'm the reason you have so much stress and heartache, so I'm sorry to add another, but I just can't live in this world anymore. Lee Alexander Roos Clarke.
>
> Btw, this is Bleach I decided to kill myself with. Don't count me as a drug overdose.

We loaded him into my car, and I drove him to Rutgers University Behavioral Health Center (UBHC), an acute psychological care facility about twenty minutes away. Because Alex was "under the influence of substances," UBHC sent him first to St. Peter's Hospital. When he returned, they assessed him as suffering from "depressive disorder (not otherwise specified); generalized anxiety disorder; opioid dependence; sedative, hypnotic and anxiolytic dependence; and alcohol dependence." While they saw his strengths as stable housing, supportive family, education, and hobbies, they described significant negatives, including impulsivity, difficulty trusting, and anxiety. He reported that what he most wanted was to "move out of the house and get paid." With respect to the suicide note, the intake interviewer reported:

> Pt reported to writer that this was the first time he had ever experienced suicidal thoughts and justified his actions because this was the first time

he had ever felt "this bad about himself." Pt reported that this response was "impulsive" and views this as a reaction due to crashing his mother's car twice in 1 day, getting apprehended by the police for looking suspicious and finally charged with possession of an illicit substance on 6/26/14. Pt reported that he owes his parents a significant amount of money and will not be able to ever get out of debt, is not able to manage his anxiety with psychotropic meds and in general is not functioning to the level that he feels his parents expect him to be. During assessment, pt minimizes his actions and was unable to recognize the seriousness and dangerousness of his lack of judgment, lack of insight and impulsivity. . . . Family is very supportive but pt says that his family is completely unsupportive. . . . Pt is receiving Xanax prescriptions from 2 different doctors. . . . It is likely that he is abusing Xanax at this time. Additionally, after pt's recent car accident, he took the train back to Metuchen and made 10 charges on his father's credit card for food and cigs. The family is very concerned about pt's safety and well-being. Additionally, there are 2 younger cousins living in the home and they are concerned for their safety.

While Alex claimed that he didn't really want to die, his note and actions said otherwise. Sadly, he spoke his truth: "I just can't live in this world anymore." As a person who used drugs, he couldn't envision a different life. He had found no alternative visions out there, no possibility of a good future. After a brief hospital stay, Alex transitioned to Summit Oaks Hospital, where he stayed for several more days and was then discharged back to home.

Just two weeks later Alex was back at JFK, this time after falling and suffering a seizure and concussion. We were terrified and at our wits' end about what we could do to keep him safe and alive. But the downhill slide continued unabated. His health deteriorated, and he protested our attempts to keep him safe. Along with the drinking and drugs, Alex's anorexia and bulimia flared. He purged almost daily. Sometimes I would find him banging around the kitchen drunk or high trying to cook pancakes. One day he poured maple syrup on the wall. Another time, when I went downstairs to the kitchen after hearing noises, I walked past the stove, and felt the heat from four burners. He couldn't figure out how to turn them off, he told me. I worried incessantly that he would burn down the house. During dinner, he sat nodding from the effects of drugs, and restricted what he ate: no rice, no pasta, no dessert. Then later at night he would eat everything in sight, especially sugary foods like chocolate or maple syrup straight from the bottle, brown sugar by the spoonful, and sugary cereals. We knew by then that research shows that habitual opioid use is associated with increased sugar intake.[2] A few hours later he'd head to the bathroom to purge. His cheeks eventually puffed up like a chipmunk's from excessive purging.

One evening when Chip was out of town at a work conference, I confronted Alex about some issue I no longer remember. We got into an argument, and he went to leave. I tried to block his way, and he stood tall in front of me as if he might strike or push me. It's the only time in Alex's years of polysubstance use that I was briefly afraid that he might harm me. I let him pass and he disappeared into the night, likely to buy (or steal) liquor or drugs. Worried about what might happen, I called my former neighbor Joe and he drove me around the neighborhood looking for Alex, to no avail. Eventually, Alex returned home, slipping quietly into his room. I was always relieved to know he was home, even if it wasn't any safer.

Even during periods of what we hoped were progress, we learned new things about addictive behavior, including buying urine to conceal drug use, or taping syringes inside his pants. Every time we found more proof of his drug and alcohol use, he denied it, then admitted it, then expressed self-loathing. From the beginning Alex was aware that drugs can change the brain's chemistry. He knew it from his high school research, and he learned it again in his college biology courses, and then again in rehabs. It intrigued him intellectually. But the highs and intoxication were a siren song. His altered brain, and his need to self-medicate, meant he couldn't escape the drugs' grip on him.

By July 22 we decided to once again send Alex to Somerset Medical Center's Eating Disorders Unit (EDU), the program that had done so well for him twelve years earlier. He and they agreed to his admission to what was rehab #4. This time his diagnoses were "depression, suicidal ideations, suicide attempt, anorexia, bulimia." They described Alex as experiencing "rational thought loss, increased stress, delusional, decreased appetite, increased sleep, restricting, binging/purging, [weight] loss, substance abuse." He reported "feeling down, depressed/hopeless . . . feeling like failure, [letting] others down . . . be better off dead/want to hurt myself." The hospital's notes continued: "Patient describes social network as very limited. Notes that he has friends but feels as they are moving on with their lives and becoming more independent. States that due to this, he has been feeling more lonely recently. Patient denies history of emotional, physical, and sexual abuse, and no other trauma, neglect, or exploitation have been reported. Does confirm a history of legal problems. 2 cases pending, both involving drug possession."

This time, Alex's stay in the EDU was a disaster. Truth be told, we were mainly trying to get him away from heroin for a few days before we could find another rehab. He butted heads with the EDU doctors and nurses. After two days, he put in the required forty-eight-hour notice to leave against medical advice (AMA). Because he was an adult, they had to let him go. In a phone conversation with us the day he left, the EDU's director told us: "All he wants to do is get high on heroin, he'll probably die." This was not a foreign thought to us, but nevertheless chilling to hear.

After leaving Somerset he headed by train to Plainfield, where the police arrested him on an outstanding warrant for missing a court hearing for the June 26 incident. When they took him to jail, they left his suitcase behind and everything he had was stolen. He called us several times that night, begging us to come bail him out. Trying yet again to teach him "consequences," we declined. The following morning, the police let him go anyway. He wandered around Plainfield wrapped in a blanket he had stolen from the EDU, the only thing left at the location where his suitcase had been. Later that day a black police officer called me, asking if we would pick him up. The officer told me quite pointedly that "he doesn't belong in this area." I readily understood what he was saying: What was this young white male doing in this poor, black neighborhood? Chip went to pick him up. I was thankful that the officer was kind and understanding, and that he called me. That wasn't the first time I told Alex that but for the color of his skin, he'd likely already be in prison.

On the Road, Scene 5: Psychiatric Hospital, Overdoses, Jail, and More Rehabs

July 30–Aug. 26, 2014: Silver Hill Hospital, New Canaan, CT (rehab #5).

Aug. 27, 2014: UBHC, Piscataway, NJ (one day).

Aug. 28, 2014: Traveled to Newark; back to Metuchen, broke into cars.

Aug. 28–Sept. 18, 2014: Middlesex County Jail, North Brunswick, NJ.

Sept. 18–Oct. 17, 2014: UBHC daily program, outpatient; dismissed, recommended for inpatient (rehab #6).

Oct. 14, 2014: UBHC to Social Services, walked out; sent to Robert Wood Johnson psychiatric ward.

Oct. 20–24, 2014: Princeton House, NJ, inpatient (rehab #7); administratively discharged for apparent mumps.

Nov. 11, 2014: Ear, nose, and throat specialist diagnosed swollen parotid glands, due to anorexia/bulimia.

Nov. 18–Dec. 17, 2014: New Life Counseling (Endeavor House), Keyport, NJ, for IOP (3 days per week) (rehab #8).

Alex's therapist from the Rutgers CRAFT program suggested Silver Hill Hospital, a well-respected psychiatric hospital in Connecticut. Their offerings looked ideal, including a dual diagnosis program that focused both on mental health and drug addiction, as well as eating disorders. They accepted him but had no opening until the end of July. In the interim, to get him out of town, Chip took him to Chick and Barbara's home in Hillsdale, in the woods of upstate New York. Those few days were tense. It was obvious that Alex took something once they arrived, probably Xanax. Chip described it as the most miserable time he'd ever spent in Hillsdale, usually his place of peace. Ever vigilant, and on edge, he looked up the geographic coordinates in case he needed to call an ambulance. They stayed several days before heading to Silver Hill.

On July 30—Chip's and my twenty-sixth wedding anniversary—Chip drove Alex to Silver Hill for rehab #5. The hospital's white clapboard building is set on a campus of forty-four parklike acres and could be easily mistaken for a quiet New England resort, rather than the psychiatric hospital and rehab that it is. Upon arrival Chip presented our insurance card and our credit card, paying nearly $30,000 upfront for thirty days of treatment. Silver Hill's price tag was not covered by our insurance. Although Blue Cross/Blue Shield reimbursed Silver Hill for bills they submitted for labs and therapy groups, we were responsible for everything else, primarily Alex's room and board. The hospital provided an accounting of these remaining charges so I could send it to Blue Cross/Blue Shield for reimbursement, although they made clear that the charges were likely not reimbursable. Although Silver Hill received prompt payment, we never did. But we should have. Many others, especially those without insurance, fare much worse. Prior to the Affordable Care Act (ACA), our insurance would likely have been canceled due to pre-existing conditions or age limitations. Even with the ACA we began to worry about what would happen when Alex turned twenty-six, when he would have automatically aged off our policy. Employer provided group healthcare was not going to be an option for him.

After I became Alex's medical heir, Silver Hill sent me a voluminous stack of documents in response to my request for Alex's medical information. The two and a half inches of records from Silver Hill made the quarter-inch bundle we received from Ambrosia, for approximately the same length of stay, pale in comparison. The records primarily comprise the notes taken by the admissions interviewers who evaluated Alex on intake; the facilitators who described his participation in each of the group activities he attended; and the residence staff who asked him about his day at their nightly wrap-ups. Also included were progress notes and assessments from the psychiatrists, social worker, and eating disorder specialist who worked most closely with Alex. Many of these notes include direct quotes from discussions with Alex, dialogue consistent with the conversations he and I had during his phone calls home and our visits to Connecticut. His voice comes through clearly. Reading the notes as the days and weeks went by, I can hear his frustration, anger, and indignation grow to the point of boiling over. Silver Hill's paper trail provides an eye-opening look into the substance treatment "industrial complex" inflexibly wedded to a 12 steps methodology applied in cookie-cutter fashion. It is a case study of nonrecovery in action.

The records revealed that when the admissions staff performed a body check, they found two empty syringes "in case," Alex told them, "he got a hold of some drugs." As part of the intake process, the admissions staff gave Alex a booklet that detailed his rights and responsibilities as a patient, including a dress code, a prohibition against any drugs and alcohol, and rules necessary to maintain a safe and therapeutic environment (e.g., body search, search of personal items, and urine drug screens). Patients were also asked to maintain the confidentiality and privacy of other patients and visiting family members.

They checked him in, and Alex began his stay in Silver Hill's "Main House" for inpatient treatment. He again described his preteen anorexia and the stresses in his life. The admission notes go on to recount:

> [Alex] minimiz[ed] . . . all his substance use, and his medication seek-
> ing for Xanax, stating that his panic disorder and anxiety are uncon-
> trolled without it. He also has been using heroin for the last year, using
> it IV for the last 8 months. . . . [He described a] "seizure disorder" that
> has been ongoing for the last 2 years, for which he takes keppra. . . .
> His drug use has also led to him isolating himself, and also feeling bad
> about himself. . . . He reports that for the last 8 months he has also had
> a resurgence of his eating disorder behaviors. . . . [He] has started to
> purge once or twice a week. . . . He does feel self conscious about his
> appearance, feels that people look and judge [him] often. He feels that
> restricting allows him to regain power over himself. . . . He does report
> ongoing depression and anxiety. He gets panic attacks, where he will
> start sweating, have a racing heart, get short of breath, and have to
> leave the situation. . . . He worries a lot, catastrophizes, and also
> ruminates. He has low energy, poor concentration. He endorses
> anhedonia [inability to feel pleasure] and also amotivation. . . . It
> was his parents who motivated him to come to SHH [Silver Hill Hos-
> pital] and [he states,] "I am upset I have to take so much time out of
> my life to deal with the mental stuff." When asked how SHH can
> help him the most he states, "Stop the cycle of eating disorder before
> it gets to a point I can't control it, and I also want to get a plan of how I
> can get back in good graces with my parents and move forward with
> my life."

The intake assessment summarized Alex's diagnosis as:

> 24 year old male with opioid dependence, benzodiazepine dependence, r/o [rule out, i.e., eliminate a diagnosis from consideration] alcohol abuse, anorexia nervosa, depressive disorder NOS [not otherwise specified], anxiety disorder NOS, r/o panic disorder who presents seeking long term treatment and management strategies for his ongoing substance abuse and eating disorder, as well as tx [treatment] for underlying anxiety and depression, with recent social stressors triggering treatment.

After two days he moved to shared living quarters in Scavetta House, which housed Silver Hill's residential Transitional Living Program for men. Common areas allowed for interaction among patients, but Alex and other patients also roamed the campus, traveling to the main house to eat, and to nearby buildings for therapy groups. On August 1, Alex met with his social worker/counselor for the first time. Initially, they seemed to hit it off: during a group meeting that day she recounted that "Pt stated 'I'm happy to be here. I'm definitely doing this for myself.'" In his one-on-one with the social worker, he described his relationship with us as "very strained right now. They love me but they're very fed up with what's been happening." He recounted the recent family stressors due to the deaths in the family, and the changing family composition, and described how "traumatizing" his hospitalization for an eating disorder had been. She noted his current stressors as "inadequate transportation, unemployment, inadequate finances, inadequate social support, isolated, parent conflicts, friends with substance abuse issues."

At first, Alex was happy to be at Silver Hill. He felt like he was finally at a place with people "like him," which I assume meant a lot of educated middle-to-upper-class young people. Of course, this was because the clients, or their relatives, could afford (or manage to afford) the hefty costs not covered by insurance. The presence of a lot of young white men from similar backgrounds as Alex, who were suffering through the same anxieties and addictions as he was, made Alex more receptive to rehab. In an early progress note, one therapist noted: "Pt reported his goal was 'to get there.' Pt reported he is grateful for his mom and dad 'willing to put me through another round.' Pt was given support for sharing in groups with staff and peers." The therapist added that early that first week Alex told his peers in the residential wrap-up that he was "grateful for the guys here in the house."

In early phone calls home, he told us that he had stimulating conversations with his housemates, and connected with several of them, who shared and validated his intellectual interests. One housemate (who left AMA soon thereafter) gave Alex his copy of Scott Stossel's *My Age of Anxiety*, which Alex spent hours reading during break times.[3] He talked with me about it several times and gave it to me to read after he came home. I readily understood why Alex found it compelling. The book recounts how Stossel overcame crippling anxieties to become a successful journalist and eventually the national editor of *Atlantic* magazine. I like to think he saw hope for his own future in Stossel's story, a potential blueprint for moving forward.

It was not long, however, before troubles emerged. It started with his being admonished for flirting, a violation of the rules governing patients' behavior. Given the re-emergence of his anorexia and now bulimia, Alex had been assigned to the eating disorder table for his meals. By August 2, the records reported Alex's "possible fraternization with a female resident," to whom he reportedly commented, "You're a vegetarian? Now I'm even more attracted to you." According to the report, Alex denied violating the rules and said he "was just being friendly and did not mean anything by it." Several days later he was reprimanded again, this time for talking with the women at his table about his recent arrest and pending legal proceedings, and for gossiping about other residents. In a group session on group crisis survival skills, a staff member described Alex in her notes as "too animated in his interactions within the group today." His language was "often" inappropriate (he had used an example of going to the strip club and buying drugs). Because of these interactions, staff eventually moved Alex from the eating disorder table to a table with his male peers. Although he was allowed to continue to participate in Silver Hill's other eating disorder treatment sessions and programs, he described the change of table to his counselor as being "kicked out" of the eating disorder program.

On August 5, Alex told his social worker that he had suffered a seizure. The social worker's documented reaction is one of disbelief: "It was observed by no one. Pt reports feeling angry toward psychiatrist for not giving him Xanax." The notes of the psychiatrist who met with Alex in response to the reported seizure did not address it, focusing instead on Alex's drug-seeking behavior, lack of engagement, and denial:

> Subjective: insisted on meeting early, "quick, simple question." Once in the office he set to complaining about his anxiety and wanting to know why I won't give him Xanax. He says nothing works except Xanax; he denies any addiction issues, and says "what I'm really here for is my eating disorder."

> Assessment: pt has not been engaging well in treatment [here] so far, and spends much of his time in testing boundaries and seeking pharmacologic comfort. Pt has been trying to switch from suboxone to methadone—though he also says he doesn't have an opiate addiction—mainly because he thinks it will reduce his anxiety. When he hears that the use of opiate replacement is a contraindication with benzos, he then backpedals and says he doesn't need ORT [opioid replacement therapy] at all.

On August 6 Alex had another run-in with his social worker, who described the incident in her notes:

> Writer entered the room to overhear pt telling an inappropriate story for a coed group. Pt was immediately asked to stop telling the story, he did not. Pt was asked again and finally stopped. Pt left the room but returned approx. 10 mins later. Pt's check in consisted of complaints about staff. Writer attempted to redirect pt to discuss how he's doing today and offering to meet with him after group to discuss his concerns. Pt displayed minimal insight into how his story may have impacted a coed group. Pt asked to switch Social Workers; writer encouraged him to try to work this out.

Later that day, Alex attended his gratitude group, which was reported thus:

> [He] stated that he was grateful for his family. He shared that if it were not for them he would not be getting help. He stated that he is grateful

that he is not as lost as he was. He stated that he was grateful for his insurance. Pt stated that he was having a hard time not eating at the [eating disorder] table. He shared that he was told that he is not working hard enough and that this upset him. He stated that he is trying to work on [his eating disorder] but [is] not allowed in groups.

Two days later (August 8), the social worker reported on a family meeting with Alex, Chip, me, and his psychiatrist, stating that Alex was "defensive throughout the family meeting" and that his "mood continues to be irritable." That same day, his psychiatrist reported:

I met with Alex several times this week to try and get to know him. He is focused on getting medication for anxiety. He does not think he has a drug problem. He says it is anxiety, and he really needs to have his anxiety addressed with medications so that he will get the most out of this program and his parents not waste money. He comes just before the change of shift to demand that something be done, and is quick to point out that the staff is not really paying attention to him. He tells me that he got all A's in college. . . . I did not feel he was a very authentic person. I feel he is always looking for a way to turn a situation to his advantage.

Assessment: Seems to be a drug addict without much insight, who may either be a psychopath or a pseudopsychopath. He may also be developing a subtle psychotic illness, possible due to his drug use. He is using his intelligence to undo himself. I feel that he is constantly trying to play me. I hope there is more substance to him than that. I hope he is salvageable. He may not be able to gain very much from this program.

On August 12, the eating disorder doctor also met with Alex, and in my opinion—unlike the psychiatrist and social worker who could not get past Alex's defensiveness—mostly got it right:

SUBJECTIVE: "Anxiety is my worst problem; it gets in the way of my life." "My eating disorder helps me cope with my life."
OBJECTIVE: Patient was open, cooperative, and forthcoming with information in the interview. Patient gazed straight ahead with a blank expression on his face and showed little emotion. Pt. appeared calm but reported that he felt very anxious.

ASSESSMENT: Pt has a longstanding history of an eating disorder beginning around age 12. Pt reports that he began experiencing severe anxiety around that time. He states that the eating disorder helped him in coping with his anxiety, gave him a sense of control and accomplishment, and helped him cope with feelings of low self-esteem and a poor self-image. He reports that he often purged as a way to lower his high anxiety. He also states that restrictive eating gave him a "real sense of accomplishment." That he "felt good about himself when he could get through a day without eating." Pt feels like "a failure" in life and he has not accomplished goals he would like for himself. Pt states that his greatest problem is his severe social anxiety with his heart pounding, racing thoughts, etc. and feels that this problem is the greatest impediment to his self-esteem and success.

The psychiatrist's August 13 treatment notes describe a session mainly consisting of the doctor lecturing Alex to stop acting like a drug addict, be less needy, tolerate discomfort, and start being "nice," along with a little name-calling thrown in for good measure:

I told Alex about Tolstoy and Churchill and how we all need to learn to suffer and work.

He will think about it. I also told him that he behaved like a sociopath and drug addict, and he needed to not act like that if he wanted to be treated differently.

Assessment: says he is very anxious, but does not look it overtly anxious [sic]. He wants benzodiapines [sic]. He really wants them. He really needs them. He is especially needy.

He needs to learn to tolerate discomfort. He needs to be nice to people.

I wish it were as easy as tolerating discomfort, and learning to be nice.

During his third week at Silver Hill, Alex and his social worker began to look for sober living options following treatment. We all agreed that New York City's Tribeca 12 seemed like a good option, because it provided both work and transportation options, two issues key to Alex's ability to maintain sobriety. After interviewing with a Tribeca 12 staff member, however, he was turned down. His social worker noted:

> At this time they are not accepting him into Tribeca 12. . . . [Their staff member] stated: "He wants to return to the use of benzos. . . . He's really not looking at ETOH [ethanol alcohol] at [*sic*] being a problem. This was more of a concern than the heroin. He's willing to abstain from ETOH if he comes to the house but he doesn't feel it's a problem for him. It seems like he will have a desire to return to this. He's not 12-step motivated. . . . If he were still wanting to come to the city we would take [him] in our IOP but he would need to find other sober living.

On August 22 the issues with his social worker bubbled to the surface once again. The social worker reported that in group, Alex "had nothing to check in about because all he was going to do was complain and he was told to stop complaining. Writer encouraged pt to think of something positive to share; pt wasn't willing to do this. Pt made rude, angry comments directed at writer and was asked to leave the group." As Alex's largely contentious thirty-day stay at Silver Hill was coming to an end, Chip and I drove to Connecticut for a long weekend of "family education" to prepare for Alex's return home. The Saturday and Sunday sessions focused on parental/family education. We found the educational sessions useful, and appreciated meeting other families who were living through the same hell as we were. The next two days we were joined by Alex and his peers. We found the most useful sessions were the ones we shared with Alex, who seemed open to exploring our interactions. Here we were, talking with a sober Alex, something that had become a rarity. Prompted by a facilitator, we wrote out responses, which we then spoke aloud to the group. When prompted to tell us "what I like and love about you," Alex responded about Chip: "1) Sense of humor, 2) Sensitivity and kindness (most of the time). Also very responsible, 3) Extremely smart & technologically proficient." About me, he wrote: "1) Extremely helpful @ times/Always willing to lend a helping hand; 2) Very good organizer; 3) Very forgiving/Always look on the bright side."

In a second exercise, we responded in writing, and then spoke aloud, to the prompt "will you forgive me for." For Chip he wrote "1) Scratching your car quarter panel, 2) Wasting your money, 3) Doing drugs/over-dosing in your office." From me, he asked forgiveness for: "1) Being mean to you, 2) Taking money from you, 3) Crashing your car."

Another communication exercise that elicited useful insights included a set of three prompts:

When you . . . [some action].

I feel . . . [some feeling].

I would like you to . . . [listing an alternative behavior].

Alex responded to this short exercise by saying that he wished Chip would not react in a sarcastic manner, and instead "take the time to listen to my point of view, and respond in a polite manner." He felt that Chip treated Hunter and Ginny differently than he treated him at the same age, and that made him feel "like you love and pay attention to them more than me." For me, he noted that he felt angry when "you micro-manage my life," and frustrated when "you repeat yourself over and over to me." His response: "I would like you to let me manage my own life more." None of Alex's responses surprised us; he had been telling us variations of these for a long time, even back in his anorexia days. In our defense, we wanted nothing more than to have Alex manage his life, but that was hard to do amid the insanity.

Despite the good feelings from our talking sessions with a sober Alex, Silver Hill's discharge report was blunt:

Primary: bipolar disorder [the first time I heard this diagnosis]; generalized anxiety disorder; opioid dependence; alcohol dependence; cannabis abuse.

Mood disorder due to general medical condition, partial seizures, epilepsy, hypothyroidism, low testosterone (likely secondary to opiate use)

Today, patient downplays this [drinking problem], makes little mention of his alcohol use and even says he aspires to "moderate drinking" and shuns AA and its message of abstinence.

Pt began using oral opiates, with progression to heroin over the past two years. He has been using benzos as well, Xanax preferred. He says he is not a daily user, but also admits that he has strong cravings and once he decides he wants to use "nothing can stop me."

The report described him as "neat/clean," but his attitude was "calm, evasive," his affect "anxious," and his judgment "impaired with poor insight." Other adjectives included in the report were "sullen," "resistant," "manipulative," "hypoactive," and "flat." He had "constricted range" and his behavior was "appropriate just barely since parents present." The report concluded: "24yo man in early contemplation stage [i.e., he is aware of his problem, seriously thinking about overcoming it, but has made no commitment to do so], still imagining he can use addictive substances moderately. He is disdainful of AA and abstinence and sees himself as primarily anxious and in need of the right medication. [His] [outpatient treater] notes that pt is brittle and hypersensitive to criticism, negative attention, etc. and is anxious/panicky in group settings."

Alex was discharged with buprenorphine/naloxone sublingual film (aka Suboxone), gabapentin (aka Neurontin, an anticonvulsant), levetiracetam (aka Keppra, used to treat epilepsy), liothyronine (for hypothyroidism), paroxetine (an antidepressant), propranolol (a beta blocker), and quetiapine (aka Seroquel). I worried then (as always) that the seizures and other symptoms he was experiencing (even though Silver Hill medical personnel doubted he even had them) came in part from the drugs he was taking, or interactions among them. He did try at several points in his life to wean himself off these drugs. He, too, tired of being a chemistry experiment. He continued to take quetiapine, to help him sleep, but nonetheless continued to suffer from severe insomnia.

As we left Silver Hill, we knew from Alex that he had a contentious relationship with some of the staff. When I received his records, I learned much more. Despite his early hopes that he would find recovery support at a facility that catered to "people like him," Silver Hill proved no better than any of his previous rehabs—and in some respects failed him more than the others by falling down on their promises and marching in lockstep with the blame-the-user philosophy that undergirds the 12-step method. Silver Hill's hefty price tag did not translate into progress, let alone success. When asked to complete a final survey, he refused: "You don't want to hear what I have to say," he told them. He felt the eating disorders doctor understood him, and her written notes suggest as much. Once he began to clash with his social worker and psychiatrist one week into the program, however, his progress stalled. We had visited him several times, and listened to his complaints, but felt he needed to address these issues himself as part of the therapeutic process. I doubt our intervention would have helped. Their records reflect a mindset toward Alex that was entrenched in the 12-step ideology from the start. While admittedly Alex was no doubt difficult (as I am sure is commonly the case), they were trained professionals who promised treatment but quickly resorted to blaming him, labeling him, and then writing him off. Alex was bitterly disappointed with Silver Hill.

As I read Silver Hill's records, it became obvious to this nonexpert that he should have been assigned a new social worker. Their relationship was contentious—on both sides—and they were immediately at loggerheads. His progress stalled only one week into the program. The medical staff charged with caring for his mental and physical health early on labeled him an "especially needy, drug-seeking liar, a sociopath, a psychopath, inauthentic," but without any documented basis except their disbelief about what he told them. He said he was anxious, but they didn't believe he looked "overtly anxious." It is no surprise that the psychiatrist's early view that "he may not be able to gain very much from this program" became a self-fulfilling prophesy. He never got beyond their labels. I remember his indignation when he told me by phone that they called him a sociopath. I remain shocked that a psychiatrist would use such labels in therapy, but those labels nonetheless stuck—both in Alex's head and the minds of the staff—for his remaining time at Silver Hill.

As Alex traveled down the second road to anorexia and substance use, he did learn to lie: he sought drugs through legal and illegal means. I, too, knew that angry and belligerent young man. But that's not all he was, and those actions don't add up to sociopathy or psychopathy. In fact, I learned that the *Diagnostic and Statistical Manual of Mental Disorders, Fifth Edition* doesn't even use these terms as diagnoses; they have been abandoned as outmoded terms. Today doctors instead diagnose such people as having an "antisocial personality disorder," which does seem more descriptive of Alex's behavior.[4]

In the 1970s Canadian psychologist Robert Hare created a Psychopathy Checklist, but the descriptors for this diagnosis do not sound anything like Alex prior to his substance use, or the person we knew him to be underneath: a sensitive, empathic, loving young man.[5] How is it that medical personnel at a psychiatric hospital would glibly throw around such terms, and not understand the effects of labeling? Alex was hurting and looking for a way out. For him that path was not the 12-step way, just as it is not for so many others. All that aside, the problem was even more basic—how could Silver Hill ever reasonably believe they could produce recovery in thirty days? Within a week it became patently obvious their program would not achieve immediate results. How do they get away with blaming Alex and writing him off?

We drove home on August 26, and the next day Alex began a new outpatient program at UBHC, which included medication management and individual and group therapy. He completed yet another intake interview, which contained nothing new. It made little difference, because on what would have been Day 2, he fell into drug use once again. In the morning, I was sitting in my office and saw him walking toward town. I jumped in the car, and slowly followed him as he headed to the train station, stopping first at the liquor store. I watched from the station parking lot as he waited for the train, trying to decide whether to try to stop him. Even if I were physically able to deter him, I realized it wouldn't make any difference. If it wasn't that day, it would be the next. I watched him get on the northbound train, presuming he was going to Newark for drugs. That day I called UBHC to cancel his attendance at the outpatient program. I knew he wasn't going back.

That night, a local police officer we had known for years brought more unwelcome news. Artie grew up in Metuchen, was a local basketball star, and played in college. He worked briefly on Wall St. before deciding to apply to the police academy. After finishing he returned to town as a police officer. He knew Alex through Little League, though his own children were closer in age to Hunter and Ginny. Artie had known Hal, and over the years he and Chip had formed a strong connection. Artie also kept in touch with Alex.

I was asleep when I heard Chip's phone vibrating. Artie wanted to stop by to talk with us, never good news coming from a police officer, let alone in the middle of the night. I let Chip sleep and went downstairs to get the news. He told me that Alex had been arrested while breaking into unlocked cars behind a local business, stealing loose change. This time Artie felt he had no alternative but to send him to the Middlesex County Jail. Alex's chances to avoid jail had run out. When I interviewed Artie for this book he said, "I thought that this might be the best course for him at that time." I remember him telling me that night he knew several young men who had turned their lives around after a few nights in jail. I wanted to believe that could happen with Alex, but I knew it wouldn't. I knew this would yield a particularly bad outcome. Artie went on to say: "I don't think that you wanted [him to be sent to jail] that night. And I think that I was trying to say, 'Look, he's going to be somewhere where maybe he can have a few days clean.' And maybe it'll change his mind. I don't know. I was just looking for answers. Maybe one thing that would resonate with him that would change the course. And obviously it didn't change the course. But I was looking for answers just like you guys were, and I felt horrible about it."

I asked Artie whether he still, all these years later, thought that jail was the best solution for Alex:

No. I think there's more options nowadays, that they're trying to understand [this] better. . . . And I don't know that they'll ever nail it, because we see all the ODs. And now we're carrying Narcan. And it's just an epidemic.

I think that Alex was a brilliant kid. When you watched him, when you spoke to him, he was so smart, so witty. People wanted to be around him. He was charismatic. I don't know what would have changed the course. I don't think, now I look back, I don't know that that was the right thing that night.

But maybe I saved him from scoring that night and getting something bad. That's how I look at it, and that's how I kind of digest it for myself. Because when you have families like yours, who have been through some tragedies in the past with Hal, and before that, with his wife. . . . How do I explain to you why I think this is the best thing for your kid?

Though Artie didn't know it, Alex later told us that he had already bought Xanax, and as they put him in the back of the police car, he swallowed every last pill rather than allow them to confiscate them. When he arrived at the jail, he was totally out of it.

During our interview, Artie and I had a long conversation about what police departments could do in response to the overdose epidemic. I spoke to him about harm reduction approaches, which were strategies he hadn't heard about. I appreciate that officers like Artie are looking for alternatives to jail for people who use drugs (PWUD). When we spoke in 2021, he estimated that about five or six young people in Metuchen had died from overdoses since Alex. And if you expand the age range to include twenty-five- to forty-year-olds, he said, the number was probably closer to twenty. I appreciate Artie's willingness to "think outside the box," as he described it, and hope other officers and police departments begin to consider and advocate for approaches other than jail for all drug users, especially the young ones.

The charges Alex faced were significantly more serious than the possession charges from his June 26 arrest. At first, we told Alex to get a public defender, again trying to learn "consequences." But it became quickly apparent that he (and we) needed someone who would manage all the charges and court appearances. It was overwhelming. So once again we hired Al. We talked with Al on September 11 and learned that Alex was facing two counts of burglary and credit card theft, felony charges that would be brought before a grand jury for indictment, with the likelihood that he would be indicted. At first, Al told us that until the case was resolved Alex would remain in jail and that the process could take three to four months. He said one possibility post-indictment would be to request a five-year probation with assignment to drug court. But, he explained, that process could take up to nine to ten months and screwing up in drug court would immediately lead to state prison. When we spoke with Al the next day, we found out that Alex was eligible for bail, for $15,000. We were not prepared to pay it at that time, still thinking along the same "tough love" lines that Artie later expressed to me.

The psychiatric and medical evaluations I later received from Middlesex County Jail describe Alex's stay, beginning August 28. The nurse who first met him on intake described him as "very weak and drowsy during intake, unable to follow up with questions, stated he took some drugs but cannot remember the drugs and that he was diagnosed [with] depression and has been to different hospital (psyche) but can't remember their names. Refer to psyche doctor for evaluation and also inmate not consistent with his answers." The intake mental health screening and assessment noted that he required routine follow-up for mental health issues and that he was likely "withdrawing from substance abuse." They "approved him for the general population with a routine mental health referral" and "medical monitoring for potential withdrawal." They noted that he seemed disoriented, flat, depressed, had slurred speech, and was unable to sit still. The Xanax he took in the police car was kicking in big time. The jail continued him on meds, including gabapentin, hydroxyzine (aka Vistaril, an antihistamine), propranolol, levetiracetam, chlordiazepoxide (aka Librium, a benzodiazepine), and thiamine (vitamin B1).

According to the jail's documents, Alex found the next few days traumatizing. On September 2, he reported he had a seizure and was taken to medical for "seizure precautions." He had a "right side hematoma and lateral-face redness and eye bruising." On September 4, he was medically cleared. The psychiatrist who treated him recorded in his September 2 progress notes:

> [Inmate] reportedly stated he had a seizure but cellmate denied seeing it. Reportedly he got up, blacked out and hit head and then knocked on door to tell COS [correctional officers] what happened. Cellmate reported to custody that [inmate] was banging his head and trying to get down here to access medications. Cellmate also reported [inmate] has been "kicking drugs and acting crazy." . . . There are contrary reports re: events. [Inmate] had been med-seeking earlier today. His mother had also called and reported [his] MH hx [mental health history] and recent suicide attempt in June 2014 [and described his] current mental status and recent events. . . . He will be placed on HiVis [high visibility] psych. Observe and reassess.

The next day, the jail psychiatrist reported Alex saying, "I told a lie yesterday—I feel like I am getting threats here. 23-hour lockdown scares me." The psychiatrist added: "Says he wants to move out of N-pod [the inmate pods were labeled alphabetically]. Says he lied by saying he had a seizure and hit his head on a toilet. Says he is scared to be in jail. . . . 'if my parents see bruises on me, maybe they will bail me out.' Says he is desperate. Speaks in a dull, flat, monotone voice." Later that evening, the psychiatrist noted that Alex said "he was put on thyroid medicine in Rehab. He has a fear of taking it because he feels it may make him fat."

When we finally talked with Alex, he was frantic. When he realized that we weren't going to bail him out, he argued that "things were going to be different, he had learned his lesson, he never would have entered the cars if he was in his right mind." He claimed that he didn't even realize he was in jail until he woke up the next morning. Then the daily phone calls from jail started. We learned that inmates can't just call collect from jail. Everything is privatized now that capitalism has arrived at the county jail. We were directed to set up a prepaid phone account at GTL Inmate Phones. Over the next three weeks, we paid $200, in $25 increments billed to our credit card, to talk with him. We twice sent him books to read, and they had to be newly purchased books from Amazon. We put money into his commissary account and paid $100 for the privilege of setting up the account—more privatized jailing.

Alex visibly deteriorated over the course of the three weeks he spent in jail. His baseline weight on admission on August 28 was 150 pounds, already slim for his six-foot frame. By September 4, he was down to 134, a loss of sixteen pounds in seven days. He reported that they kept him in his cell twenty-three hours a day, not allowing him to mix with the general population, likely "for his own safety" the police told us. At one point, we didn't hear from him for several days. He reported he had been in solitary confinement. We visited him twice, through a video hookup. It wasn't like in the movies or TV. We didn't get to hug him, or even see him clearly. He was in a different part of the jail, and we could barely hear him with other families conversing around us. He looked worse when we saw him the second time, and we could tell his physical and mental health was deteriorating. On September 16, we agreed to bail him out, writing out a check to the state of New Jersey for $15,000. All told, he was in Middlesex County Jail from August 28 to September 18. That money was eventually returned to us, but not until Alex died, a high price indeed.

Alex worked with Al to apply for pretrial intervention (PTI). Two months before he died, Al informed him via a March 16, 2015, letter that he had been accepted for PTI, for which he would be enrolled for thirty-six months, on condition that he: (1) remain enrolled in substance abuse treatment until medically discharged; (2) submit to random urine monitoring; and (3) obtain and maintain lawful employment.

Alex died before he could enroll. Reading these conditions now is ironic. While the first two are certainly appropriate, the last—finding lawful employment—is simply wishful thinking. Once substance use took over his life, Alex spent years looking for jobs, mostly unsuccessfully. And after these arrests, he knew it would be that much harder and probably impossible. I know from the criminal justice literature that "checking the box" dooms most work applications.

Alex continued to move down the second road, as he tried several more rehabs, none of which proved successful. He was stressed to the breaking point, and we were trying anything we thought (hoped) might work. After being released from jail on September 18, Alex returned to UBHC's full-day outpatient program—rehab #6. According to written notes I made at the time, the presiding doctor told me, "You should have kept him in jail, he's not ready. He admitted Xanax. His way was not working, and he was belligerent." We were seeing that belligerent Alex at home every day, and it was clear that UBHC was not working. On October 5, UBHC transported him to Social Services in New Brunswick to apply for Medicaid benefits. He didn't get home until 8 P.M., having ended up at Robert Wood Johnson University Hospital (RWJUH)'s psych unit for part of the day. He told UBHC staff the next day that "he got bored at social services, so he got drunk"—so Social Services staff sent him to RWJUH. UBHC kicked him out of the program on October 17, telling us (again) that they could not help him and that he needed an inpatient program.

Alex was then accepted into Princeton House's inpatient facility (rehab #7). He arrived Monday, October 20, but was there for only four days. On intake, he was found to be positive for cocaine and opiates. The facility's records state that Alex said he had used crack cocaine the previous Friday. Then, on his second day in rehab, the staff diagnosed him with mumps. I had noticed his swollen glands when we dropped him off but wasn't sure what to make of it. I thought at the time that he looked weird. Alex noticed it too and told staff: "I don't know why my face is swelling up like this. It hurts to touch and feels really hot." I found the lab results stating a "positive" mumps diagnosis in the medical paperwork, with the notation: "Results suggest response to immunization or prior exposure to the virus." Online descriptions through the Mayo Clinic Laboratories are consistent with that notation, suggesting that " individuals testing positive are considered immune to the mumps virus."[6]

A registered nurse confirmed with me at the time that Alex had had the measles, mumps, rubella (MMR) vaccine when he was a child; nevertheless, and for reasons unknown, the staff instituted a mumps protocol. As noted in the medical paperwork: "VSS [Vital signs stable] bilateral swollen painful parotid gland. No testicular pain. Per parents received mmr. Nursing supervisor advised." Even erring on the side of caution, the staff did the worst possible thing for Alex, isolating him and requiring he remain in his room, even during mealtimes. When he left his room, he was required to wear a mask. He was alone, unable to interact with other patients or even use the patient phone. Chip and I were allowed to visit if we wore masks and gloves, but for no more than thirty minutes. At that point, he was none too happy with either of us, describing me to the intake staff as "boring," and his relationship with Chip as "rocky, he doesn't really like me anymore." He reported that we were threatening to kick him out, describing himself as having "control over myself but I feel like I don't have control about things outside of me." And always his unwavering belief: "I want to stop doing drugs, I don't want to stop drinking altogether. I just want to reset my mind and stop thinking about alcohol all the time."

On October 24, Princeton House administratively discharged Alex for "non-compliance": not wearing a mask and twice inviting a female peer into his room. He readily admitted it: "I'm so bored out of my mind. I'm sorry for what I did." He didn't play by their rules. Indeed, he didn't play by anyone's rules. As I learned from the ear, nose, and throat (ENT) physician I took him to several weeks later, he never had mumps. The ENT diagnosed the real explanation for the enlarged parotid glands: bulimic purging.

I looked for another program that might accept Alex, and again tried an outpatient program. On November 18, I drove him three days each week to Keyport, New Jersey, for a program run by Endeavor House called New Life Counseling (rehab #8). Keyport is an interesting little Jersey town, which I explored while waiting for Alex to finish his program. I walked around to see the sights, took my book to read at the local library, and bought fresh fish for dinner. As I later learned, Alex was meeting other patients who introduced him to yet more drug suppliers. .

Alex refused to sign a consent form for us to be involved in his treatment at New Life Counseling. At that time we were not aware of what he was telling the staff, or what his treatment there comprised. After receiving his records, I learned Alex was still reporting seizures. Although I had seen one seizure, he was never diagnosed with a seizure disorder. Curiously, he denied ever having been in jail. He saw "unemployment, lack of direction in his life, and living under his parents' roof as his main sources of stress." The intake staff identified his strengths as "capacity for analytic thinking, good expressive language and communication skills, good physical health, and patient has a college degree." The intake interview summary, excerpted below, reveals Alex seemingly going through the motions of retelling his story—this time leaving out his history of anorexia, but continuing to identify the deaths of family members as the reason for his coping difficulties:

> Client's affect during the interview was bland. . . . The client shared that he has felt aimless and perhaps a bit unmotivated since his graduation from college. Client has lacked direction since college and he feels that this lack of direction and motivation precipitated his drug problems. Client spoke about a series of deaths in his family that he has had difficulty coping with or accepting. He believes his inability to cope with these deaths has caused him to intensify his drug use. Client also reports that he has Generalized Anxiety Disorder, Social Anxiety, Panic Disorder and shared that he does not like to talk about his feelings rather he usually bottles them up and attempts to cope with them alone. . . . The client has an understanding of his problems and the consequences but lacks a clear understanding of how to alleviate the causes. Client feels a tremendous amount of pressure from his parents to

succeed in his life, as they are professionals with extensive formal educations.

It wasn't clear to us at the time that he was feeling pressure from us to succeed. But he clearly believed that I was "overly involved in all aspects of his life and thinks that he would benefit more from treatment by excluding [us]." He reported a paternal family history of alcoholism and claimed to feel triggered by Chip's drinking. He told intake that he "accidently found where his father hides alcohol at home," which he confronted him about. Chip remembers that incident: Alex had broken into an old safe looking for liquor that Chip had locked away. We threw away the safe.

During his four weeks at Endeavor's New Life Counseling, Alex managed to find a job as a server at Benihana restaurant, which he promptly lost when he stayed after his first shift to drink at the invitation of his boss (who knew Alex had a problem with alcohol when he hired him). In addition to going to Endeavor three days a week, he continued to see Dr. O on a regular basis and twice during that time met with a new psychiatrist. On December 17, his twenty-fifth birthday, Alex turned to drugs yet again, and Endeavor "therapeutically discharged" him from IOP.

On the Road, Scene 6: 25th Birthday, and More NJ Rehabs
Dec. 17, 2014: Twenty-fifth birthday, heroin overdose at home.
Dec. 17–19, 2014: JFK Hospital, Edison, NJ; developed pneumonia.
Dec. 27, 2014–Jan. 16, 2015: Discovery Institute, NJ (rehab #9); kicked out for heroin use.
Jan. 16–28, 2015: Endeavor House North, Kearney, NJ (rehab #10).
Jan. 28–Feb. 4, 2015: Endeavor House South, Keyport, NJ.
Feb. 4–18, 2015: Endeavor House, Cliffwood, NJ.
Feb. 18–Mar. 3, 2015: Oxford House (South), NJ, sober house; kicked out for relapse.
Mar. 3–9, 2015: Sunrise Detox, Toms River, NJ.

By Alex's twenty-fifth birthday, we felt helpless, and at a total loss. The next five months were a blur of detoxes, rehabs, and sober living houses, in both New Jersey and Florida. Living with a loved one with substance use and mental health issues is like being on a carousel ride from hell. Again and again, we'd repeat the only strategies we knew: rehab, release, overdose, Narcan, detox, rehab research, rehab, guarded hope for the future, overdose, repeat. It was all so repetitious, and obviously wrong-headed. But there was nothing else, no other options. We saw no alternatives. All of us, especially Alex, wanted off that carousel, but round and round we went, over and over again. We began increasingly to recognize that death might be the only way that carousel ride would end. That looming realization didn't keep us from hoping against hope that someone or something would reach Alex, to help him turn his life around.

That birthday morning—December 17, 2014—Alex shot up several bags of heroin. His door was locked, but when we awoke we could hear his labored breathing. We used our skeleton key to open his door. He was unresponsive, with grey mucous coming out of his nose and mouth. I'll never forget the sound of his breathing. I was sure he was brain dead. Later, when I looked at his phone messages, I saw that he had told a friend he wished we'd found him several hours later. But he didn't die that day. Narcan worked its magic yet again, the paramedics resuscitated him and took him to JFK. He ended up staying until December 19 because he developed pneumonia. Hospitals were never safe places for Alex. Reflecting the stereotypes about substance use, nurses and doctors regularly lectured him about his "life choices." I would have preferred more caring from medical personnel, and less lecturing. But I recognize those feelings; we too were beyond frustrated with Alex's actions. Unlike the doctors and nurses, however, we knew it wasn't just a matter of "choice," and our Alex was still in there, somewhere.

After his discharge Alex begged to be allowed to stay home for Christmas. We agreed, but I used the time to look for a new rehab. Christmas with the three kids was a subdued affair that year. Once I knew that he was scheduled to enter a new rehab on December 27, I slept in his room the night of December 26, until he fell asleep and then in the living room to listen for him. I didn't want him to run away. The next day we took him to rehab #9—the Discovery Institute, where it was more of the same. He suffered from "post-acute withdrawal symptoms during his first few days of treatment, and once they subsided client appeared to still have a flat affect and somber mood, reporting he still had anxious symptoms." Alex made little to no progress clinically during his three weeks there and was vocal about disliking the place: "The client stat[es] that he does not 'like the facility' or 'feel it is productive being in rehab again.'" On January 16, Discovery kicked him out: "On [Alex's] 13th day of treatment he was suspected of using drugs or alcohol. When given the opportunity to admit to using or taking place in any other negative behaviors the client denied. The client had visible symptoms of being high such as dilated pupils, slurred speech, flat affect, and appeared to be 'nodding out.' At a later time the client admitted to using and did not seem to express any remorse for his actions. [We] decided to administratively discharge the client on this date."

On January 16 we picked up Alex at Discovery Institute and drove him directly to another Endeavor House program—this one in Kearney, New Jersey (rehab #10). This time Alex consented to have us involved in the program. He cycled through Endeavor House's three integrated programs, spending January 16–28 at Endeavor North (Kearney), January 28–February 4 at Endeavor South (Keyport), and February 4–18 at Endeavor House Cliffwood. This time, he made progress. When he arrived at Kearney, he narrated his same history and admitted using heroin at Discovery, for one and a half to two weeks. The intake summary assessed Alex's relapse potential as "high, [but he] does not see this as a major problem in his life."

When Alex reached Endeavor South, a clinician reported: "He is having a lot of panic attacks, last was 45 minutes ago, reports heart racing, sweating 'feels like I am about to have a heart attack.' [On February 4] reports that he has been happier while he is here but could not describe what was making it easier to be here. Despite being happy, client reports that he is ready to move on from here and start his life." We visited him often and participated in parent-client meetings. On the day he entered Endeavor South, his list of prescriptions included levetiracetam, quetiapine, hydroxyzine, trazodone (an antidepressant), and the muscle relaxant cyclobenzaprine, in addition to several nonprescription medicines.

I wrote in my journal about driving to Cliffwood to take Alex to lunch. He wanted to get his hair cut, and color his grey, something he was sensitive about. But what I really remember about that visit was a conversation we had while driving to lunch. Reflecting on how well he was doing at Endeavor, I suggested he and I write a book on recovery together. To do so, I told him, we needed a "happy ending." He seemed open to the possibility. But, of course, it never happened, and I was left to write "our" book alone.

While Alex was at Cliffwood, we helped him search for an Oxford sober living house. He had several interviews, and moved into a house in Beachwood, New Jersey, on February 18. We paid $550 to get him set up, a $250 deposit and two weeks of rent. Chip helped him move in, brought his bicycle so he'd have some mobility, and visited him several times. When we talked, he reported that he rode his bicycle for hours each day looking for entry-level service jobs, but nothing panned out.

Ominously, Alex called me one night to say he just couldn't do it any longer. He could not live this sober life we wanted so much for him. Nothing I said gave him any solace. As I hung up, I knew it was just a matter of days, if not hours, until he turned to drugs once again. When he did his housemates took him to Sunrise Detox in Toms River, which he entered voluntarily at 2 A.M. March 3. Alex told the intake staff that he had relapsed the "day he discharged from Endeavor House and entered Oxford House." They reported that he "tested positive for drug screen" and admitted to "using the entire time at the Oxford House." He "was asked to leave and suggested to go to detox." He reported that his last use of IV heroin was March 2, and described himself as "homeless."

Alex's sense of hopelessness, and the inability of the recovery system to help him, is manifest in the Sunrise Q&A intake form:

What worked from previous treatment? Nothing works. Every time I leave a treatment facility I use that day.

What did not work from previous treatment? Coupling with females, bringing drugs into the facilities.

How long did the patient stay sober/abstinent after completing treatment? None, possibly a day or two.

Evaluation of relapse history/patterns: Patient goes to the liquor store directly after leaving treatment.

202 DESCENT INTO INSANITY

How does Lee [Alex's given name] pay for his drugs/alcohol? Boosting [shoplifting], stealing from friends and family [and selling on the black market].

What precipitating events lead to Lee's relapse (i.e. triggers)? Patient reported boredom and loneliness. Patient reported the urge to use does not go away.

Does Lee appear to be concerned about his drinking/drug use? Yes. Patient reported he wishes he could use without consequences.

Lee level of motivation for treatment appears to be? Low.

The Sunrise records state that he was authorized for the following medicines: quetiapine, diazepam (aka Valium), trazodone, gabapentin, hydroxyzine, buprenorphine/naloxone, Augmentin (an antibiotic), and the antihypertensive clonidine. A nutritionist described him as "thin and undernourished."

The Sunrise counselors encouraged Alex to go to a rehab in Florida and told him that the rehab would pay his way there. We wanted him to move to the Caron Foundation in Pennsylvania, but I couldn't convince the insurance company to pay for it. The same time Blue Cross/ Blue Shield was saying no to Caron, it said yes to a Florida rehab. From a treatment perspective this made no sense. Caron is a well-respected dual diagnosis program, which would have kept Alex closer to home, enabling us to visit during his treatment. From an insurer's perspective, however, one rehab is the same as the next, and Florida's are cheaper.

On the Road, Scene 7: Back to Florida, and the End of the Road
Mar. 9–14, 2015: Gardens of Lake Worth, FL (rehab #11).
Mar. 16, 2015: Wandering the streets of West Palm Beach, FL, area; met Joaquin.
Mar. 16, 2015: The Shores, Port St. Lucie, FL (refused entry, back on streets).
Mar. 16–17, 2015: Beaten up on the streets and taken to Lawnwood Regional Hospital, Fort Pierce, FL.
Mar. 17–Apr. 16, 2015: Joaquin arranged pickup, back to The Shores, Port St. Lucie, FL (rehab #12).

Apr. 17–18, 2015: Pathways to Recovery, Boca Raton, FL (sober living house).

Apr. 19–24, 2015: U Turn, Delray Beach, FL (sober living house).

Apr. 25–26, 2015: Redemption, Delray Beach, FL (sober living house).

Apr. 27–30, 2015: Away and Means, Delray Beach, FL (sober living house).

Apr. 29, 2015: Accepted to College Recovery, New Brunswick, NJ.

Apr. 30, 2015: Dr. G's Urgent Care, Delray Beach, FL: prescriptions for 90 Xanax and 30 Ambien.

Apr. 30, 2015: Delray Medical Center, Delray Beach, FL.

May 1, 2015: Flight back to Newark, NJ; met the plane, and pickup by College Recovery.

May 1–6, 2015: Serenity Detox, Union, NJ.

May 6, 2015: Refused entry to Footprints to Recovery rehab, Hamilton, NJ; train to Newark.

May 11, 2015: Official date of death.

May 12, 2015: Newark police officers arrived.

By March 9, 2015, two months before Alex died, we were back on that carousel ride from hell. On the recommendation of Sunrise Detox, Alex moved to a rehab in Florida. Because he was an adult, we had no say in the matter, except to provide our insurance information. Gardens of Lake Worth paid his way there. I'm surprised Alex even agreed to more treatment; he was fed up with the 12-step recovery process by this time.

On March 9, he arrived at Gardens of Lake Worth rehab (rehab #11), a sister program to Advanced Health and Education in New Jersey, the very first rehab Alex attended. The intake picture was terrible, his deterioration obvious. This time he lied on his intake interview. He denied having an eating disorder, any history of suicide attempts, or suicidal ideation. He signed for us to receive confidential information. The initial psychiatric evaluation reported:

25 year old white male with a history of addiction presents with a relapse onto heroin. He was living at the Oxford House in NJ and relapsed after 2 weeks there. He was struggling with severe anxiety, esp. social anxiety, and was miserable going to all the meetings. He was using several bags a day for over a week. He was caught with a urine test. He still has bad

heroin cravings. His anxiety is very high. . . . He noted a good response to Suboxone. . . . Very scared and passive behavior; anxious, fearful affect. . . . Vegetative signs: dysphoria, anhedonia, hopelessness, helplessness, anergia, preoccupation, decreased concentration, decreased sleep.

All those descriptors well describe Alex's decline. I had to look up what some meant, and they are horrifying: dysphoria is a generalized dissatisfaction with life, anergia is an abnormal lack of energy, and anhedonia is the inability to feel pleasure. Even before I understood their meaning, I knew he was circling the drain, and that there was little we could do to halt the decline. Heartbreakingly, he described us as providing "no familial support." The staff reported that he was only marginally involved in group activities.

Within five days of arrival, Garden's clinical director called to let us know that Alex had walked out with two other guys. He had no wallet or ID, which were still in the rehab's safe. He spent several days on the streets of West Palm Beach. We had no idea where he was. His discharge evaluation reported:

Client left AMA 3/14/15; client is at high risk for relapse and continued use; against staff advise; unknown where discharged to since AMA; instructions: reenter a treatment facility as soon as possible.

The client has consistently failed to meet treatment objectives and further progress is not likely to occur, despite persistent therapeutic efforts and treatment plan revisions. . . . The client is experiencing a worsening of drug-seeking behaviors such as craving or return to regular use of psychoactive substances despite continued interventions, to such an extent that he/she requires treatment in a more intensive level of care.

Alex had a few guardian angels during his time using substances. One of them was Joaquin. On March 16, two days after he left Gardens of Lake Worth, I received a phone call from Joaquin, who had Alex with him. Earlier that day, Joaquin had been headed to a work meeting at the Panera Bread in Boynton Beach, just a mile or so from where Poo lives. When I interviewed him, he remembered Alex as soon as I mentioned the Boynton Beach Panera: "[My colleagues and I] pull up to the Panera and there Alex and someone else was there. They were in full-on nodding off mode. They were apparently very high, and slouched in the seat with their suitcases. . . . I walked up and I said, 'Hey man, are you okay? Do you need any help? What can I do to help?' And he says, 'Well I just came out of this treatment center, and I need help.' And I said, . . . 'It just so happens that I help people get to treatment.'"

Joaquin was working with The Shores treatment center, among others, to help direct substance users to treatment. The Shores records identified him as the one who referred Alex. When Joaquin met Alex, he brought him back to his office to call me. I don't know how he reached Alex. Perhaps living on the streets for several days pushed Alex to recognize that he needed more security, not to mention adequate housing and food. Joaquin convinced him to go back into treatment. I have no idea whether Joaquin received any payment for this referral, but I presume he did. Patient brokering is rampant in the rehab industry. Recently Florida has cracked down on it. In an online search I later found that Joaquin was arrested in 2017 for illegal sale of insurance and violating Florida's patient brokering law. When I contacted him again to ask about that report, he told me that the arrest originated in 2007 for his previous car accident business. He was convicted and put on probation. Since then, he has established several new businesses.

But when Joaquin called me that day, I was simply a desperate mom, and I didn't care whether he was earning a referral fee. I was only happy that he convinced Alex to return to treatment. Joaquin called The Shores, a rehab an hour north of Boynton Beach, and staff members came down to drive Alex to Port St. Lucie. Joaquin described the director there as a mentor and the rehab as "a very, very strong treatment center that really focused in on the spiritual piece that I know that a lot of places don't really hone into."

I knew Joaquin was a character. He's typical of many who work in the addictions field, in that he is in long-term recovery himself and previously had spent time in rehabs and jail:

I'm someone who has been in recovery now for a long time. I battled with addiction ever since I was thirteen years old. . . . I was in my third treatment center when I was fourteen.... I understand how difficult it is to get clean. Eight years ago, when I got sober, I knew that the only way that I was going to maintain sobriety was ... to rely on service [giving back].

Yeah, I had a couple of different types of addictions. In my teens, I went into a treatment center for crack cocaine when I was thirteen. Then later, when I got out of there, out of that treatment center that I was in for ten months, I immediately relapsed and got into the designer-type of drugs, club drugs and all of that. Then of course I went back into drinking and cocaine pretty heavy.

I got sober for about three years in Alcoholics Anonymous, then I had a relapse.... I came into Alcoholics Anonymous when I was twenty-four. I left around the age of twenty-eight, and then used for six years after that, then I got sober. And I've been sober for the past eight years now.

Joaquin is a big fan of 12-step programs—the community aspect of the program worked well for him:

The community factor is a big one. Especially when you're considering basic life skills, building relationships and communication. And the fellowship is something that you can live such an awesome life in the fellowship of alcoholics and narcotics in these fellowships. And sometimes going back into the rat race, per se, you kind of don't get to enjoy that early beginning. I think the book about Alcoholics Anonymous describes it really well when it talks about it's kind of like the feeling of being rescued from a shipwreck. Where comradery and everybody is high-fiving, and we made it, and we've gotten through this. That feeling is very present in a good sober home. [But in] a bad [sober home] you have no chance of getting better, because everybody is getting high and the management and everything is rotten, and all they can think about is money.

Joaquin's story illustrates what our local police officer Artie had hoped for Alex:

I thank God for the police who stopped me and put me in jail. And when I went to jail, I had what a lot of people describe as the "white light experience." And it's not like it really happened that way. I didn't realize that I had a white light experience until way into the recovery process.

What had happened [was] that I went into jail, and as soon as you get to jail they always ask you, "What are you here for?" And the guy I was going to be rooming with for the next couple months asked me, "Why are you here? What did you do?" And my honest answer to him was, "Man, I'm an alcoholic." That was the reason I was there is because I was an alcoholic. Yes, I got the DUI, two in a row. . . . He said, "You're kidding. I've been sober by the grace of God for eleven years thanks to the 12 steps of Alcoholics Anonymous. I'm here for a suspended license."

As Joaquin described it, it was at that point that he dedicated himself to a life of sobriety, service, and therapy. That was his aha moment, his "white light experience"—an image others in AA have described. After a second DUI, his bond was revoked. In addition to his own strength and resilience, however, Joaquin was also very lucky to meet up with a compassionate judge when he faced five years in prison for his second DUI:

And I had a judge who to this day I go to her courtroom and thank her on my anniversary every year. I have pictures with her every single year. She's the mental health judge. I don't know why, I don't know how . . . I ended up in her courtroom, but with a mental health judge they have more compassion, I guess. There's more sympathy for you. I had just had my little white light experience, I came out of jail, I had a courtroom full of people from church. I had people . . . because I'm not a bad guy either, you know what I mean? I had people there. And my wife was pregnant at the time.

I said, "Your honor, listen. I need help. I need real help. And if you give me help, I'll be able to help other people." And she said, "Okay, I'm going to put you in treatment." So that's how I got the treatment. . . . Something else that I've learned is that compassion and empathy go a very long way. Right?

I wish Alex could have spent more time with Joaquin and wish he could have met more people like him in his rehab experiences. Joaquin was more consequential in his short time interacting with Alex than many doctors and therapists who treated him over the years. Joaquin may speak the 12-step language, but his actions are harm reduction in action. He recognizes the larger, systemic factors holding back PWUD, and he knows to "meet people where they are at." When Poo called him to let him know that Alex had died, Joaquin was devastated.

Thanks to Joaquin's intervention, on March 16 Alex was driven to The Shores in Port St. Lucie, Florida (rehab #12). Even then, however, he initially refused entry, ending up back on the streets. That night he was beaten during an assault on U.S. Highway 1. Fire Rescue brought him to Lawnwood Regional Medical Center in Fort Pierce, Florida, which reported:

> Patient is 25-year-old male who presents to the ER today complaining of pain to neck, face, nose, head and right elbows following alleged assault. Unknown loss of consciousness. Patient is alert and oriented at this time. Denies any chest pain, shortness of breath, nausea, vomiting or abdominal pain.... [A CT scan of the brain found] no evidence of acute intracranial process; [a CT scan of the cervical spine without contrast] found no acute fracture or dislocation; [a CT scan of facial bones without contrast] found no evidence of acute osseous abnormality...[Primary diagnosis:] head injury; [secondary diagnosis:] abrasions, contusion.

Alex reported to the Fire Rescue unit that he had been beaten up and robbed. The paramedics who treated him noted that he "was found to have previous injuries from another altercation a couple days ago." After The Shores called to alert me that Alex had refused treatment, I began to call around to hospitals in the area, including Lawnwood. No one would confirm that Alex was there. I appealed to those I spoke with as a mother fearful about her child, but Health Insurance Portability and Accountability Act (HIPAA) regulations meant that no clerical or medical staff member would speak with me, a mom looking for answers about my missing son. I described the scenario I worried most about, that he would be unconscious without an ID. It was only when the hospital submitted insurance claims that I learned he had been at Lawnwood all along.

Several days on the street, multiple beatings, and another night in a hospital finally convinced Alex to try institutionalized rehab living yet again. He called Joaquin, and on March 17 staff from The Shores came to pick him up. This time, Alex agreed to stay. The Shores staff described him as "cooperative, appeared to be very dirty due to living on the streets, physically beaten as evidence by bruises and wounds on face and slightly disheveled." This comment broke my heart. I can't imagine him dirty and disheveled; he was always so fastidious about cleanliness and his appearance.

The Shores' records contain both positive and negative descriptions of Alex's time there, noting that "client [was] well received by peers and staff." Alex told them he had "never had much clean time after rehab. But am planning my future now. Using and what I want from life is not compatible." By April 6, he reported that "he has no complaints. Said he saw his family. His family is happy with him right now. Trying to get his parents to ok his after plan which is to finish his master's degree." At the same time, his counselor was worried: "His speech was articulate, his judgment poor, and he had poor insight into his addiction and denial of illness. His affect was flat, and he's very guarded and resistant, and he's experiencing an elevated level of anxiety and feelings of hopelessness. Risk for relapse: extremely high. He doubted that he can stay sober and wasn't sure that he wants to stay sober."

Alex consented to our communicating with his counselor, who reported his concerns to me. I tried to be optimistic, but I wasn't. On March 19, he told his counselor that he had "been stressing about talking to his parents. Dad is mad at him but knows that his dad is coming from a good place and really worries about him. Something is keeping him alive for a reason. He has a purpose." He described his relationship with me as "strained because of drugs, sober, safe, will be loving and ask for help." With Chip, he reported that their relationship was "strained, drinks, safe in moderation, will love from a distance."

Poo and her daughter Sara visited Alex several times during the month he was at The Shores. Poo took pictures of them eating oysters, walking on the beach, and enjoying each other's company. He looked good, albeit too thin. I talked regularly with his counselor, providing him with as much information as I could. I was never a big fan of rehabs, but there are clearly dedicated people in the recovery community. We were impressed with several people over Alex's rehab years, and those at The Shores were more successful than most in reaching him. Poo told us that Alex quit smoking while he was there, a habit he began after starting drug use. All those addicted, it seems, smoke—it's another addictive behavior that's also self-medicating. Breaking that habit was good news.

Most importantly, Alex was starting to think about his future. At The Shores he developed a "three-year plan" that entailed coming back to New Jersey and re-entering his Rutgers graduate program. He did this all on his own, reporting it to us as a work in progress. He re-applied to the Rutgers program, was accepted, and began to call around to inquire about sober living environments. He reached out to Rutgers Alcohol and Drug Assistance Program (ADAP), a nationally known program for students with alcohol and drug problems. Because he needed more clean time to be eligible, ADAP put him in touch with College Recovery in New Brunswick. We checked out the program and facilities and were impressed. He would live in a terrific apartment complex one block from the Rutgers campus. We toured the facilities on April 29, and I took a picture of the apartment and sent it to Alex. They had a linked IOP program, a fitness facility, nutritional counseling, and a strict drug and alcohol monitoring policy.

At College Recovery there was a community, one that could support him while he was in school. Alex was accepted and planned to move there and start summer school in late May. Everything was set. The three-year plan was put in motion, and he was ready once again to transition onto the first road. Alex asked me whether I knew how expensive it would be, and I assured him that we were on this road with him and were willing to pay what was necessary to keep him on it. Insurance would have picked up most of the cost, so we understood, but our contribution would still have been over $2,000 each month—the cost of a mortgage for many people—for at least a year. But, finally, he had worked to set up a long-term program, and we hoped it would provide him the support he needed. And, best of all, he seemed hopeful, for the first time in a very long while.

But then Alex made a critical mistake. On April 17, a month after he entered The Shores, Alex headed to halfway houses in Delray Beach. Joaquin had warned him against these places, calling them "body snatchers." We implored Alex to come back to New Jersey, in preparation for his new sober living housing and summer classes. But he wanted to spend a few weeks down in Florida before heading back to classes. He called it the "recovery capital of the world," but we knew it better as a community of addiction and relapse. There were dealers everywhere, hanging outside halfway houses and 12-step meetings. For the next two weeks, he cycled through four houses, Pathways to Recovery, U Turn, Redemption, and finally Away and Means. He was in and out so fast, I didn't even bother to write them for paperwork. Each house was connected to IOPs, and he spent several days at their clinics, with charges made to our insurance. The last halfway house—Away and Means—asked me to send them $250 to supplement our insurance, and when I said no, they kicked him out. In a 2019 article, Jeremy Roebuck reported on one Philly rehab owner (thirty-one-year-old Joseph Lubowitz) who received kickbacks for providing referrals to recovery facilities in Delray Beach, Florida (Real Life Recovery and Halfway There sober living home, run by Eric Snyder). Roebuck described how the fraud worked:

> [Real Life Recovery] offered patients free airfare, rent, and other perks while ignoring rampant drug use and using clients "like cattle" for their urine samples, submitted for frequent, pricey, and unnecessary drug tests. Patients were subjected to urine testing as often as four times a week, each costing their insurance company as much as $9,000. One woman was tested 11 times in about a month, with results showing continued drug use. In all, the facilities billed her insurance more than $488,000 for urine testing and other services. . . . Patients' urine was the "liquid gold" used to earn the scheme's illegal gains.[7]

These predatory recovery facilities target young people like Alex. And as we know all too well, many of them don't survive.

After cycling through four sober houses, on the morning of April 30 Alex was back on the streets. I learned about Alex's last days in Florida from Liz, a young woman Alex met at his last sober house. Knowing that he was back on the streets, I tried to call him several times. Later that day, Liz called me and said that Alex had gone to Dr. G's, an urgent care facility in Delray Beach, for prescription drugs, and then next door to buy alcohol. The records I received from Dr. G's office were brief, as brief I suspect as the time the doctor spent with Alex:

Current meds: Xanax, Ambien. Past medical history: anxiety disorder, insomnia, depression. . . . General examination: in no acute distress, well developed, well nourished (no other issues noted). Psych: alert, oriented, good eye contact, normal. Denies fainting. Assessments: ADHD; insomnia, anxiety. Occupation: medical researcher. He responded "no" to "Do you Smoke?" "occasionally" to "Do you drink," and "never" to "Do you use drugs?"

After that minimal evaluation, the doctor prescribed: "Start Xanax Tablet, 1 mg, 1 tablet, Orally, Three times a day, 30 days; 90 tablets. Start Ambien Tablet, 10 mg, 1 tablet at bedtime as needed, Orally. Once a day, 30 days, 30 Tablets."

What doctor, especially a doctor in Delray Beach, would give someone right off the street ninety Xanax and thirty Ambien? It's like dropping a recovering alcoholic on Bourbon Street during Mardi Gras.

I learned much more from Liz. She described how they met, and what happened that April 30: "He was actually in the sober house before I got there. . . . Alex and I just started talking. . . . I just started hanging out with him. We would go to the meeting, because it was mandatory meetings, and I would just stay in the room with him when we were at the house. And, we started doing drugs together there at the house." She learned quickly that he was purging: "And then, as I started staying with Alex more frequently, I also learned that he was bulimic. . . . When I first got to the sober house he made a bunch of pancakes, and ate them all, and then went to the bathroom. I was like, 'Well, we all have issues.' So, I was like, 'Well, maybe this is one of his issues that he's trying to deal with.'"

I asked what she found appealing about Alex: "Just himself. He was the smartest individual I had ever met. Very kind, down to earth, caring. And unfortunately, in the drug world, you don't really find anybody like Alex. We didn't know each other very long, and I hate to say it, but we kind of met and then rushed into things. We were kind of living with each other right off the bat because we were in the sober house and they didn't really seem to care about anything." When I expressed surprise that they permitted relationships, Liz said:

With the sober houses, . . . some of them just collect money and then let you do whatever you want. So, that was one of them. But, from the time that I got there until the situation happened where I had to call his aunt [on April 30], we were together 24/7. . . . He was so intelligent. For me, a lot of people that I had hung out with and befriended down in South Florida who were addicted to drugs portrayed themselves in a totally different manner. Very self-centered, selfish, angry. And Alex was the complete opposite. Very kind and loving, didn't really seem to have any malice towards anybody, any hard feelings. You could tell he was sad. He was just a sad individual. But, at least with me and everybody else that was there, he treated all of us with respect. Always was asking everybody if they needed anything.

Liz reported that she and Alex used drugs together the entire time they were at Away and Means. She said that Alex purchased drugs from people outside the house. When I expressed surprise that he had any money, Liz reported, "He had money. I don't know . . . who sent it to him, on a few different occasions; one of the times he went down to get. . . . Someone wire transferred him money." Except for a $100 deposit we put into his account on April 23 for food, we had stopped giving Alex any money months earlier, because we knew all too well where it would go.

Liz was with Alex the day he went to Dr. G's and received his prescription for the boatload of Xanax and Ambien. That morning, April 30, 2015, they learned that they were both being kicked out of Away and Means for drug use. Alex decided to head to a walk-in clinic a mile down the road. Liz continues the narrative:

So, we left and walked down to the walk-in clinic. They gave it to him pretty quickly. He was in and out within twenty-five minutes and right next door was a pharmacy, so he filled the prescription. And of course, I was still getting high from crack cocaine. And, he filled the prescription and he took almost the whole bottle. Also, there was a package store in the same plaza, so he got a small bottle, like a pint, of alcohol and he was drinking that as well.

And we were just sitting in the parking lot of that plaza. . . . He was so disoriented. He would stumble behind the dumpster of the plaza, and it seemed like he would pass out. It was more than nodding out, but not enough to pass out. . . . He was very disoriented. Didn't know what I was saying. He tried to run away, but he couldn't really function enough to run away. So, I ended up calling an ambulance, and then I called the number for his aunt that was in the phone, and that was over. . . . We sat there while he was doing the Xanax and drinking the alcohol for probably three hours. So, this was an all-day occurrence.

Liz was another guardian angel for Alex. She went on Alex's phone, and began texting with Poo, and then called me as well. Liz had been talking with Alex about Poo and knew that she lived close by. She stayed with Alex until the ambulance picked him up and saw Poo pulling into the parking lot as she left. Her brief relationship with Alex was instrumental in Liz's exit from both Florida and the drug life. By the time she gave up drugs, she had lost fifteen of her friends to overdoses. Liz saw sober houses charge insurance millions of dollars for things that never happened. She described what others call the "Florida shuffle," where you'd go to detox, then rehab, then to a sober house where you'd get high again, and then start all over again. She left for home the very next day:

South Florida just wasn't for me. I didn't want to sit in a parking lot all day, and get high, and do nothing. To be completely honest, I think that incident with Alex pushed me to get sober. Seeing how Alex was this incredibly intelligent kid, and life really was nothing. So, it kind of just pushed me to go home and be with my family. . . . Yeah, I also didn't want my family to go through what you guys went through with Alex. And I just felt like I was . . . I didn't want to live that life anymore. I didn't want to wander around the streets doing nothing.

In my interview, Liz told me that, once she arrived home, she entered methadone treatment, and began to work with a counselor who believed in her. By then, she wanted a "normal life." After six years on drugs, and ten rehabs, she finally began to work with her family to get sober. She has remained sober and is now a mother, has a good job, got her Bachelor of Science degree, and is enrolled in a master's program.

Poo sent me her texts with Liz, which began at about 5:30 P.M. on April 30. Liz told her that they likely took Alex to the Delray Medical Center, so Poo headed there where she found Alex incoherent and delirious. Luckily, they let her into Alex's room as he recuperated, and she stayed with him the entire night. In the meantime, she was on the phone with us, and we were booking a plane back to New Jersey for him the next day.

The records I received from Delray Medical Center described Alex as arriving at 5:28 P.M. on April 30 in an "altered level of consciousness" and "too intoxicated" to sign the health forms. Alex had sixty-five alprazolam (Xanax) and ten zolpidem (Ambien) in his possession, meaning that he had likely already swallowed twenty-five of the ninety Xanax and twenty of the thirty Ambien he had received just a few hours earlier. At 9 P.M., he asked his nurse for additional Xanax and Ambien, but understandably was denied. At midnight, the nurse on duty gave his meds to Poo. By 2 A.M., the nurse described him as steadier on his feet, and starting to make more sense when talking. By 7:28 A.M., he was "in no apparent distress . . . no deficits noted. Level of consciousness is awake, alert, oriented to person, place, time, gait is steady." He was discharged at 7:29 A.M. on May 1.

Poo was able to provide a more detailed description of Alex's time at Delray Medical Center, and it wasn't always pretty. The Delray medical staff must deal with overdoses daily, and one can understand how weary and jaded they must be. Poo took notes about Alex's actions that night, as well as his and her interactions with the doctors and nurses who cared for him. Five hours after he arrived, Alex was still asleep. He would wake up occasionally but remained incoherent. When he awoke at 2 A.M., he began staggering around and was hungry. He wanted his meds, which of course they had taken away.

Poo continued the story: "[He ate one sandwich] and then he asked for another sandwich, then I'm sure he hadn't eaten in a long time. Then the last nurse that came in, she was really pissed, and she said to me, 'This isn't a restaurant.' [I responded,] 'Well, you know he's sick and he was hungry.' She brought a sandwich and some graham crackers and milk. And she said, 'That's it, as soon as we clear him as able, he's out of here, we want this bed for somebody who needs it.'" At 2:40 A.M., Alex was asleep, and the nurse asked Poo to come outside and said, "We want him to leave." At 3:50 A.M., another nurse stated, "I'm tired of being his babysitter. I will not give him more food."

All in all, Alex ate three sandwiches. Poo argued with the hospital staff that he was impaired and needed to stay in the hospital. The nurses wanted to make him medically stable and release him—with the legal drugs he brought in. Instead, Poo was there to remind them that this was someone's son, and that he had a flight to New Jersey the next day. After talking with Poo and then us, the doctor finally agreed to keep him for the rest of the night. We were thankful for that. Poo got rid of the drugs, and when Alex found out he was furious. They were legally prescribed, after all. But Poo did the right thing, saving Alex from himself.

When they finally discharged him, Poo first drove to his last sober house to get his belongings, and then to her home where he took a shower. Because they had time before his flight, she took him to Brooklyn Bagel for breakfast: "He ate like he hadn't eaten in a year, and he got, he never told you this, he got a huge iced coffee and, you know what, those places like Starbucks, where they have the syrup pump? He walked over to the pump station, and he stood there, and he kept pumping syrup. I mean, to the point that it was just disgusting." As she drove him to the airport, Alex said, "Pull over, I'm going to be sick." They pulled over on the side of I-95, and Alex "just puked his guts out."

At the West Palm Beach airport, Poo talked with the airport staff about trying to keep Alex from ordering drinks on the plane. The pilot, who was wary of letting him on the plane, said they would try to monitor his drinking. She waited until he boarded the plane:

> He didn't want me anywhere near him. He was full-blown angry, and he couldn't get away fast enough. . . . He really just gave me the silent treatment. He wouldn't talk to me, and he kept trying to get away from me. He was one of the last ones to get [on the plane]. He wouldn't hug me, then he wouldn't talk to me, just walked to the gate, to the ticket agent person at the jetway. . . . [And then] he turned around and from a distance from where I was standing, he just whispered, "I love you." He turned around and he left.

Alex loved Poo, and as he walked away toward the plane, a bit of that love and his humanity returned. We regretted the trauma he put her through, but she treasures that signal of his love for her. The real Alex was in there somewhere.

I decided to meet Alex's plane at 1:58 P.M. that May 1, and I'm glad I did. The United staff allowed me to go to the gate when I alerted them to the circumstances. He was starving, so I bought him a sandwich. He ate the meat and threw away the roll. He was close to emaciated, his pants nearly falling off. As I walked him toward baggage claim, where he was to meet the College Recovery staff member, I could tell he was impaired. Because of his drug intake the previous day, and likely alcohol consumption on the plane, College Recovery insisted he go again to a detox and then rehab. He was upset, anxious to start his three-year plan. I wish I could say we had a meaningful conversation, but it was rather mundane, organizing for his next steps. I gave him a hug goodbye, said I love you, and then he was off to Serenity Detox in Union, New Jersey. I always worried when he left that I would never see him again, but this time it was true.

The Serenity paperwork assessed Alex's current state. He admitted using heroin the previous day, along with cocaine. On intake, he tested positive for benzodiazepine (Xanax):

> Client was alert and oriented during the session.... [Client] appeared flat and hopeless as evidence of his saddened facial expressions and pessimistic outlook on the process.... [Client] reported no family history of mental illness or addiction ... reported not being happy or finding anything that could make him happy throughout his life until he used heroin.... [Client is] in the pre contemplation stage of change and although he has suffered numerous consequences (loss of family support, loss of motivation, legal involvement, inability to find and maintain a job) client does not see his using as a problem. Client has limited insight into the recovery process and has not engaged in treatment to follow any treatment. Client has a college degree and is currently looking to complete Master's courses. Client has no family support and cannot return home after treatment.

The clinical session notes from May 5, 2015, indicated "affect (flat); mood (hopelessness); cognitive (oriented); judgment and insight (poor judgment with no insight into the recovery process; behavior (appropriate). Client is at risk for relapse. Level of progress: no progress. Barriers: impulsivity, lack of sober support, poor engagement in treatment, difficulty managing distractions, non-compliance with treatment, limited insight, poor judgment."

I didn't learn until my interview with Alex's college friend Connor that he was working at Serenity Detox when Alex was there. Connor told me:

> I looked at the chart that morning and saw Clarke's picture. And I said, "Holy shit." So, I went to my manager and I said, "Listen, I know this guy . . ." It's like this was a very good friend of mine. . . . It was 7:00 A.M., so I went into his room, and I woke him up. And I said, "Hey man, how you doing? It's good to see you." . . . And I mean he was a model patient. He was quiet. He was clean. He went to every meeting. And there's two ways that can go. One of them is you really believe it, and you're fine. And the other one is "I'm not engaging. This is stupid. I'm just doing my time." Ready to get out.

Connor worked for three of the days Alex was at Serenity. Because he was working twelve-hour shifts at the time, he spent much of his downtime with Alex. Chip talked with Alex several days into his detox at Serenity and had a good conversation. I tried to call him the next day, but because of HIPAA rules, they would "neither confirm nor deny" Alex was there. They insisted on that stance even when I told them that Chip had talked with him the previous day. This was not the first time I was stymied by what I was told were HIPAA privacy rules, but it was the worst. Occasionally, people would break a small rule, and tell me something, but mostly these regulations hindered our ability to help Alex.

On Wednesday, May 6, Alex was due to be transferred from Serenity Detox to Footprints to Recovery, in Hamilton, New Jersey—step two on his road to College Recovery. A staff member from Footprints came to drive him there. Connor provided some information about that morning. He had been hitting golf balls at the public golf course across the street from Serenity. They were heading to a hot dog place after:

> I stopped at a 7-Eleven to go get cash . . . and directly next to me is Alex in shotgun, in somebody's car. So, what happened was, so I was immediately red alert. Like this is not good. . . . I knew he was supposed to leave. I said goodbye to him the day before. . . . And I was like, "What's going on, man?" And I was like, "Are you going now? Or are you going after you get one more shot? . . . Because that guy's [the driver's] pupils

are very small. He looks like he's f-cked up, what's going on dude?" And he was like, "No man, I'm going."

After getting money at 7-Eleven, Connor gave Alex his phone number, telling him, "This is my number, please call me . . . just call me." And Alex did call him, at 12:08 P.M., for a two-minute conversation, according to our phone records. Connor reported on their conversation: "He was very upset at how I acted. Yeah, he was like, 'You're supposed to be my friend,' this and that. And was very upset with me. . . . I was assuming he was going to get high and not on his way to treatment. Because I didn't know he was going to get picked up by someone in civilian clothes, in a Subaru." I said to Connor, "Not a good last conversation. Right? We all have those." He replied: "I've thought about that to this very day. . . . Yeah, I still think about it."

I interviewed Connor almost seven years after Alex died. Within a week of our interview, I was drawn to the sites Connor talked about. I sat in the same 7-Eleven's parking lot, and in the parking lot outside Serenity down the street, trying to reconstruct what it must have been like that day. I imagined Alex in that parking lot, and in that facility. Chip and I even got a bite to eat at the hot dog place Connor mentioned. We tried to imagine scenarios that would have led to a different outcome.

But that day back in 2015, we assumed all was going according to plan until we got a call around 6 P.M. from the College Recovery staff who were coordinating his transfer. Consistent with Connor's story, a tech from Footprints drove him down, but Alex refused to enter what would have been rehab #13. I called Footprints, and they reluctantly told me that he had asked them to take him to the train, and they had obliged. We knew he was headed back to Newark. His train would have gone right through Metuchen on his way there. We figured out his route by looking at his bank and phone records. While still in Florida, he had figured out how to get a $100 advance added to his debit card. Upon arriving in Newark, he headed directly to the Walgreens near the train station, looking for syringes no doubt. At approximately 4 P.M., he had three outgoing phone calls and one text to "Mimi," who was a drug dealer he had used in the past. I texted and called him repeatedly over the next few days:

May 6, 2015, 7:28 P.M.

Alex there is a warrant out for your arrest. If the police pick u up they will take u to jail in Newark.

May 6, 2015, 10:40 P.M.

Alex there is a warrant out for your arrest. If the police pick u up they will take u to jail in Newark.

May 7, 2015, 10:15 A.M.:

Alex, remember your 3-yr plan. Contact [staff person at College Recovery] to get back on track.

May 9, 2015, 11:37 A.M.

I'm going to police to file a missing persons report on you. If you get this please call me.

May 12, 2015, 8:16 A.M.

We got an announcement about your PTI. . . . You must appear in court with [Al] on May 20th to accept the PTI. Otherwise there will be another warrant for your arrest and the $15,000 bail we paid will be forfeited.

Alas, he never responded, and I don't know if he ever read my texts (the last one, of course, came after he died). The one thing Alex never let go of was his cell phone. Chip thought that meant that he was either in jail or dead. Beginning that Wednesday evening, his phone was off for several days, until Saturday morning, when it was powered on again for fifteen minutes. We guessed it was probably not him, but rather someone who either stole his phone or received it in trade for drugs. I walked to the Metuchen Police Station that Saturday and filed a missing person report. They began to check their connections in New Jersey and New York City. Nothing. On Sunday, May 10, Chip made us a Mother's Day dinner. Mostly we were terrified. He had never been gone that long. On Monday, Chip spent hours walking in and around the Newark train station, and the neighborhoods that bordered it. It was a desperate search, a last-ditch effort to find Alex. Alex would be found, but not by Chip.

We heard nothing more until Tuesday afternoon, May 12, when those two Newark law enforcement officers came to the house. After that moment we knew our lives had changed irrevocably. The certified time of death was approximately 10:30 A.M. Monday, May 11, which meant that he could have died earlier, perhaps even on Mother's Day, certainly before Chip was in Newark searching for him.

We had always hoped he could somehow dodge death, if we did enough, cared enough, loved enough. Nothing was enough. As I noted at the start of this book, we wanted to remember Alex living and breathing, so we didn't view his body. We lived in a small town, and the funeral director had been Alex's Little League coach, so he was able to confirm that it really was Alex. Nonetheless, I held out hope that he'd eventually return home. I would "see" him walking downtown. The finality of it was and is impossible to comprehend. Even today I marvel at how people—friends, neighbors, colleagues—go on with their daily lives when our lives were forever shattered that day in May. They walk around being normal. We just walk around.

The day after Alex died, we drove to Newark to meet again with the detective. We wanted to see if there was anything more to learn. Chip asked if they found a note, and she indicated they had, in his back pocket. The very existence of a note meant that they labeled Alex's death suicide, and assigned it to the Robbery and not the Homicide division. I took a picture of the note then. When they returned the note several weeks later, it was nearly impossible to read, with black splotches from the dusting they had done for fingerprints. But still it was clearly written to us, in his sloppy, but recognizable, penmanship:

Mom and Dad, . . . I am sorry I am taking the easy way out. But I can't deal with my life anymore. I'm tired of hurting you and going down this downward spiral. I will love you forever, Alex.

These sentiments rang true and were consistent with previous notes Alex had written to us over his years in addiction. He didn't feel he could do what was required to live a sober life. The rehab and hospital records consistently described him as hopeless, and highly likely to return to drugs. In his mind, Alex no longer had a reason to live. To our minds, this was always inexplicable.

The state bureaucracy lumbered on. The medical examiner reported on the official Certification of Death that Alex died "Approx 05/11/2015; Presumed 1039." He was found outdoors in an empty lot, in Newark. In

November 2015 I sent for a copy of the autopsy report, which was completed on May 12. It reported the "cause of death as acute heroin intoxication, and the manner of death suicide." The toxicology tested positive for alcohol, heroin, and nordiazepam (a benzodiazepine). Physically Alex's heart weighed only 357 grams, less than a pound. That was hard to believe: Alex's heart was so big, I expected it to weigh much more.

CHAPTER 11

Making Sense

> I don't really miss who he is at all. But who he was—I'm pretty
> sure I'm right about who he was, and I miss that person
> so much. And the person I thought that person would turn into,
> I miss him, too, with all my heart.
>
> —Carol, mom of incarcerated son Krishna, interviewed in
> Andrew Solomon, *Far from the Tree*

WHAT HAPPENED to my family? Like the mom Andrew Solomon interviewed, I miss my sweet son Alex, the delightfully funny, smart kid, and then young man he became, before mental health and substance use disorders stole his life away. And now, I'm really missing the person he could have become, the marriage he could have had, the family he could have raised—and our grandchildren. I miss the laughter, the sensitivity, the friendship. But I don't at all miss the angry, sullen, young man he was when he was in full-fledged addiction. Living with Alex during those years was hell.

Before Alex died, I spent nearly every spare moment finding treatment centers, rehabs, and sober living houses, and dealing with the crises that daily landed on our doorstep. After his death, I continued to ask how it was that we found ourselves in this terrible dead end. It mystified me how everything could have spiraled so terribly out of control despite our best efforts to save him. I started reading as much as I could. I gathered "data" from my journals, scrapbooks, and photo albums. I interviewed those who had known Alex before and during our seasons of hell. I read his writings and collected the records from the health care and rehab facilities that collectively became Alex's second home. To learn more about the experiences of others and the public policies surrounding drug use in the United States, I became involved in social communities, both personal (such as Naranon, grief groups) and policy-oriented (such as addiction groups). I quickly realized that I would do things differently if I were dealing with Alex's addictions today. Indeed, there are now other options that were not available to us then. I also learned that our current political, medical, and criminal justice institutions are still not up to the task. And, of course, what we experienced and what my reading has confirmed is that the self-proclaimed system of help for those with such disorders and their families is largely a Potemkin village.

In this chapter I revisit the three approaches I discussed in chapter 3, considering my experiences with Alex as he traversed the organizations responsible for treating and policing addiction. Another important lesson: Much as we wish we had control over our children's lives, they have their own paths. Ultimately, I wanted to better understand Alex's.

He Never Wavered

Most people, and most American institutions, view addiction as a voluntary "choice," evolving from individual "defects of character." This conventional wisdom undergirds how our society understands, treats, and polices addiction. Specifically, we have a treatment system based on the 12 steps of Alcoholics Anonymous (AA); a political sphere and criminal justice system focused on punitive remedies; an insurance system that discourages alternative treatments; and overall an integrated societal, governmental, and business system that fails to adequately monitor or hold providers accountable for their rates of failure or success. These, and popular media and culture, amplify the choice paradigm. That the 12 steps might work for some individuals is a weak endorsement for its monopolistic stranglehold on treatment options. I learned from living within the insanity of Alex's addictions that we need to think more broadly, to think outside the organizational boxes that have shaped our country's one-size-fits-all addiction treatment and policy to date. The singular focus of 12-step programs is on "choice"—that is, you can choose to use or choose not to use. There is no denying that choice is a piece of the puzzle, and so it was with Alex.

But it's never the whole story, and for many not even a major part of it. Let's begin by considering how Alex made sense of his addictions, and how he justified his search for legal and illegal drugs. It is draped in the language of his "choices," but I'll explain why in large measure they were anything but.

Alex was unwavering in his belief that he needed alcohol and drugs to soothe his anxieties, insecurities, and panic attacks. He insisted on this both to us and to everyone at his treatment facilities. He didn't believe in the 12 steps—at least half of which are about God, and Alex wasn't religious—he wanted to achieve control of his demons and compulsions in a way he could accept. And when he didn't get what he needed—when what was offered to him did not work—he self-medicated, in the last few years primarily with Xanax and heroin.

Certainly there are individuals—like Joaquin and Connor—for whom the 12 steps seem to have worked. I applaud their success. To try to understand why AA's methods work for some, I asked Connor for his take. His answer is consistent with what I've heard from AA advocates over the years. In March 2014, about a year after his graduation from Dickinson, Connor entered his first rehab—the Caron Foundation—for his heroin addiction. He soon fully embraced AA's precepts, which he continues to follow. He remains sober today. Although he is a strong advocate for the 12-step message, Connor knows he might be more the exception than the rule: only a few of the guys he met at Caron are still alive. In fact, he told me, the high failure rate was explicitly discussed in his 2014 therapy groups: "They were even saying it when I was there. They're like, 'Yeah, maybe two of you will be alive in five years.' . . . Those are the stakes. That's how serious this is." Connor explained why he was one of those who "chose" sobriety:

> For me, I came in and I was terrified. . . . I knew I was going to die if I didn't get clean. I knew that intimately and as such, I did everything I was told. I went through rehab. When I was taken out of the medical wing and finally able to join groups, I broke down immediately. I was scared and I was miserable and I didn't want to die for the first time in a long time . . . and that changed everything for me.
>
> If I had a belief in something and someone's like, no, you're wrong, I'd be like, well, what do you mean? Not just like well f-ck you, or no I'm not

or, okay you're right. And then not interrogate that thought further. I
wanted to know why and how I was wrong. I wanted to know how I could
learn the lesson that I was trying to be taught . . . so that I could not die.

Connor sounded much like Liz in his commitment to get and stay clean.
Why didn't it work for Alex? With Alex there were deeper roots, underlying mental health issues. If Connor and Liz had similar issues, they did
not share them with me. Even at twelve Alex lacked self-esteem; he knew
he was in pain, and in his mind restricting food helped him to control that
pain. He was already angry that we "ran his life," a theme that recurred
throughout his eating disorder and rehab experiences. In his rehab writings, he described the shame, embarrassment, and insecurity that followed his anorexia diagnosis. He felt he wasn't progressing emotionally or
socially the way he should. Despite academic, social, and sports successes,
his insecurities, body image issues, and resurgent panic attacks followed
him for the rest of his life. His self-medication, first through anorexia as a
preteen, then with drinking starting at age thirteen, and then to drugs in
high school and harder drugs in college, followed him as well. Drinking
and taking drugs were the behaviors that bolstered his self-esteem and
reduced his feelings of inadequacy.

As Alex grew older, he expressed that if he could get a job, he would be
fine. He repeatedly insisted that he could drink in "moderation" and live
a "normal" life. He saw that adults in his life drank and they did fine.
Why not him? He railed against us and the rehabs/hospitals he attended
when we questioned these assumptions. We knew he would have to
learn to control his drinking, something he had a hard time doing. He
mostly didn't like the rehabs/hospitals he attended, and the staff didn't
much like him either. He told them repeatedly that they weren't treating
his anxiety, and bristled when one psychiatrist told him he didn't appear
"overtly anxious." I suspect that if he had shown the requisite anxiety, it
would have been dismissed as so much fakery. How do you win in a situation like that? He wanted Xanax to treat his anxiety and resurgent panic
attacks, but rehabs and hospitals were not about to give him benzos.
Instead, steeped in the 12-step orthodoxy, the doctors and staff he
encountered repeatedly portrayed him as drug-seeking, resistant to AA
programs, and likely to fail. And at Silver Hill, they further labeled him a

sociopath and psychopath. Once his thirty days were over, all these medical facilities were happy to move him along to sober living houses or outpatient programs. Once there, as predicted, he returned to drugs, again and again. Did they discharge him after thirty days because he was anything like "well"? Not in the least. Simply, that's how long the insurance lasts, so that's how long they get. In this, as in so many other ways, it is the needs of the organizations that are served, not the needs of those in treatment.

As he cycled through the dozen outpatient and inpatient programs he attended, Alex's hopelessness, despair, isolation, and, ultimately, fatalism, grew. He didn't fear dying; he was resigned to it. He had already faced death and survived multiple overdoses. We heard that hopelessness when he was twelve and hospitalized in the eating disorder unit. He told me flat out that he hoped the eating disorder would kill him, so he wouldn't have to disappoint us: "If I weren't around, you wouldn't have to worry so much." He described dying as the "rational" thing. It didn't occur to him that our rational response to his death would be despair and depression.

That same hopelessness and despair re-appeared throughout his rehab experiences, perhaps most pronounced in his three suicide letters, which I've shared before but that are worth revisiting here. In the first, from February 2014, he stated, "I know I am acting selfish and self-centered by taking my own life, but I just can't go on like this. . . . I wake up every day hating my life, what I have become, and what I have done to you all." In the second, from June 27, 2014, his despair was searing: "I will preface this message by saying there is no good end in sight for me. I can't stand my life. Nothing seems to work out. And now with this on my record I literally have no hope of being successful." And, his third and final suicide letter from May 2015: "I am sorry I am taking the easy way out. But I can't deal with my life anymore. I'm tired of hurting you and going down this downward spiral. I will love you forever, Alex."

Breaking the Brain

As I searched for explanations, as a sociologist I knew that this singular focus on "choice" was too simplistic, too moralistic. The idea that Alex's brain was "broken" made more sense. This view is also inherently more compassionate, and it feels right to me that programs designed to help people who use drugs should be more empathic. The idea is that the brain is hijacked, and it's the drugs that are doing the hijacking. That first shot of heroin floods the brain with pleasure-providing dopamine, and it is on the hunt for that feeling thereafter. Addiction's negative consequences are, as researchers describe them, "total compulsions."[1] Brain imaging research supports this. Opiates and similarly addicting drugs reduce the ability of the prefrontal cortex to exert control, meaning that those who use substances eventually do so just to feel normal, not to derive pleasure. Drug use in the key years from around age twelve to twenty-five—when the brain is undergoing critically important developments—is especially destructive. In this view, those suffering from addiction deserve compassion, respect, and treatment, not punishment—clearly an improvement over a simple choice/defects-of-character argument.

From our vantage point, it sure looked as though heroin had taken over Alex's brain. The sweet, empathic, engaging Alex disappeared when he was high or trying to get high, replaced by a drug-seeker with a maniacal drive for Xanax and heroin. He lied, cheated, and stole to get more. It didn't matter where he was—in New Jersey, New York City, up and down the east coast of Florida, or even in our small central Jersey town—he always knew where to find his substances of choice and he knew how to get money to pay for them. He sold drugs to support his habit, a common occurrence among low-level drug users. We all have our networks and so it is with drug users. Heroin users seem able to find each other even if they've never met. Gone were his circle of neighborhood and school friends. He now mixed with a lot of unsavory characters, some with guns. He sometimes lived on the streets. He was beaten up several times, and ended up in the hospital.

I know what drugs did to him. Drugs did break his brain. But I also know that this explanation, too, only goes so far. How and why did he get to the point that he took that first hit of heroin? And, most importantly, beyond brain chemistry, what other factors pushed him to keep injecting heroin when he knew it was destroying his life? What was driving his insatiable search for legal and illegal drugs? The obvious answer is "to get more dopamine." If that were enough of an explanation, no one would ever stop searching and shooting, yet many do. Dopamine was an incomplete answer to my questions. I was looking for more.

We're Doing It All Wrong

If the answer to the mystery of what happened to my family was neither fully choice nor the result of broken brain compulsion, what was it? How did Alex reach that level of hopelessness, loneliness, and despair that led him to the end of the road? Why did he keep moving down that second road, when so many of his friends successfully traversed the first one, even those who themselves spent some time on their own second roads? Why could someone able to exert intense determination to learn to wakeboard in a day, to skateboard like a pro, to not eat and then to relearn to eat not move beyond substance use? I realized early on that to fully understand "why" we need to raise our gaze higher, to examine systemic factors outside of his and our control.

As I struggled to find answers during Alex's early addiction years, I came across the work of Maia Szalavitz and had my first aha moment. In an opinion article for the *New York Times*, she tells of how she became addicted: "I had told myself that I'd never try heroin because it sounded too perfect. It's like 'warm, buttery love,' a friend told me. When I did yield to temptation . . . that's what I experienced. It wasn't euphoria that hooked me. It was relief from my dread and anxiety, and a soothing sense that I was safe, nurtured and unconditionally loved."[2] Szalavitz's description is rooted in social science research. It finally helped me to make sense of Alex's substance use and mental health disorders. I began to see the reasons 12-step treatments work for some individuals, but only some. By better understanding the role of systemic factors driving substance use, we can more effectively shape addiction treatment remedies and policies for all. In my reading, I also learned that we need to better appreciate the history of addiction in the United States as well as borrow effective strategies to treat addiction developed in other countries. Why put on blinders to what doesn't work and turn a blind eye to what does? Why start from scratch when countries like Portugal and Canada have demonstrated track records in addressing addiction? That's a topic I return to in chapter 13.

We still don't know enough about addiction to explain it or make it go away. Lots of people are in pain and don't inject heroin into their arms. So the strategies we choose to use to combat addiction are paramount, and AA has long been the major player in that arena. 12-step programs are based on a set of beliefs from the 1930s, when Bill Wilson and Margaret "Marty" Mann jointly established AA, essentially a social community that revolutionized addiction treatment. Wilson was Mann's sponsor, and held his first AA meetings in his Brooklyn, New York house. Wilson provided his story for this fledgling organization, while Mann was the "brilliant strategist and a public relations genius" who worked with Wilson to advocate for alcoholics.[3] The AA model remains the core of addiction treatment today. In addition to its history, AA's primacy is bolstered by a network of social communities, treatment providers, insurance providers, policymakers, agencies (such as law enforcement and the judiciary), the media, and a multitude of other organizations. Alex's experiences gave me an insider's perspective on all those organizations.

Szalavitz disagrees with the broken brain theory and, based on her own experience, argues instead that addiction is a pattern of learned behavior: "Drugs can only be addictive in the context of set, setting, dose, dosing pattern, and numerous other personal, biological and cultural variables. . . . It only develops when vulnerable people interact with potentially addictive experiences at the wrong time, in the wrong places, and in the wrong pattern for them. It is a learning disorder because this combination of factors intersects to produce harmful and destructive behavior that is difficult to stop."[4] Viewed this way, substance use is best seen as a coping mechanism for pain, not as a character flaw or brain disease. Instead, pre-existing conditions or vulnerabilities such as psychological disorders (e.g., depression or anxiety) or socioeconomic factors (e.g., poverty, unemployment, incarceration, and racism) are the real precursors to addiction.

This explanation was the proverbial lightbulb turning on over my head. It put into words what I was seeing from my front-row seat to addiction, and it led me to like-minded social and behavioral scientists who have documented the insufficiency of the traditional U.S. treatment system, the failure of the punitive responses that are applied with near ubiquity against substance users, and the broken public policies. Searching for alternatives to choice-based, punitive strategies, I found more clarity and hope in "harm reduction," a recent and developing paradigm gaining adherents in the fight against addiction, a topic I address more fully in chapter 13.

One of the most compelling interviews I did after Alex died was with one of his therapists. We had known Dr. O for decades. For over twenty years, Chip had relied on Dr. O's wisdom, and once Alex began using drugs, both Chip and I spoke with him, singly and together. We suggested Alex meet separately with Dr. O, and he did so. As I learned, Alex opened to Dr. O, who described his diagnoses as

> generalized anxiety, that would be part of it. I think major depression, major depressive disorder. . . . When we look at eating disorders, it's like some people think that is kind of a borderline personality disorder. . . . I think an addictive personality disorder [that young] with alcohol. . . . There was always some substance in him that made him feel okay. That if he was doing the substance he could then operate.
>
> As he related it to me, early on in his life, he'd avoid anything he thought he may not be good at. That was really important to him. And not to be embarrassed by it among his peers, for him to feel good about himself. That's the way he managed. Don't do anything I won't feel good at doing, or competent. . . .
>
> Was there some kind of predisposition, or something developmental early on? And the eating disorder was when he was twelve or so? So, something was happening before puberty so that sort of began the course of living his life.

Dr. O described Alex as having to "quiet down the engine running inside of him in order to be social around his friends, in order to be at ease. . . . There was chatter in his head about what he had done wrong that day; he would never play a sport he couldn't do well (e.g., basketball vs. baseball). He worried about being laughed at, not being good enough terrified him. He was popular because he only tried things he knew he could do well. His constant refrain was "I need to control myself." Alex felt, Dr O. believed, he needed to control "that motor, that anxiety, that thing that then said to him 'I'm not coping well, I cannot cope well [as with anorexia], I know there are lots of control issues, and if I can control this, and I can control what is going on out there ...' Early on at twelve years old, and before that, he was seeking a way to be able to control himself in order to control the environment."

Dr. O also discussed Alex's inability to accept that he ultimately could not, however, control his self-medicating: "That is the self-deception, if you will—he thinks there is somehow he could self-medicate and do it in the right amount to make it work. And that's what got him in trouble, that fight he had in college where they knocked his tooth out.... He goes over the top and someone is not amused by it and socks him."

When I asked Dr. O whether he thought Alex died by suicide, he did not rule it out: "I don't know that he cared anymore. 'My well-being, my soul, and there's no future for me.' Everything I think he was saying to you, 'I don't have a future, I'll never be anything,' and that kind of lament, despair. I would use the word 'despair,' that's his message here. And so that I would imagine that at some point he was so low that he'd think he might kill himself." Dr. O was a compassionate clinician, and we were then (and still now) glad Alex had someone to confide in. He told us about one session during which Alex, like Szalavitz, described heroin as "blissful, not torture." Alex felt his life was tortured, and heroin was one of the things he used to take him away from that. He was a tortured soul and was looking for something to self-medicate with.

Dr. O described Alex as having insecurity at the very core of his being, which made him feel totally stuck. After anorexia, he never really made the transition from adolescence to adulthood. That observation, in fact, may point to one of the key factors at play for Alex. I remember sitting with Alex on the back porch one late night during his last year of life and his telling me that he felt like Peter Pan, never really growing up. I think he understood the truth of that description.

As I noted earlier in chapter 5, we had histories of alcoholism and mental health issues in our families, which likely contributed to Alex's susceptibility to drug-taking. Alex was also traumatized by the many deaths in our family that occurred the summer of 2012 when he graduated from college. Hal and Granny died that summer, and Kathy and Lexi even earlier. He verbalized his pain over these events with us, his friends, and the staff at multiple rehabs and hospitals over the years. At fourteen, he spoke at Kathy's service, in front of hundreds of people. But he could not bring himself to speak at Hal's or Granny's service. The difference is important, because he was a different person by the time Hal and Granny died. His social anxieties were resurfacing that year; at the same time, his career plans collapsed. While his friends were making progress, his inability to move ahead on his long-term career plans devastated him, exacerbating his hopelessness.

As he devolved into despair, his continued drug use meant that he ran afoul of the law. The DUI was bad (and expensive) enough, but he could have moved beyond that charge. Once he was accused of possession of illegal drugs and charged with breaking into a car, his situation became dire. He found himself in jail, and his insecurities, panic attacks, and self-medicating took over his life. In his eyes, that was when any possibility of future success faded away.

What about the rehabs and psychiatric hospitals charged with recovery? I searched for reputable programs that might provide Alex some hope, some way out of his loneliness and despair. They all failed. That isn't to say there weren't good people along the way. There clearly were, even in the 12-step programs Alex loved to hate. There were moments of progress, glimpses of the old Alex, and glimmers of hope. He produced insightful writing during his time at Ambrosia Treatment Center, however problematic that rehab was for him. His time at the three linked Endeavor programs successfully provided him encouragement to move on with his life. And he made progress at that last rehab, The Shores in Florida, where he took the initiative to re-apply to the Rutgers Professional Science master's program. Not only was he re-admitted, but through his own initiative he was accepted to an off-campus sober living program for college students right off campus, which could have supported a sober lifestyle.

But along with the better, there was the worse. It didn't matter if it was a big psychiatric hospital, or a small doctor's office, rehab, or detox, medical personnel and rehab staff failed him. Two weeks before he died, a doctor in Florida gave him ninety Xanax and thirty Ambien pills when he walked in off the streets. Maybe the doctor felt she was doing the right thing, keeping a user from doing illegal drugs. But even if strictly legal, those prescriptions were morally abhorrent. Given the Florida overdose epidemic, doctors in Delray Beach should know better. But it wasn't just Florida doctors. Many of the doctors and nurses who cared for Alex in ERs and rehabs in multiple states bought into the stigma of addiction, attributing his substance use to "choice," and negatively labelling him when he resisted their AA paradigm.

We too bought into the AA paradigm and myth of thirty-day recovery programs. How could we not? We were desperate and found nothing else. We always hoped that maybe this new program was "the one," that he'd meet the perfect therapist who'd help him move beyond his hopelessness. Instead, when their therapy failed, they passed him along to the next program or sober living house, which also didn't work. It worked well for the bottom line of the organizations involved, but much less so for the suffering individuals who needed help.

In the same December 2021 *New York Times* op-ed where Maia Szalavitz talks about heroin's "warm, buttery love," she points to what she sees as important social explanations for overdoses: "times of uncertainty and economic inequality" and "social disconnection and using alone."[5] This focus on isolation is important. From my vantage point, it's critical for understanding Alex's movement down the second road. Alex himself often mentioned his isolation and loss of friends during the years between his May 2012 college graduation and his death in May 2015. We saw it daily in the lack of friends coming to see him, especially once he started using heroin. As he got closer to the end of the road, most of his friends understandably kept their distance from his drug-taking behavior. His singular focus on alcohol and drugs left him increasingly isolated from the very social communities that might have provided links to a future without drugs.

Definitionally, isolation comes from loss of community. In one of the best studies in the field, Kai Erikson's *Everything in Its Path* demonstrates the massive social effects of the flood that devastated Buffalo Creek, West Virginia, on February 26, 1972. After the flood, "the community no longer surrounds people with a layer of insulation to protect them from a world of danger. There is no one to warn you if disaster strikes, no one to rescue you if you get caught up in it, no one to care for you if you are hurt, no one to mourn you if the worst comes to pass."[6] The friends I interviewed invariably brought up their lost social connection with Alex. They did so spontaneously during our interviews, and always with immense regret. At the time, it was too painful for them to watch the friend they loved deteriorate. They thought the "old Alex" was still in there, and being young, they expected that he'd grow up, snap out of it, kick the habit, and be back in their lives again. Some told me that they still wonder today if they could have made a differ-ence, and somehow prevented his death. What if they had invited him to their parties? What if they had come to see him more often during those last few months? I understand those feelings; it's what all of us who loved him felt (and continue to feel). What could any of us have done to make a difference? And the sad truth is that toward the end we didn't want to be around that Alex either. It was beyond sad to see Alex's need for heroin, to find syringes hidden all over the house. We loved Alex, and he loved us. There's no adequate description of the pain we felt watching our child circle the drain of death. We felt guilt, and help-lessness. Despite our efforts, we couldn't find out how best to help him. It was like there was a secret to which we'd never been given the key.

The answer, however, is not the individual actions of relatives and friends, although those too are important in ensuring continuing social communities. We need to operate on an entirely different level, address-ing factors that are more systemic and organizational in nature. We need to recognize, as C. Wright Mills argued, how our "personal trou-bles" are clearly linked to "public issues," and determine what to do about it.[7] Those are the tasks I turn to next.

RE-CREATING A LIFE

CHAPTER 12

Social Communities

I look the worst full in the face. What I see is frightening but enlightening. I believe that knowing a thing permits more comfort with that thing. Sometimes the comfort comes from greater control. Sometimes it comes from knowing the enemy, or the scary thing, which proffers a way forward, toward greater safety. There is horror in disaster. But there is much more, for we can use calamity to glean wisdom, to find hope.

Tragedy is with us now as never before. . . . We can learn a lot about how society works, and fails to work, by looking at the worst. We can learn about the imagination, about politics, and about the wielding of power. We can learn about people's capacities for despair and callousness, and for optimism and altruism. As we learn, our possibilities for improvement increase.

—Lee Clarke, *Worst Cases*

L ITTLE DID CHIP REALIZE when he wrote *Worst Cases* that we would soon be living our own worst case. Although neither of us could have predicted it, his words did propel me to "glean wisdom" and "find hope" from the personal disaster we still live through.

When Alex fell fully into addiction insanity in 2013, along with the all-consuming practical challenges of finding treatments, detoxes, rehabs, sober houses, and insurance coverage, I began an intellectual search for understanding. I would later describe this as my recovery. I started by reading the scholars and nonacademics writing about eating disorders, addiction, and resilience. After a while, I returned to my sociological roots and began to ask how the skills I developed as a researcher and teacher might help me answer the "why" and "how" questions in my own life. I explored studies about community and social integration to see how others address their own worst cases. I learned how researchers study stress, suicide and despair, mental health, grief, bereavement, and resilience, areas typically outside my own academic expertise. I learned a lot about stigma, and how the power of those who stereotype and stigmatize is more important for stigma's reproduction than the characteristics of those harmed. I read historical studies of opioid (and other drug) crises and studied policy research on addiction and the strategies designed to combat it. I learned about harm reduction, and what some U.S. states, such as Oregon and Vermont, and other countries, such as Portugal, are already doing to effectively combat the epidemic.

While intellectualizing my experiences was helpful, I soon realized I needed more than reading to help my recovery and find understanding. I needed to talk to people. And so, I began looking for communities of people to ease my grief, and, with this turn, not only did I make new friends and contacts, I broadened my social communities. This book presents my own story of living within the insanity of addiction. But my larger goal is for my story to make a positive addition to the growing moral community of action against addiction. This is not a "happy ending" book, but rather one that ends with hope and calls to action.

Online Communities

Early on in Alex's addiction journey, I searched for social community online. One of the first things I did was join online support groups of "addict's moms."[1] Online support groups connected me with moms who, more than anyone, understood my grief. I craved those connections. No one wants to be a member of these groups, but alas many of us find ourselves there. These groups were the brainchild of Barbara Theodosiou, a Florida mom who started "The Addict's Mom [TAM] Public Page" on Facebook in 2008 when she learned two of her four children suffered from addiction. She lost her son Daniel in March 2015, just two months before we lost Alex. She also started an offshoot group, "TAM Grieving Moms," for those whose children have died.

Reflecting the surging overdose epidemic, the numbers of moms joining these and similar groups is staggering. Many moms—too many—
share my pain. In 2015, when I first followed the TAM Public Page, it had
over 25,000 followers. When I last checked in 2023, over 197,000 people
followed it, and over 4,000 were members of TAM Grieving Moms. All
fifty states have TAM chapters. In 2016, the Obama administration
awarded Theodosiou the White House Champion of Change Award,
and she has since published a book that depicts her story, *Without
Shame.*[2]

In my TAM posts, I mostly wrote about the harm reduction strategies and the evidence-based research I was beginning to learn about. I
railed against criminal justice approaches. Some days, however, I just
posted articles about grief and resilience. On what would have been
Alex's twenty-seventh birthday, December 17, 2016, I published a tribute to him on TAM Grieving Moms and took my first steps toward
advocacy:

> Alex was born at 1:24 a.m. 27 years ago today. We lost him way too soon.
>
> Not a day goes by that I don't think about him. Typically, it's my first
> thought when I awake, sometimes it takes me until breakfast, or my
> shower, to remember. I fill my life with checklists, but the pain is there
> each and every day. Alex once told me that we'd be better off without
> him . . . he was wrong.
>
> I attach the picture I have on my phone, one I look at multiple times a
> day. It's one of my favorites. We got Lexi [our German shepherd] when
> Alex was in the hospital back in [seventh] grade. She helped Alex
> recover from his eating disorder, and Alex loved that dog fiercely. He
> sobbed with us when Lexi died five years ago this month.
>
> I am thankful to those who have been there for us. Thanks for not
> telling us that it's time to move on, thanks for not telling us that it's god's
> will. Our only option is to simply put one foot in front of the other, tak-
> ing one step at a time, integrating our sorrows into our lives. We have
> each other, and we have Hunter and Ginny. And we have our family and
> friends.
>
> I've been privileged to get to know other families over the last few
> years whose loved ones suffer with addiction, as well as other families

who have lost their child to addiction. There is a striking similarity about many of our lost children, their brilliance, their humor, and most of all their sensitivity, almost too sensitive for this world.

I'm fearful for what the future holds for those still struggling with addiction. The recovery system is broken. Please help me to be vigilant against those who promise walls and law and order. We need fewer jails, and more local police supporting diversion programs. We need a greater recognition of the addiction-mental health link. We need more focus on the demand side, and longer recovery programs that actually work.

We need the Affordable Care Act, which provides support for the most vulnerable among us, and we need to ensure insurance parity between medical/surgical vs. mental health services for those of us who do have insurance.

Without these, we risk a rupture in the very social bonds that make us human and keep us civilized.

Over time, I became more overtly political. In August 2016 I posted my thoughts about a low-level dealer who was being prosecuted for murder:

I'd love to hear what you all think of this. My heart goes out to Hernandez's family. But the further I've gone along in this process of addiction, recovery, and death, I've gone to a different place than Peggy Hernandez. I wonder how common my reaction is? I don't think there is one right or wrong attitude/behavior, I'm just saying I now think differently. At the beginning (in full addiction mode), we turned over all the evidence we could to the police. We blamed the dealers, and did whatever we could to try to stop them. I absolutely hated them and what they were doing to my son. But I eventually came to the realization that my son was going to find drugs in one way or the other, and he did, in multiple states, from rehabs, to sober living groups, to doctors, you name it, he found them. Shut down one low-level dealer, he'd find a new one. It's like whack-a-mole. For all I know, he could have re-sold drugs to other addicts, that's what addicts do to make money [I learned later that he did sell drugs]. Now that my son has died, I realize quite personally that the criminal justice approach to drugs has failed, and we need a more humane, less stigmatized, medical approach—one that focuses on demand, and not just supply. Was this dealer an addict too? He doesn't sound like he was very high on the supply chain. Yes, let's go after those making millions off our kids, let's go after the doctors making millions from over-prescribing addictive drugs. They deserve a life behind bars. And low-level dealers have to take responsibility too. But let's not assume that a criminal justice approach will save our kids. It hasn't worked thus far, and it's only gotten worse. Let's look for more humane methods that will help our kids get out of the addiction cycle, that will reduce their need for drugs. The recovery system is broken.

I wanted to know what others thought about my developing anti-punitive stance. The online responses were cordial. Some agreed with me, while others argued for long prison sentences.

As I turned toward advocacy, I largely moved on from TAM and similar sites. I remain thankful that they exist, and especially that they were there for me when I needed them the most. They gave me the opportunity to begin to write about addiction, and to hone my political beliefs.

12-Step and Grief Groups

When Alex began actively using in 2013, I joined Nar-Anon, the 12-step program for family members connected to Narcotics Anonymous (NA). After trying out several groups, I found one that was right for me. Like Alex, Chip had never been enamored with the 12 steps. He went to a few family meetings with me, but never went back. He did, however, attend multiple 12-step programs with Alex over the years, taking him whenever and wherever Alex could find a meeting, whether it be Alcoholics Anonymous (AA), NA, Cocaine Anonymous, or Smart Recovery. I was thankful for that. Chip told me later that Alex preferred AA over NA, because there was "always a heroin dealer at NA."

Although I too had difficulties with the 12-step approach, I was able to find a Nar-Anon community that sustained me. Once I found my group, I went every week. I was very nervous the first night. I could tell that everyone knew each other and were happy to be there. The group's facilitator came up to welcome me. We all sat around in a circle in comfy chairs and couches; typically there were twenty or so of us. I didn't speak much that first meeting, until the end when I talked about Alex.

Everyone was interested in hearing my story but didn't push me to talk. Just as the Nar-Anon literature assures, I quickly felt a part of the group, and connected with several attendees. Being "in the rooms" with others who understood what I was going through was soothing.

Taking turns, we read "The Twelve Steps of the Nar-Anon Family Groups" and "The Twelve Traditions of Nar-Anon." I did feel "powerless over the addict" and "that our lives had become unmanageable" (step 1). I was uncertain about many of the other steps. I wasn't sure a "power greater than [me] could restore [me] to sanity" or that I had "defects of character." By then, I had mostly lost the religious connections to my Catholic childhood and didn't buy into any organized religion. Nevertheless, I found comfort in the weekly repetition of the same readings from the little blue book, *Nar-Anon Family Groups*. Every week, the same words, the same ideas, somehow proved soothing, giving me respite from the trauma I was dealing with at home. For me, as for many, my "higher power" was the group itself.

During the years I attended, the people I met in Nar-Anon kept me sane. And while many of the steps didn't speak to me, step 12 always did: "Having had a spiritual awakening as a result of these steps, we tried to carry this message to others . . ." One thing I always felt strongly about was the need to alert other families to the dangers of addiction, and to use my experiences to help others.

When Alex died in May 2015, I took a break from Nar-Anon, but in mid-July I returned. Chip was visiting family in Florida, and I needed human connection. In my journal I described how I got what I needed from the meeting: "It was so good to feel the love and warmth. You just feel totally accepted, no need to explain. . . . I feel at peace around them." At an October meeting, I gained insight into why that group gave me such peace. The topic was "no longer alone." I spoke a lot, unusual for me. Several men in the group spoke as well, talking about what the group meant to them. It struck me this was one of the reasons I liked this group—the men actually opened up. I wished Chip had been there. I wanted him to feel the same community. I was beginning to realize how differently we responded to our grief. As I saw it then, Chip had decided to go it alone. When we discussed it later, he instead described it as a preference for privacy. He certainly talked with friends, family, and Dr. O, but he was reluctant to talk in group settings. He already "knew" their story—he was living it. Why should he tell them of his own misery, guilt, and sense of ruin? In contrast, I was out there looking for a community of those who understood my grief and would talk with me about it.

We each took turns leading the meetings. One evening in December, close to Alex's birthday, and seven months after losing him, I agreed to facilitate. My role was different than before, when I had been one of the parents whose child was still in the throes of addiction. I felt like a visitor from a different reality. All Nar-Anon family members fear losing their loved one; the potential is always in one's consciousness. That evening I wanted to show I had survived, that I was dealing with my complicated grief and moving through the pain. I still have the notes I wrote up for the meeting. The topic I chose was "Memories/Remembering." I read several paragraphs from the eulogy I gave at Alex's "Celebration of Life." I talked about our good memories, how Alex was the kind of kid parents brag about on social media. I also spoke about the terrible day the police officers came to our door, and how recovery systems are failing our loved ones. I made an argument for an activist community. I talked about how Chip and I were on those two roads with Alex, and we were now navigating a new road on our own.

I also spoke about step 12, and how I was struggling with how best to carry the message to others, and what my role should be after Alex's death. I felt it was my job to provide "reports from the front." I asked for volunteers to read three of the most compelling daily readings in *Sharing Experience Strength and Hope*: on "Grief" (August 30), "Joy" (September 14), and "Missing the Addict" (July 11).

Even as I was often annoyed at the guidelines governing our conversations—indeed I regularly broke the 12-step rules against crosstalk and incorporating unapproved readings—I met wonderful people at Nar-Anon. They were immensely supportive and put up with my grumpiness about process. We did more than just commiserate. We had a get together at my house over the summer, enjoying the pool, potluck food, and comradery. We learned the importance of social community as we prepared for the possibility of the worst, and then the aftermath for some, like me. Nearly all my Nar-Anon friends were at

Alex's memorial service. As I presented my eulogy, I searched for their supportive faces among the hundreds there. I knew they were hurting along with me. I represented their worst nightmare.

In June 2015, Chip and I began attending a grief group of parents who had lost family members (mostly children) to addiction. For a while I continued to attend Nar-Anon, but eventually it became too much to hear about active addiction. On Mondays we drove an hour each way to the "Grief and Bereavement Group," run by a counselor who facilitated the group pro bono. He began each session with a reading that helped to structure a free-form discussion, and ended it with a meditation. Like my Nar-Anon group, these were people just like us, their stories just as heartbreaking as ours. Chip spoke quite a bit that night, narrating our story. I wasn't sure Chip would keep going. We left the group after about a year, but I remain in touch online with several "grief buddies," and we continue to support and learn from each other.

Self-Care

As Alex descended into addiction, my predisposition toward anxiety went into overdrive. My physician prescribed the anti-depressant Effexor, which I reluctantly tried. I've never been one for medicine. I hated it and weaned myself off within a year. It never did anything for my anxiety, and the long list of possible side effects worried me. More helpfully, I found a therapist who, as it happened, had encountered similar problems with her sons. She provided help for coping with Alex's addiction, and I stayed with her several years. She was a fan of wilderness programs, but we had concerns about such strategies so never further researched that option.[3]

After Alex's death, I searched for a way forward emotionally, including finding solace from friends who had also experienced loss. My friend Dorothy told me over breakfast that, although the loss of her young son had shaped her life, she had come to the decision that she didn't want it to define her life. It had been ten years since her son died, and she was once again finding joy. Her comment resonated with me, as I hoped to eventually find joy again.

I found that it helped to stay active and be with people. I took exercise and yoga classes at the Y and did weight training with a personal trainer. I also found Dana, an acupuncture therapist. I had been wary of needle therapy but spent more than a year relaxing each week into her soothing therapy. I also walked with friends, something I always enjoyed. When the COVID-19 pandemic lockdown hit in 2020, my visits to the Y and acupuncture stopped abruptly. But I continued walking, usually alone, often listening to podcasts as a distraction from my still ever-present grief. Sometimes my friend Dori would join me at the proper social distance. During the summer months when our pool was open, I swam each day, twenty minutes of my slow crawl up and back, with breast strokes every five laps to break the monotony. Although I seldom see Alex in my dreams, I sometimes did during my daily swims. I would envision Alex walking into the back yard to let me know he'd been away on a trip, but he's back now. It was always when I got to the deep end that I'd see his legs and then come up to rest on my arms to talk with him. But then, of course, he's gone. One of the few dreams I do remember occurred after Chip brought home some of Alex's clothes left at Poo's in Florida. I picked through them quickly before falling asleep. A few hours later I woke with a start and had a distinct vision of Alex leaning over to give me a hug.

To replace our Y yoga sessions, Dori organized a few friends for Zoom yoga two mornings a week. Even if I'm not in the mood, yoga stretching gets me up and moving. I've kept up with those yoga sessions even after leaving New Jersey. I also took an eight-week program on mindfulness meditation. The mindfulness-based cognitive therapy (MBCT) approach spoke to me.[4] I'm certainly one to ruminate over the bad times in my life, so I was open to finding ways to avoid negative thinking. MBCT points to the dangers of focusing on the "doing mode," where we tend toward automatic thoughts and ideas, leading to negativity and rumination. Instead, MBCT encourages being aware of the "present moment" and responding with "kindness and compassion to ourselves and our experience."[5] "Being" rather than "doing" makes a lot of sense to me, even if it's hard to accomplish.

Meditation didn't change my life, and I haven't kept up with it. But there are several aspects of the practice that have been useful for me.

First, the observation that "thoughts are not facts, but mental events" helped me to understand that my negative thoughts and tendency toward rumination need not control me.[6] Second, "the 3-minute breathing space is the single most important practice in the MBCT program."[7] Most of us might not have the time nor desire to devote to lengthy meditation rituals, but all of us have three minutes. Those three minutes of mindfulness settle me. And third, "the cornerstone of the whole MBCT program is learning to respond to unpleasant and difficult experiences by, as a first step, intentionally taking a breathing space rather than reacting automatically with aversion."[8] I tend to rely on meditation in the middle of the night, when I have difficulty falling back to sleep. Sometimes it helps to quiet my sleeplessness. If not, I still rely on Ambien.

At one point, my search for recovery took a more mystical turn. A few months after Alex died, I had lunch with my friend Ann who had been visiting a psychic for years and swore by her. She encouraged me to come with her, and even paid for my visit. Ann was convincing about the value it provided her, and by then I was ready to try almost anything to assuage my grief. I was skeptical. When he learned about it, Chip was even more dubious.

But there I was, six months after Alex died, driving south on Route 1 with Ann for our sessions with Colleen (a pseudonym). I asked Ann not to mention my full name to Colleen or tell her anything about why I was coming. I wanted to be a blank slate and didn't want her to google me. I went first, then Ann. Afterward, Ann and I compared notes over dinner.

Colleen began my session with a tarot card reading. She told me I'd had very long lives, by which I assume she meant I'd lived many lives. Right away, she asked if I'd experienced a recent loss, and when I said yes her very next question was whether I'd lost a son to overdose. Without my asking, she assured me Alex did not die by suicide. Colleen described Alex as having already achieved a "high level of awareness," and was surprised he had only been gone six months. As she described it, it normally takes a lot longer to "get to that level," but that Alex had learned what he needed to advance quickly. "Your mother did a lot of praying," she told me, "and that helped him to move up levels." Later, when I told my mother about Colleen's comment, she was happy to hear it. She was always praying for us.

Colleen assured me that Alex was not in pain when he "passed over." My father, who "had been in the military," was there to help. She also assured me Hal, Kathy, and especially Granny were with him. Alex didn't want us to feel guilty; he loves us, and his death "had nothing to do with us." "We did everything we could." She also told me Alex loves Hunter and Ginny very much and will be there for them: "They're going to be okay." She saw Alex "very strongly on my right side." He mentioned "writing" several times, and Colleen asked what that meant to me. I confided that I wanted to write a book about losing Alex. She told me that "it will be published" and that I'd be "standing in front of groups." This project "will lead me away from my current job to a new focus." She was right about that point: even before I retired or found a publisher, I dramatically changed my research and writing to focus on mental health and substance use.

I didn't tell Chip about my going to a psychic until afterward. Neither of us quite knew what to make of it. We talked about it in one of our sessions with Dr. O. He believed, as do I, that some people are more intuitive than others, exceptional at reading people's verbal and non-verbal cues. Whether she was really speaking for Alex is something else entirely. I decided not to overthink it. My visit with Colleen was surprisingly comforting. I was happy to hear Alex wasn't in pain when he died, and that he loves us and is with other loved ones. It also comforted me to think his death was accidental. I still question the medical examiner's determination of suicide based solely on the note he left. I hope instead that he was thinking about us those last few days, carrying the note around in case something happened to him. I hope he wanted to spare us from the blame of what might happen. That would have been the Alex we knew.

As a postscript to my visit with Colleen, we attended our grief group shortly after, and I described it to my grief buddies. Three of the moms, but none of the dads, had been to a psychic. Given my years of studying gender differences in attitudes and behaviors, this didn't surprise me. As we discussed our respective visits to psychics, our talk turned to our children and how sensitive they were and how they might want to connect with or comfort us. We realized we were all searching for answers our traditional recovery groups could not provide. Others I've talked with over the years have also been to psychics or had close friends who have. Although I remain skeptical, I can't deny that at some basic psychological level, it worked for me.

Turning Grief into Action

In January 2016, Chip and I had a session with Dr. O and spoke about the different ways we grieved. Those differences were stark. As Dr. O observed, in dealing with Alex's loss each of us was searching for a new "authentic self." Chip was looking for the "old normal." Being around "normal" people—friends we knew from before Alex died—is what made him feel normal. Getting back to his research allowed him to approach normality. Trauma had marked each of us, leaving us without our normal, good defenses, and he was searching for what he should allow back into his psyche. He was looking for things that mattered, not things that increased his vulnerabilities. By contrast, I was "trying on" a wide range of reactions and digging into my vulnerabilities. I read grief books and self-help writings online. I went to Nar-Anon and grief groups. I visited a psychic, did acupuncture, began meditating, and exercised religiously. I sampled a wide range of strategies, trying to see what if anything felt right. Most importantly, I began to write.

Dr. O helped us to see that Chip's grief was more immediate, so deep it often got in the way of his writing and teaching, not to mention sleeping. On the other hand, I tried hard to compartmentalize, and as long as I got enough sleep, I could do my work and get through the day. We recognize and appreciate our different grieving strategies. Chip couldn't understand how I could keep returning to the trauma. From my perspective, I was reliving the trauma to make sense of it. As Chip describes it, our different ways of grieving are really just different ways to suffer. I disagree. As I see it, I have been trying to find a way to put joy back in my life, into our lives.

In my academic career as a researcher, teacher, and administrator, I was a social activist on gender issues. After Alex's death I wanted to become involved in the politics of addiction, and to use my social science skills to make a difference. I came across the phrase "turning grief into action" and that felt right. There are others who have expressed similar sentiments. In his book about the death of his son Beau, Joe Biden talks about the need to "have a purpose." Maria Kefalas describes how her "superpower of grief" helped "harness" her pain over her daughter Cal's diagnosis of a fatal genetic disease by raising funds toward finding a cure. Kefalas wrote her book while Cal was still living.[9] Sadly, in March 2022, Cal died at the age of twelve, outliving all expectations. She also outlived her dad, my Rutgers colleague Pat Carr, who died of cancer on April 16, 2020.

I started small. My first "action" was to fight the stigma of substance use and mental health disorders by being open about Alex's cause of death in his obituary, in a Facebook post, and at the Celebration of Life. As the weeks turned to months and then years, I explored several ways to become involved, and in the process learned more about public advocacy in the addiction field. I found that there were already multiple groups advocating for enlightened and effective approaches to substance use crises, at both the state and federal levels. In November 2015, I attended a breakfast conference at a local hotel ballroom sponsored by the Partnership for a Drug-Free New Jersey, a nonprofit coalition of communication, corporate, and government professionals dedicated to substance use prevention and the reduction of substance use and misuse. There I found a community of like-minded people who shared my mission to reduce overdoses.

The keynote speaker that day was Dr. Andrew Kolodny, then the chief medical officer for Phoenix House, and now the medical director of Opioid Policy Research at the Heller School for Social Policy and Management at Brandeis University. Kolodny spoke about Purdue Pharma and the prescription opioid misuse it spawned. It was the first I'd heard of it. Kolodny raised several points that resonated with me. Back in 2015, increases in addiction were due almost entirely to an increase among whites, as heroin was moving into the suburbs. A major explanation for whites' shift to heroin was a consequence of their greater reliance on prescription opioids, which at that point were being prescribed more aggressively for whites. Ironically, racial stereotyping was protective in this instance. As I show in chapter 3, historians have found that protection to have been short lived.[10] Drug overdoses have disproportionately impacted blacks in other historical time periods, and racism continues to shape the physical and social consequences of substance use. For example, blacks began to suffer higher mortality rates when fentanyl and other synthetic opioids arrived on the scene.

Dr. Kolodny's presentation was also the first I heard of the "evidence" pharmaceutical companies used in their advertising to justify sales of OxyContin, at ever-increasing dosages.[11] My biggest takeaway from the breakfast was that as much as I loved what I was learning, I wasn't cut out to be part of the professional anti-drug lobby. Although I'm glad such organizations exist, my heart just wasn't in this form of advocacy. I was drawn to smaller groups, wanting to connect with people on a more personal, grassroots level. Nonetheless, I was determined to learn as much as I could, whenever and wherever I could. Over the years I have attended excellent conferences and/or training sessions and deepened my knowledge of addiction, trauma, treatment, and harm reduction.[12] Along the way, I met a host of dedicated activists and clinicians and learned about their work to stem the tide of substance use.

Through online contacts, I joined a group called "Denied Treatment," which focused on mental health insurance parity in New Jersey. Given my experience confronting insurance reimbursement denials, this was a cause that directly spoke to me. Working with Denied Treatment, I used my social science skills to dig into research, make sense of data, craft evidence-based arguments, and write for a broader public to advocate for change. The group's founder, Valerie, told me an attorney working pro bono wanted "to meet with individuals and/or family members regarding [insurance denials]." The attorney was looking for personal stories.

Beginning in March 2016, I worked with a small group to change New Jersey's insurance law for those facing insurance denials. I heard heartbreaking stories, even worse than mine, from families who had spent hundreds of thousands of dollars trying to save their children. Many of those active in this effort were also part of a larger Parity Coalition group, focused on ensuring parity between insurance reimbursement for physical and mental health issues. Along the way, I made some good friends, especially Valerie and Rocky, longtime activists on parity issues. Valerie successfully fought her insurance company, eventually receiving reimbursement for her family's expenses. Rocky told her story about unsuccessful fights with her insurer in multiple venues, including with reporters, a television special, and in testimony before the 2017 President's Commission on Combating Drug Addiction and the Opioid Crisis, chaired by former New Jersey governor Chris Christie. Even with such public exposure, she still hasn't been reimbursed for the over $300,000 her family spent for her sons' mental health and substance use treatment.

Discussion at our first meeting that March revolved around hopes the New Jersey attorney general might be persuaded to follow New York State's precedent in guaranteeing insurance parity for physical and mental health issues. The Paul Wellstone and Pete Domenici Mental Health Parity and Addiction Equity Act of 2008, passed by the U.S. Congress and signed into law by then president George W. Bush, prohibits insurance companies from imposing higher financial requirements, in-network requirements, and similar treatment limitations on people seeking mental health or substance use disorder (SUD) treatment than for other health care services. The passage of the federal law was an important success, even though it includes several exceptions and implementation at the state level has lagged. Thousands of New Jersey residents remain at risk for insufficient treatment options and prohibitive expenses. The Denied Treatment group was attempting to close the loopholes reducing the federal law's efficacy. Through my affiliation with Denied Treatment, I wrote an op-ed that appeared on *Insider NJ* on November 25, 2018, where I documented the appeals process I had gone through:

> Alex was just days away from entering a year-long program when he died. Few, if any, of the charges for the program he was about to enter would have been covered by our insurance provider, Horizon Blue Cross/Blue Shield. We would have paid the thousands of dollars needed over that next year to help make him better. But it was too late.
>
> Horizon Blue Cross/Blue Shield has also repeatedly denied us reimbursement for mental health/SUD services we pre-paid for Alex at a psychiatric hospital in 2014. The appeals process is a bureaucratic

nightmare, not for the faint of heart. We have gone through multiple appeals, both through our insurance company and the state's regulatory appeals process. . . .

Perhaps four years isn't a lot of time for an insurance company to drag out an appeals process, but the nine months between August 2014 and May 2015 when Alex was still alive, we were holding our breath, hoping he would survive. Since that day in May when our lives were forever shattered, I've continued the appeals process—for us, but also for other families struggling with SUDs. My family, and countless other families, have gone through more than a lifetime's share of defeat and heartbreak because this insurance system is broken.[13]

I also made a direct appeal for a bill then wending its way through the New Jersey legislature:

Insurance discrimination is illegal. The national parity law is on the books, it needs to be enforced. As the Kennedy Forum has argued, the leadership on parity is not happening at the federal level. The recently passed opioids legislation contains no parity provisions. It's time for New Jersey public officials to take a more active approach. A new bill (A.2031/S.1339) being debated in the New Jersey legislature would require insurance companies to file annual reports that demonstrate compliance with the federal parity law. Health advocates [have been arguing that] regulators should require insurance companies to demonstrate that they comply with federal parity requirements before they are allowed to sell their plans, monitor compliance through data auditing, and provide direct assistance to help consumers secure their right to equal coverage.

On January 17, 2019, alongside Valerie and Rocky, I testified before the New Jersey State Senate Commerce Committee, detailing our family's experience with Horizon Blue Cross/Blue Shield (BCBS) and the New Jersey State Health Benefits Commission, the state's regulatory apparatus for dealing with such disputes.[14] I made many of the same points as I did in my op-ed. Specifically, I pointed out:

Upon Alex's admission, we pre-paid $29,600 for room and board through Silver Hill's transitional living program (TLP). Per their suggestion, we requested a detailed accounting for room and board. Silver

Hill billed Horizon BCBS for intensive outpatient program only, and BCBS reimbursed them directly for labs and therapy groups.

We had no indication that BCBS would never reimburse us for room and board.

... In their December 4, 2018, letter the State Health Benefits Commission gave two specific reasons for their denial:

- "The Commission denied the appeal because the services received at Silver Hill Hospital, an out of network facility, were Intensive Outpatient Services only. Room and board is not a covered expense for Intensive Outpatient Services."
- "Silver Hill Hospital is not a licensed facility for Residential Services. In accordance with the provisions of the plan, a location must be licensed to provide the services for which reimbursement is requested."

This BCBS decision puts families in an impossible situation.

The fact is that Silver Hill did provide supervised living—room and board—24 × 7, paid for by us. The entire time Alex was at Silver Hill he remained on the Silver Hill campus, in a clinically managed setting, consistent with ASAM [American Society of Addiction Medicine] criteria. All the patients were housed in residential facilities, where they were checked by Silver Hill staff, and given medicine prescribed by Silver Hill doctors.

I urged the state senate, this time directly, to support parity: "To move in this direction, the NJ Assembly voted 73-2 to achieve greater oversight and transparency, and I'm hopeful that the NJ State Senate will soon follow suit in supporting Bill S1339."

Our group's efforts were successful: the New Jersey State Senate supported the bill, and on April 11, 2019, Governor Phil Murphy signed the parity legislation into law. As the Office of the Governor's press release detailed, the law "requires health insurers to provide coverage for mental health conditions and substance use disorders under the same terms and conditions as provided for any other sickness and to meet the requirements of the Paul Wellstone and Pete Domenici Mental Health Parity and Addiction Equity Act."[15] One long battle, at least, had ended successfully.

With respect to my personal attempts to receive reimbursement for our Silver Hill costs, I contacted Horizon BCBS immediately after Alex left the hospital. He was in residence at Silver Hill for approximately one month, from July 30 to August 26, 2014. I kept detailed notes on all my paperwork and filings, and a log of contemporaneous conversations with my insurer. My first request was dated September 19, 2014, followed by two additional letters dated December 12, 2014, and January 16, 2015. Those initial requests were followed by a comedy of errors involving lost paperwork, information never entered into the system, and delay after delay after delay. I was initially denied because my request allegedly was missing certain required codes, even though Silver Hill reported they were properly included on the provided paperwork. I received another denial for an untimely filing, although I began my reimbursement request one month after Alex left Silver Hill. Over the years I talked with multiple staff and supervisors, without success.

As noted in my testimony to the New Jersey State Senate, eventually Horizon BCBS denied reimbursement for our Silver Hill bills because "supervised living is not a covered benefit." The "final" denial letter was dated September 23, 2016, fully two years after I first requested reimbursement. This was Horizon BCBS's final argument, and they stuck with it. I argued, to no avail, that Alex had been in "supervised living services" at many other rehabs over the years. Horizon BCBS paid for room and board elsewhere, while denying payment for residential room and board at Silver Hill. There is no meaningful justification for providing payment for these services directly to the rehabs but not for identical services paid for by us.

I took advantage of the Horizon BCBS appeals process. On May 22, 2017, I wrote a "first-level administrative appeal" to Horizon BCBS, followed by supplementary information I sent on July 25, 2017. When that appeal was turned down, on November 1, 2017, I filed a "second-level administrative appeal" to Horizon BCBS, and on June 1, 2018, I appealed another denial directly to the State Health Benefits Commission. On July 27, 2018, I directly addressed Horizon BCBS's response to my June 1 letter, noting their response failed to address any of the specifics I had raised in my letter. Rather, they simply reiterated their previous denial that "supervised living is not an eligible benefit under [Horizon BCBS].

On November 8, 2018, I made an in-person appeal to the State Health Benefits Commission, but that appeal was denied 5-0. I received the final disposition of my appeal in a December 4, 2018 letter: "The Commission denied the appeal because the services received at Silver Hill Hospital, an out of network facility, were intensive Outpatient Services only. Room and board is not a covered expense for Intensive Outpatient Services." I made one last appeal to the regulatory State Health Benefits Commission, dated January 16, 2019, but never heard back. Finally, I gave up.

The system was stacked against us. I have always suspected if Alex had a well-recognized physical rather than mental health illness, these costs would have been covered without issue. And we had these problems despite being fortunate enough to have, thanks to our Rutgers employment, what I've often described as "Cadillac insurance," compared with coverage available to most Americans. Both Chip and I have had various physical maladies over the years since Alex died, including very costly breast cancer surgery and a hip replacement for me. All these bills were fully covered, with reasonable copays. When Chip was at Robert Wood Johnson University Hospital for four hours of COVID-19 treatment in January of 2022, Horizon BCBS paid approximately 57 percent of the nearly $3,000 the hospital charged for his care, the lower figure a function of payment agreements between the state and health care providers. We paid only $100 for the copay. It's important to recognize that these decisions are very much organization-level judgments, with organizations such as Silver Hill, Robert Wood Johnson University Hospital, insurance companies, and state regulatory bodies negotiating among themselves about payment strategies. We need more transparency about how such negotiations occur, and how they affect those receiving health care, for both physical and mental conditions.

Writing for Recovery

From the very first days, my sister Marianne knew I would write about our family's experiences with addiction. She has read drafts of much of my writing over the years and has encouraged me to keep writing. She knew I'd spent much of my career trying to understand systemic patterns of inequality, and that those skills would help me as I dove into research and writing about addiction. Even Colleen, the psychic I visited, told me I'd publish a book. I knew how to write, and I felt I had to write. As sociologist C. Wright Mills noted: "When you keep waking up in the middle of the night to scribble a note, always about one topic, you may as well realize it: you are writing a book."[16]

Throughout my career, I wrote a great deal about gender inequality and work, family, and community. After losing Alex I shifted my attention to mental health and substance use disorders and began to write with nonacademic audiences in mind. The ideas I had earlier written proved useful as I tackled addiction. I had been interested in how various mechanisms of inequity reproduce gender inequality in the workplace, through workplace interactions and institutionalized policies and procedures. This focus on subtle as opposed to overt explanations for how inequality gets reproduced, I reasoned, also applied to explanations for the overdose epidemic and Alex's addiction. Rather than focus on individual-level "choice" or "brain disease" arguments, I directed my attention to the larger social context in which choices—an individual-level behavior—are made.

My first attempts at writing for a nonacademic audience in the fall of 2016 involved long-form essays, which mostly came to nothing. Occasionally, a magazine editor would respond with suggestions, but no one was interested in publishing my essays. To commemorate what would have been Alex's twenty-seventh birthday, I posted to "Pantsuit Nation," a Facebook group celebrating Hillary Clinton's 2016 run for president. This post was then adapted and included in an eponymous collection of stories by group members.[17] I was astounded and humbled by the response: 12K reacted, and 1.5K took the time to write comments. An astonishing number talked about their addicted family members in recovery, and many had lost loved ones. I was not alone.

As I began to figure out my take, I experimented with writing op-eds, which I saw as trial balloons for my developing arguments. On November 12, 2017, I published my first op-ed on the opioid epidemic, in New Jersey's *Star Ledger*: "My Son Died of a Heroin Overdose. Trump's

Commission Could Help the Crisis—If He Listens."[18] I framed my article as a critique of the Trump administration's policies on the overdose crisis. While the administration's Commission on Combating Drug Addiction and the Opioid Crisis provided useful recommendations, the administration's policies directly contradicted the commission's report.

On March 15, 2021, I published another op-ed, also in the *Star Ledger*.[19] As President Biden was closing in on his first hundred days in office, I wrote to urge him not to forget those struggling with addiction. In "Promise Me, Joe, That You'll Remember Alex in Your First 100 Days," I reminded President Biden we both lost sons in May 2015, and that he had spoken movingly about his son Hunter's recovery from drug and alcohol addiction. I urged him to move beyond a reliance on incarceration and toward support for harm reduction and medication-assisted recovery strategies. I closed with an appeal for a larger moral community of action: "Any story about addiction has to address the stigma that those with substance use and mental health disorders and their families face. We need education and moral support, not shame and moral indignation. We need noise where there is now deafening silence, action rather than passivity. We need political achievements as opposed to delay and inaction at both the state and federal levels. The moral community already exists. We now need a larger community of action."

In the academic year of 2018–2019 I was a fellow at the Rutgers Institute for Research on Women's seminar "Public Catastrophes, Private Losses," where I put some of my early ideas into writing. I worked with a sociology graduate student to gather relevant social science research on addiction and recovery.[20] Thanks to her work, I was able to read widely in the social sciences, learning much about the literature on communities, social interaction, stigma, grief and bereavement, stress and anxiety, suicide, despair, and resilience. These proved therapeutic and helped me better understand Alex's and our stories. They also shape my take on addiction. In the spring of 2019, I developed and then taught a course on addiction in the Rutgers School of Arts and Sciences Honors Program called "Addiction: Epidemic, Devastation, Loss."[21]

Ken, the *Rutgers News* staff member I worked with on my long-form articles and op-eds, told me I had already written enough for several book chapters. Following his advice, I began to chart out my narrative of insanity and recovery. I view this book as part of my activism, in search of a moral community of action. I thought about writing this book years before I sat down to draft my first words. I wrote multiple drafts of chapter outlines, proposals, and queries to agents and presses. On January 1, 2021, in the middle of the COVID-19 pandemic lockdown, I finally began to draft chapters. As I wrote, I realized my work as a sociologist was increasingly shaping my story, and I began to envision my book as a sociological memoir.[22] For the first time in my professional life the words just came pouring out of me. I felt I had to write. I have a mission: to champion a third way to combat addiction that focuses on anti-punitive, harm reduction activism. My expanded social communities have given me support, encouragement, and purpose. And, of course, so too has my family. While I have a wound that I know will never completely heal, the process of telling my story and calling upon my decades of work as a sociologist to promote change and reduce stigma has, in short, helped me feel better.

CHAPTER 13

A Community of Action

I have learned that trauma can steal everything from you that is most precious and rip joy right out of your life. But, paradoxically, it can also make you stronger and wiser, and connect you more deeply to other people than you ever imagined by enabling you to touch their misfortunes and integrate their losses and pain with your own.

—Jamie Raskin, *Unthinkable,* on the loss of his son Tommy to suicide

ADDICTION, LIKE SUICIDE, does indeed "steal everything from you that is most precious." Representative Jamie Raskin well attests to the horror and loss he faced when his son Tommy died by suicide on the last day of December 2021. In this chapter I focus on Raskin's second insight: the yin and yang of trauma and loss. As he discovered—and as I found through my travels alongside Alex on the addiction road—connecting with others, learning from their experiences, and integrating their pain with your own can make you stronger, wiser, and yes, happier. I want to help families affected by mental health and substance use disorders to better understand the insanity and provide strategies to help them. My message is simple: "You are not alone; many of us are walking down that same road." And, for those untouched by the drug overdose crisis, you should know that if it happened to my family, it could happen to yours. We might not be able to banish this devil but by being open about it we can reduce stigma and prejudice and champion more compassionate strategies for mental health and addiction disorders. We can make things better.

Dealing with addiction requires uncomfortable conversations. In this book I meet that silence head on. I move beyond the entrenched explanations for addiction—personal choice or brain disease—that currently shape most of the available treatment and govern most of our public policy. I probe a broader set of explanations—ones that view addiction as a learning disorder and a coping mechanism for psychological pain. My reading of social science and policy writings has convinced me that the best remedy (if not the cure) for such pain is harm reduction, an approach based on a fuller understanding of the causes of addiction, combined with less punitive policies to reduce the stigma that impedes recovery. From those who work in harm reduction, I learned that activists on the ground focus on two concepts: "big harm reduction" likens harm reduction to a social justice movement akin to the war on drugs, racism, LGBTQIA+, and so forth, while "little harm reduction" refers to the set of principles, practices, and strategies to reduce harm.[1]

Unlike most memoirs about addiction, the hero of this book has not lived to tell the tale. *Surviving Alex* is my way of sharing Alex's and my family's story. But I hope it proves to be more than that. The number of overdose deaths is staggering and has increased in recent years. As I noted, the twelve-month overdose death count ending February 2023 was an astonishing 105,000.[2] Fentanyl—fifty times more potent than heroin—is now frequently mixed with other drugs such as cocaine, Adderall, and Xanax. It's killing young people, many merely casually experimenting with drugs, at an alarming rate. To understand the enormity of these numbers, we need to move beyond personal stories to address the larger systemic factors that have led to the epidemic and the policies that have failed to halt it. Mine is not a personal-choice story of "you can't try heroin even once." Rather it is a story of bankrupt organizational systems, among them ineffectual treatment options and processes, an insurance system that rewards an entrenched "industrial treatment complex" irrespective of results, lack of insurance parity between mental and physical health, Big Pharma–fueled prescription drug use, punitive criminal justice policies, and the lack of political will to address systems that are clearly failing. In this chapter, I move toward this broader agenda.

Combating Stigma

In *Undoing Drugs*, Maia Szalavitz tells the story of Heather Edney, an activist in the harm reduction community: "She spoke powerfully about the stigma she was subjected to as a target of the war on drugs. She discussed specific examples, like overdosing, being revived, and then being left in severe withdrawal in a hospital's janitorial closet.... In that closet, she'd been seated in a disused dentist's chair with an IV and ignored for hours, while nauseated, sweaty, and shaking. Occasionally, a nurse would stop by and berate her, telling her she should be ashamed of herself and saying things like 'This is what you get' for being addicted."[3] The first challenge to be addressed is stigma.

Just as Heather Edney experienced, some of the worst stigma Alex faced came from those who cared for him in the many rehabs and hospitals he attended. Sadly, it was sometimes the nurses and doctors who berated, shamed, and labeled him. It was doctors who prescribed legal drugs like Xanax and Ambien in excess, which contributed to his addictions and overdoses, but which he then got blamed for taking. It was rehab psychiatrists who turned Alex into a failed chemistry experiment, and it was a rehab psychiatrist who, based on no apparent evidence, excused the ineffectiveness of his treatment by labeling Alex a sociopath and psychopath. We had no such negative experiences when Alex was hospitalized with anorexia in middle school: health care workers were wonderfully supportive, compassionate school administrators facilitated his return to classes, and Alex's friends welcomed him back with open arms. Treatment was sometimes tough, but there was compassion surrounding his mental health challenges. The stigma Alex experienced ramped up dramatically during high school and college, when he began to drink heavily and use drugs, and especially after college when he turned to heroin. His mental health was no longer "in the mix." Though still young, he was now seen as someone responsible for his actions and for inflicting harm upon himself. Of course, there is some truth to that view, but it is not anywhere close to the full truth. Left unanswered by personal explanations is why Alex's addictions emerged when they did, and why they persisted, and why there were no treatments to help him make different choices.

Sociologists view Erving Goffman's classic 1963 book *Stigma* as the pioneering work on the topic.[4] Since then, social scientists in a variety of fields—those studying stigma specifically, as well as those researching prejudice and discrimination, social psychology, mental illness, addiction, and inequality—have updated Goffman's conceptions of stigma.[5] The word itself refers to "the mark, the condition, or status that is subject to devaluation."[6] Stigmatization is the process whereby that mark negatively affects the lives of those affected. This progression is social because it occurs through interaction with people of different status and power. Differences are distinguished and labeled and associated with negative stereotypes. Social actors then create "us" versus "them" categories, resulting in status loss and discrimination for the stigmatized.

Put another way, "stigma sorts and stratifies people, assigning them to categories against their will. Powerful forces then attach moral and political value to those categories that cut some people out of public life."[7] When stigma is institutionalized, agents of social control label and disadvantage the stigmatized. For example, doctors label those they believe are "mentally ill" and the criminal justice system designates those under their jurisdiction as "criminals."[8] One important conclusion of this research—and one I entirely agree with—is that understanding how stigma works requires seeing the stigmatized not as victims but as people being discriminated against.

Researchers have learned that those who use illicit substances experience high levels of stigma, greater even than other stigmatized groups such as those labeled as having schizophrenia.[9] Moreover, it's not just the user him or herself who experiences stigma. Goffman coined the term "courtesy stigma" to refer to the stigma that arises by association to families who have a proximate social relationship with those marked by stigma. Researchers use the term to describe the isolation and shame parents and families experience from negative labeling, or even outright discrimination.[10]

I can attest to the truth of this. Stigma arrives the day you learn that your child suffers from substance use disorder, and it continues well after he or she recovers (if you are lucky) or dies (if you are not). As my activist friend Rocky described it, your friends and neighbors typically don't bring casseroles to your home when your loved one overdoses or dies from addiction. And that was mostly our experience.

My personal conception of stigma, and of its relationship to grief, has evolved since Alex was diagnosed with anorexia at twelve years of age. Later, his substance use created a whole new level of stigma. When Beau Biden died of brain cancer just two weeks after Alex in May 2015, I recognized immediately that his death would be viewed differently than Alex's of an overdose, and not just because his father was the sitting vice president. My view evolved further when my friend Nancy and I visited the 9/11 National World Trade Center Museum in Manhattan a year after Alex died. No one who visits the 9/11 museum can forget the small room with the photos of those who died so violently that beautiful September day. Nancy and I spent a long time there, reading all the inscriptions and looking at the photos, feeling the enormous grief those photos engendered. Of course, grief was already on my mind, and that day Nancy and I spoke a lot about Alex. The quote inscribed on the 9/11 Memorial wall, "No day shall erase you from the memory of time" (Virgil), continues to resonate with me.

Yet, I am starkly aware that some deaths are viewed as more virtuous than others. Those of us who know grief, know that it exists on a hierarchy. Among the most virtuous are certainly those who died on 9/11. We can all agree they were innocent victims of terrorists. Equally virtuous are the children of Sandy Hook, Parkland, and Uvalde, and too many other places to count, who were victims of America's horrific gun violence. Cancer deaths like Beau Biden's and the like aren't far behind. In contrast, many view overdose deaths as less virtuous, far lower on any collective hierarchy of grief.

Those of us who have lost children to overdose sometimes contend with thoughtless observations that illustrate collective views of less virtuous deaths. To the extent that such deaths are viewed as a consequence of personal choice, some would say that Alex "brought it on himself." Or they may think there was something Chip and I as his parents could have done. For example, someone expressed to me that Alex might not have died if I had sent him to the local Catholic school. Those lower on the hierarchy of grief feel greater direct or courtesy stigma. If addiction is a way of medicating psychic pain, why should it be stigmatized? Rather, compassion should be the proper response. Continuing stigma traumatizes those still in the throes of addiction, as well as their families. Certainly, we need to reconsider how we think about such difficult topics. Learning about different strategies to treat addiction can further that effort. And, of course, we won't stop stigma if we're incarcerating those who use drugs.

Moving Forward

In *The Year of Magical Thinking*, Joan Didion writes, "I also learned from this literature, two kinds of grief. The preferred kind, the one associated with 'growth' and 'development,' was uncomplicated grief, or 'normal bereavement.' . . . The second kind of grief was 'complicated grief,' which was also known in the literature as 'pathological bereavement.'"[11] Many of us who experience grief have been encouraged to move on, even by well-meaning family and friends. As Didion describes it, moving on would be the "normal," expected way to move beyond grief. Friends have told me how strong I am, how well I've handled Alex's death. I'm thankful for their admiration, but I don't feel strong, just determined. From the beginning, I described myself as moving forward, putting one foot in front of the other, day by day, week by week, year by year. In contemplating how best to re-create my life without Alex, I explored insights of social scientists who write about grief, bereavement, and resilience, naming the complicated grief that has structured our lives since Alex was first diagnosed with anorexia. Like many who contend with such grief, I didn't want to move on, or erase memories of Alex. As I struggled with Alex's death, I wanted to move forward, somehow integrating his death into my significantly altered life.

Social psychologists describe grief symptoms as typically lasting from six to twenty-four months, although a child's death can elicit more intense symptoms.[12] Those suffering from complicated grief have difficulty continuing everyday responsibilities and are more likely to suffer from physical ailments. The American Psychiatric Association recently recognized prolonged grief as its own disorder, adding it to its hugely influential *Diagnostic and Statistical Manual of Mental Disorders, Fifth Edition*.[13] Deaths from substance use can be especially devastating because they are often untimely, sudden, and censured.[14] Not only are people not bringing casseroles, but they're also not bringing caring or empathy.

As I've described, society can and does attribute social and moral stigma to overdose deaths. Because these deaths are viewed as self-inflicted, the grief of families left behind is devalued.[15] Psychosocial and sociological approaches can reshape our thinking about how best to address complicated grief, by viewing it as "a dynamic experience of moving between the past and grieving what has been lost and the future and adjusting to life without the person, gradually and unevenly becoming more focused on restoration . . . a kind of "meaning reconstruction," a crucial aspect of which is 'storying grief.'"[16] This is how I came to view my own recovery process.

The idea of continuing bonds plays a central role in the rich research traditions of grief, bereavement, and resilience. According to this research, grief reflects the loss of a relationship. As described by Julia Samuel, "Death steals the future we anticipated and hoped for, but it can't take away the relationship we had. The connection to the dead is maintained internally through our memories, which are probably the most precious we will ever possess; they become part of us, our guides and our witnesses as we carry on with our lives."[17] Continuing relational bonds between families and lost loved ones fosters healthy grieving and broadens societal conceptions of "normal grief."[18] In one of my first forays into this topic, I read my sociologist friend Carolyn Ellis's remarkable, multiyear descriptions of the long-term grief she suffered after her brother Rex died when his Air Florida plane crashed into the Potomac River during takeoff in January 1982. What compounded her grief was that Rex was on his way from Washington, DC, to visit her in Florida. Over the years Carolyn learned to cope with her grief through photos and stories, which kept her connected to Rex. She found it therapeutic to write about Rex, the crash, and her loss, first in an initial exploration of grief written in 1993, and later in reflections written twenty-five and then more than thirty years after his death.[19]

Others writing about bereavement have developed practical strategies. Following the death of her twelve-year-old daughter Abi in an automobile accident in 2014, Lucy Hone turned the experience of her grief into a book providing valuable advice for others confronting loss. She encourages survivors to actively search for a rich life after their loved one's death.[20] I am particularly drawn to the way she conceptualizes resilience: "We are often told that grief will reduce over time, but what really happens is that your grief stays the same, your world and your life grow around it. . . . I have noticed how our lives have grown around Abi."[21]

My high school friend Rosemary, whose thirty-four-year-old son died by suicide three months after Alex, reported a similar process of rediscovering herself. When she and I first spoke several years ago about the loss of our sons, she described her journey as "moving through." But she soon realized that phrasing suggested a new and different end. Much like Lucy Hone, she now frames her journey as "carrying him with me into my family's new life, a life with purpose, love and hope." While part of her will always be devastated, "building a bigger life helps to balance the pain and make it more manageable. We don't have to let them go. We need to carry their fire."

Harm Reduction Policy Goals

A well-known harm reduction principle is "Meet them where they are, but don't leave them there."[22] As I wondered how to move forward on the second road, the sociologist in me went looking beyond micro-level approaches. I searched more broadly for systemic explanations for Alex's addiction, and alternative treatment and policy approaches. Alex, Chip, and I lived within our personal set of relationships, of course, but we also operated within an organizational sphere that included health care agencies (e.g., hospitals, rehabs), our insurance company, the criminal justice system, educational institutions, self-help groups, governments (local, state, and federal), and advocacy organizations. We interacted repeatedly with all these organizations during Alex's mental health and addiction challenges, and as I've described in previous chapters, they all shaped his addiction journey. To focus solely on addiction as "choice" or "brain disease" misses multiple other explanations for why and how Alex turned to substance use in the first place, and why he remained in its thrall despite his and our best efforts.

As I was digging into social science and policy research, I came across the harm reduction movement, and learned that it addresses many of the macro-level factors I was exploring. Sadly, by the time I found and learned its name, it was too late to save Alex. As I write this on May 11, 2022, the seventh anniversary of Alex's death, I can't help but wonder if I had known more about harm reduction early on whether I might have saved him, or at least found better treatment options to give him more time. I was immediately drawn to harm reduction's more empathic approach, and to its guiding principle to meet people where they are, even if that means supporting them while they continue to use illicit substances. These compassionate methods are in sharp contrast to the punitive ones Alex encountered throughout his addiction ordeal.

Although the harm reduction policy community is now quite active, amid Alex's substance use I heard nothing about it, not even the name. And I was an educated consumer, actively looking for treatment alternatives. I wasn't alone: the vast majority of those I interviewed, and those with whom I've discussed my book, hadn't heard about harm reduction either. Even years after the approach was introduced, most still haven't. Several of my academic colleagues knew about it because it overlapped with their research interests (e.g., criminal justice, sociology of medicine, history of medicine), but to this day, as far as I can tell, most academics are unaware of this perspective and alternative approach. Even those professionals I met whom I thought might have come across it in their work—police officers, school administrators, and physicians—hadn't heard about it either.

In my forays into addiction policy and treatment I learned that while policy types now regularly talk among themselves—there is, for example, an active Twitter community and set of groups focusing on harm reduction that I follow—those conversations have yet to reach a broader audience. Most people like me and Chip—moms and dads trying to save their kids—still aren't hearing their messages. Every single rehab and sober living house Alex attended was based on the 12 steps, and none were open to using medications for opioid use disorder (MOUD),[23] except perhaps to use suboxone to detox. Most still aren't. Frankly, at that point I didn't even know the right questions to ask, and I was constantly frustrated in my search for treatment alternatives. There were no harm reduction rest stops available on my addiction road. Now that I know more, I hope to build stronger bridges from the harm reduction policy world to the lives of families facing addiction. There is substantially more to the explanation of overdoses than bad choices made by young people in the throes of addiction. Understanding the larger, systemic picture is key to understanding how to fix the problem, and the kinds of roles that government and private partnerships can play in developing solutions.

In their world, activists have long strategized how best to move from punitive approaches to harm reduction strategies. An important aspect of this is the language we use. A shift to person-centered language, which puts people first, is well underway. Moving away from "addict" or "substance abuser" to "substance use" and "people who use drugs" (PWUD) has become standard for those writing in the field, including me. I and many others eschew talk about "hitting rock bottom," a common touchstone and oft-used phrase in 12-step meetings.[24] The notion that somehow hitting bottom was important to recovery never made sense to me. I remember telling my Nar-Anon group that when Alex hit bottom, he'd be dead.

It never felt right to me that abstinence programs focus on the concepts of enabling, hitting bottom, and codependency. The focus there is on doing wrong, apologizing, and seeking redemption, to the exclusion of family support. Approaching the chaos of addiction in that way hurts rather than helps those who use. It also hurts families.[25]

Inspired by harm reduction beliefs, the activist group Partnership to End Addiction recommends a different approach:

- recognize that changing substance use is a process, making quitting "cold turkey" unrealistic,
- use early intervention when problems are less severe,
- avoid rhetoric about "hitting bottom,"
- recognize that relapse is common, and not a failure,
- encourage family support and recognize positive behavior as more effective than punishment,
- prefer use of medications, along with treatment and counseling, and finally
- understand that recovery requires long-term and, often, repeat treatment.[26]

Perhaps the most important philosophical underpinning in the harm reduction approach is the need for community, for connection. As well-known activist Johann Hari described it, "The opposite of addiction isn't sobriety. It's connection. . . . If you are alone, you cannot escape addiction. If you are loved, you have a chance."[27] Researchers and activists generally agree with this message. Because "stigma is fundamentally a social phenomenon rooted in social relationships and shaped by the culture and structure of society, [its solution] must similarly be embedded in social relationships and changing the structures that shape social relationships."[28] Researchers have begun to call for more study on the role of social bonds in treating addiction.

The History of the Modern Harm Reduction Movement

Harm reduction has a long history, and yet only recently has it reached into the policy space. More people are learning about what it offers for addiction treatment and policy, and how it differs from traditional approaches. Rehab programs based on the 12-step philosophy were the only game in town when Alex needed treatment, and very little has changed since then. To illustrate, I came across several books published in the mid- to late 2010s that critiqued 12-step programs and the rehab industry more generally. Although each espoused harm reduction principles, there were still few to no explicit references to the movement.[29] It was not until 2021 that Maia Szalavitz's *Undoing Drugs* provided the first authoritative history of American harm reduction, and more recent studies of addiction have given it more play.[30] Harm reduction offers a strong counter to the traditional punitive approach to addiction that has dominated American drug policy for the last century. As Hari explains, the war on drugs has been an utter failure, and Maia Szalavitz offers an alternative that succeeds.

Harm reductionists reframe their strategies to target harm rather than highs.[31] It is sometimes described as radical empathy that recognizes all lives have value. In her history of the movement, Szalavitz analogizes the harm reduction model to drivers wearing seat belts, physicians wearing masks during surgery, and all of us wearing masks during the COVID-19 pandemic. Because of the United States' long-standing punitive approach toward drug users, ultimately aimed at incarceration, much of the early work on harm reduction was pursued in other countries. Many trace the birth of the modern international harm reduction movement to the UK city of Liverpool in the 1980s, and to John Marks, a physician in the United Kingdom's National Health Service (NHS).[32] The NHS was then interested in trying to stem the HIV/AIDS epidemic. Dr. Marks's clinic spearheaded a harm reduction strategy of prescribing both injectable (with clean needles) and smokable heroin and cocaine to drug users, to great advantage. Research data demonstrated his success: in contrast to other cities such as Edinburgh in Scotland, which suffered greatly from increasing HIV/AIDS cases, Liverpool became a world leader in reducing HIV/AIDS among drug injectors.[33] Data showed a decline in crime due to fewer thefts and illegal drug transactions. Because they had access to drugs through the NHS, clinic users had less need to steal to procure drugs or to find drugs on the streets.[34]

What was happening in the United Kingdom was in stark contrast to the U.S. war on drugs, which to this day shapes addiction policy in this country. The goal of the war on drugs is to stop substance use through prohibition and punishment, while harm reduction recognizes the humanity of people by seeking to make people's lives better, "meeting people where they're at," both physically and psychologically.[35] The simplicity of its branding was brilliant: activists focused on reducing harm that saved lives in the process. Who could disagree with saving lives?

Any discussion of early harm reduction efforts must also include Portugal's impressive success in reducing heroin overdose deaths.[36] In the 1980s, Portugal had one of the worst heroin drug problems in the world. The country had tried the prohibitionist policies common in the United States and elsewhere—criminalization and incarceration— but they had failed miserably. A family doctor in Algarve, João Goulão, had seen the worst of it. He described heroin addiction as starting among the more marginalized but moving quickly to the middle and upper classes. At its worst, an estimated 10 percent of the Portuguese population was addicted to heroin. In the early 1990s, Goulão established the country's first drug treatment center in Algarve, dedicated to treating PWUD with compassion rather than condemnation. By 1997,

Portugal's government asked Goulão to develop addiction policies at the national level, and, in 1999, he joined with a team of doctors and judges to develop a comprehensive national plan on how best to treat drug addiction. The team's recommendations were based on two foundational tenets: (1) those who use drugs should be viewed as full members of society, and (2) all drugs should be decriminalized. The team advocated for the money saved from punishing and incarcerating users be used for addiction education and recovery.

In 2001, Portugal's parliament adopted the recommendations and decriminalized the possession and use of drugs. It remains illegal to sell, however, and the country's drug problem has not evaporated. Criminal gangs still supply illegal drugs on the street, and people still become addicted. The catastrophe predicted by the country's right wing has not come to pass, due in large measure to the ripple effects of the legislation: "There were two dimensions to Portugal's drug revolution. The panel didn't simply lift the legal penalties and leave people to it. They took the big, lumbering machinery of the drug war and turned it into an equally big, active machine to establish a drug peace. . . . In the United States, 90 percent of the money spent on drug policy goes to policing and punishment, with 10 percent going to treatment and prevention. In Portugal, the ratio is the exact opposite."[37]

These policy changes worked. Even the chief of the Lisbon Drugs Squad, João Figueria, who had expected an explosion of drug use, has acknowledged that the opposite was true. In the decade following decriminalization, Portugal's drug use remained below the European average, its number of problematic drug users halved. Compared with Spain and Italy, only Portugal has shown declines in problematic drug use. In a testament to the importance of bipartisan cooperation, both conservatives and leftists have supported Portugal's decriminalization: governments on both the left and right have kept the law in place. "All the Portuguese society accepts it completely. It is a system that is settled."[38] In recent years some have begun to question Portugal's status as a progressive model of drug decriminalization. Even João Goulão, one of the architects of Portugal's drug decriminalization, was quoted recently to that effect: "What we have today no longer serves as an example to anyone," although he is quick to blame lack of resources.[39]

Vancouver, in British Columbia, Canada, has also earned a significant reputation in the history of the international harm reduction movement.[40] Ann Livingston and Dean Wilson, of the Vancouver Area Network of Drug Users, were early supporters of safe injection sites (also called overdose prevention sites, or supervised consumption sites).[41] These sites provide clean needles to users who furnish their own drugs, and have naloxone on hand to reverse any overdoses that might occur. In September 2003, Livingston and Wilson established Insite, Vancouver's first safe injection site. With the support of Vancouver's conservative mayor, Insite was modeled on similar successful sites in Europe. A companion program, Onsite, was co-located in the same building, and provided services for those who wanted to get off drugs. As of 2021, there were a hundred injection sites in ten countries, and after millions of injections, not one person has died, quite a remarkable achievement. Despite the success of this harm reduction method, such sites were illegal in the United States until December 2021, when two injection sites opened in New York City (East Harlem and Washington Heights).[42] Continuation of these sites is continually threatened by lack of sustainable funding streams.

To this day the United States remains far behind other countries such as Portugal and Canada in its harm reduction policies, perhaps because of its strong initial roots in stigmatized HIV/AIDS activism, which faced enormous resistance due to a combination of homophobia, racism, and sexism. Despite that, these homegrown efforts in the 1980s served as important forerunners to a growing harm reduction movement in the United States, and many of these initiatives occurred initially at the local level. As HIV/AIDS spread it infected not only gay men but also straight men and women who injected drugs; it also spread to infants infected in utero. The frequent connection between sex work and drug use compounded that spread. The number of infections among IV drug users increased dramatically between 1978 to 1981: in those three years the percentage of IV drug users infected with HIV/AIDS increased from 20 to 50 percent.[43] Advocacy groups such as the Association for Drug Abuse Prevention and Treatment (ADAPT) emerged to support IV drug users infected with HIV/AIDS by among other things providing clean needles. Also important in these efforts was the AIDS Coalition to Unleash Power (ACT-UP) founded in New York in 1987 by Larry Kramer. ACT-UP soon joined forces with ADAPT to support needle exchange, which was still illegal in the early 1990s. In April 1991, eight ACT-UP defendants went on trial for a misdemeanor needle possession charge, facing six months in jail.[44] Szalavitz was in the courtroom when the verdict was read. Sounding like a harm reductionist herself, Judge Laura Drager decreed: "This court is also satisfied that the harm the defendants sought to avoid was greater than the harm in violating the statute. Hundreds of thousands of lives are at stake in the AIDS epidemic. The crime of possessing a hypodermic needle was enacted as a weapon in the war on drugs. Although law enforcement officials believe the statute essential in this fight, available evidence suggests it has had limited success. . . . With respect to one count of criminally possessing a hypodermic needle, the court finds each of the defendants not guilty."[45] Thanks to the ACT-UP defendants, needle exchange and syringe possession are now legal in New York State.

A black activist social worker named Keith Cylar linked up with ACT-UP to import the idea of harm reduction to housing.[46] With his partner Charles King, Cylar spun off ACT-UP's Housing Committee to establish a new nonprofit Housing Works in 1996. The new organization quickly generated revenue—$27 million by 2004—and had established a track record of success in providing housing, as well as health and other services, for people with or at risk for HIV/AIDS or other chronic illnesses, including substance users. Since that time, it has grown substantially, and is still thriving today.[47] Housing Works demonstrates action in the face of nonaction, particularly with regard to homelessness. It's really "harm reduction in action," one of many such actions that deal with real-life problems. Such initiatives filled an important need not addressed by abstinence-based policies. Housing Works' philosophy has been "housing first," recognizing that users would have little chance of achieving sobriety without a safe place to live.

There are several additional names important to know in the nascent American harm reduction movement. When Gary Comer, the owner of Land's End, took his company public in 1986, he set up a family foundation to oversee the distribution of proceeds. In 1991 he asked his daughter to run it. Having lived in both New York and San Francisco,

Stephanie Comer was aware of the devastation of HIV/AIDS. The Comer Foundation became an early supporter of needle exchange, funneling initial donations to Dave Purchase, who had established a needle exchange program in Tacoma, Washington, with the support of his local government and the police. By 1991, twelve needle exchanges existed in the United States, across nine states.[48] Since 1994, philanthropist George Soros has been a significant donor to harm reduction programs.

In 1993, Stephanie Comer contacted Chicagoan Dan Biggs.[49] A year earlier, Biggs had founded the Chicago Recovery Alliance (CRA), which ran the city's nonprofit needle exchange program. He had big goals, including wrenching recovery from its abstinence roots, and Biggs worked relentlessly with others to revolutionize what recovery could and should look like. They came up with a definition of recovery, which I believe hits the mark: "any positive change, as defined by the person him- or herself." With funding from the Comer Foundation, Biggs and others organized the Harm Reduction Working Group, which met in October 1993 to establish a U.S. organization for harm reduction policy and practice. Hoping to catch up to the Europeans, the group was a veritable who's who of American harm reductionists, including, among others, Biggs, Purchase, and Edith Springer (an early harm reduction trainer). The working group developed a definition of harm reduction and statement of purpose: "Harm Reduction is a set of strategies and tactics which encourages users to reduce harm done to themselves and their communities by licit and illicit drug use. By allowing users access to the tools to become healthier, we recognize the competency of their efforts to protect themselves, their loved ones and their communities."[50] This framing recognizes the importance of those who use drugs to speak for themselves: "nothing about us without us." This motto, popularized by the disability community, became a rallying cry for those active in this community.[51]

The Harm Reduction Working Group eventually birthed a larger organization, the Harm Reduction Coalition. Many harm reduction conferences followed, including an inaugural four-day one in September 1996, held at the Oakland Convention Center in California. The conferences helped institutionalize the harm reduction movement, generated favorable publicity, and developed important bridges to a wide variety of professionals, including leading psychologists in the field who have become important proponents of the method, such as Alan Marlatt (who founded the University of Washington's Addictive Behaviors Research Center in 1981) and Andrew Tatarsky (who founded the Center for Optimal Living in New York City in 2011).[52]

Meanwhile, in Chicago, Biggs and the CRA were also responsible for laying the groundwork at the local level for making Narcan more available to laypeople for reversing overdoses. Prior to their advocacy, naloxone was available only to hospitals and ambulances. Biggs's advocacy did much to rebut the claim that the availability of Narcan enabled users or sent the wrong message about drug use. Immediately after the program began in 2001, its early efforts bore fruit: the number of overdose deaths in Chicago declined by 20 percent and continued to decline by 10 percent in each of 2002 and 2003.[53]

Today, researchers and activists focus on five precepts of harm reduction:

- Trying to ban or criminalize nonmedical use of intoxicants will not be effective
- maximization of individual autonomy and dignity, leading to a people-centered approach
- having a hierarchy of needs; establishing goals to accomplish, or meeting the person where they are
- serving as an alternative to the criminalization or medicalization binary
- maximization of noncoercive and appropriate intervention options, as appropriate for each individual.[54]

While policymakers and activists began the process of institutionalizing harm reduction philosophy and methods, revamping treatment programs to incorporate harm reduction philosophy and methods has proven more elusive. As my experience in the addiction world demonstrates, harm reduction was mostly invisible to moms like me looking for treatment programs. The only available treatment for us was the Minnesota/12-step program based on Alcoholics Anonymous (AA)'s 12-step philosophy, which insists on abstinence and views addiction as a chronic progressive brain disease.[55] The Hazelden Betty Ford

Foundation is representative of this treatment, which typically lasts one month, followed by longer-term stays at sober living houses. Also available were longer-term programs such as therapeutic communities, which sometimes used more forceful "tough love" strategies. At most, selected harm reduction principles, such as relapse prevention, were sometimes incorporated into 12-step programs, reinterpreted to encourage abstinence. Although some programs like Hazelden have begun to incorporate medications into their treatment program, that was not an available option for Alex at any treatment facility we researched (and given what I did for a living, I researched them all as best I could).

Adding to the mix, advocates of abstinence actively opposed, and continue to oppose, harm reduction approaches to treatment for substance use. Battles between the two factions are ongoing. In *Undoing Drugs*, Szalavitz discusses early research on controlled drinking conducted by Linda and Mark Sobell, who found that controlled drinking was more effective than abstinence.[56] Their initial research was published in a 1973 article in *Behaviour Research and Therapy*, and three years later they published a follow-up article that reported the same results. A media and scientific firestorm ensued, fueled by 12-step advocates. Media reports, including a 1983 *60 Minutes* segment and an article in *Science*, vilified the Sobells. Though intensely scrutinized, their research and findings have held up. Their vindication proved an important win for U.S. harm reduction. Ideally, of course, these philosophies should not be seen as diametrically opposed or as presenting an "either/or" scenario. One can practice harm reduction and still desire abstinence.

Historically, the federal government has provided inconsistent leadership around mental health and substance use disorders; changes implemented by one administration are routinely ignored or overturned by the next. For example, while the Obama administration implemented important policy initiatives, including a beefed-up Office of National Drug Control Policy (ONDCP), most of these initiatives languished or were rescinded during the Trump administration. Trump did, however, create a Commission on Combating Drug Addiction and the Opioid Crisis, chaired by former New Jersey governor Chris Christie, which published its final report November 15, 2017.[57] The report provided a policy roadmap, but the administration failed to listen to its recommendations. Instead, Attorney General Jeff Sessions rescinded the Obama administration's easing of penalties for nonviolent drug arrests and called for the harshest possible charges against offenders. Trump agreed with this approach, promising more drug prosecutions, jail sentences, and programs to keep young people from trying drugs. He adamantly refused to consider harm reduction initiatives already shown to be effective in other countries. As we all know from the failure of the national war on drugs, "just say no" didn't work during the Reagan years. It didn't work during the Trump years either, and it won't in the future.

President Biden has charted a welcome change of course. Toward the end of his 2022 State of the Union Address, he offered a "Unity Agenda for the Nation."[58] The first point on that agenda was to "beat the opioid epidemic" and the second was to "take on mental health." Significantly, he highlighted harm reduction, and several of his appointees publicly support these policies, including Surgeon General Vivek Murthy and ONDCP director Rahul Gupta. Through the ONDCP, the Biden administration has issued a National Drug Control Strategy that details a comprehensive path toward addressing the overdose epidemic.[59] Moreover, on October 6, 2022, in a decent good-faith effort, President Biden issued a "full, complete, and unconditional pardon" to any U.S. citizen or permanent resident charged or convicted [federally] of simple possession of marijuana, and encouraged state governors to do the same.[60] More such pardons are needed. All these harm reduction goals promise to "meet people where they are" by expanding access to treatment for those who need it; promoting greater availability of naloxone, drug test strips, and syringes; and ensuring access to evidence-based treatment. Goals are important, but we also need funding to back up these ambitions. Signaling bipartisan support, all but fifteen states have made it legal either to possess fentanyl test kits or to freely distribute them, including states such as Georgia, New Mexico, Wisconsin, Tennessee, and Alabama, and Mississippi, South Dakota, and Texas are headed in the same direction.[61]

One important harm reduction goal at the federal level must be to unlock the "liquid handcuffs" on methadone treatment to bring Food and Drug Administration (FDA)-approved treatment into the medical mainstream.[62] Current methadone regulations are over fifty years old. They reflect the inflexibility of the time they were adopted and fail to adequately serve those with opioid use disorder. At present, methadone must be delivered daily and only at licensed opioid treatment programs. This inflexibility negatively affects the employment and family care responsibilities for those relying on this medicine. The most affected have been poor black and brown communities, particularly those in suburban and rural areas. In the past few years, the COVID-19 pandemic has forced the Substance Abuse and Mental Health Services Agency, which regulates methadone, to issue waivers to users to bring their medicine home. There is hope that these waivers will be extended and that pharmacies will be permitted to dispense methadone. Such improvements would move methadone closer to the model currently in use for buprenorphine (aka Suboxone), an FDA-approved medication already prescribed at medical offices and taken at home.[63] Some recent successes have loosened restrictions for clinicians who treat opioid use disorder with medicine: through its bipartisan Mainstreaming Addiction Treatment Act of 2021, the Biden administration eliminated the "X-waiver," doing away with a Drug Enforcement Administration certification previously required to prescribe buprenorphine.[64]

In addition to advances at the federal level, progressive efforts at the state level are also beginning to show promise. In November 2020, voters in New Jersey supported a constitutional amendment to legalize marijuana. On February 22, 2021, marijuana was decriminalized in the state for those twenty-one and older, and fully legalized on April 21, 2022. In addition, as I noted earlier, New Jersey is one of the national leaders in parity legislation, requiring health insurers to provide coverage for mental health and substance use disorders comparable to what they offer for physical conditions. Governor Phil Murphy signed the parity legislation into law on April 11, 2019. Recognizing the importance of language, New Jersey has renamed the Statewide Drug Court as the Statewide Recovery Court and taken additional efforts to support harm reduction.[65] Changing language goes only part way toward a solution. For example, the evidence suggests that drug courts, which have now been established in all fifty states, do reduce harm compared with existing punitive sentencing. But incarceration remains a sentencing option and can lead to increased harm, because (1) people who use drugs can be sentenced to longer terms if they fail to remain clean, and (2) many drug courts ban the effective use of methadone and buprenorphine. Instead, to reduce risk we need to move toward noncarceral strategies.[66]

As I was completing this book in 2022, I attended a virtual opioid summit sponsored by the New Jersey Department of Human Services and learned more about why New Jersey is at the forefront of state responses to the overdose epidemic.[67] The state has developed a comprehensive and collaborative approach to the crisis that involves multiple state offices and other nonprofit organizations, including Human Services, the Office of the Attorney General, NJ Cares, Corrections, Labor and Workforce Development, Children and Families, Health Services, Drug Monitoring and Analysis, NJ Harm Reduction Coalition, and Prevention Resources. Impressively, they have established a 24/7 addiction helpline.[68] This is truly government at its best, working effectively for its citizens.

Finally, as an emeritus faculty member of Rutgers University, I am proud that Rutgers was the first university in the United States to establish a Recovery House. In 1983 Rutgers hired Lisa Laitman, a licensed clinical alcohol and drug counselor, as the founding director of the Rutgers Alcohol and Other Drug Assistance Program. She established the Recovery House in 1988. On May 17, 2022, I attended the Thirteenth Annual Rutgers Recovery Graduation. In addition to celebrating their graduates, the ceremony recognized Lisa for her decades of service.

An alumna of the Recovery House also received an award that night: the CEO of Prevention Links, Morgan Thompson, a leader in alcohol and drug prevention. Prevention Links was instrumental in establishing the Raymond J. Lesniak Recovery High School, an alternative high school for students who have substance use–related issues and who are looking for a self-contained, public school conducive to meeting the needs of their education and recovery.[69] Thompson, like all the graduates and alumni who spoke that night, directly credited their success, and their lives, to the Rutgers Recovery House.

Several U.S. states have gone further than others in instituting harm reduction approaches. Modeling its policies on Portugal's reforms, and supported by the Drug Policy Alliance, Oregon in 2020 passed a state-wide ballot initiative (Measure 110) to legally decriminalize drugs, garnering 58 percent of the vote.[70] The law applies to possession of cannabis and psychedelics, as well as possession of small amounts of all drugs. The law eliminated criminal penalties for possession, relying instead on treatment (construed broadly) or paying a $100 fine. Access to other resources like housing and employment is part of the process. Significantly, there is bipartisan support for these efforts. It's too early to tell whether Oregon's reforms will be successful. The pandemic and the dramatic rise of fentanyl use have negatively impacted the law's effectiveness, but lack and delay of sufficient resources and treatment options are also key. It's also clear that criminalizing addiction is the wrong strategy to eliminate this scourge. The failure of years of the war on drugs has demonstrated that.[71]

Colorado and Washington State have also made significant progress. Both states successfully promoted and won ballot initiatives in 2012 to legalize, tax, and regulate cannabis in their states, although they went about it in very different ways.[72] In Colorado, activists made the harm reduction argument that marijuana was less dangerous than alcohol. Switching from alcohol to cannabis, they argued, would reduce risky behavior and hence crime, benefiting not only the individual but the broader society as well. In contrast, Washington activists never argued that marijuana was safe. Instead, they claimed that the state needed to counteract the harms of marijuana by targeting funds from the new law to drug prevention efforts in schools and treatment. Despite their different approaches, both states supported the measures by significant margins: 55 percent of those in Colorado and Washington supported the bills to legalize cannabis possession in small amounts.

Another set of states are addressing substance use disorder at the grassroots level by instituting the "hub and spokes model" designed by Dr. John Brooklyn and operationalized by the Vermont Department of Health's Division of Alcohol and Drug Abuse Programs. Vermont has become well known for adopting this model, a compassionate alternative to traditional, more punitive methods, and California and Washington State have followed suit. Using funds from the Affordable Care Act's Medicaid waiver, Vermont set up nine regional hubs to provide daily, intensive support to those dealing with substance use disorder. For follow-up care, the hubs link with over seventy-five doctors, nurses, and counselors who serve as "spokes" at the local level. The program is set up to take full advantage of MOUD, including methadone, buprenorphine, and naltrexone (aka Vivitrol), an injection that has been used to prevent the return to drugs. As the parent of someone who had no access to such services, this program looks promising to me, both because it uses medications and because it locates services at the community level. More than six thousand families have benefited from these services in Vermont. As one addiction provider noted about a patient in her care: "It's all about reaching the patients who ... are sick and tired of being sick and tired, but not sick and tired of being high."[73]

We need support at the federal and state level for treatment programs that offer empathy and compassion, as well as evidenced-based therapies. Policies that expand syringe programs, naloxone distribution, diversion programs, medication-assisted treatment, and partnerships between public health and law enforcement are baby steps in the right direction. We need to protect the Affordable Care Act and expand Medicaid participation. The Trump administration supported neither. To move forward, health care needs to be viewed as a right, not a privilege. Such programs have already been shown to be effective in other countries, and in several U.S. states.

While progress remains slow at the federal level, activists at the local level are making headway, just as they did at the beginning of the U.S. harm reduction movement. A new cast of characters has replaced the early activists such as Dan Biggs, Keith Cylar, and Edith Springer. In *American Fix*, Ryan Hampton reports on his 2016 visits in twenty-two states hit hardest by the addiction crisis. In these communities he found "ordinary people doing extraordinary things to fight back against the crisis."[74] In *Raising Lazarus*, Beth Macy documents the actions of a host of local activists from North Carolina, Indiana, West Virginia, and Virginia.[75] Similarly, Sam Quinones's *The Least of Us* highlights the local activism important in the fight against resurgent fentanyl and meth epidemics by Will Pfefferman in Kenton County, Kentucky; Lou Ortenzio in Clarksburg, West Virginia; and Angie Odum, in Tennessee.[76] This is harm reduction on the ground, and these activists are fighting the overdose epidemic where it is most virulent, in America's rural areas, which tend toward political conservatism. As Macy points out, we can learn a lot from the "grounded, service-oriented kind of harm reduction embodied in the work being done right now."[77] But as she also argues, this can't be accomplished solely by individuals because the problem is systemic. Drug overdoses need to be addressed by institutions and all levels of government.

Nevertheless, the benefit of such on-the-ground, local activism is that these are precisely the people who know their dying neighbors, understand local politics, appreciate that harm reduction strategies cost less than incarceration, and can change the hearts and minds of their fellow citizens. To change those hearts and minds, we need activists like Christina Dent, a conservative Christian in Mississippi, who founded the nonprofit End It For Good. She argues for a more nuanced approach, addressing addiction as a health issue rather than resorting to incarceration.[78] We also need local harm reduction activists like Pennsylvania's Jordan Scott, and others I've met through my participation in Mobilize Recovery's Family Caucus. Jordan has been active in forming the Lehigh Valley Walk for Recovery (which fundraises for local grassroots organizations), speaks on panels and lobbies for legislation, has worked to expand Good Samaritan laws (which provide immunity for those who witness overdoses and call for medical services), and does local street outreach to drug users.[79]

Harm reduction on the ground is analogous to what sociologists have long taught us about response to disasters—hurricanes, earthquakes, even nuclear meltdowns. We think someone has to be in charge, a strong leader who can tell us how to be and what to do. But that's just the popular view, the stuff we see in movies. What really happens in disasters of all types is that they happen to "regular" people, people in their homes at night, or at work, or at leisure. When the thing we call a disaster comes, *they* are the leaders; *they* are in charge if for no other reason than that they're in the middle of the calamity of the moment. So it would be a more accurate representation of reality—and therefore a more safety-producing response—if we thought of parents, cousins, siblings, and neighbors as "first responders." The real point here is that our worlds are not regulated and organized by officials at the top of our organizations. Our worlds are organized by the institutions of which we are a part. And that, I think, is where we need to direct more attention and resources to harm reduction. Doing that will save more lives than hiring more people in uniforms and funding more drug interdiction. If we really care about saving people who use drugs, and giving them more time to save their lives, this should be our approach.[80]

As I wrote in a 2017 op-ed published in New Jersey's *Star Ledger*, the overdose epidemic must remain at the top of our political agenda.[81] We cannot allow it to be lost in tweetstorms, as occurred during the Trump administration. The federal government must be an important partner in these efforts, along with state and local governments. We also need the will of the people to move beyond shame and stigma to demand action. More will die until action—both presidential and congressional—replaces rhetoric. Those who have lived the insanity can play a critical road in the process of recovery, providing clues to the road forward. Those without firsthand experience with substance use should realize that if it happened to my family, it could happen to anyone.

Harm Reduction in Action

In addition to reading about the history of harm reduction, I wanted to learn about the nuts and bolts of how it operates in practice. Toward that end, in May 2022 I participated in a two-day training session on "integrative harm reduction psychotherapy" sponsored by the Rutgers Center of Alcohol Studies and New Jersey's Center for Great Expectations. Most of the attendees were New Jersey clinicians. Andrew Tatarsky, who founded and runs the Center for Optimal Living in New York City, conducted the training to introduce us to the paradigm he uses to treat addiction. I rely heavily on the presentations and reading materials from that training, as well as other publications I have read, to describe harm reduction in practice.[82]

Tatarsky's description of one male patient struck a particular chord with me:

I had one patient who entered my group about two years ago heavily drinking and his initial goal was to moderate. Over the course of six months, he discovered that he was just having an impossible time of it and began to attend AA while he was attending my group. He stopped drinking with the support of AA and about three months later, decided to leave group so that he could just focus on AA. Eighteen months later, he called me up to say he had been abstinent for eighteen months and was now interested in re-exploring whether moderation is something that he can be successful at. About a month ago, he re-joined our group and there were still some of the same members that knew him from back when, and he has begun to experiment with occasional moderate drinking and approaching it in an extremely thoughtful, systematic way with an experimental attitude, which is what we suggest people bring to any positive change goals and strategies that they may be exploring.[83]

There are several things that strike me about this clinical interaction. First, the patient Tatarsky describes sounds like Alex. He told us, and all the rehab staff who treated him, that alcohol moderation was his goal. Not one psychiatrist engaged him on that goal; for them, abstinence was always the only approach, the only goal. They stigmatized him for not following the AA orthodoxy and kicked him out of programs when he used drugs. Within a few days of exiting the programs, he always resumed his drug use. We weren't much better. Based on what we had learned, and in our frustration, we also didn't believe Alex could learn to moderate his drinking.

Second, the patient's goals shifted realistically over time, from moderation to abstinence and back to moderation, as he gained skills and control over his actions. Importantly, the process respects the patient's autonomy. And third, this interaction makes clear that harm reduction and 12-step programs need not be in conflict or mutually exclusive. Rather, they can be effectively used in tandem, a point I return to below.

As I've noted, the idea of harm reduction emerged as a compassionate alternative to extant theories of personal and disease models of addiction, one that builds on both psychodynamic and cognitive-behavioral traditions. Following in the footsteps of American psychologist Alan Marlatt, and echoing the definition of recovery advocated by CRA, Tatarsky argues that the harm reduction philosophy and treatment used an approach that embraced "the full range of harm-reducing goals including, but not limited to, abstinence. . . . Small incremental positive changes are seen as steps in the right direction."[84] Harm reduction recognizes that many of those who use drugs do not want to stop drinking or taking drugs, or at least are not yet ready to do so when they start treatment. Importantly, a harm reduction therapist is open to support moderation attempts—anathema to those relying on 12-step philosophies. If someone reduces their drinking, or drug-taking, they need interaction and support, not condemnation. The chief goal is to keep the interaction going, and the user alive. If they're alive, it's generally because they want to be alive. While it might be better if they didn't drink, or take drugs, perhaps they'll still get there. In the meantime, they don't feel abandoned, which facilitates interaction with people who aren't using. While harm reduction isn't harm elimination, we know that abandonment more likely leads to death. A common refrain in harm reduction: "There is no harm reduction possible if one is dead."

A main goal of harm reduction is to engage the active user in a collaborative therapy relationship, and to view any reduction of harm as a valuable outcome. These goals are in the service of reducing the stigma of addiction and using the client's strength to produce behavioral change. The treatment is individualized, requiring integrative therapeutic psychotherapy to develop personal skills and enhance the client's ability to set goals and manage change.[85] Overall, the goal of this "psychobiosocial process model of addiction" is to revolutionize how we treat people who use drugs, moving from a culture of stigma to "compassionate pragmatism," and treatment as opposed to incarceration.

In learning about alternative approaches to substance use, there was one topic I repeatedly came back to: comparisons of harm reduction and 12-step programs. On the one hand, many have found 12-step programs immensely useful for them over the years. I found my own Nar-Anon experience helpful when Alex was in active addiction, and many of those I admire in the addiction community, and some of those I interviewed, swear by these self-help groups. With respect to providing an important community of like-minded people searching for answers, the Minnesota model has thrived. I, nevertheless, had qualms about this method along the way, and it was decidedly not helpful for Alex, and ultimately not for me. He was stigmatized and shamed throughout the treatment process because he did not adhere to AA/Narcotics

Anonymous (NA) goals of abstinence. I am convinced we need multiple paths to recovery. As Szalavitz describes it, "The real problem is claiming that one approach is the only way and contains the only truth about addiction—rather than as one twelve-step slogan has it, telling people to 'take what you like and leave the rest.'"[86]

As the Sobells's research discussed above and other data have shown, harm reduction approaches are more humane and ultimately better at saving lives and helping people manage their drug use than jail, prisons, and rehab programs that rely solely on AA/NA fellowships. If such abstinence-based programs help some people, that's great—whatever it takes to keep them alive. But it's not the only way. The community focus of harm reduction programs provides social support for those chained to the destructive carousel of addiction. In this context, I appreciate early harm reductionist Dave Purchase's pithy observation: "A dead person can't two-step, let alone twelve-step."[87]

There are new approaches that seek to broaden 12-step methods beyond simply abstinence only.[88] Researchers and practitioners in this tradition are investigating the role of integrating quality-of-life measures into both research and medical services. This approach has promise specifically because it acknowledges the importance of problematic negative life experiences that can lead to self-medicating substance use in the first place. The goal in this developing model is not simply to promote abstinence, but to improve the substance user's quality of life. Adherents first assess the "patient's perception of how his or her health status affects physical, psychological, and social functioning and well-being" and then evaluate the patient's functioning, but also their "environment, safety, finances, access to transportation and health services, and opportunities for recreation and leisure."[89]

Some in the field have begun to broaden the very idea of addiction recovery by attempting to produce benefits in other aspects of life such as housing, health, employment, and criminal justice outcomes, along the lines of Housing Works, for example, and other programs and initiatives I've discussed throughout this book. Researchers have made headway in developing patient questionnaires and ratings— called patient-reported outcome measures—that more effectively integrate the patient's own health and quality-of-life assessments into the clinical relationship.[90] Found to be empirically valid and reliable, the resulting Substance Use Recovery Evaluator (SURE) assessment tool focuses more directly on recovery than on abstinence per se. Additional research is needed to further assess SURE's effectiveness in aiding recovery, but focusing on improving one's quality of life is all to the good.

Further, activists and researchers have noted that significant research support already exists for harm reduction approaches such as MOUD, naloxone, and overdose prevention sites. And yet, fearful that such approaches will increase drug use and overdose deaths, opponents continue to argue for incarceration and detox/treatment interventions for those who use drugs. Such strategies remain the go-to solutions for many politicians and treatment providers, even though the data do not bear out their effectiveness. Indeed, such approaches can actually increase the risk of overdose, because it's well known that those who return to the same drug levels they used previously no longer have the same tolerance. Contrary to public opinion, jails, detoxes, and rehabs don't keep people safe or sober.

Learning about harm reduction, and the new clinical and research developments since 2015, is both immensely sad and inspiring for me because of the promise it offers. We may have lost our struggle to keep Alex alive, but others can and will benefit from these developments. I hope harm reduction approaches continue to revolutionize the way the United States addresses substance use and mental health disorders. Focusing on improving the quality of life of those suffering with these public health issues is a step in the right direction. We need to champion more compassionate strategies, approaches that will save lives that would otherwise be lost. Some of those saved could be your children.

As this chapter makes clear, we need a more effective community of action. Thankfully, there are many good organizations now working on these issues. To mention just a few, the Drug Policy Alliance provides a useful yearly roadmap for those who seek to reduce the harms of drug use. The Kennedy Forum offers policy suggestions for transforming mental health and substance use disorders, especially parity issues. The Recovery Advocacy Project focuses on recovery projects and action at the local level (including through Mobilize Recovery and its Family Caucus). Shatterproof, founded by Gary Mendell who lost his son to addiction, recommends national principles of care and innovative recovery strategies. On June 8, 2022, it sponsored a daylong virtual "Stigma of Addiction Summit." Originally founded as the Center on Addiction and Substance Abuse at Columbia University, the Partnership to End Addiction seeks to link effective care to research. In November 2022, it partnered with Paramount to produce the documentary *Untreated and Unheard: The Addiction Crisis in America*, which I highly recommend.[91] This documentary should be shown in schools, police stations, communities, indeed everywhere that might enable us to save lives. The National Harm Reduction Coalition and the New Jersey Harm Reduction Coalition support strategies to reduce the negative consequences of drug use. The American Society of Addiction Medicine focuses on addiction medicine, treatment, science, and advocacy. The New Jersey-based Prevention Resources and the Center for Great Expectations offer multiple prevention and support services, education campaigns, as well as in-person and virtual conferences on substance use issues and harm reduction training. The Center for Motivation & Change uses evidence-based strategies to effect change, providing outpatient services, residential treatment, family services, and trauma treatment. It is well known for *The Beyond Addiction Workbook for Family & Friends*. Finally, as I was finishing up this book, I participated in the Family Recovery Summit, the brainchild of Karen Bernetti. From her interviews I learned about many other resources founded by parents who struggled with the substance use of their family members, among them, Truth Pharm and Trail of Truth (founded by Alexis Pleus) and Moms for All Paths to Recovery (founded by Kathleen Cochran).[92]

Ultimately, in comparison to the current treatment system of rehabs, hospitals, and abstinence programs, harm reduction is fundamentally a social process rooted in sound sociological perspectives. It recommends social interaction with those who don't judge you for your substance use and mental health disorders, and engagement in a collaborative therapeutic relationship meant to reduce harm. It demands the input of those voices affected by substance use into the development of effective solutions. There is no one true road to recovery. If the AA/NA abstinence method of recovery had worked, Alex would still be with us today. He tried that approach, time and time again. For him, however, that strategy led only to the common result sociologist Émile Durkheim identified: a sense of isolation and hopelessness. By the end of his life, Alex felt alone, in despair, and dug in a hole so deep he thought it impossible to climb out. Evidence suggests that harm reduction strategies save lives. I wish one of those lives had been Alex's.

CHAPTER 14

A Dad's Story

I Failed My Son

LEE CLARKE

Author's note: This book is my personal story, and while Chip shares much of my sorrow, pain, and trauma, our experiences, opinions, reactions, and manifestations of grief are not the same. I do not speak for him in this book. Yet, I feel it's important that he not be a silent bystander to our shared trauma. Although less inclined toward sharing, he acquiesced. Here, Chip gives voice to his story.

WHEN SOMEONE ASKS YOU TO TELL A STORY, they're asking you to make coherent something that may not have been coherent at the time. Just so with this chapter. I'm reasonably certain about the facts I use but I have found it impossible to relay the confusion, incoherence, and sheer insanity that Alex brought to our lives. It must have been worse for him, and the wisest course of action for me may well be to say heroin was his answer to the vexing questions of his life and be done with it. Obviously, that is not what I have done, but I do want to stress that I'm forcing coherence on things that were decidedly not coherent.

To this day I do not have satisfying answers to key questions, and I've mainly given up on trying to answer them: Why heroin? Why do some people become addicted while others can walk away? Why was Alex addicted and not a walker? I understand that he backed himself into a corner so confining that suicide was the only way out. But why get to that point? We never beat him, nor was he abused (the first and favored explanations of medical professionals). Was it just an accident? I think drug use is generally an answer to a question, even if that question is no deeper than "How can I get outside my head to have a little fun or relaxation?" But why was Alex's life so bad that opiates became the answer? We were never abusive or poor, although sending him to an expensive private school often made him feel that way. Once he asked, "Daddy, are we rich? Are you famous?" In fact, I was a little famous because of my work on disasters, including TV and radio appearances, being quoted in big newspapers, giving talks to the New York Fed, etc. The *New York Times* even profiled me. But fame of any sort and depth doesn't translate easily into a better lifestyle. It takes money for that. And I explained to Alex that we were richer than most people in the world, but we were very far from the kind of rich he was asking about. He had friends with three- and four-car garages, European vacations, and so on. Some of those people were nice, but some weren't, which is normal for the super-rich because they come to believe not only that they are rich because they deserve it, but that other people are not rich because they don't. Still, plenty of Alex's friends, rich or not, were easy to be with and kind, smart people. There just was no good reason to use heroin because its risks are easily assessed, and they are high, so why take the chance? And now, with fentanyl, it's even worse. Frankly, I have no idea why Alex went down that road.

But my ongoing confusion is not what I've been asked to write about.

From the moment I first saw Alex, I loved him as I'd never loved before or since. When someone asked me what it was like to be a father, I'd say that you can imagine hating your mother, imagine leaving your spouse, imagine any friendship turning sour. And siblings? Please. But with your child there is nothing you would not do for him, or her, nothing that would diminish my love for my son. Then heroin came along. I don't care if there are studies that show heroin addiction is like other addictions—relatively easily conquered with the right social support. I don't believe them. I don't care if withdrawal is easier in supportive, socially accepting situations. I don't care if we're not supposed to say "junkie" or "drug addict" ("substance use disorder" is the politically correct term, hiding the horror of life with a heroin addict while pretending that heroin isn't special).

My son turned into someone I didn't know and didn't want to know. He wanted heroin more than anything else. Sure, he wanted to be loved and accepted, as his mother says. But when he was jonesing for dope (meaning craving like a maniac), he was the most despicable person I'd ever met. At a multifamily meeting at a Connecticut hospital, we all went around the room and said how it made us feel when we saw our loved one high on heroin. I told the truth. "I hate him," I said, and Alex looked surprised.

But I still loved him more than life itself. As Pat shows in this book we did everything we could think of at the time to help. I was determined not to let Alex's addiction drag us into the poorhouse, and it didn't, but I wrote a lot of checks for $10,000, $20,000, and $30,000. I dare not try to add it all up in a spreadsheet. What's the point? We spent the money and he's dead anyway.

Here's the thing that eats away at my soul. I loved him while hating his behavior. I gave up hope but grasped any straw that seemed plausible to lead him away from the destruction. I broke laws. I lied to police. I lied to my wife. I lied to Alex. I told him he could still be successful and that I didn't think worse of him for getting caught in heroin's trap. Ultimately, I failed at everything. It's sexist and even stupid to say this but a friend from a death group (aka a bereavement group) hit the nail on the head when he said, "Fathers are supposed to fix things." This, though, I could not fix. I wake up and go to sleep with the monsters of guilt and shame gnawing away at my life. People say we did everything we could. Just as Alcoholics Anonymous (AA) or Narcotics Anonymous (NA), those generally useless organizations of the dreadful, say, it's no one's fault but their own. By now I should be over it, like I'm over the death of my dog or the deaths of my grandmothers? Bullshit. The editor of two of my books lost his son to heroin. He's the only person who has ever said anything close to useful about my own suffering. He said (and I think he was quoting another sociologist who had lost his child to the H), "You never get over it. You just get used to the idea that you'll never get over it." I can't imagine a truer thing to say. Still, doctors write in my charts that I have not success-fully dealt with my son's death, which is as vacuous as it is true. F-ck the doctors. I want my son back.

What makes you scream? Many of us scream inside all the time. That's what I do. It leads me to do stupid things, make out-of-the-blue idiot remarks, and think dark thoughts. For example, I wonder about ways to commit suicide. Not as a plan. I'm no more going to kill myself than I am going to bring my son back to life. No. I just wonder. What do people feel like just before they do try it? How did Alex feel? Is it like I feel right now, how I felt this morning, how I'll feel when I go to bed? Do they make good plans for it and, if so, what's the best one? I'm sure they don't want to leave a mess or an ugly visage for their loved ones to find. Robin Williams hung himself. Discovering his body must have been a repulsive sight. I've seen dead people, some of whom were people I loved—my mother, my brother, my sister-in-law, but not Alex. My mother was the worst because she'd taken her false teeth out when she was in the hospital and her jaw jutted to one side when she passed. It was nearly gruesome. My brother and sister-in-law just looked like they were lying down. They were the wrong color, a sort of blue one doesn't otherwise see, but hardly gruesome or in pain. I even kissed my brother's forehead before leaving the room, four times I think I remember, once for each of his children, once for my son, and once for our other niece. Yet I wanted to scream then too. But I never did. Maybe writing this is my way of screaming through my unending pain and guilt and unhappiness and surety of how worthless I was to him.

Why that latter sentiment? Simple. Because fathers fix things. That's what they're supposed to do. I can fix a lot of things. But I couldn't fix the most important thing and that haunts me in ways only another father who should have fixed important things but failed could really understand. My plan here is to spend a few pages spilling my guts, tell-ing what it was like, and a few pages of sociological analysis of some collective issues involving the road Alex took. I have no central mes-sage. This may be because there is none to be had, or it may be that I'm not smart enough to figure one out. Clichés certainly don't help, so I'll try to avoid those. I don't really care about saving the world, or even other substance use disordered people. That's cold, I know, and I like to think of myself as a warm, caring liberal. Reading my own words over and over, I may be wrong about that.

At the hospital, one of the emergency services (EMS) guys said he was "royal blue" when they arrived at our home. That's how they found Alex after one of his overdoses. By that time, our neighbors were consoling Pat in the living room, I think some cops were already there (I hate having cops in the house), and I'd stopped doing CPR on my son. What the EMS fellows didn't realize—why should they?—was he was in fact coming out of the royal blue when they got to our house. Just moments (seconds, minutes, whatever) before, I heard a scream from my wife that I never again want to hear. I was in the TV room, vaguely aware that Alex had taken a shower (people shoot up in the bathroom because it's natural to lock the door and demand privacy there) and was now in my office, when the scream came. All I remember is that she yelled at the top of her lungs, "Alex!" but in a horror-movie tone, unreal in both its register and what it did to me. I jumped out of my chair. I knew what was happening. I knew what I would find. I didn't know if he was dead, but I was prepared for it. I did my own scream: "Call 911!"

Alex was lying on his back, a trickle of blood coming from his nose which came from banging his head on my desk as he passed out. I flung my office chair out of the room and straddled my son. I saw him slip from white to blue—first his lips then the rest of his face, then anywhere I looked. I slapped him and yelled his name, as if that would matter. No response. I'd taken CPR years before and it all came back to me as if I practiced it every day. I ripped his shirt down the front, straightened his head to make sure nothing was in his mouth, traced my fingers up his abdomen to the xiphoid process, and started my ABCs—airway, breathing, compressions. The current thinking (I need a refresher course) was that the precordial thump was a waste of time and so was an initial breath. In a situation like that the brain needs oxygen right away and the only way to get it there is to get the oxygen that's in the blood at the moment to the brain. So, I started compressions right away. I did pause to give a couple of breaths after a while and to see if it was working. Initially, it wasn't. Back to work.

I had the thought of getting my phone out of my pocket to take his picture. I'd show it to him later and then maybe, just maybe, he'd experience the same horror I was feeling. Maybe it would scare him straight. But maybe the time it would take to photograph his face would be just enough time for him to have brain damage or die. So, I didn't take a picture (I can still see it as clearly now as then). I kept pushing on his chest. I kept thinking I was looking at my dead son, that my efforts would be fruitless. Why bother? He seemed determined to die anyway.

Then he took a breath on his own. Not a whole breath. A small breath. Holy shit! The next thing I remember is yelling to Pat and my neighbors, who had come when they saw the ambulance lights, "We have him back." Or something like that. Faint breaths, though he was still blue. EMS guys took over, which was a relief. I was exhausted and the enormity of the situation was dawning on me. By the time they loaded Alex onto a gurney he was white again. Thank goodness. Blue is not a proper color for human skin.

There were a lot of rescues in Alex' life, as Pat has covered in such excruciating detail. Some of these were the result of rich, white privilege. One of my most memorable is the night I got a call on my cell phone from an officer from the Edison, New Jersey, police department. I had fallen asleep on my deck, the result of too much gin and too much worry—worry because I knew Alex had taken Hunter's car. There's only one place he'd be going in the middle of the night: his favorite dealer in South Plainfield, New Jersey. Anyway, the officer told me Alex had been in a single-car crash. He was alright, but I should come right away. The Edison cop started to give directions, but I knew immediately where they were because I knew Alex was on his way back from South Plainfield. I told the officer I'd be right there, then brushed my teeth and washed my face. After all, I didn't want to be arrested for drunk driving. The rescue could wait for a few minutes. I think if Alex had been black, he would already have been arrested.

When I made the turn onto the road—this was the middle of the night—there were a lot of flashing red and blue lights. When I got out of my car an officer came over to talk to me. Alex had veered off the road and crushed the right front fender of Hunter's car by slamming into a mailbox on a post near the side of the road. Alex told the officers that he had a seizure the night before and hit his head on the floor. He told them he believed he momentarily blacked out from the undiagnosed, untreated concussion.

The officer asked me if what Alex said was true, and there was just enough truth in it that I could convincingly lie: "Yes, my wife and I saw the seizure and subsequent fall. No, we did not take him to the hospital." The officer then began to berate *me* for "not taking these things seriously." As my grandmother was fond of saying, I was laughing with my throat cut. I could think of only two things: I had to save my son from being arrested, and how ridiculous it was that I was getting yelled at by this cop. I was the knight in shining armor here. I galloped to the rescue on my white stallion. I was doing what fathers should do, and you're giving me shit about it?! I apologized to the officer, promised I'd take Alex to the hospital later in the day. I didn't say what I was thinking: Have you shoved your hand in his pocket? Did you find the heroin and the syringes? Did you give him a field sobriety test? Alex went to sit in my car (I had the keys) while I went to survey the damage to Hunter's car. He'd pulled off to the side of the road, where the car spent the rest of the night. I also went to the house of the damaged mailbox and told the guy who came to the door that I'd pay for the damage. He just shook his head. "No, that's not necessary."

So, I saved him again. I got in my car to drive away. "You motherfucker," I said. I couldn't think of anything else to say. Later I would find the heroin and the syringes in his pockets.

We had a lot of interaction with officialdom because of Alex's heroin use. I have always had cop-friends and had many more as I got older. This was partly because of my scholarship on disaster. I lecture to and about so-called first responders, and I made a lot of friends because of that. It was nearly always surprising for rooms of cops, firefighters, and the like to hear that disaster researchers regard them as essential in disaster even though they are rarely the first to respond. They should be called "official responders" rather than first responders, I would say. This is for the simple reason that people who are in the throes of calamity—the earthquake, school shooting, or whatever—are the first on the scene. Take, for instance, the example of 9/11. About 420 official responders died that day, and it is surely right to say they were heroes and that they saved some people. But the total number of dead was about three thousand, the vast majority of whom were just regular people (indeed, contrary to many other disasters, they were disproportionately well-educated, white males), and while I have not tried to count the actual number of people rescued by regular people, it was a large number. Most of the dead, by the way, were above where the planes struck the World Trade Center. There wasn't anything anyone could have done for them. Indeed, by the time official responders arrive at a disaster scene of any type, most of the people who are going to die are already dead.

In the present context, the implication of this gruesome fact is that if we are going to save people from dying by heroin, we're going to have to give instructions and tools (anti-opioids) to the people most likely to cross paths with the victims. This includes schoolteachers, office managers, young people, and even other (to be politically incorrect) addicts. Our lives are organized by institutions (by which I mean ways of thinking and behaving), social networks, and formal organizations, and that's how disasters (most of them anyway) do whatever damage they're going to do. If harm reduction is really going to matter much, we must take account of the cultures and social structures in which people live. This—not some fantastical higher power—is why AA works for some people. To get control of or quit drinking alcohol for most people, it seems to help to be around people who have struggled similarly. This is why despite my deep skepticism about 12-step programs, I took Alex to AA and NA meetings as often as he would go. It proved to be in vain. He never connected. When Alex's networks of people who did not live and breathe for their fix left him, the end was inevitable.

That's the source of my guilt. This was one of the very few times that Dr. O, whose advice I sought when large crises pushed me toward the abyss, got it wrong. He thought my way of dealing with Alex's death was essentially one of denial, as if acting like things were normal again would allow me to think things really were normal. That was not at all what was going on with me. Rather I was overwhelmed with things to do, contradictory feelings I didn't want, and loss that was so great that I sometimes thought my brother was right to eat and drink himself to death. I was trying to deal with my own pain of losing my mother, my brother, his wife, and a score of normal failures all at once. I knew I would be facing new challenges, even if I didn't really understand what that was going to mean. My family was shrinking, but my responsibilities were growing. There do not exist two more delightful people in the world than my nephew Hunter and niece Ginny. I got to the point of not feeling odd at all when I introduced them to other people as my son and daughter. But I needed to be left alone to do all that, to get to that point. Instead, there were cops in the house, insurance bills to pay, lawyers to deal with and pay, doctors, nurses, rehab staff to manage, and so forth. It was like a black hole of officialdom was sucking me into its soul-crushing weight. I couldn't see straight or do my academic writing or get control of things. It got to the point where I knew the rehabs we forced Alex into were a complete scam. It took years for Alex to so completely lose his self to heroin that even his drug-using friends (Adderall, weed, cocaine, mushrooms, constant drinking—all kinds of stuff, but not heroin) left. It took far longer for me to give up on him. We pushed Alex into rehab after rehab, but they were all only twenty-eight or thirty days long, because that's what insurance pays for. The logic, if there is any logic in it, is that someone can kick the habit in twenty-eight days even though it probably took years to develop. It doesn't make sense. And as Pat recounts, they don't work except as revenue generators. Most rehabs should be summarily shut down. Yet they provided relief to me because they got the biggest source of chaos out of my house if only for a short time and for completely wrong reasons. I needed peace, longed for it. Real peace would come only if Alex beat his habit. But that wasn't happening. I saw him in complete withdrawal once. It was suffering one wishes only on their worst enemies. My thought was, "Good. Maybe he really has a chance of coming out the other side."

But I was wrong. And ultimately, I abandoned him too. That was wrong, yet another thing I could not fix. It is what I mean when I say that I failed my son.

There's nothing good about heroin. That seems stupid to say aloud, I know, but there are a great many people who think it's just dandy. I'll grant that it must feel divine. Alex said it was like having God wrap

His arms around you, and I've heard similar variations of that metaphor. But it's still not good. It makes people crazy to get the drug, devoted to it as one might long to be with a lover who's out of reach. It makes otherwise honest people into thieves. People sell their bodies for it, give you the shirts off their back, sell their possessions, go to the ends of the earth. I suppose it makes a sort of macabre sense to be willing to do so much to get what you need more than anything else in the world. That's why there's nothing good about heroin.

It must feel good though. I did a lot of drugs in my day. At least it seems to me now, it was a lot of drugs. Not just weed, but there's a story there. My friend and I smoked our first joint, or maybe two, at a Friday night dance. I think we were in the ninth grade. When Monday came everybody in the school knew what we'd done, including, I have no doubt, my mother who taught in the school (Mama didn't tell Daddy, thank goodness). Teachers who thought I was the cat's meow told me how disappointed they were. Of course, within four to six weeks all my middle-class, white friends were asking me where they could cop some dope ("dope" meant marijuana then). And we smoked with more than one high school teacher. But part of the full story here is that when I lost all those friends, I gained other friends—my black contemporaries with whom I had nothing in common before the big dope-smoking incidents. I lost some friends yet gained others. It was worth it.

I did plenty of drugs back in the day. There's a whole class of drugs called hallucinogens that I loved. The highly synthesized stuff like acid was far too unpredictable. Mescaline was good but never really lived up to its promises. Mushrooms, though, were great. I grew up in South Florida. It rains a lot there, especially in the summer. After a monsoon we drove to cow fields, sometimes twenty miles away, and picked shrooms. Someone had taught me how to recognize the good ones, that is to say the ones that got you high but didn't kill you. And they were free! I was genuinely surprised to discover after moving to Long Island that people paid good money for mushrooms, stuff I was not long before picking out of cow shit. And if you had a valium or a Quaalude to take after the mushroom high wore off it was stupendous. That way, you didn't have to grind your teeth and stay up all night. They also had to be used sparingly, which we did.

The second thing was more dangerous: cocaine. I was in college in the late 1970s and coke was all the rage. The high was too short, for sure, but the cure for that was . . . more cocaine. We'd do coke all Saturday night but then take Sunday to sleep and otherwise recover, then go back to class on Monday. No problem. We didn't think of it as addictive.

Why tell these stories? Because they bring up issues of shame and regret. Pat is strong in her belief that we should do away with shame as a response to heroin use. I am not as sure about that. During most of the time I used drugs, they were intermittently available. I am frankly shocked at the omnipresent smell of marijuana when I walk about New York City. We smoked a lot of weed back in the day, but its illegality meant we mostly kept it a secret. But in all my smoke-filled days and bleary-eyed nights, heroin never once crossed my path. There was no demand for it. Maybe I would have tried it, but I doubt it. Then, heroin use was highly stratified. I never met a middle-class white kid who did heroin (maybe a few music makers, but their use didn't last long). Heroin was, as far as we knew, confined to poor black people in urban ghettos. I hope that doesn't sound racist, but racism might be unavoidable when talking about drugs.

Things are different now. Heroin is readily available to anyone seeking it out. High school kids see it as just another drug to try. They don't realize until it's too late that it will ruin their lives. There's no shame in using heroin, and I think that's part of the problem.

ENDING 1: THE ROLE OF SHAME

Shame is important in this story. The idea suffuses this book, and Pat goes a long way to make us not feel it.

Feel it or not it cannot be avoided.

The truth is that when I found out Alex was using heroin, I was flabbergasted. Truly, he was smarter than most people I know, and don't forget I swim in an ocean of PhDs. But using heroin is just stupid. Pot, sure. What did I care? I think you should be able to walk into your local convenience store and buy pot, which is increasingly possible. I smoked a lot of pot. But as I said, heroin never crossed my path. It was in a special category. It's not that we were wiser than to get mixed up with something that would wreak so much devastation. We just didn't come across it, and by "we" I mean people who were happy to try many other drugs. I think that was mainly because it was a shameful thing to do, even if our conception of shame wasn't well formed. We were cool if we had good weed from Columbia or, more rarely, Thai stick. But heroin. Are you kidding me?

But now that stigma is gone. For young people—a lot more of them than in the past at least—it is just another drug. They know it can be dangerous, but young people do a lot of dangerous things and get away with it. Heroin is especially dangerous when it's mixed with fentanyl, but that's just exaggerated danger to many. Also, many of them would feel shame if they stuck a needle in their arm. If shame keeps them from trying heroin, then it isn't all bad. Maybe we should just say it's not going to help to heap shame upon people already addicted. Prevention may not be everything, but it's not nothing.

ENDING 2: DANCING WITH DEATH

This book started with a description of two "black-clad officers" from Newark approaching our front door. One was in a black suit. She was a detective. The other wore a Newark police uniform. He was an officer. I would see them both again.

They rang the doorbell, and I knew before we opened it that Alex was dead. We'd had a lot of police cars from our little town of Metuchen in front of the house. It was a familiar sight. But a Newark police car? Those cops were far out of their jurisdiction. It could only mean one thing. Actually, I'd expected and imagined this day just as it happened. A few nights before we had some friends at our house. Alex had been missing for several days. I told my friend Joe that I thought Alex was either arrested or dead. He wasn't answering his phone. That was the tell. Through all the years of madness Alex and his beloved heroin brought into our lives, and the slow ruination of his own life, Alex never lost his phone. It was his lifeline to his dealers, after all. It was also his lifeline to us when he'd get in trouble. But now he wasn't answering it. We knew he had it when he got to Newark. He'd made a call or two to a Newark area code. I couldn't tell exactly who he called but I could see on our phone bill that he had indeed done some calling. It was just like the $2.59, or some similarly low number, he spent at the Walgreens close to the Newark train station. That was probably enough to buy maybe a week's worth of syringes. So, the failure to answer the phone now meant he was either in jail and didn't want to call us, or it meant he was dead. The phone was turned on briefly after he arrived in Newark. Then the phone went dead too. My best guess is that he traded the phone for dope and had to turn it on to show a dealer that it worked, but that afterwards the SIM card was taken out and discarded. The phone disappeared forever. Just as Alex disappeared forever.

I said above that I'd see those officers again. I did, the next day, on NJ.com, the state's largest news website. I'd asked one of the Newark cops who came to the house where they found Alex. The officer told me the name of a big street in Newark, adding that "at one end are the restaurants, close to the restaurants you know. But people like you would never go to the other end." By people like me he meant white and middle-class who would have no legitimate business at the other end of that street. So, I knew what to search for on the internet. It's hardly unusual to see articles about people who are stabbed or shot to death in Newark. Sometimes even overdose qualifies as news there. Newark can be a violent place. However, because the officer had told me the street name, a few internet searches led me to the article on Alex's death. They didn't list his name, of course, or publish pictures of his body. But there, plain as day, were the officer and detective who stood in my living room the day before. You can still find the article. In it, the reporter explains that Alex had been found in an empty lot by someone who worked close by. There's a picture of someone from the Essex County coroner's office pushing a gurney with a body bag on it into a large SUV. My son was in that body bag. All I could do was stare and cry.

Well, it wasn't all I could do. I did two other things. I emailed the article's author to ask some questions that were raised by comments. He responded to one comment that the cops didn't think it was a violence-related death (which meant there would be no investigation) partly or mainly because they found a suicide note in his pocket. Not long after, Pat and I were in the Newark Police Station, where a cop let us take a photo of the note. The other thing I did was not tell Pat about the article. I regret this. At the time, though, it felt like the right thing to do. As I say, you couldn't see Alex's body in the photos. But your imagination can put him right there. The pain at the time, for both of us, was more searing than I can describe. Why add to Pat's pain for no obvious purpose? Of course, she's seen the article now, and the pictures, and the snarky comments posted at the time. Things disappear on the net quickly, so I downloaded and screenshot all that was related to the article right away. This isn't a big part of the overall story. But it doesn't feel entirely irrelevant either.

That's it. There are no happy takeaways about heaven or defeating adversity. I don't believe in heaven, and in my case at least the only thing defeated was my family. There are only other endings, all of which end up at the same place. So, I guess, really, in the end, I am left with only this reality: Alex needed one of those endings and he found it. I guess he needed it so much that he couldn't bring himself to care about the absolute carnage he'd leave behind. The odd thing is that he was loving and caring. And smart. So how could he have done that? I don't know, and I suspect he didn't know either. He just needed the pain to stop. I failed my son, and he died. I regret. I grieve.

Epilogue

> Most people are on some kind of pilgrimage, whether or not
> they recognize it as such. If you put your writing in the
> form of a quest you will make a connection with your
> readers that will surprise you with its power.
> —William Zinsser, *Writing about Your Life*

We Walk Alone

My quest for understanding brought me along the two roads Alex
traveled. On the first road, Chip and I hoped to rear Alex through an
ideal childhood to a life of his own. When we moved onto that second,
bumpy road, our hope was simply to navigate the potholes to get back
onto the first road. When anorexia and addiction led to dreadful
detours, we hoped simply to save Alex. Now, in our grief, we walk alone.

In this book, I want to give meaning to Alex's life and to suggest a
possible roadmap for more effectively addressing the overdose crisis. I
researched and wrote this book to honor my beautiful boy, to learn
more about the whys and hows of addiction, and to inspire my community and my country into action through greater adherence to harm
reduction approaches. Alex was a person who used drugs, and I want
others to hear his voice, and the voices of all those who use drugs and
their families. It's well past time to set aside the blame we have placed
on those shattered by addiction. The moral argument is bankrupt,
and yet it persists. Instead, we must broaden our gaze to those practices and institutions that are complicit in Alex's (and so many others')
addiction and death. We must address the systemic factors that produce

307

and reproduce addiction. And we must support public policy solutions, both governmental and private, that promote treatment and prevention strategies over incarceration. We need an approach that operates for the larger societal good.

This book presents only a fraction of what I learned during Alex's years of anorexia and addiction and since his death. I am not on the road I had envisioned, but I am still walking, learning, and now sharing my story—with what I hope will be a broad audience. Even years out, I feel the pain of Alex's loss, a hurt that will never go away. I remember the first pain I ever saw flicker across Alex's face as a newborn. I was staring at him when he got his first shot, and saw his face contort with pain. It pained me to be the reason he was feeling such distress. Even then I realized that it was just the beginning of the pain we all go through. Now the hurt is different. I learn about the grandchildren of my friends, and I'm truly happy for them. But I'll never be a grandmother to Alex's kids. I hear about the engagements, marriages, children, and career successes of Alex's friends, and I'm excited for them. But I miss the experiences I could have shared with Alex. I recently sold Alex's bass and amp to a local Metuchen kid. I'm thankful for the music he'll enjoy, but I miss the beautiful (and not so beautiful) music Alex would have played on that bass.

I keep in touch with his friends, and I wonder what Alex would be doing in his early thirties. I also realize how strange life is. Hunter and Ginny lost their parents, and we lost our son. But we found each other, and we are family. They have given us the opportunity to continue to parent, and we're so proud of the young adults they have become.

What can I say to others who have lived, or will have to live, with active addiction and mental health disorders in their families? What have I learned in my quest to understand addiction and survive its aftermath? In this book, I have tried to provide some useful answers when I could. Yet, there are many unknowns and questions that elude answers. In this pilgrimage I have also sought to answer some of my own questions. Too many unknowns remain, and that is sometimes the most difficult reality to contemplate during those long nights when I cannot fall back to sleep. Why didn't Alex get off the train on his way to Newark that last Wednesday? What did he do in Newark those last six days? Where is the red canvas suitcase full of clothes that he brought home from Florida? Where are the things that were in his backpack? Did he sell his clothes and phone for drugs, or were they stolen? Did he really refuse entry at that last rehab? Who gave him that last dose of heroin, the one that killed him? Was he thinking of us that last day? While I learned answers to some of my questions, mostly I learned that our love and our efforts were not enough to save him, a lesson many families learn about their addicted loved ones.

Chip has it right when he describes our future—any self you think you will be tomorrow, anything you plan to do for the next week, for the rest of the year, and indeed for the rest of your life, assumes your child will be alive. When that assumption proves false, your world crumbles, and you need to reorganize yourself and your family's future. Chip and I were on those two roads with Alex all those years. We shared those pathways to potential futures and got a future without him—a destination on a road we didn't want to walk. We, and Hunter and Ginny who survive with us, must now navigate without Alex. Although we may grieve differently, for me despair is a dead end. The road I hope we can follow involves integrating our pain, our reorganized selves, into lives that allow for future peace and joy. That road beckons.

A Counterfactual Exercise

What I really want, though, is a do-over. Of course, I know that's not possible, but I have thought deeply about it and can imagine a different outcome. To close this book, I consider alternative history, or what historians call counterfactual inquiry.[1] Such thinking addresses questions such as "What if John F. Kennedy had lived?"[2] Or more recently, "What if Hillary Clinton won the 2016 election?" I do this because, as historian Niall Ferguson has written, "decisions about the future are—usually—based on weighing up the potential consequences of alternative courses of action, it makes sense to compare the actual outcomes of what we did in the past with the conceivable outcomes of what we might have done."[3]

Everything I've learned about harm reduction convinces me that it might have worked for Alex. Although he never used that language, that is precisely the life he wanted, one that would have permitted him to drink in moderation. But no program he attended allowed him that option. And, frankly, we were so ensconced in the existing recovery orthodoxy, we couldn't see it either. Maybe it's a fantasy that could never have been realized. But then again, maybe harm reduction could have worked—it certainly has for others.

What might have happened if the historical context our family lived through had been different? What if we had lived in a world steeped in compassionate, paradigm-shifting harm reduction methods, as opposed to the punitive, choice-based approaches we faced? Perhaps Alex would not have moved so far down the second road, perhaps he would even have shifted back to the first. Maybe we could have kept him alive long enough that he would have rejected heroin. Maybe we could have helped him make different "choices" if there had been more than one option available to him.

It's hard not to think first about chance. How different might our story have been if things had happened in different ways in Alex's travels down the second road. Some of this is clearly serendipitous, when for example he survived several car crashes while driving impaired; our friend Ken found him at Love's Truck Stop in Fort Pierce, Florida; the Plainfield police officer called us to pick him up; Joaquin found him disoriented outside the Boynton Beach Panera's; Liz called him an ambulance that last day of April in 2015; and Poo was always there to care for him. Clearly Alex had people who cared about him as he trekked along the second road, a community that saved and protected him, even when he resisted.

But chance cuts both ways. Neither Alex nor we had any control over the deaths that devastated our family the summer he completed college. Maybe he'd have gotten a higher score on his dental school exam if they'd allowed him extra time, and maybe he could have succeeded in his career plans without detours if a dental program had accepted him. If he hadn't gone to that New Jersey bar that night, Alex might not have met the guy who sold him his first heroin. If that police officer on the New Jersey turnpike hadn't seen Alex's friend move marijuana from the trunk to the front seat at the rest stop, he wouldn't have pulled them over. If the passenger standing in line next to him as he headed to Ambrosia hadn't had Xanax, and if he wasn't also getting the free drinks in first class (the only seat available), he wouldn't have had the altercation with police when he got to West Palm Beach. We sure wish his counselor hadn't suggested Silver Hill Hospital, and the Princeton program hadn't incorrectly diagnosed him with mumps. If there had been a program in place so that our local police officer could have sent him to a treatment program rather than jail, he might not have been incarcerated. And if someone with Narcan found him the night he took the heroin that stopped his heart, maybe he could have survived once again. Perhaps then he could have succeeded in his Rutgers master's program and his College Recovery sober housing. And so on, and so on.

Looking back to Alex's middle school years, it's notable that his teachers and classmates were instrumental in easing him back to health after his bout with anorexia, providing him with an embracing community that welcomed him. When he ran afoul of the school rules against alcohol in his senior year of high school, however, that same school took a punitive, zero tolerance approach and suspended him. Perhaps if his high school had restorative justice methods in place, it might have chosen a different method of discipline, one that might have worked better for Alex and others like him.

During college, Alex faced reasonable, compassionate sanctions for his excessive drinking behavior, including arrests and hospital visits that were eventually stricken from his record. But after his 2012 graduation, the unexpected deaths of family members and the collapse of his career plans shattered his already shaky sense of self. His drinking and drug-taking put him on a collision course with New Jersey's criminal justice system.

And it is here, in the criminal justice arena, where alternative approaches might have made the most difference in Alex's trajectory. According to its adherents, harm reduction strategies strive to "meet people where they are, but not leave them there." They also remind us that "dead people can't recover."[4] If marijuana had been decriminalized in New Jersey before April 2014, rather than in February 2021, Alex would never have been charged with possession in the first place. No doubt Alex would have cheered President Biden's October 6, 2022, proclamation pardoning marijuana possession. Moreover, if possession of small amounts of all drugs was decriminalized, as has been true in Portugal since 2000, Alex would not have been charged with heroin possession in June 2014, and hence not faced a warrant for his arrest in Plainfield, New Jersey. Instead of deteriorating in jail in August and September 2014, he might have participated in lengthy, nonpunitive mental health treatment, care that had no automatic thirty-day limit. Or what if, like Joaquin, a mental health judge had sent Alex to treatment rather than jail? And what if those treatments had been long enough to seriously address his issues, and be fully covered by insurance? It's clear from Alex's suicide letters that his hopelessness and despair stemmed primarily from his belief that he'd never be able to get beyond the criminal charges he faced. As he saw it, his life was already ruined, and there was no reason to live. We understand his despair because we know the criminal justice research: those who "check the box" that they've ever been convicted are likely unemployable. In a harm reduction world, legislation could "ban the box," providing much needed second chances.

Ideally, families with loved ones lost to overdose would stand shoulder to shoulder, advocating for policies known to reduce the harms of drug use. But there is a growing contingent of families demanding tougher criminalization laws to address (especially fentanyl) drug supply, even calling for prosecuting drug suppliers as murderers. I understand their heartache and their fury. Early on I found some of those who sold Alex drugs and forwarded their names to the police, who were wholly uninterested in the results of my detective work. As my journey progressed, I came to realize that a far more complex web of social factors and institutional failures lead to addiction and that is where we must concentrate our efforts. More punitive drug laws aren't the answer. More important is doing something about the demand for drugs and saving those in the midst of the insanity.[5]

Furthermore, it's not enough to adhere to Alcoholics Anonymous (AA)'s "fake it 'til you make it" mantra, which preaches that by following AA's 12 steps to abstinence, sobriety will come. As I witnessed firsthand, abstinence programs are often ineffective, but they are virtually the only treatment method out there. We need ways to provide safe, maintenance doses of therapeutic drugs under controlled conditions, while still encouraging those reliant on drugs to wean themselves off when they're ready. There should be greater access to methadone and buprenorphine to those who want these medicines. Supervised injection sites should be available for those still reliant on drugs, safe places where substance users can test and ingest drugs. Such sites have existed for decades in places like Vancouver, Canada. For the first time in the United States, in December 2021 two sites opened in New York City. If those sites had existed in Newark in May 2015, or in locations even closer to our home, Alex might have found a haven that could have saved his life. We know such sites do save lives—no one has died at the Vancouver site since it opened in 2003. A February 2023 article in the *US News & World Report* reported that about 2,300 people have used the New York City injection sites a total of 55,000 times since they opened, and there have been more than 700 overdose interventions and no deaths.[6] When people are ready to quit, there are opportunities co-located to encourage recovery. And yet, NYC's supervised injection sites face funding shortages, and the U.S. attorney for the Southern District of New York is threatening to shut them down, claiming they violate federal, state, and local law.[7]

I wish that in March 2015 our insurance had approved Alex for treatment at Caron, located outside Philadelphia. If Sunrise Detox had recommended a local program, rather than flying him on the rehab's dime to Florida, the "non"-recovery capital of the world, we would have been close enough to participate in his treatment, and perhaps protect him from the predatory sober houses he encountered in the month before he died, saving him from the infamous "Florida shuffle." He wouldn't have visited the doctor who prescribed him ninety Xanax and thirty Ambien when he walked in off the street, the drugs that landed him nearly comatose in the Delray Medical Center less than two weeks before he died.

When it comes to the AA treatment methods and drug addiction, there is little evidence of AA's success in helping those who use drugs become sober.[8] It is well beyond time to examine other paths to recovery, such as programs that incorporate medications for opioid abuse disorder. In his 2022 book, Carl Erik Fisher reported that "only one in twenty legally referred people getting treatment for opioid addiction receives these potentially life-saving medications."[9] Peer support programs like AA need to be open to the use of medicine in recovery, which for the most part they are not. While the 12 steps work for some, they fail for most, and they failed Alex. The rigidity of current treatment models reinforces the stigma of addiction and chips away at self-esteem. Alternative paths to recovery offer the hope of a more compassionate approach that eschews the labels and blame Alex faced during his time in rehabs and hospitals. These institutions operate by establishing the categories by which they evaluate patients. If you don't go along with the way they define "normal" or "recovery," it's evidence of deviance or defiance. AA was considered the norm—the gold standard—at every single rehab Alex attended. And as his experience demonstrates, there is little room for deviance in such programs. The medical staff described him as "disdainful of AA and abstinence" (which was true enough), but then as a consequence he was essentially written off as "not salvageable," "inauthentic," "brittle and hypersensitive to criticism," and even a "sociopath" and "psychopath." Their approach placed the blame for the ineffectiveness of their program on Alex's young shoulders and amounted to a classic self-fulfilling prophecy. Tellingly, not one of the dozen rehabs or hospitals Alex attended ever did a follow-up survey with him or with us. No doubt they didn't—and don't—want hard data demonstrating their failures. It's no wonder that no one really knows the success rates of most addiction programs. While some organizations learn how to avoid failure by closely examining their mistakes, that realization is nearly nonexistent in the drug treatment world.[10]

Frank Greenagel is a New Jersey clinical social worker with a long association with Rutgers Recovery House and Rutgers School of Social Work. I originally met him back in the spring of 2015 when Alex was re-accepted to the graduate program in business and science and applying for sober living at College Recovery. I reconnected with him again at the New Jersey Recovery High School's 2022 graduation. He sent me some of his writings about his years of experience in addiction treatment, and his views are largely negative, and consistent with what we experienced: "I advocate on behalf and work in the addiction treatment industry. I do this despite [the] fact that very few programs are any good and most are horrendous. This is true for both in-patient and out-patient programs. They dress themselves up with fancy websites, glossy brochures, and friendly marketers. Back in the late 90s when I was a private first class (PFC) in the Army, [my sergeant] occasionally told me that 'You can't polish a turd.' . . . [But as one of my students responded,] 'Yeah, but you can roll it in glitter.'"[11]

Greenagel nevertheless offers useful advice for treatment program owners and families looking for programs: ensure that (1) therapists and workers are adequately supervised, (2) there is adequate individual therapy, and (3) existing effectiveness data is collected by a neutral outsider. When we were amid our insanity, I would have benefited from asking those questions of all the rehabs Alex attended.

There are existing treatment alternatives to AA's methods that have demonstrated success, but they are few and far between. As a newly minted psychiatrist (and harm reduction supporter), Carl Erik Fisher had access to a lengthy, specialized rehab program for medical personnel when he misused drugs. These physician health programs do effectiveness studies and claim a five-year success rate of 75 percent or more. To someone with my experience in the addiction field, this seems amazing.[12] No other program even comes close. It's not just the social capital that those attending bring to such programs that accounts for these success rates, it's the institutions themselves and the strategies they employ. Fisher's physician health program effectively used strategies such as negative contingency management, which required him to undergo years of mandatory, random urine screening to keep his medical license. These strategies worked for Fisher; he's a psychiatrist in good standing today. If such approaches are generating success with medical personnel like Fisher, they could also help others. Perhaps, they could have helped Alex.

Another important detail differentiated Carl Erik Fisher from most rehab patients: he and his medical colleagues typically had a profession to go back to. Alex was desperate to work and earn money, a theme he repeated often during his rehab years. Success seemed out of reach. Even when he searched for low-paid service jobs at restaurants and stores, he couldn't land a job. And if he couldn't find a job, his goal of living a "normal" life was beyond reach, and he was dependent on us. How different his future might have been if he'd had access to a program like Fisher's. These programs should be available for all those who use drugs, along with help to find safe, clean housing.

As long as we're rewriting history, what if Alex had gotten off the train as he headed to Newark that last week of his life, after he refused entry to that last rehab and dropped out of sight? The Northeast Corridor line goes straight through Metuchen. If he'd gotten off that train, we would have told him to come home. We'd done it many times before. We always knew the alternative was Newark's drugs. Perhaps it wouldn't have made a difference, but we would have liked the opportunity to try again.

What I really believe in my heart of hearts is that we needed more time, so that Alex could have better realized the options available to him. There is research evidence that extra time could have made a difference: 70 percent of those with alcohol problems get better with no interventions; most people using illegal drugs age out by thirty; and by age thirty-seven fully "75% of people who have had severe substance problems have no symptoms whatsoever."[13] Keri Blakinger describes getting sober in prison but doesn't attribute her sobriety to incarceration. Instead, early in her prison career, she no longer saw drugs as an escape. At age twenty-eight, she was a classic case of aging out.[14] Alex was only twenty-five; he needed more time to let his prefrontal cortex develop, to find solutions, and to learn to hope again. In her brilliant novel *Demon Copperhead*, Barbara Kingsolver reveals an important truth about addiction: never give up on people, even when they fail repeatedly; the next time your efforts might well succeed.[15] A different historical context, steeped in harm reduction compassion, might well have given Alex that extra time. If only.

> I sheltered him as best I could, searching for the sound
> of his breath above the rushing water. A long time passed
> before I could accept that he no longer needed me.
>
> —Richard Powers, *Bewilderment*

We tried our best for Alex. We nurtured him, we supported him, we searched unremittingly for ways to protect and help him. But then "in the ordinary instant" (as Joan Didion describes it), he no longer needed us, the "sound of his breath" was stilled. We ran out of time.

Eulogy at Celebration of Life, May 17, 2015

Lee Alexander Roos Clarke

(December 17, 1989–May 11, 2015)

Our family knows grief. We know to put one foot in front of the other, and keep moving forward. We did it for Kathy, we did it for Granny, and we did it for Hal. I thought I knew grief, but this is a new kind of grief—raw, screaming, overwhelming grief. My neighbor Dori and I used to trade gruesome stories about the horrible things that happened to children, mostly things we read in the newspaper. I think it was kind of a naïve hope that if we talked about it, if we learned from it, bad things wouldn't happen to our families, to our children. But we have to reckon with the real world here, and bad things happen to good people.

And Alex was a very good person, a "good kid." He was movie-star good-looking, smart, and wickedly funny. Definitely takes after his father in that regard; no one describes me as funny. I am still in awe of the eulogy he gave for his Aunt Kathy when he was fourteen. He wrote it because of his love for Kathy. He was an excellent athlete, excelling in baseball in high school and earning a black belt in karate. He was kind, and generous to those he loved, and he loved fiercely and was fiercely loyal. Among those he loved were Hunter and Ginny. He was a bit peeved that his "only child" status was threatened when Hunter and Ginny came to live with us. Frankly it was funny to see Alex and

Hunter's attempts at one-upmanship: "You gave Alex this!" or "You never let me do those things, when I was Hunter's age!" They became like brothers, squabbles and all.

Here is what Hunter remembers: "He was my friend, my role model, and my brother. I always looked up to him and aspired to be as outgoing and intelligent as he was and I still do. My favorite memories growing up were being around Alex, Ellis, Joe and Mark and even though I was five years younger, Alex would include me, somehow finding the perfect balance between little brother and best friend. I'll always be grateful for everything he taught me and everything he did for me and my sister. No one will ever come close to having the same impact on my life that Alex did and because of that I'll miss him forever." For her part, Ginny remembers how kind Alex was: "I could have been that annoying younger cousin, but he helped me with my math homework, came into my room to chat, and played video games. He was a brother to me."

But Alex also had his demons. He had an eating disorder that almost killed him when he was twelve. After being hospitalized, he fought back with the help of our dog Lexi, good doctors, and his Wardlaw friends to mostly recover. But significant anxiety and panic attacks remained with him for the rest of his life, fueling self-medication through drinking, drugs, and a resurgent eating disorder. These got particularly bad in the last few years of his life. He was searching for something to fill the void. But drinking and drugs did the opposite—they drove away his friends, the friends who loved him so much. Alex had to deal with much grief in his short life: when Lexi died, followed by Granny, followed shortly by Hal, he had a hard time coping. It was all the more difficult that their deaths occurred as his career plans fell through, and he didn't have a fully realized Plan B. He knew he could do science, he knew how to study—he was an A- student in biology and computer science at Dickinson College after all. And it was all the more difficult when he could see his friends moving ahead with their lives. He felt left behind and overwhelmed by life.

I need to be honest about Alex's addictions. The first thing we need to do is break down the stigma of drug abuse. This is happening to your friends, to your friends' families, even if people don't like to talk about it. It's happening right here in Metuchen, and in your towns. Once you do start talking about it, you hear the stories of friends or family members suffering the insanity that is drug abuse. In addition to breaking down the stigma, we need to better understand that addiction is a disease, a devastating and horrendous disease that physically changes one's brain chemistry. It's not simply a matter of personal choice, and especially not once addiction has a stranglehold over your life. People struggling to understand how this happened to Alex want to be able to blame someone or something. They are looking for rational explanations when there are none. The Nar-Anon Family Group describes it in this way: "We have learned that addiction is an illness. It is a physical, mental, and spiritual disease that affects every area of life. It can be arrested but never cured. We have found that compulsive use of drugs does not indicate a lack of affection for the family. It is not a matter of love, but of illness. The addicts' inability to control their use of drugs is a symptom of the disease of addiction. Even when they know what will happen when they take the first drink, pill or fix, they will do so. This is the 'insanity' we speak of in regard to this disease."

To you young people: If you have friends with mental health or drug issues, tell their families. Once we learned from a few of Alex's friends that his drug use had escalated in especially destructive ways, we began a years-long struggle to help him. We and he worked so hard over so many years, but ultimately he was unable to climb high enough to reach sustained recovery. I am in awe of those who are in recovery for years, because I now realize how difficult their battles are. It used to seem easy—just make the right life choices, find God—but such attitudes are not in touch with the realities and challenges of mental health and drug addiction. I fervently hope that you won't have to go down the long road we have traveled with your loved ones, but I know some of you already have, and more of you will. Find support right away.

One reason I want to be open and honest about Alex's struggles is to find a way in which his life can continue to have meaning, for me and for those who suffer from this disease. If I can be part of a larger movement, I want to do that. If I can help people better understand the difficulties and challenges our young people face, I want to do that. Otherwise, too many more of our loved ones will die. Yes, it happens to people who look like us, and yes it happens to people who come from good families like ours. It can happen to anyone. *Let me repeat: Yes, it happens to people who look like us, and yes it happens to people who come from good families like ours. It can happen to anyone.*

What I do know is that we could not have walked down this long road, and dealt with the grief we have faced, and are facing, without so many of you. As academics, of course, we now have a shelf full of books about addiction. That helps. But what really helps are our families and communities. This last week has been a blur, but we wouldn't have survived without our Metuchen and Sociology communities. I've learned from our years of grief how to ask for and accept help. Those of you who know me well know how hard that is for me. I want to mention each and every one of you by name, but it would simply take me too long. Thanks to Chip's and my families, especially Poo, who did so much for Alex. My local Metuchen friends are always there for us, and have been with us since Hour 1. And our Sociology colleagues readily stepped up to the plate, completing my grading for the semester and giving Chip's final exam. My students are likely happier, since they gave somewhat more A's and B's than I would have. Other colleagues, members of my book club, and other locals showed up with food and companionship, and organized so much for us. A number of Alex's buddies stopped by to offer their support, and many more have called and written. We heard from so many others by phone, by email, and by text. And I received much support from the Saturday night Nar-Anon Serenity Group; you were always collectively and individually supportive, and I am thankful. As you know more than anyone, this is the outcome that terrorizes us more than any other. As I begin to pick up the pieces of my shattered life, I'm sure I'll learn more about other acts of kindness or support. To all, I thank you.

In closing, I want to highlight some excerpts from the comments Alex's friends or teachers made to us in the past few days. I chose just a few, to represent the different parts of Alex's life.

Sangya, adviser for the Rutgers Business and Science Program: "I spoke with Alex several times recently and helped him with the readmission process. He was so excited about coming back and finishing up the course work. . . . He told me that he was looking forward to coming back to NJ. He sounded so positive and hopeful."

Adam, Wardlaw friend: "I met you when I was 7 yrs old in the 2nd grade at Wardlaw Hartridge. . . . I will never forget those times. . . . You and your family helped me out in many ways back then and [then] again . . . when I took your dad's class at Rutgers. I'll always be embarrassed of the time your dad put up a slide in the middle of Sociology 101 of you and I in the 2nd grade acting like fools."

Latisha, Wardlaw friend: "Clarke; You were a fun guy, a great friend to many, smart, talented and you always knew how to make someone smile! My fondest memories of you were from senior year of HS and your amazing dance moves in the senior lounge! . . . To quote Maya Angelou, 'I've learned that people will forget what you said, people will forget what you did, but people will never forget how you made them feel.' You made those around [you] feel wonderful, important and appreciated! Not to mention you were SO funny and laughter helps us along so much in this life!"

Amy, Dickinson friend: "You were one of my closest friends and we shared so much together. I remember once Lexi ate your retainer and at first we thought it was funny until we realized that it was actually extremely expensive. Senior year, we told the school that I was your roommate [living on campus] so you could have a gigantic double to yourself while I lived off campus. . . . I shared every detail of my life with you and you were always there to listen and give advice, but never once did you judge me. . . . My favorite memories are from us going skeet shooting together. . . . You never put me down and always encouraged me to be better—until I got as good as you then it turned into a weekly competition. . . . Love you always Clarke."

Tim, Dickinson roommate: "From the first time I met you freshman year of college I knew it was the start of something amazing. The charisma, the energy, the style, and the overall manner with which you went about your everyday life was something I envied and tried to incorporate into my own life. We laughed, we fought, we cried, we went on adventures, we learned, and no matter what it was, we were always up for everything if we got to do it together. . . . Living with you were two of the best years of my life . . . and man did we make them count. You taught me confidence and you were always there for me when I needed you. You were much more than just a roommate, partner in crime, and best friend. You were a brother to me. . . . I will never forget the way you could always light up a room simply by walking in and busting out one of your classic Clarke phrases. From sharing clothes to sharing time together, I spent more time with you than anyone else those four years at Dickinson and after and I would never have it any other way. I am never going to forget how you helped me become the person I am today. . . . I will always love you Alex Clarke."

To all of Alex's young friends, I implore you: Have no regrets, celebrate the joy and laughter Alex had back in those days. Keep a piece of him in your soul as you journey through your life. He would have liked that. And keep in touch—I want you to have a life well lived.

I've gone on too long, so to Alex, as I kissed you good night and read you stories as a child, I would hesitate at your door and say, "Remote hug." Then later, when we were separated and talking on the phone, we would say, "Remote hug," as a ritual of our love. I hope you continue to feel my "remote hugs" envelop you, now and forever.

Please donate to Rutgers University Alcohol and Drug Assistance Program (ADAP), so that others suffering in recovery might live again:

Lisa Laitman, Director
ADAP Recovery Program
Rutgers University
17 Senior Street
New Brunswick, NJ 08901

ACKNOWLEDGMENTS

One's social communities make all the difference. I've survived these last years because I surrounded myself with loving family and supportive communities. Some read what I wrote, and others were just there when I needed them to help me live and manage my life.

I am thankful to my family, who supported my efforts throughout. My sisters and mom read a few early chapters. Marianne Roos has long supported my writing, editing my work with a critical eye. As a former nurse, Libby Roos helped me decipher medicalese from the hospital records I combed through. As a STEM researcher, Christine Roos Montague helped me understand the scientific language I came across. All three helped me pull together images for the book. My sister-in-law, Lynn Clarke Moran (Aunt Poo), was always there, and especially so when Alex was in Florida treatment facilities.

Back in the dark days of 2015, *Rutgers News* staff member Ken Branson read several op-eds and long-form essays I'd written. He encouraged me to use my grief for good, and to translate those writings into a book. During the summer of 2018, sociology graduate student Allegra Pocinki provided valuable research assistance, both for this book and for the Rutgers honors course I taught in spring 2019, "Addiction: Epidemic, Devastation, Loss." My niece, Clara Montague, filmed a documentary podcast, *About Alex*, that semester as part of her schoolwork at Ithaca College's Roy H. Park School of Communications. My excellent honors students, a few of Alex's friends, and Maia Szalavitz, participated in the filming.

During the academic year 2018–2019, I was fortunate to participate as a fellow at the Rutgers Institute for Research on Women's (IRW) Seminar on Public Catastrophes, Private Losses. The yearlong seminar was the brainchild of then IRW director Arlene Stein and associate director Sarah Tobias and brought together interested faculty and graduate students. The fellows that year read through my early writings and provided academic support and friendship. Arlene provided significant support then, and later, by reading drafts of my writings, and providing advice on publishing my work. Evelyn Duffy, of Open Boat Editing, and my sociology colleague Joanna Kempner also provided valuable advice on framing my work for publication.

Several friends and colleagues read and provided significant feedback on all or portions of the book. Two friends read the entire manuscript, and I'm especially indebted to them. Both knew and loved Alex, so for them, reading the book was a labor of love. In the process, they made my writing a good deal better. Mickey Neuhauser provided detailed editorial comments on every chapter, exactly what academics crave. My former Stony Brook colleague Nancy Tomes also provided thorough comments, as well as friendship and solace, at our monthly Zoom sessions. Jessie Dunleavy, a fellow traveler in grief, and memoir author and activist, read multiple chapters, and continues to provide me wisdom beyond measure.

Kayla Crawley, Paul Hirschfield, Jackie Litt, Julie Phillips, Pamela Stone, and Rebecca Vogel advised me during my early writing days. I am indebted as well to several activists in the addiction field who provided valuable advice. Rocky Schwartz and Valerie Furlong worked with me on Denied Treatment, provided friendship, and acted as sounding boards whenever I had questions during my initial forays into activism. Lisa Laitman, Morgan Thompson, and Jordan Scott read the activism chapter, "Community of Action," and thankfully caught errors and omissions. Participants in Mobilize Recovery's Family Caucus, and especially its Chair Jaclyn Brown, offered useful advice as I was finishing my book. Other friends and colleagues talked with me about issues that occurred along the way, or sent relevant readings: David Bland, Nancy DiTomaso, Carolyn Ellis, Judy Gerson, Devra Golbe, Frank Greenagel, Jon McLeod, Priti Narayan, Melissa Sarsten Polito, and Sarah Rosenfield.

I thank Lisa Laitman, and the Rutgers Recovery House, for establishing a fund in Alex's memory. The monies collected have thus far supported sober living students traveling to academic meetings, book scholarships, community dinners, and other sober social events. I hope to support more such activities in the future.

Support comes in many forms, and I'm thankful for so much from so many. Our closest neighbors, Dori and Joe Meoni, witnessed our anguish up close and always provided us comfort. They knew and loved Alex, for nearly his entire twenty-five years. Other members of our local tribe—Carolyn and Joe Nesi and Janis and John Lewandowski—were similarly available when we needed them. Our legendary local get-togethers over the years sustained us. And Dori, Carolyn, and Janis often served as my nonacademic control group.

Local and far-flung friends and colleagues provided support along the way, including Crystal Bedley, Steve Brechin, Nancy Cantor, Debby Carr, Phaedra Daipha, Donna DiDonato, Mary Gatta, Linda Hartig, Dorothy Hodgson, Maria Iosue, Jim Jasper, Chris Mariano, Paul McLean, Chick and Barbara Wareck Perrow, Judy Tanur, Martha Weinstein, and Greg Youchock. Thanks as well to Tina Zaccagna, Dana Cappa, Ewa Piosik, and Kristina Kopec, friends and life helpers for many years. Thanks as well to April Gosdick, who helped organize Alex's Celebration of Life, and to the hundreds of people who joined us to remember Alex.

Along my travels, I met many others dealing with addiction, including those in my Nar-Anon and bereavement groups who helped me immeasurably. I am indebted to those I interviewed. Most had no problem with me using their first names, and I thank them for that. Regardless, I thank all my interviewees for providing me key insights into Alex's thoughts and behaviors. They too loved him and grieve for him still.

I appreciate the hospitals, rehabs, detoxes, and other institutions in which Alex spent time for complying with my request for medical information as Alex's legal medical heir. Some of these organizations sent lots of information, some sent much less. I hope all of them learn from my story. Large or small, they could have done a better job caring for Alex. We need to move toward a more humane, empathic, harm reduction philosophy to treat mental health and substance use disorders. We're not anywhere near there yet.

As soon as I decided on an academic press, I realized that Rutgers University Press was the perfect choice. Micah Kleit saw the book's value and promise, and my editor Peter Mickulas helped to craft my Jersey story into a more readable book. They recognized and believed in my goal to turn grief into action. Helpful in that regard were the two reviewers the Press selected, medical sociologist Debby Carr and an anonymous reviewer. The production group at Rutgers University Press and Westchester Publishing Services, including Daryl Brower, Michelle Scott, Paul Vincent, and Robie Grant, were terrific partners.

Finally, last, but certainly not least, to Alex: through continuing bonds our love survives. To Hunter and Ginny, you allowed us to continue to parent, even after losing Alex, and for that I am grateful. And, to Chip, thanks for reading every word of my story, several times, and for agreeing to write your story as well. Somehow, we managed to survive with our love intact. It was no easy feat.

Washington, DC
October 2023

NOTES

Prologue

1. Centers for Disease Control and Prevention (CDC), "National Vital Statistics System: Provisional Drug Overdose Death Counts," accessed August 3, 2023, https://www.cdc.gov/nchs/nvss/vsrr/drug-overdose-data.htm.

2. CDC, "Drug Overdose: Death Rate Maps & Graphs," accessed June 22, 2022, https://www.cdc.gov/drugoverdose/deaths/index.html.

3. U.S. Department of Health and Human Services, "SAMHSA Announces National Survey on Drug Use and Health (NSDUH) Results Detailing Mental Illness and Substance Use Levels in 2021," accessed August 3, 2023, https://www.hhs.gov/about/news/2023/01/04/samhsa-announces-national-survey-drug-use-health-results-detailing-mental-illness-substance-use-levels-2021.html#:~:text=46.3%20million%20people%20aged%2012,having%20a%20drug%20use%20disorder.

4. Justin McCarthy, "Drugs Have Been a Problem in Family for 32% of Americans," Gallup, November 11, 2021, https://news.gallup.com/poll/357134/drugs-problem-family-americans.aspx.

5. Patricia A. Roos, "My Son Died of a Heroin Overdose. Trump's Commission Could Help the Crisis—If He Listens," *Star Ledger*, November 12, 2017, https://www.nj.com/opinion/2017/11/my_son_lost_his_battle_to_heroin_addiction_trumps.html#incart_river_mobile_index.

Chapter 1 Day 1

1. In 1959, C. Wright Mills wrote one of the most famous quotes in sociology. If you ever took a sociology course, you've likely heard it: "The sociological imagination enables us to grasp history and biography and the relations between the two

within society." C. Wright Mills, *The Sociological Imagination* (New York: Oxford University Press, 1959), 6.

Chapter 2   Week 1

1. Joan Didion, *The Year of Magical Thinking* (New York: Vintage International, 2006), 35–37.
2. Carolyn Ellis, *Final Negotiations: A Story of Love, Loss, and Chronic Illness* (Philadelphia: Temple University Press, 1995).

Chapter 3   Context

1. Maia Szalavitz, *Unbroken Brain: A Revolutionary New Way of Understanding Addiction* (New York: St. Martin's Press, 2016); Maia Szalavitz, *Undoing Drugs: The Untold Story of Harm Reduction and the Future of Addiction* (New York: Hachette, 2021); Anne Case and Angus Deaton, *Deaths of Despair and the Future of Capitalism* (Princeton, NJ: Princeton University Press, 2020); Johann Hari, *Chasing the Scream: The First and Last Days of the War on Drugs* (New York: Bloomsbury, 2015); Carl Erik Fisher, *The Urge: Our History of Addiction* (New York: Penguin, 2022).
2. Centers for Disease Control and Prevention (CDC), "Drug Overdose: Death Rate Maps & Graphs," accessed June 22, 2022, https://www.cdc.gov/drugoverdose /deaths/index.html.
3. CDC, "National Vital Statistics System: Provisional Drug Overdose Death Counts," accessed August 3, 2023, https://www.cdc.gov/nchs/nvss/vsrr/drug -overdose-data.htm. See also American Medical Association, 2022 Overdose Epidemic Report, 2022, https://end-overdose-epidemic.org/wp-content/uploads /2022/09/AMA-Advocacy-2022-Overdose-Epidemic-Report_090622.pdf. The COVID-19 pandemic intensified the crisis. As of June 2022, the number of deaths in the United States due to COVID-19 was approximately 1.01 million. CDC, "Covid Data Tracker," accessed June 22, 2022, https://covid.cdc.gov/covid-data -tracker/#datatracker-home.
4. Andrew Kolodny, "Where We Stand & How We Move Forward: The Current State of the Opioid Crisis" (keynote address, Knock Out Opioid Abuse Day, Learning Series Webinar, Partnership for a Drug-Free New Jersey and NJ Cares, October 6, 2022), https://knockoutday.drugfreenj.org/wp-content/uploads/2022 /10/KOOAD_10_6_webinar.pdf.
5. CDC, "Data Brief 356: Drug Overdose Deaths in the United States, 1999–2018," fig. 3: "Age-Adjusted Drug Overdose Death Rates Involving Opioids, 1999–2018," accessed June 24, 2022, https://www.cdc.gov/nchs/data/databriefs/db356_tables -508.pdf#page=1. The CDC and other agencies use "age-adjusted" death rates to account for the fact that most health outcomes occur differentially across age

groups. For example, cancer, stroke, and diabetes typically occur among older people, while injuries due to risky behavior and accidents occur primarily among the young. CDC, "CDC 24/7: Saving Lives, Protecting People. United States Cancer Statistics, Hints for Reading Tables and Graphs," accessed November 3, 2022, https://www.cdc.gov/cancer/uscs/about/hints.htm.

6. Kolodny, "Where We Stand & How We Move Forward," 15.

7. Kolodny, "Where We Stand & How We Move Forward," 8.

8. CDC, "Number and Age-Adjusted Rates of Drug Overdose Deaths by State, US 2018," accessed June 24, 2022, https://www.cdc.gov/drugoverdose/deaths/2018 .html.

9. CDC, "Drug Overdose Deaths in the United States, 1999–2018," NCHS Data Brief No. 356, January 2020, https://www.cdc.gov/nchs/data/databriefs/db356-h.pdf.

10. CDC, "Table 27: Drug Overdose Death Rates, by Drug Type, Sex, Age, Race, and Hispanic Origin: United States, 1999–2016," 2017, https://www.cdc.gov/nchs /data/hus/2017/027.pdf.

11. Case and Deaton, *Deaths of Despair*, 113.

12. In this section I rely heavily on David Herzberg, *White Market Drugs: Big Pharma and the Hidden History of Addiction in America* (Chicago: University of Chicago Press, 2020).

13. Herzberg *White Market Drugs*, 2.

14. Herzberg *White Market Drugs*, chs. 1–2.

15. I rely heavily here on Johann Hari, *Chasing the Scream*.

16. Hari, *Chasing the Scream*, 32.

17. Michelle Alexander, *The New Jim Crow: Mass Incarceration in the Age of Colorblindness*, rev. ed. (New York: New Press, 2010). See also Samuel K. Roberts, "The Impact of the US Drug War on People of Color," in *The Oxford Handbook of Global Drug History*, ed. Paul Gootenberg (New York: Oxford University Press, 2022), 474–494.

18. Herzberg, *White Market Drugs*, 130.

19. Herzberg, *White Market Drugs*, 268–278.

20. Jane Porter and Hershel Jick, "Addiction Rare in Patients Treated with Narcotics," *New England Journal of Medicine* 302, no. 2 (January 10, 1980): 123.

21. Sam Quinones, *Dreamland: The True Tale of America's Opiate Epidemic* (New York: Bloomsbury, 2015); Ryan Hampton, *Unsettled: How the Purdue Pharma Bankruptcy Failed the Victims of the American Overdose Crisis* (New York: St. Martin's Press, 2021).

22. Herzberg, *White Market Drugs*, 274.

23. Herzberg, *White Market Drugs*, 278.

24. Herzberg, *White Market Drugs*, 243. See also Julie Netherland and Helena Hansen's fascinating work on "white opioids," which clarifies how definitions of addiction, as well as its proposed solutions, operate historically to reinforce racial

hierarchies. Shifts in viewing addiction as a brain disease makes the study and practice of opioid use appear race-neutral when it most assuredly is not. Julie Netherland and Helena B. Hansen, "The War on Drugs That Wasn't: Wasted Whiteness, 'Dirty Doctors,' and Race in Media Coverage of Prescription Opioid Misuse," *Culture, Medicine and Psychiatry* 40 (2016): 664–686.

25. Szalavitz, *Undoing Drugs*; Hari, *Chasing the Scream*; Fisher, *The Urge*; Jeneen Interlandi, "One Year inside a Radical Approach to America's Overdose Crisis, *New York Times*, February 22, 2023, https://www.nytimes.com/2023/02/22/opinion /drug-crisis-addiction-harm-reduction.html; "America Has Lost the War on Drugs. Here's What Needs to Happen Next," editorial, *New York Times*, February 22, 2023, https://www.nytimes.com/2023/02/22/opinion/harm-reduction -public-health.html.

26. Herzberg, *White Market Drugs*, 285.

27. Quinones, *Dreamland*; Beth Macy, *Dopesick: Dealers, Doctors, and the Drug Company That Addicted America* (New York: Little, Brown, 2018).

28. Sam Quinones, *The Least of Us: True Tales of America and Hope in the Time of Fentanyl and Meth* (New York: Bloomsbury, 2021).

29. Quinones, *The Least of Us*, 182, 336. "P2P" refers to phenyl-2-propanone, a clear liquid used to produce meth.

30. Case and Deaton, *Deaths of Despair*, 57.

31. Case and Deaton, *Deaths of Despair*, 62.

32. This increase shows up dramatically in Case and Deaton, *Deaths of Despair*, fig. 5.2, p. 66.

33. Case and Deaton *Deaths of Despair*, 66, 121.

34. David Sheff, *Beautiful Boy: A Father's Journey through His Son's Addiction* (Boston: Mariner Books, 2008); William Cope Moyers with Katherine Ketcham, *Broken: My Story of Addiction and Redemption* (New York: Penguin, 2007); Szalavitz, *Unbroken Brain*; David Carr, *The Night of the Gun: A Reporter Investigates the Darkest Story of His Life, His Own* (New York: Simon and Schuster, 2008); Hunter Biden, *Beautiful Things: A Memoir* (New York: Gallery Books, 2021); Ryan Hampton, *American Fix: Inside the Opioid Addiction Crisis—and How to End It* (New York: All Points Books, 2018); Harriet Brown, *Brave Girl Eating: A Family's Struggle with Anorexia* (New York: Harper, 2011); Marya Hornbacher, *Wasted: A Memoir of Anorexia and Bulimia* (New York: Harper Perennial, 1998); Nic Sheff, *Tweak: Growing Up on Methamphetamines* (New York: Atheneum Books for Young Readers, 2008); Nic Sheff, *We All Fall Down: Living with Addiction* (New York: Little, Brown, 2011); Keri Blakinger, *Corrections in Ink: A Memoir* (New York: St. Martin's Press, 2022); Matthew Perry, *Friends, Lovers, and the Big Terrible Thing: A Memoir* (New York: Flatiron Books, 2022). Barbara Kingsolver, Demon Copperhead. (New York: Harper, 2022).

35. Jessie Dunleavy, *Cover My Dreams in Ink: A Son's Unbearable Solitude, a Mother's Unending Quest* (Loyola University, MD: Apprentice House Press, 2020).

36. W.J.T. Mitchell, *Mental Traveler A Father, a Son, and a Journey through Schizophrenia* (Chicago: University of Chicago Press, 2020).

37. Szalavitz, *Unbroken Brain*, 36.

38. Addiction researchers have since critiqued Volkow's brain imaging work for among other things relying on data from one point in time rather than over time, restricting claims of causality. See Carl Hart, *Drug Use for Grown-Ups: Chasing Liberty in the Land of Fear* (New York: Penguin, 2021).

39. Fisher, *The Urge*, 7.

40. National Center on Addiction and Substance Abuse at Columbia University (CASA), *Addiction Medicine: Closing the Gap Between Science and Practice*, June 2012, https://drugfree.org/reports/addiction-medicine-closing-the-gap -between-science-and-practice/.

41. CASA, *Addiction Medicine*, 19.

42. CASA, *Addiction Medicine*, 26.

43. Szalavitz *Unbroken Brain*, 36.

44. Stanton Peele's website is https://peele.net/.

45. National Institute of Mental Health, "The Teen Brain: 7 Things to Know," 2020, https://www.nimh.nih.gov/health/publications/the-teen-brain-7-things-to-know.

46. Szalavitz, *Unbroken Brain*, 4; see also Fisher, *The Urge*, 274.

47. Szalavitz, *Unbroken Brain*, 134.

48. Case and Deaton, *Deaths of Despair*, 113, 122; Hart, *Drug Use for Grown-Ups*.

49. Fisher, *The Urge*, 37–38. For additional information on dislocation theory, see also Bruce K. Alexander, "Dislocation Theory of Addiction" (expanded version of speech given at the New Directions in the Study of Alcohol Group, Fortieth Annual Meeting, Bradford, United Kingdom, April 24, 2016), September 9, 2017, https://www.brucekalexander.com/articles-speeches/dislocation-theory -addiction/290-addiction-a-hopeful-prophecy-from-a-time-of-despair-2.

50. Case and Deaton, *Deaths of Despair*, 123.

51. Szalavitz, *Unbroken Brain*, 37–38.

52. Szalavitz, *Unbroken Brain*, 134–135.

53. Leslie Jamison, *The Recovering: Intoxication and Its Aftermath* (New York: Little, Brown, 2018); Michael Pollen, "How Should We Do Drugs Now?," *New York Times*, July 13, 2021, https://www.nytimes.com/2021/07/09/opinion/sunday/drug -legalization-mdma-psilocybin.html.

54. Szalavitz, *Unbroken Brain*; Hari, *Chasing the Scream*.

Chapter 4　"A Good Family"

1. Hanya Yanagihara, *A Little Life* (New York: Doubleday, 2015), 248–249.

2. One of Alex's best friends during lower and middle school was also named Alex. To avoid confusion with my Alex, I call him "AlexF" (because his middle name is Fred).

Chapter 5　Widening Cracks

1. National Eating Disorders Association, "Eating Disorders in Men & Boys," 2022, https://www.nationaleatingdisorders.org/learn/general-information /research-on-males.

Chapter 6　Calm before the Storm

1. Paul Hirschfield, "Trends in School Social Control in the United States: Explaining Patterns of Decriminalization," in *The Palgrave International Handbook of School Discipline, Surveillance, and Social Control*, ed. Jo Deakin, Emmeline Taylor, and Aaron Kupchik (London: Palgrave Macmillan, 2018), 57. One prominent example of such policies was Drug Abuse Resistance Education, or D.A.R.E. Founded in 1983, D.A.R.E. was very visible in many school districts.

2. Hirschfield, "Trends in School Social Control," 45.

3. Thanks to Kayla Crawley and Paul Hirschfield for providing me the benefit of their wisdom on this topic. Some further readings: Paul Hirschfield, "The School to Prison Pipeline," in *Live Free's Agenda for Ending Mass Incarceration and Criminalization*, ed. Pastor Michael McBride and Andrea Marta (Merced County, CA: Live Free, 2016), 40–45; Kayla Crawley and Paul Hirschfield, "Examining the School-to-Prison Pipeline Metaphor," in *Oxford Research Encyclopedia of Criminology*, June 25, 2018, https://doi.org/10.1093/acrefore/9780190264079.013.346; Brenda E. Morrison and Dorothy Vaandering, "Restorative Justice: Pedagogy, Praxis, and Discipline," *Journal of School Violence* 11, no. 2 (2012): 138–155, https://www.tandfonline.com /doi/abs/10.1080/15388220.2011.653322?journalCode=wjsv20.

4. U.S. Bureau of the Census, "QuickFacts, Metuchen Borough, New Jersey," 2022, https://www.census.gov/quickfacts/fact/table/metuchenboroughnewjersey. Race categories include those Hispanic and not. Hispanics include those of any race.

5. Street Law, Inc., "*New Jersey v. T.L.O.* / You Decide: Is This a Legal School Search?," 2020, https://s3.amazonaws.com/landmarkcases.org/TLO/Student /Activity_You_Decide_TLO_Teacher.pdf.

6. I assume Bruce was referring in his comment to the number of students suspended yearly just for drug or alcohol use, not for all possible infractions. I was able to find published data on "student disciplinary removals" on the New Jersey

Department of Education website that record a higher number of suspensions. The NJ School Performance Reports detail the number of in-school and out-of-school suspensions for each school in the state from the 2011–2012 academic year to 2020–2021 academic year (to date). For the pre-COVID academic year of 2018–2019, I found estimates of twenty-five out-of-school suspensions, substantially higher than Bruce's estimate of three to five. Students might also be suspended for behaviors such as truancy; tardy behavior; cutting class; harassment, intimidation, or bullying other students or teachers; damage to property; fighting; theft; vaping; sexual activity; or inappropriate behavior at an athletic event. I corresponded with personnel in the New Jersey Department of Education in July 2022, who confirmed their tables refer to individual students (e.g., if a student was suspended three times, he/she would count as one student). See "NJ School Disciplinary and Bullying Actions," *NJ Spotlight News*, accessed June 28, 2022, https://www.njspotlightnews.org/tables/nj-school-disciplinary-and-bullying-actions/#/co2/Middlesex/co6/Metuchen; https://rc.doe.state.nj.us/; New Jersey Department of Education, Office of Fiscal and Data Services, *Student Safety Data System Guidance, 2022–2023*, 2022, https://homeroom4.doe.state.nj.us/ssds/doc/SSDS_Guidance.pdf.

Chapter 7   College Days

1. Through the online New Jersey court system, I came across two additional interactions Alex had with the criminal justice system that I hadn't known about: an arrest for misuse of a handheld wireless phone (3/7/12) and disorderly conduct (1/13/12).

Chapter 9   Worst Case

1. Anne Case and Angus Deaton, *Deaths of Despair and the Future of Capitalism* (Princeton, NJ: Princeton University Press, 2020), 66, 121.

2. Bruce Weber, "Philip Seymour Hoffman, Actor of Depth, Dies at 46," *New York Times*, February 2, 2014, https://www.nytimes.com/2014/02/03/movies/philip-seymour-hoffman-actor-dies-at-46.html; Matthew Perry, *Friends, Lovers, and the Big Terrible Thing: A Memoir* (New York: Flatiron Books, 2022).

3. Carl Erik Fisher, *The Urge: Our History of Addiction* (New York: Penguin, 2022), 274. See also Maia Szalavitz, *Unbroken Brain: A Revolutionary New Way of Understanding Addiction* (New York: St. Martin's Press, 2016), 4.

4. David Brooks wrote an excellent article about his friend Peter Marks, who died by suicide in April 2022. This article underscores many of the themes I discuss in this book. David Brooks, "How Do You Serve a Friend in Despair?," *New York Times*, February 9, 2023, https://www.nytimes.com/2023/02/09/opinion/despair-friendship-suicide.html.

5. During that academic year, Alex took courses in Principles of Financing and Accounting, Mobile Application Development from Concept to Market, Fundamentals of Personal Care Science, Drug Discovery from Concept to Market, Introduction to the Fundamentals of Applied Colloid and Surface Chemistry, Science and Technology Management, Principles for Communication and Leadership for Science and Technology Management, Virtual Social Media Marketing.

6. Szalavitz, *Unbroken Brain*, 135.

7. Centers for Disease Control and Prevention, "Today's Heroin Epidemic," *CDC Vital Signs*, July 2015, https://www.cdc.gov/vitalsigns/pdf/2015-07-vitalsigns .pdf.

8. Stephen Stirling, "N.J. Heroin Overdose Death Rate Is Triple the Soaring U.S. Rate," NJ.Com, July 8, 2015, https://www.nj.com/news/2015/07/nj_heroin _overdose_death_rate_is_triple_the_soarin.html#:~:text=As%20dire%20is%20 the%20situation,of%20death%20in%20othe%20state.

9. Sam Quinones, *Dreamland: The True Tale of America's Opiate Epidemic* (New York: Bloomsbury, 2015); Beth Macy, *Dopesick: Dealers, Doctors, and the Drug Company That Addicted America* (New York: Little, Brown, 2018).

10. I call her "KatieK" to distinguish her from Alex's high school girlfriend.

11. More like ninety days is the minimum. See William Stauffer, "Addiction Treatment Is Broken. Here's What It Should Look Like," *Stat Madness*, January 2, 2020, https://www.statnews.com/2020/01/02/addiction-treatment-is-broken-heres -what-it-should-look-like/.

12. Christine Stapleton, "Sober Home Task Force Score: One-Fourth Already Have Pleaded Guilty," *Palm Beach Post*, October 20, 2017, https://www .palmbeachpost.com/story/news/2017/10/20/sober-home-task-force-score /6986728007/.

Chapter 10   End of the Road

1. W.J.T. Mitchell, *Mental Traveler: A Father, a Son, and a Journey through Schizophrenia* (Chicago: University of Chicago Press, 2020), 63–64.

2. David J. Mysels and Maria A. Sullivan, "The Relationship between Opioid and Sugar Intake: Review of Evidence and Clinical Applications," *Journal of Opioid Management* 6, no. 6 (2010): 445–452.

3. Scott Stossel, *My Age of Anxiety: Fear, Hope, Dread, and the Search for Peace of Mind* (New York: Alfred A. Knopf, 2014).

4. According to the American Psychiatric Association, behaviors consistent with this disorder include (among other things) committing unlawful acts, deceitfulness, impulsivity, and irresponsibility. See "DSM-IV-TR Diagnostic Criteria for Antisocial Personality Disorder (301.7)," *Psychiatric News*, January 2, 2004, https://psychnews.psychiatryonline.org/doi/full/10.1176/pn.39.1.0025a.

5. "Hare Psychopathy Checklist (Original) (PCL-22)," accessed January 11, 2023, https://psychology-tools.com/test/pcl-22.

6. Mayo Clinic Laboratories, "Mumps Virus Antibody, IgG, Serum," Test ID MPPG, 2023, https://microbiology.testcatalog.org/show/MPPG#:~text=The%20 presence %20IgG,considered%20immune%20to%20mump.

7. Jeremy Roebuck, "Philly-Area Rehab Owner Who Illegally Profited from Others' Addictions Will Spend 18 Months in Prison," *Philadelphia Inquirer*, December 9, 2019, https://www.inquirer.com/news/joseph-lubowitz-humble -beginnings-philly-opioid-rehab-eric-snyder-real-life-recovery-delray-beach -20191209.html.

Chapter 11 Making Sense

1. Carl Erik Fisher, *The Urge: Our History of Addiction* (New York: Penguin, 2022), 7.

2. Maia Szalavitz, "Opioids Feel Like Love. That's Why They're Deadly in Tough Times," *New York Times*, December 6, 2021.

3. Fisher, *The Urge*, 151, 156.

4. Maia Szalavitz, *Unbroken Brain: A Revolutionary New Way of Understanding Addiction* (New York: St. Martin's Press, 2016), 134–135.

5. Szalavitz, "Opioids Feel Like Love."

6. Kai T. Erikson, *Everything in Its Path: Destruction of Community in the Buffalo Creek Flood* (New York: Simon and Schuster, 1976), 240.

7. C. Wright Mills, *The Sociological Imagination* (New York: Oxford University Press, 1959), 8.

Chapter 12 Social Communities

1. Here I use the preferred language of Barbara Theodosiou, founder of "The Addict's Mom Public Page" on Facebook in 2008. Elsewhere, I employ the "person-centered language" that activist groups promote (e.g., "person with addiction"). See Jennifer Taylor, "Stigma Can Kill: Words Matter in Addiction," *Treatment Magazine*, February 16, 2021, https://treatmentmagazine.com/stigma-can-kill-words -matter-in-addiction/.

2. Barbara Theodosiou, *Without Shame: The Addict's Mom and Her Family Share Their Stories of Pain and Healing* (Center City, MN: Hazelden Publishing, 2020).

3. Anguished parents have sometimes turned to wilderness therapy programs for their addicted children. Such programs rely on camping and hiking, with group and individual therapeutic exercises. Many young people then transition to therapeutic boarding schools. Proponents argue that such programs offer long-term specialized care that doesn't exist elsewhere. Others argue that there is little

evidence that such programs work; they are expensive, and some have involved abusive behavior. Adiel Kaplan, "Does Science Support the 'Wilderness' in Wilderness Therapy?," _Undark_ [a nonprofit digital magazine exploring the intersection of science and society], January 29, 2020, https://undark.org/2020/01/29/does -science-support-the-wilderness-in-wilderness-therapy/.

4. John Teasdale, Mark Williams, and Zindel Segal, _The Mindful Way Workbook: An 8-Week Program to Free Yourself from Depression and Emotional Distress_ (New York: Guilford Press, 2014), 4–5.

5. Teasdale et al., _The Mindful Way Workbook_, 17, 27.

6. Teasdale et al., _The Mindful Way Workbook_, 65.

7. Teasdale et al., _The Mindful Way Workbook_, 99.

8. Teasdale et al., _The Mindful Way Workbook_, 124.

9. Maria J. Kefalas, _Harnessing Grief: A Mother's Quest for Meaning and Miracles_ (Boston: Beacon Press, 2021).

10. David Herzberg, _White Market Drugs: Big Pharma and the Hidden History of Addiction in America_ (Chicago: University of Chicago Press, 2020).

11. I refer here to the one-paragraph letter to the editor published in the _New England Journal of Medicine_ claiming an addiction rate of less than 1 percent among those with no history of addiction. Jane Porter and Hershel Jick, "Addiction Rare in Patients Treated with Narcotics," _New England Journal of Medicine_ 302, no. 2 (January 10, 1980): 123. See chapter 3 for additional discussion.

12. Conferences and/or training sessions I have attended include "Overdose Prevention Centers: Promoting Health & Harm Reduction," Drug Policy Alliance and The College of New Jersey, April 5, 2019; "Trauma at the Core: Building Resiliency across the Lifespan," Center for Great Expectations and the College of New Jersey, December 6, 2019; "Integrative Harm Reduction: A New Paradigm for Risky and Addictive Behavior," a two-day training on harm reduction offered by the Center for Great Expectations and the Rutgers Center of Alcohol and Substance Use Studies, May 19–20, 2022; "Opioid Summit: The Evolving Opioid Crisis: A Collaborative Approach," NJ Human Services, September 21, 2022 (zoom, online); Andrew Kolodny, "Where We Stand & How We Move Forward: The Current State of the Opioid Crisis" (keynote address, Knock Out Opioid Abuse Day, Learning Series Webinar, Partnership for a Drug-Free New Jersey and NJ Cares, October 6, 2022), https://knockoutday .drugfreenj.org/wp-content/uploads/2022/10/KOOAD_10_6_webinar.pdf.

13. Pat Roos, excerpt from "Denying Our Insurance Rights," _Insider NJ_, November 25, 2018, https://www.insidernj.com/denying-insurance-rights/?fbclid =IwAR0Di3sFDLDmS_1V93SZ6sPVdq_He-QiAStY9psH _PJsckoHVa8VTlemXoo.

14. Lilo H. Stainton, "New Jersey Comes Closer to Approving Mental-Health Parity Law," _NJ Spotlight News_, January 18, 2019, https://www.njspotlightnews.org /2019/01/19-01-17-new-jersey-comes-closer-to-approving-mental-health-parity-law/.

15. State of New Jersey, Governor Phil Murphy, "Governor Murphy Signs Mental Health Parity Legislation" (press release), April 11, 2019, https://www.nj .gov/governor/news/news/562019/20190411a.shtml#:~:text=The%20law%20 (A2031%2FS1339),Parity%20and%20Addiction%20Equity%20Act.

16. C. Wright Mills, "On Intellectual Craftsmanship," in *Symposium on Sociological Theory*, ed. Llewellyn Gross (Evanston, IL: Row, Peterson, 1959), 52.

17. Libby Chamberlain started the Pantsuit Nation Facebook page on October 20, 2016, to support the candidacy of Hillary Clinton for president. It grew from a small group of friends to 24,000 members in one day and reached one million by election day. The permanent link to my post is https://www.facebook.com/groups /pantsuitnation/permalink/1236132799817653/. In 2019, Supermajority Education Fund bought out this group, and chose to pause the community as of June 6, 2023. A selection of the site's essays with accompanying photos appeared in Libby Chamberlain, ed., *Pantsuit Nation* (New York: Flatiron Books, 2017). My post appears on pp. 238–239.

18. Patricia A. Roos, "My Son Died of a Heroin Overdose. Trump's Commission Could Help the Crisis—If He Listens," *Star Ledger*, November 12, 2017, https:// www.nj.com/opinion/2017/11/my_son_lost_his_battle_to_heroin_addiction _trumps.html#incart_river_mobile_index.

19. Patricia A. Roos, "Promise Me, Joe, That You'll Remember Alex in Your First 100 Days," *Star Ledger*, March 15, 2021, https://www.nj.com/opinion/2021/03 /promise-me-joe-that-youll-remember-alex-in-your-first-100-days-opinion.html.

20. I thank Rutgers sociology graduate student Allegra Pocinki for her excellent research work.

21. Also that year, my niece Clara Montague decided to film a documentary podcast about Alex's life as part of her coursework at Ithaca College's Roy H. Park School of Communications. Clara filmed hours with family, friends, and my Honors Addiction course in the spring of 2019, combined with family photos and videos, and an interview with Maia Szalavitz. Her podcast, *About Alex*, is in progress. See Clara Montague, "About Alex Long Trailer," YouTube video, 2:48, May 17, 2020, https://youtu.clarabe/wsUBNbKLn_4.

22. I thank my colleague Arlene Stein for suggesting this framing. Arlene was the director of Rutgers Institute for Research on Women (IRW). She, Sarah Tobias, and their IRW colleagues sponsored the 2018–2019 seminar "Public Catastrophes, Private Losses" that encouraged my early memoir writings. My seminar colleagues provided early support and critical insight.

Chapter 13   A Community of Action

1. I thank Jordan Scott, a Pennsylvania harm reduction activist, for explaining this distinction to me.

2. Centers for Disease Control and Prevention (CDC), "National Vital Statistics System: Provisional Drug Overdose Death Counts," accessed August 3, 2023, https://www.cdc.gov/nchs/nvss/vsrr/drug-overdose-data.htm.

3. Maia Szalavitz, *Undoing Drugs: The Untold Story of Harm Reduction and the Future of Addiction* (New York: Hachette, 2021). Szalavitz tells the story of Heather Edney, an activist in the harm reduction community (200).

4. Erving Goffman, *Stigma: Notes on the Management of Spoiled Identity* (Englewood Cliffs, NJ: Prentice-Hall, 1963).

5. Important reviews of stigma include Sarah Rosenfield, "Labeling Mental Illness: The Effects of Received Services and Perceived Stigma on Life Satisfaction," *American Sociological Review* 62 (1997): 660–672; Bruce G. Link and Jo C. Phelan, "Conceptualizing Stigma," *Annual Review of Sociology* 27 (2001): 363–385; Bernice A. Pescosolido and Jack K. Martin, "The Stigma Complex," *Annual Review of Sociology* 41 (2015): 87–116.

6. Pescosolido and Martin, "The Stigma Complex," 91.

7. Tressie McMillan Cottom, "What's Shame Got to Do with It?," *New York Times*, April 12, 2022, https://www.nytimes.com/2022/04/12/opinion/whats-shame-got-to-do-with-it.html.

8. Pescosolido and Martin, "The Stigma Complex," 93. See also Elevyst, *How Bad Is It, Really? Stigma against Drug Use and Recovery in the United States*, April 2022, https://elevyst.com/stigma-initiative.

9. Patrick W. Corrigan, Sachiko A. Kuwabara, and John O'Shaughnessy, "The Public Stigma of Mental Illness and Drug Addiction: Findings from a Stratified Random Sample," *Journal of Social Work* 9 (2009): 139–147; Emma E. McGinty, Howard H. Goldman, Bernice Pescosolido, and Colleen L. Barry, "Portraying Mental Illness and Drug Addiction as Treatable Health Conditions: Effects of a Randomized Experiment on Stigma and Discrimination," *Social Science & Medicine* 126 (2015): 73–85; Johns Hopkins Bloomberg School of Public Health, "Study: Public Feels More Negative toward People with Drug Addiction Than Those with Mental Illness," October 1, 2014, https://publichealth.jhu.edu/2014/study-public-feels-more-negative-toward-people-with-drug-addiction-than-those-with-mental-illness.

10. Ara Francis, *Family Trouble: Middle-Class Parents Children's Problems, and the Disruption of Everyday Life* (New Brunswick, NJ: Rutgers University Press, 2015). Although Francis addresses addiction, her research is focused more broadly. She well describes the isolation, shame, and rejection families face when they are viewed as different: "Goffman's concept of courtesy stigma to examine accounts of parents whose children have disabilities; caring for a child with disabilities alters one's place in the prevailing social order, undermines claims to "normalcy" and disrupts valued relationships. The stigma can be felt or enacted—parents sometimes experience isolation and shame because they anticipate negative labeling,

while, in other cases, rejection and discrimination are directly manifest in interaction" (60–61).

11. Joan Didion, *The Year of Magical Thinking* (New York: Vintage Books, 2006), 48.

12. Deborah Carr, *Worried Sick: How Stress Hurts Us and How to Bounce Back* (New Brunswick, NJ: Rutgers University Press, 2014), 30–32.

13. American Psychiatric Association, "Prolonged Grief Disorder," 2022, https://www.psychiatry.org/File%20Library/Psychiatrists/Practice/DSM/DSM-5-TR/APA-DSM5TR-ProlongedGriefDisorder.pdf.

14. Christine Valentine, Linda Bauld, and Tony Walter, "Bereavement Following Substance Misuse: A Disenfranchised Grief," *OMEGA, Journal of Death and Dying* 72 (2016): 286.

15. Valentine et al., "Bereavement Following Substance Misuse," 291.

16. Valentine et al., "Bereavement Following Substance Misuse," 293.

17. Julia Samuel, *Grief Works: Stories of Life, Death, and Surviving* (New York: Scribner, 2017), xx.

18. These academic traditions, of course, reflect existing religious and cultural beliefs. As my friend Mickey Neuhauser pointed out to me, in the Jewish tradition immediate family members who have died are remembered annually on the anniversary of their deaths, and on certain holidays, by lighting a twenty-four-hour "yahrzeit candle" and by going to synagogue to publicly recite a prayer of remembrance that is part of every Shabbat service.

19. Carolyn Ellis, "Seeking My Brother's Voice: Holding onto Long-Term Grief through Photographs, Stories, and Reflections," in *Stories of Complicated Grief: A Critical Anthology*, ed. Eric D. Miller (Washington, DC: National Association of Social Workers Press, 2014), 3–21. See also Greg Roberts's beautiful tribute to his young daughter. Roberts's doctoral dissertation helped him understand how his daughter remained in his life even after her death. Greg Roberts, "Into the Mystic: Bereaved Parents, Love and Spontaneous Creativity" (PhD diss., Deakin University, Melbourne, Australia, 2015).

20. Lucy Hone, *Resilient Grieving: How to Find Your Way through a Devastating Loss* (New York: The Experiment, 2017).

21. Lucy Hone appears on an episode of the *Hidden Brain* podcast; see Shankar Vedantam, host, "Healing Your Heart," *Hidden Brain* (podcast), April 5, 2022, 49:35, https://hiddenbrain.org/podcast/healing-your-heart/.

22. One hears this harm reduction principle everywhere. Some of the best recent work on harm reduction can be found in Szalavitz, *Undoing Drugs*. While not directly focused on harm reduction, several other authors accept its principles; see Johann Hari, *Chasing the Scream: The First and Last Days of the War on Drugs* (New York: Bloomsbury, 2015); Carl Erik Fisher, *The Urge: Our History of Addiction* (New York: Penguin, 2022). Harm reduction is now the official position of the Biden administration; see White House, "Fact Sheet: White House Releases 2022

National Drug Control Strategy That Outlines Comprehensive Path Forward to Address Addiction and the Overdose Epidemic," April 21, 2022, https://www .whitehouse.gov/briefing-room/statements-releases/2022/04/21/fact-sheet-white -house-releases-2022-national-drug-control-strategy-that-outlines-comprehensive -path-forward-to-address-addiction-and-the-overdose-epidemic/.

23. Many in the treatment community use the term medication-assisted treatment (MAT). I use these terms interchangeably.

24. Carrie Wilkens, "Who Needs to 'Hit Rock Bottom'?," Center for Motivation & Change, February 8, 2016, https://motivationandchange.com/who-needs-to-hit -rock-bottom/.

25. Maia Szalavitz published an op-ed piece in the *New York Times* that addresses this issue directly. Maia Szalavitz, "Codependency Is a Toxic Myth in Addiction Recovery," *New York Times*, July 8, 2022, https://www.nytimes.com/2022/07/08 /opinion/codependency-addiction-recovery.html.

26. Partnership to End Addiction, "9 Facts about Addiction People Usually Get Wrong," August 2019, https://drugfree.org/article/9-facts-about-addiction-people -usually-get-wrong/.

27. Hari, *Chasing the Scream*, 293. See also Maia Szalavitz, "Opioids Feel Like Love. That's Why They're Deadly in Tough Times," *New York Times*, December 6, 2021. Academics make this same point; see, for example, Robert Waldinger and Marc Schulz, *The Good Life: Lessons from the World's Longest Scientific Study of Happiness* (New York: Simon and Schuster, 2023). Since I first heard Hari's point about the need for connection several months ago, I now hear it all the time, most recently at the Thirteenth Annual Rutgers Recovery House Graduation on May 17, 2022, and at a training session on harm reduction methods.

28. Pescosolido and Martin, "The Stigma Complex," 105.

29. Anne M. Fletcher, *Inside Rehab: The Surprising Truth about Addiction Treatment—and How to Get Help That Works* (New York: Viking, 2013); Lance Dodes and Zachary Dodes, *The Sober Truth: Debunking the Bad Science behind 12-Step Programs and the Rehab Industry* (Boston: Beacon Press, 2014); Adam Bisaga, *Overcoming Opioid Addiction: The Authoritative Medical Guide for Patients, Families, Doctors, and Therapists* (New York: The Experiment, 2018). Fletcher mentions harm reduction only twice, Bisaga four times, and Dodes and Dodes not at all. Even Hari's *Chasing the Scream*, which is a broader examination of the rise and fall of the war on drugs, has no endnotes on harm reduction.

30. Szalavitz, *Undoing Drugs*; Carl L. Hart, *Drug Use for Grown-Ups: Chasing Liberty in the Land of Fear* (New York: Penguin, 2021); Fisher, *The Urge*.

31. Szalavitz, *Undoing Drugs*, 7. I rely heavily on Szalavitz's *Undoing Drugs* to highlight the key historical time points in the development of the harm reduction movement. See also the National Harm Reduction Coalition website: https:// harmreduction.org/.

32. Szalavitz, *Undoing Drugs*, ch. 2. Szalavitz visited Marks's clinic in the early 1990s. See also Hari, *Chasing the Scream*, ch. 15.

33. Szalavitz, *Undoing Drugs*, 42.

34. Szalavitz, *Undoing Drugs*, 36.

35. Szalavitz, *Undoing Drugs*, 55.

36. Hari, *Chasing the Scream*, ch. 16. I rely heavily on Hari's *Chasing the Scream* to describe Portugal's experiences. Two other easily available articles on Portugal include Susana Ferriera, "Portugal's Radical Drugs Policy Is Working. Why Hasn't the World Copied It?," *Guardian*, December 5, 2017, https://www.theguardian.com/news/2017/dec/05/portugals-radical-drugs-policy-is-working-why-hasnt-the-world-copied-it; and Caitlin Elizabeth Hughes and Alex Stevens, "What Can We Learn from the Portuguese Decriminalization of Illicit Drugs?," *British Journal of Criminology* 50 (2010): 999–1022, https://www.researchgate.net/publication/249284847_What_Can_We_Learn_From_The_Portuguese_Decriminalization_of_Illicit_Drugs.

37. Hari, *Chasing the Scream*, 239.

38. Hari, *Chasing the Scream*, 249, 251. Hari describes drug policies in a number of other countries, including Argentina, Brazil, and Uruguay (ch. 17). The International Doctors for Healthier Drug Policies (IDHDP) has recognized successful efforts to stem overdoses in Australia, Germany, Greece, Italy, Luxembourg, Norway, and Switzerland. IDHDP, "Seven Countries Have Been Effective in Reducing Overdose Deaths—How?," May 29, 2017, https://idhdp.com/en/resources/news/may-2017/seven-countries-that-beat-an-overdose-crisis.aspx.

39. Anthony Faiola and Catarina Fernandes Martins, "Once Hailed for Decriminalizing Drugs, Portugal Is Now Having Doubts," *Washington Post*, July 7, 2023, https://www.washingtonpost.com/world/2023/07/07/portugal-drugs-decriminalization-heroin-crack/.

40. See Szalavitz, *Undoing Drugs*, ch. 20, and Hari, *Chasing the Scream*, ch. 14, for extended discussions of Vancouver's experiences. See also Gabor Maté, *In the Realm of Hungry Ghosts: Close Encounters with Addiction* (Berkeley, CA: North Atlantic Books, 2009), for an excellent examination of Downtown Eastside, a Vancouver neighborhood beset with problematic drug use.

41. The VANDU [Vancouver Area Network of Drug Users] website is https://vandureplace.wordpress.com/.

42. See the OnPoint NYC website for descriptions of these Overdose Prevention Centers: https://onpointnyc.org/. See also Jeffrey C. Mays and Andy Newman, "Nation's First Supervised Drug-Injection Sites Open in New York," *New York Times*, November 30, 2021, https://www.nytimes.com/2021/11/30/nyregion/supervised-injection-sites-nyc.html; "Tough-On-Drugs Policies Have Failed. Supervised Injection Sites Will Save Lives," editorial, *Washington Post*, December 7, 2021, https://www.washingtonpost.com/opinions/2021/12/07/tough-on-drugs-policies-have-failed-supervised-injection-sites-will-save-lives/.

43. Szalavitz, *Undoing Drugs*, 17.

44. Szalavitz *Undoing Drugs*, ch. 6. Szalavitz's description of this trial reads like a crime novel. It's fascinating in its descriptions of ACT-UP, the defendants, expert witnesses, and the judge.

45. Szalavitz, *Undoing Drugs*, 109.

46. Szalavitz, *Undoing Drugs*, ch. 8. Housing remains an issue today. Policymakers continue to debate the link between substance use and homelessness. See Jim Hinch, "Why Won't Policymakers Talk More about Drugs and Homelessness?," *Zocalo Public Square*, May 23, 2022, https://www.zocalopublicsquare.org/2022/05/23/policymakers-drugs-and-homelessness/ideas/essay/.

47. Its current website is https://www.housingworks.org/.

48. Szalavitz, *Undoing Drugs*, 139.

49. Szalavitz, *Undoing Drugs*, chs. 10–12.

50. Szalavitz, *Undoing Drugs*, 156.

51. Ralf Jurgens, *Nothing about Us without Us: Greater, Meaningful Involvement of People Who Use Illegal Drugs: A Public Health, Ethical, and Human Rights Imperative* (Toronto: Canadian HIV/AIDS Legal Network, International HIV/AIDS Alliance, Open Society Institute, 2008), https://www.opensocietyfoundations.org/uploads/b99c406f-5e45-4474-9343-365e548daade/nothing-about-us-without-us-report-20080501.pdf.

52. Szalavitz, *Undoing Drugs*, ch. 14.

53. Szalavitz, *Undoing Drugs*, 170.

54. Samuel Kelton Roberts (speaker and moderator), with Terrell Jones, Sam Rivera, Maia Szalavitz, in New York Academy of Medicine, "Then & Now: Drug Policy and Harm Reduction Services," YouTube video, 1:02:04, May 16, 2022, https://www.youtube.com/watch?v=f9aAkDaPUlM.

55. Szalavitz, *Undoing Drugs*, ch. 13.

56. Szalavitz, *Undoing Drugs*, 193–195. Szalavitz refers to G. Alan Marlatt's description of the controversy; see G. Alan Marlatt, "The Controlled Drinking Controversy: A Commentary," *American Psychologist* 38, no. 10 (1983): 1097–1110. See also Carl Erik Fisher's description of a similar 1970s controversy between the National Council on Alcoholism (NCA) and the RAND Corporation. RAND was set to publish a report on forty-five treatment centers established by the National Institute on Alcohol Abuse and Alcoholism (NIAAA), which found similar relapse rates for post-AA moderate drinkers and those who were abstinent. The NCA tried to quash the RAND publication. Withstanding intense media and political pressure, the NIAAA stood by RAND. Fisher, *The Urge*, 250–251.

57. The President's Commission on Combating Drug Addiction and the Opioid Crisis, *Final Report*, November 1, 2017, https://trumpwhitehouse.archives.gov/sites/whitehouse.gov/files/images/Final_Report_Draft_11-15-2017.pdf. In addition to the chair, Governor Chris Christie, there were five other commissioners: Governor

Charlie Baker, Governor Roy Cooper, Congressman Patrick J. Kennedy, Professor Bertha Madras, and Florida Attorney General Pam Bondi.

58. Joe Biden, "State of the Union Address," White House, March 1, 2022, https://www.whitehouse.gov/state-of-the-union-2022/.

59. White House, "Fact Sheet," April 21, 2022.

60. Joe Biden, "A Proclamation on Granting Pardon for the Offense of Simple Possession of Marijuana," White House, October 6, 2022, https://www.whitehouse .gov/briefing-room/presidential-actions/2022/10/06/granting-pardon-for-the -offense-of-simple-possession-of-marijuana/.

61. Robert Gebelhoff, "A Quiet Revolution in Drug Policy: States Embrace Fentanyl Test Kits," *Washington Post*, February 9, 2023, https://www .washingtonpost.com/opinions/2023/02/09/fentanyl-drug-test-kits-harm -reduction-republicans/.

62. Zoe Adams, Noa Krawczyk, Rachel Simon, Kimberly Sue, Leslie Suen, and Paul Joudrey, "To Save Lives from Opioid Overdose Deaths, Bring Methadone into Mainstream Medicine," *Health Affairs*, May 27, 2022, https://www.healthaffairs.org /do/10.1377/forefront.20220524.911965/.

63. National Academies of Sciences, Engineering, and Medicine, *Opportunities to Improve Opioid Use Disorder and Infectious Disease Services: Integrating Responses to a Dual Epidemic* (Washington, DC: National Academies Press, 2020), ch. 3. There is also dissension among those fighting opioid addiction, with the American Association for the Treatment of Opioid Dependence lobbying against rolling back methadone regulations; see Leigh Ann Caldwell and Theodoric Meyer, "The Under-the-Radar Battle over Opioid Addiction Treatment Legislation," *Washington Post*, December 1, 2022, https://www.washingtonpost.com/politics/2022/12/01 /under-the-radar-battle-over-opioid-addiction-treatment-legislation/.

64. Amanda D'Ambrosio, "The X-Waver Is Officially Dead," *Medpage Today*, January 5, 2023, https://www.medpagetoday.com/special-reports/features/102520.

65. Ann Forline, "New Jersey Drug Court Switches Name to Recovery Court," *South Jersey Observer*, December 29, 2021, https://www.southjerseyobserver.com /2021/12/29/new-jersey-drug-court-switches-name-to-recovery-court/. Many such as Beth Macy (*Raising Lazarus: Hope, Justice, and the Future of America's Overdose Crisis* [New York: Little, Brown, 2022]) and Sam Quinones (*The Least of Us: True Tales of America and Hope in the Time of Fentanyl and Meth* [New York: Bloomsbury, 2021]) point to drug court successes. But they also have their detractors. As Szalavitz (*Undoing Drugs*, 158) notes, many drug courts ban medicine for OUD. Moreover, participants often face higher prison sentences if their treatment fails than if they hadn't sought help in the first place. On other harm reduction initiatives, see "Governor Murphy Signs Legislative Package to Expand Harm Reduction Efforts, Further Commitment to End New Jersey's Opioid Epidemic" (press release), State of New Jersey Department of Health, January 18, 2022, https://www

.nj.gov/health/news/2022/approved/20220118a.shtml?fbclid=IwAR2VyrfIUHPMl
2Ou4GygGgRqpgmjVkriR2QJVC7iYkoKoNtfsRlm5Iw-aJ8; Alex Norcia, "New
Jersey Governor Signs Bills to Expand Harm Reduction," *Filter*, January 18, 2022,
https://filtermag.org/new-jersey-governor-harm-reduction/.

66. Szalavitz, *Undoing Drugs*, 158; see also David Sheff, *Clean: Overcoming
Addiction and Ending America's Greatest Tragedy* (Boston: Eamon Dolan, 2013), 296.

67. The summit, called "The Evolving Opioid Crisis: A Collaborative Approach,"
occurred on September 21, 2022, and was sponsored by the New Jersey Division of
Mental Health & Addiction Services, a division of the New Jersey Department
of Human Services. For more information, see the summit's website: https://
njopioidsummit2022.vfairs.com. I learned a lot about New Jersey's response to the
epidemic that I hadn't known earlier, and certainly knew none of this when my
family was dealing with Alex's substance use. The challenge of such activism is to
effectively link to families in crisis.

68. The New Jersey Department of Human Services ReachNJ.GOV online
addiction helpline is https://www.nj.gov/humanservices/reachnj/.

69. "About Our School," Raymond J. Lesniak Recovery High School," accessed
January 2, 2023, https://eshrecoveryschool.org/about/.

70. I rely heavily on Szalavitz, *Undoing Drugs*, ch. 22. Other useful articles
include Philip Smith, "How Oregon Is Turning the Page on America's Disastrous
Drug War," *Nation of Change*, December 3, 2021, https://www.nationofchange.org
/2021/12/03/how-oregon-is-turning-the-page-on-americas-disastrous-drug-war/;
Maia Szalavitz, "Treating Addiction as a Crime Doesn't Work. What Oregon Is
Doing Just Might," *New York Times*, January 26, 2022, https://www.nytimes.com
/2022/01/26/opinion/oregon-drug-decriminalization-addiction.html?fbclid
=IwAR2Q9rHVLiCUNcfL7Al_sBAj9ROx2k1GogFeC3jOEs
_SsUZWsvbRf1gnVQM; Drug Policy Alliance, "Drug Decriminalization in
Oregon, One Year Later," November 2021, https://web.archive.org/web
/20211114012304/http://links.drugpolicy.mkt7185.com/servlet/MailView?ms
=NDU5MzMxMTAS1&r=MTExMjExNTI5MTc3NwS2&j
=MjEyMTM3MDk1NgS2&mt=1&rt=0.

71. Jan Hoffman, "Scenes from a City That Only Hands Out Tickets for Using
Fentanyl," *New York Times*, July 31, 2023, https://www.nytimes.com/2023/07/31
/health/portland-oregon-drugs.html?te=1&nl=the-morning&emc=edit_nn
_20230804; Jim Hinch, "What Happened When Oregon Decriminalized Hard
Drugs," *The Atlantic* (July 19, 2023), https://www.theatlantic.com/politics/archive
/2023/07/oregon-drug-decriminalization-results-overdoses/674733/; Drug
Policy Alliance, "In Context: Overdose Deaths in Oregon," May 5, 2023, https://
drugpolicy.org/wp-content/uploads/2023/05/DPA_OR_OD_factsheet_branded
.pdf; Jordan Bollag, "Drug Decriminalization Policies Work—with Properly
Funded Treatment Services," rsn.org, August 13, 2023, https://www.rsn.org/001

/drug-decriminalization-policies-work-with-properly-funded-treatment-services
.html.

72. I rely heavily on Hari, *Chasing the Scream*, ch. 18.

73. State of Vermont Blueprint for Health, "Hub and Spoke," accessed May 30, 2022, https://blueprintforhealth.vermont.gov/about-blueprint/hub-and-spoke. See also German Lopez, "I Looked for a State That's Taken the Opioid Epidemic Seriously. I Found Vermont," *Vox*, October 30, 2017, https://www.vox.com/policy -and-politics/2017/10/30/16339672/opioid-epidemic-vermont-hub-spoke. I found reports that California and Washington State have also adapted the hub and spoke model; see Abby Goodnough, "This ER Treats Opioid Addiction on Demand. That's Very Rare," *New York Times*, August 18, 2018, https://www.nytimes.com /2018/08/18/health/opioid-addiction-treatment.html; State of California, "CA Hub and Spoke System: MAT Expansion Project," accessed May 30, 2022, https:// web.archive.org/web/20220403120310/https://www.uclaisap.org/ca-hubandspoke /html/project-info.html; Washington State Health Care Authority, "Washington State Hub and Spoke Project," accessed May 30, 2022, https://www.hca.wa.gov /about-hca/behavioral-health-recovery/washington-state-hub-and-spoke-project.

74. Ryan Hampton, *American Fix: Inside the Opioid Addiction Crisis—And How To End It* (New York: All Points Books, 2018), 215.

75. Macy, *Raising Lazarus*. Macy describes the work of local activists such as North Carolinians Michele Mathis and Karen Lowe (who cofounded a harm reduction ministry) and Tim Nolan (a nurse practitioner who goes door to door to help those who use drugs with buprenorphine and hepatitis C drugs). She also interviewed Nikki King (a community hospital addiction specialist in Indiana); Mark Willis (opioid response director for Surry County, North Carolina); Lill Prosperino (former addictions counselor, now a West Virginian harm reduction-ist); attorneys Mike Moore and Mike Quinn, fighting the good fight against Purdue Pharma; parents Shelly Young, Ginny Lovitt, and Alexis Pleus; Stacey Kincaid (sheriff of Fairfax, Virginia) and Fairfax Jail's Laura Yager; and activist protester Nan Goldin.

76. Quinones, *The Least of Us*.

77. Macy, *Raising Lazarus*, 290.

78. The End It For Good website is https://www.enditforgood.com/.

79. Local community activists are developing several useful strategies to address the overdose crisis, including sharing information in real time about drugs that kill and examining wastewater for opioids. See Lenny Bernstein and Meryl Kornfield, "To Curb Drug Deaths, Communities Turn to Reddit, Texts and Wastewater," *Washington Post*, February 5, 2023, https://www.washingtonpost.com/health/2023 /02/05/drug-deaths-prevention/.

80. I thank Lee Clarke for his insights into the sociology of disasters, and its connection to the overdose crisis. For additional research, see Lee Clarke, *Worst*

Cases: Terror and Catastrophe in the Popular Imagination (Chicago: University of Chicago Press, 2006).

81. Patricia A. Roos, "My Son Died of a Heroin Overdose. Trump's Commission Could Help the Crisis—If He Listens," *Star Ledger,* November 12, 2017, https://www.nj.com/opinion/2017/11/my_son_lost_his_battle_to_heroin_addiction_trumps.html#incart_river_mobile_index.

82. For those interested in further reading, see Dr. Tatarsky's website: https://www.andrewtatarsky.com; William L. White, "Bridging the Worlds of Harm Reduction and Addiction Treatment: An Interview with Dr. Andrew Tatarsky," 2016, https://www.chestnut.org/resources/79e5f464-a21d-4dd9-a24a-4ec9d81b2210/2016-Dr.-Andrew-Tatarsky-v2.pdf; Andrew Tatarsky, "Harm Reduction Psychotherapy: Extending the Reach of Traditional Substance Use Treatment," *Journal of Substance Abuse Treatment* 25 (2003): 249–256; Andrew Tatarsky and Scott Kellogg, "Integrative Harm Reduction Psychotherapy: A Case of Substance Use, Multiple Trauma, and Suicidality," *Journal of Clinical Psychology* 66, no. 2 (2010): 123–135; Andrew Tatarsky, "The Challenge of Harm Reduction: Changing Attitudes toward Addiction Treatment," *Psychotherapy Networker,* September–October 2019, https://www.psychotherapynetworker.org/article/challenge-harm-reduction. Psychologist G. Alan Marlatt was also instrumental in bringing harm reduction to clinical practice. G. Alan Marlatt, "Harm Reduction: Come as You Are," *Addictive Behaviors* 21 (1996): 779–788, https://openlab.citytech.cuny.edu/nehhealth2013/files/2013/11/G-Alan-Marlatt-Harm-Reduction-Come-As-You-Are.pdf.

83. White, "Bridging the Worlds."

84. Tatarsky, "Harm Reduction Psychotherapy," 249; see Marlatt, "Harm Reduction."

85. Tatarsky, "Harm Reduction Psychotherapy," 250–252.

86. Szalavitz, *Undoing Drugs,* 182–184.

87. Szalavitz, *Undoing Drugs,* 139.

88. I thank Lisa Laitman for her suggestion to explore this research tradition. See Alexandre B. Laudet, "The Case for Considering Quality of Life in Addiction Research and Clinical Practice," *Addiction Science & Clinical Practice* 6, no. 1 (2011): 44–55, https://www.ncbi.nlm.nih.gov/pmc/articles/PMC3188817/pdf/ascp-06-1-44.pdf; Joanne Neale, Silia Vitoratou, Emily Finch, Paul Lennon, Luke Mitcheson, Daria Panebianco, Diana Rose, John Strang, Til Wykes, and John Marsden, "Development and Validation of 'SURE': A Patient Reported Outcome Measure (PROM) for Recovery from Drug and Alcohol Dependence," *Drug and Alcohol Dependence* 165 (2016): 159–167.

89. Laudet, "The Case for Considering Quality of Life," 44–45.

90. Neale et al., "Development and Validation of 'SURE.'" See also Joanne Neale, "SURE Recovery APP—Two Years on after Its Launch," King's College

London News Centre, September 30, 2021, https://www.kcl.ac.uk/news/sure
-recovery-app-two-years-on-after-its-launch.

91. Partnership to End Addiction, "Untreated & Unheard: The Addiction Crisis
in America—Full Film," YouTube video, 1:17:10, March 29, 2023, https://www
.youtube.com/watch?v=raDfR_Ztyyo&ab_channel=PartnershiptoEndAddiction.
See also Riley Kirkpatrick, "Access Point Documentary—Rough Cut (Unofficial),"
YouTube video, 18:16, April 15, 2023, https://www.youtube.com/watch?v=3
_6k6dqFCoA&ab_channel=RileyKirkpatrick (about harm reduction in Georgia).

92. Among many other excellent websites for organizations and activists focused
on substance use and mental health disorders, there are a number I've found
especially useful: Drug Policy Alliance (https://drugpolicy.org/); Kennedy Forum
(https://www.thekennedyforum.org/); Recovery Advocacy Project (https://www
.recoveryvoices.com/); its Family Caucus (https://www.recoveryvoices.com
/family-caucus/); Shatterproof (https://www.shatterproof.org); Partnership to End
Addiction (https://drugfree.org/); Prevention Resources (https://njprevent.com/);
National Harm Reduction Coalition (https://harmreduction.org/); Mobilize
Recovery (https://mobilizerecovery.org/); American Society of Addiction Medicine (https://www.asam.org/); Center for Great Expectations (https://www.cge-nj
.org/); Center for Motivation & Change (https://motivationandchange.com);
Family Recovery Summit (https://www.familyrecoverymovement.com); Truth
Pharm (https://truthpharm.org) and Trail of Truth (https://www.trailoftruth.org),
founded by Alexis Pleus; and Moms for All Paths to Recovery, founded by Kathleen
Cochran (https://www.facebook.com/groups/momsforallpaths/).

Epilogue

1. Niall Ferguson, ed., *Virtual History: Alternatives and Counterfactuals* (New
York: Basic Books, 1997).

2. Diane Kunz, "Camelot Continued: What If John F. Kennedy Had Lived?," in
Virtual History: Alternatives and Counterfactuals, ed. Niall Ferguson (New York:
Basic Books, 1997), 368–391.

3. Niall Ferguson, "Introduction: Virtual History: Towards a 'Chaotic' Theory
of the Past," in *Virtual History: Alternatives and Counterfactuals*, ed. Niall Ferguson
(New York: Basic Books, 1997), 2. I use the term "counterfactual" loosely.
Ferguson makes the distinction between "what did happen and what could
plausibly have happened . . . we are concerned with possibilities which seemed
probable in the past" (84). Because harm reduction cohered as a plausible option
only recently, some might not consider it a "probable" alternative to the moral or
brain disease approaches.

4. Joanna Slater, "He Started a Movement to Help Drug Users. He Couldn't Save Himself," *Washington Post*, August 5, 2022, https://www.washingtonpost.com /nation/2022/08/05/jesse-harvey-opioids-addiction-maine/.

5. Zachary Siegel, "Their Kids Died of Fentanyl Overdoses. Republicans Can't Wait to Exploit It," *New Republic*, June 27, 2023, https://newrepublic.com/article /173425/kids-died-fentanyl-overdoses-republicans-cant-wait-exploit-it; Sam Snodgrass, "Bereaved Parents Weaponized by DEA to Back More Drug War, *Filter*, June 6, 2023, https://filtermag.org/parents-overdose-fentanyl-dea/amp/?fbclid =IwARoiWswo_TxjFwa2BvebmHRjDAMVh-1qRe9- -b4fnoZJNpuH2lCbL8AX9nQ; Maia Szalavitz, "We Know What Happens When We Prosecute Drug Dealers as Murderers," *New York Times*, July 28, 2023, https:// www.nytimes.com/2023/07/28/opinion/fentanyl-mandatory-drug-sentences .html#:~:text=But%20doubling%20down%20on%20 counterproductive,availability%20of%20drugs%20and%20death.

6. Steven Ross Johnson, "Safe Injection Sites Have Gained a Foothold in the U.S. Are More on the Way?," *US News & World Report*, February 2, 2023. See also Joseph Goldstein and Joshua Needelman, "Fentanyl Helps Push Overdose Deaths to Record Level in New York City," *New York Times*, January 13, 2023, https://www .nytimes.com/2023/01/13/nyregion/new-york-overdose-record.html?smid =nytcore-ios-share&referringSource=articleShare.

7. Sharon Otterman, "Federal Officials May Shut Down Overdose Prevention Centers in Manhattan," *New York Times*, August 8, 2023, https://www.nytimes.com /2023/08/08/nyregion/drug-overdoses-supervised-consumption-nyc.html.

8. Anne M. Fletcher, *Inside Rehab: The Surprising Truth about Addiction Treatment—and How to Get Help That Works* (New York: Viking, 2013); Lance Dodes and Zachary Dodes, *The Sober Truth: Debunking the Bad Science behind 12-Step Programs and the Rehab Industry* (Boston: Beacon Press, 2014); Adam Bisaga, *Overcoming Opioid Addiction: The Authoritative Medial Guide for Patients, Families, Doctors, and Therapists* (New York: The Experiment, 2018).

9. Carl Erik Fisher, *The Urge: Our History of Addiction* (New York: Penguin, 2022), 238–239. See also National Center on Addiction and Substance Abuse at Columbia University, *Addiction Medicine: Closing the Gap between Science and Practice* (New York: National Center on Addiction and Substance Abuse [now the Partnership to End Addiction], June 2012), https://drugfree.org/reports/addiction -medicine-closing-the-gap-between-science-and-practice/, 6–14.

10. See the scathing report on U.S. addiction medicine and treatment by the National Center on Addiction and Substance Abuse at Columbia University, *Addiction Medicine: Closing the Gap Between Science and Practice*, June 2012, https://drugfree.org/reports/addiction-medicine-closing-the-gap-between-science -and-practice/.

11. Frank Greenagel, "The Three Questions You Should Ask of Treatment Programs," February 11, 2018, https://web.archive.org/web/20201127093950 /http://greenagel.com/2018/02/11/the-three-questions-you-should-ask-of -treatment-programs/. See Greenagel's website for additional writings: https:// greenagel.com/.

12. Fisher, *The Urge*; Carl Erik Fisher, "Alcoholism and Me: 'I Was an Addicted Doctor, the Worst Kind of Patient,'" *Guardian*, February 8, 2022, https://www .theguardian.com/profile/carl-erik-fisher. Fisher cites the following study of physician health programs: Thomas McLellan, Gregory S. Skipper, Michael Campbell, and Robert L. DuPont, "Five Year Outcomes in a Cohort Study of Physicians Treated for Substance Use Disorders in the United States.' *BMJ* 337 (2008): a2038, https://www.bmj.com/content/bmj/337/bmj.a2038.full.pdf.

13. Fisher, *The Urge*, 274.

14. Keri Blakinger, *Corrections in Ink: A Memoir* (New York: St. Martin's Press, 2022), 213.

15. Barbara Kingsolver, *Demon Copperhead* (New York: Harper, 2022).

RELEVANT SOURCES

Substance Use/Drugs

Alexander, Michelle. *The New Jim Crow: Mass Incarceration in the Age of Colorblindness.* New York: New Press, 2010.

Bisaga, Adam. *Overcoming Opioid Addiction: The Authoritative Medical Guide for Patients, Families, Doctors, and Therapists.* New York: The Experiment, 2018.

Dodes, Lance, and Zachary Dodes. *The Sober Truth: Debunking the Bad Science behind 12-Step Programs and the Rehab Industry.* Boston: Beacon Press, 2014.

Fisher, Carl Erik. "Alcoholism and Me: 'I Was an Addicted Doctor, the Worst Kind of Patient.'" *Guardian*, February 8, 2022.

———. *The Urge: Our History of Addiction.* New York: Penguin Press, 2022.

Fletcher, Anne M. *Inside Rehab: The Surprising Truth about Addiction Treatment—and How to Get Help That Works.* New York: Viking, 2013.

Foote, Jeffrey, Kenneth Carpenter, and Carrie Wilkens. *The Beyond Addiction Workbook for Family & Friends: Evidence-Based Skills to Help a Loved One Make Positive Change.* Oakland CA: New Harbinger Publications, 2022.

Hampton, Ryan. *American Fix: Inside the Opioid Addiction Crisis—and How to End It.* New York: All Points Books, 2018.

———. *Unsettled: How the Purdue Pharma Bankruptcy Failed the Victims of the American Overdose Crisis.* New York: St. Martin's Press, 2021.

Hari, Johann. *Chasing the Scream: The First and Last Days of the War on Drugs.* New York: Bloomsbury, 2015.

Hart, Carl L. *Drug Use for Grown-Ups: Chasing Liberty in the Land of Fear.* New York: Penguin, 2021.

Herzberg, David. *White Market Drugs: Big Pharma and the Hidden History of Addiction in America.* Chicago: University of Chicago Press, 2020.

Kingsolver, Barbara. *Demon Copperhead.* New York: Harper, 2022.

351

Macy, Beth. *Dopesick: Dealers, Doctors, and the Drug Company That Addicted America*. New York: Little, Brown, 2018.

———. *Raising Lazarus: Hope, Justice, and the Future of America's Overdose Crisis*. New York: Little, Brown, 2022.

Maté, Gabor. *In the Realm of Hungry Ghosts: Close Encounters with Addiction*. Berkeley, CA: North Atlantic Books, 2008.

National Academies of Sciences, Engineering, and Medicine. *Opportunities to Improve Opioid Use Disorder and Infectious Disease Services: Integrating Responses to a Dual Epidemic*. Washington, DC: National Academies Press, 2020.

National Center on Addiction and Substance Abuse at Columbia University. *Addiction Medicine: Closing the Gap between Science and Practice*. New York: National Center on Addiction and Substance Abuse at Columbia University, 2012.

Netherland, Julie, and Helena Hansen. "White Opioids: Pharmaceutical Race and the War on Drugs That Wasn't." *BioSocieties* 12, no. 2 (2017): 217–238.

New York Academy of Medicine. "Then & Now: Drug Policy and Harm Reduction Services." YouTube video. 1:02:04. May 16, 2022. https://www.youtube.com/watch?v=f9aAkDaPUlM.

Quinones, Sam. *Dreamland: The True Tale of America's Opiate Epidemic*. New York: Bloomsbury, 2015.

———. *The Least of Us: True Tales of America and Hope in the Time of Fentanyl and Meth*. New York: Bloomsbury, 2021.

Roberts, Samuel K. "The Impact of the US Drug War on People of Color." In *The Oxford Handbook of Global Drug History*, edited by Paul Gootenberg, 474–494. New York: Oxford University Press, 2022.

Sheff, David. *Clean: Overcoming Addiction and Ending America's Greatest Tragedy*. Boston: Eamon Dolan, 2013.

Szalavitz, Maia. *Unbroken Brain: A Revolutionary New Way of Understanding Addiction*. New York: St. Martin's Press, 2016.

———. *Undoing Drugs: The Untold Story of Harm Reduction and the Future of Addiction*. New York: Hachette Books, 2021.

Mental Health

Carr, Deborah. *Worried Sick: How Stress Hurts Us and How to Bounce Back*. New Brunswick, NJ: Rutgers University Press, 2014.

Case, Anne, and Angus Deaton. *Deaths of Despair and the Future of Capitalism*. Princeton, NJ: Princeton University Press, 2020.

Earley, Pete. *Crazy: A Father's Search through America's Mental Health Madness*. New York: Berkley Books, 2006.

Ellis, Carolyn. "Seeking My Brother's Voice: Holding onto Long-term Grief through Photographs, Stories, and Reflections." In *Stories of Complicated Grief: A Critical*

Anthology, edited by Eric D. Miller, 3–21. Washington, DC: National Association of Social Workers Press, 2014.

Francis, Ara. *Family Trouble: Middle-Class Parents, Children's Problems, and the Disruption of Everyday Life*. New Brunswick, NJ: Rutgers University Press, 2015.

Jamison, Kay Redfield. *Night Falls Fast: Understanding Suicide*. New York: Vintage, 1999.

Laitman, Lisa, Linda Lederman, and Irene Silos, eds. *Voices of Recovery from the Campus: Stories of and by College Students in Recovery from Addiction*. New Brunswick, NJ: CreateSpace, 2003.

McGhee, Heather. *The Sum of Us: What Racism Costs Everyone and How We Can Prosper Together*. New York: One World, 2021.

Powers, Ron. *No One Cares about Crazy People: The Chaos and Heartbreak of Mental Health in America*. New York: Hachette, 2017.

Roberts, Greg. "Into the Mystic: Bereaved Parents, Love and Spontaneous Creativity." PhD diss., Deakin University, Melbourne, Australia, 2015.

Siddiqi, Arjumand, Odmaa Sod-Erdene, Darrick Hamilton, Tressie McMillan Cottom, and William Darity Jr. "Growing Sense of Social Status Threat and Concomitant Deaths of Despair among Whites." *Social Science and Medicine* 9 (2019): 100449.

Solomon, Andrew *Far from the Tree: Parents, Children, and the Search for Identity*. New York: Scribner, 2012.

Sontag, Susan. *Illness as Metaphor and AIDS and Its Metaphors*. New York: Picador, 1977.

Stossel, Scott. *My Age of Anxiety: Fear, Hope, Dread, and the Search for Peace of Mind*. New York: Alfred A. Knopf, 2014.

Teasdale, John, Mark Williams, and Zindel Segal. *The Mindful Way Workbook: An 8-Week Program to Free Yourself from Depression and Emotional Distress*. New York: Guilford Press, 2014.

Memoirs of Addiction, Grief, Resilience

Alexander, Elizabeth. *The Light of the World: A Memoir*. New York: Grand Central Publishing, 2015.

Barrington, Judith. *Lifesaving: A Memoir*. Portland, OR: Eighth Mountain Press, 2000.

Berube, Michael. *Life as We Know It: A Father, a Family, and an Exceptional Child*. New York: Vintage, 1996.

Biden, Joe. *Promise Me, Dad: A Year of Hope, Hardship, and Purpose*. New York: Flatiron Books, 2017.

Biden, Hunter. *Beautiful Things: A Memoir*. New York: Gallery Books, 2021.

Blakinger, Keri. *Corrections in Ink: A Memoir*. New York: St. Martin's Press, 2022.

Bowler, Kate. *Everything Happens for a Reason: And Other Lies I've Loved*. New York: Random House, 2018.

Brown, Harriet. *Brave Girl Eating: A Family's Struggle with Anorexia*. New York: Harper, 2011.

Carr, David. *The Night of the Gun: A Reporter Investigates the Darkest Story of His Life, His Own*. New York: Simon and Schuster, 2008.

Dean, Madeleine, and Harry Cunnane. *Under Our Roof: A Son's Battle for Recovery, a Mother's Battle for Her Son*. New York: Convergent, 2021.

Didion, Joan. *Blue Nights*. New York: Vintage International, 2011.

———. *The Year of Magical Thinking*. New York: Vintage International, 2006.

Dunleavy, Jessie. *Cover My Dreams in Ink: A Son's Unbearable Solitude, a Mother's Unending Quest*. Loyola University, MD: Apprentice House Press, 2020.

Ellis, Carolyn. *Final Negotiations: A Story of Love, Loss, and Chronic Illness*. Philadelphia: Temple University Press, 1995.

Finkbeiner, Ann K. *After the Death of a Child: Living with Loss through the Years*. Baltimore: Johns Hopkins University Press, 1996.

Greene, Jayson. *Once More We Saw Stars: A Memoir*. New York: Random House, 2019.

Hone, Lucy. *Resilient Grieving: How to Find Your Way through a Devastating Loss*. New York: The Experiment, 2017. [Lucy Hone appears on an episode of the *Hidden Brain* podcast; see Vedantam, Shankar, host. "Healing Your Heart." *Hidden Brain*, podcast. April 5, 2022, 49:35. https://hiddenbrain.org/podcast/healing-your-heart/.]

Hornbacher, Marya. *Madness: A Bipolar Life*. Boston: Mariner Books, 2008.

———. *Wasted: A Memoir of Anorexia and Bulimia*. New York: Harper Perennial, 1998.

Kefalas, Maria. *Harnessing Grief: A Mother's Quest for Meaning and Miracles*. Boston: Beacon Press, 2021.

Laitmon, Emily, and Terry Toll. *Our Children, Our Hearts*. Tuckahoe, NY: Bereavement Center of Westchester, 2008.

Lamb, Sharon. *The Not Good Enough Mother*. Boston: Beacon Press, 2019.

Marshall, John, and Liza Marshall. *Off Our Chests: A Candid Tour through the World of Cancer*. Oakton, VA: IdeaPress Publishers, 2021.

Miller, Chanel. *Know My Name: A Memoir*. New York: Viking, 2019.

Mitchell, W.J.T. *Mental Traveler: A Father, a Son, and a Journey through Schizophrenia*. Chicago: University of Chicago Press, 2020.

Moyers, William Cope, with Katherine Ketcham. *Broken: My Story of Addiction and Redemption*. New York: Penguin, 2007.

Perry, Matthew. *Friends, Lovers, and the Big Terrible Thing: A Memoir*. New York: Flatiron Books, 2022.

Raskin, Jamie. *Unthinkable: Trauma, Truth, and the Trials of American Democracy.* New York: Harper, 2022.

Rosenthal, Jason B. *My Wife Said You May Want to Marry Me: A Memoir.* New York: Harper, 2020.

Rosman, Katherine. *If You Knew Suzy: A Mother, a Daughter, a Reporter's Notebook.* New York: Harper Perennial, 2010.

Sandberg, Sheryl, and Adam Grant. *Option B: Facing Adversity, Building Resilience, and Finding Joy.* New York: Alfred A. Knopf, 2017.

Sheff, David. *Beautiful Boy: A Father's Journey through His Son's Addiction.* Boston: Mariner Books, 2008.

Sheff, Nic. *Tweak: Growing Up on Methamphetamines.* New York: Atheneum Books for Young Readers, 2008.

———. *We All Fall Down: Living with Addiction.* New York: Little, Brown, 2011.

Epigraph Sources

Brockes, Emma. "Toni Morrison: 'I Want to Feel What I Feel. Even If It's Not Happiness.'" *Guardian*, April 13, 2012.

Callard, Agnes. "Parenting and Panic." *The Point Magazine*, October 21, 2019. https://thepointmag.com/examined-life/parenting-and-panic-agnes-callard/.

Clarke, Lee. *Worst Cases: Terror and Catastrophe in the Popular Imagination.* Chicago: University of Chicago Press, 2006, ix.

Didion, Joan. *The Year of Magical Thinking.* New York: Vintage International, 2006, 3–4.

Hari, Johann. *Chasing the Scream: The First and Last Days of the War on Drugs.* New York: Bloomsbury, 2015, 152.

Mills, C. Wright. "On Intellectual Craftsmanship." In *Symposium on Sociological Theory*, edited by Llewellyn Gross. Evanston, IL: Row, Peterson and Company, 1959, 25–53.

Mills, C. Wright. *The Sociological Imagination.* New York: Oxford University Press, 1959, 8, 226.

Powers, Richard. *Bewilderment.* New York: W. W. Norton & Co., 2021, 274.

Raskin, Jamie. *Unthinkable: Trauma, Truth, and the Trials of American Democracy.* New York: Harper, 2022, xiv–xv.

Senior, Jennifer. 2021. "What Bobby McIlvaine Left Behind." *Atlantic* (September 2021), https://www.theatlantic.com/magaine/archive/2021/09/twenty-years-gone-911-bobby-mcilvaine/619490/.

Solomon, Andrew. *Far from the Tree: Parents, Children, and the Search for Identity.* New York: Scribner, 2012, 581.

Szalavitz, Maia. *Unbroken Brain: A Revolutionary New Way of Understanding Addiction*. New York: St. Martin's Press, 2016, 135.

Trethewey, Natasha. *Memorial Drive: A Daughter's Memoir*. New York: Ecco Press, 2020, 52.

Yanagihara. Hanya. *A Little Life*. New York: Doubleday, 2015, 574.

Zinsser, William. *Writing About Your Life: A Journey into the Past*. New York: Marlowe & Company, 2004, 182.

INDEX

Food and Drug Administration (FDA),
methadone maintenance and, 37,
279–280
Footprints to Recovery, Alex and, 203,
218, 219
fraternity, Alex and, 110, 111, 112, 115, 158
fraud, sober living houses and, 211
friends, Alex's: on Alex's darker side,
118–120; childhood, 59–60, 74, 77–78,
86–87; knowledge of heroin use,
144–145; loss of at height of addiction,
167–168, 234; reminiscences about
Alex, 21, 24–26, 100–103, 109, 115–116,
118–120, 321–322; solace from while
grieving, 246–247
Friends, Lovers, and the Big Terrible Thing
(Perry), 42

gabapentin (Neurontin), prescribed for
Alex, 157, 188, 193, 202
Gardens of Lake Worth (rehab #11), Alex
and, 202, 203–204; discharge evaluation, 204
gender, eating disorders and, 69–70
generalized anxiety disorder, Alex
diagnosed with, 174, 187, 231
genetic predisposition to addiction, 48
geographic distribution of overdose
deaths in United States, 34
Georgetown University, 85
Goffman, Erving, 264
"good family," addiction and, 15, 20, 31, 53,
65, 165, 168
Good Samaritan laws, 284
Goulão, João, 272–273
Granny (Chip's mom): Alex finding his
way to condo, 149, 159–160; at Alex's
college graduation, 123; Alex's relationship with, 56, 58, 110; death of, 125,
129, 134
Greenagel, Frank, 314–315
Greg (cousin), 58; on Alex in Kansas City,
128–129

grief: Chip on own, 293–306; complicated, 266–267; continuing bonds and,
267; hierarchy of, 265; kinds of, 250, 266
grief, coping with: exercise and, 247;
practical strategies, 267–268; turning
into action, 251; writing and, 27, 28, 250.
See also social communities
grief group, Chip and Pat and, 224, 246,
249–250
guilt, Chip on own, 300–301
Gupta, Rahul, 279

hallucinogens, decriminalization of in
Oregon, 282
Hampton, Ryan, 42, 283
Hare, Robert, 190
Hari, Johann, 32, 137–138, 271
harm reduction: "big" vs. "little," 262;
emphasis on empathy, 271–272; goals
of, 268–271, 287; possibility could have
helped Alex, 309–310; in practice,
285–291; precepts of, 277; principles of,
6; strategies, 49, 231; 12-step programs
vs., 287–288, 290–291
Harm Reduction Coalition, 276–277
harm reduction movement, 268, 269;
abstinence opposition to, 278; activism
at local level, 283–284; history of,
271–285; in the United States, 274–285
harm reduction policies, 38–39; Biden
administration and, 279; states and,
280–283
Harm Reduction Working Group, 276
Harrisburg Hospital, Alex volunteering
at, 122
Hazelden Betty Ford Foundation, 277–278
health insurance: addiction treatment
and, 227; Alex's injuries from incident
at Penn State and, 116; lack of choice of
programs and, 313; lack of parity between
mental and physical health and, 4,
252–257; paying for College Recovery
and, 210; for rehabs, 147, 179, 202

ABOUT THE AUTHOR

PATRICIA A. ROOS was a professor of sociology at Rutgers University when in 2015 she lost her son Alex at twenty-five years of age to a heroin overdose. After Alex's death, she realigned her research and advocacy interests, turning her grief into activism. She hopes to inspire a moral community of action that will realign public health policy to address the overdose crisis, and she has the particular set of skills necessary to do so. Roos spent much of her sociological career investigating systemic patterns of inequality by sex and race, focusing on how subtle mechanisms of inequity get reproduced. In *Surviving Alex* she uses these same skills to examine extant explanations and treatments for the ever-growing overdose epidemic and finds them wanting. Weaving together the personal and the sociological, she learns about the broader set of factors implicated in mental health and substance use disorders. Instead of focusing on individual-level choice and brain disease arguments, she directs her attention to the larger social context in which those individual-level actions occur. Ultimately, she imagines a world steeped in compassionate, paradigm-shifting harm reduction methods, as opposed to the punitive, choice-based approaches that currently exist.